France and the Cult of the Sacred Heart

STUDIES ON THE HISTORY OF SOCIETY AND CULTURE

Victoria E. Bonnell and Lynn Hunt, Editors

RAYMOND JONAS

France and the Cult of the Sacred Heart

An Epic Tale for Modern Times

UNIVERSITY OF CALIFORNIA PRESS

BERKELEY   LOS ANGELES   LONDON

University of California Press
Berkeley and Los Angeles, California

University of California Press, Ltd.
London, England

The author wishes to acknowledge *Historical Reflections/
Réflexions historiques, French Historical Studies,* and the
Délégation à l'Action artistique de la Ville de Paris for their
kind permission to republish portions of works that
originally appeared in their pages.

Library of Congress Cataloging-in-Publication Data

Jonas, Raymond Anthony.
    France and the cult of the Sacred Heart : an epic tale
for modern times / Raymond Jonas.
        p.   cm.—(Studies on the history of society
and culture; 39)
    Includes bibliographical references (p.) and index.
    ISBN 0-520-22136-2 (cloth : alk. paper)
    1. Sacred Heart, Devotion to—History of
doctrines.   2. France—Church history.   I. Title.
II. Series.
    BX2157.J57   2000
    232—dc21   99-058920

Manufactured in the United States of America
09 08 07 06 05 04 03 02 01 00
10 9 8 7 6 5 4 3 2 1

For Patricia

CONTENTS

ILLUSTRATIONS

ACKNOWLEDGMENTS

EARLY FUNDING FOR THIS project was provided by the National Endowment for the Humanities and by the Royalty Research Fund of the University of Washington. The Howard and Frances Keller Fund of the Department of History at the University of Washington provided funding for some key research trips. Designation as a Fulbright Senior Scholar by the Franco-American Commission gave me access to major research funding and support for an extended stay in France. A Howard Foundation Fellowship gave me the year's leave during which I completed the manuscript.

In Paris, I was pleased to work in the archives of the Archdiocese of Paris, the library of the Institut Catholique, the Bibliothèque Nationale, the archives of the Prefecture of Police, the Bibliothèque Historique de la Ville de Paris, the National Archives, the archives of the department of the Seine, and the Archives de l'Armée de Terre at Vincennes. I have been able to carry out research in the Vatican Archives in Rome, in diocesan archives in Chartres, Angers, Luçon, and Poitiers and in public archives in Mâcon, Nantes, La Roche-sur-Yon, Poitiers, Angers, Marseille, and Toulouse. In Seattle, I was ably and cheerily supported by Cynthia Blanding and Barbara Grayson of the Interlibrary Borrowing Office and by Nancy Wilson, Associate Director of Libraries, who kindly responded to my entreaties to renew my faculty study, thus guaranteeing a quiet place to work. At the University of California Press, I would like to thank Sheila Levine, Juliane Brand, Dore Brown, and Hillary Hansen. Charles Dibble, as copyeditor, asked questions and made suggestions that resulted in a much-improved text.

The Sacred Heart as an object of religious devotion, as a Parisian monument, and as an emblem of counter-revolution, is a richly visual topic. The images I have collected over the course of my research and included here as illustrations are from among dozens I have gathered in archives and libraries. I offer sincere gratitude to the archivists and curators who allowed me to photograph this material while working with their collections.

Thoughtful acquaintances, resourceful archivists, good colleagues, and concerned friends have helped in various ways. They include Susannah Barrows, James Leith, June Hargrove, Gérard Besson, Gabby and Odile of La Bonnetière, Timothy Tackett, Tom Kselman, Denise Salomon, Jacques Gadille, Marcel Launay, Françoise Martin, Howard Bloch, Gérard Cholvy, Eugene Vance, Nancy Wood, Michel Peronnet, Yves-Henri Nouailhat, Joseph Anderson, Victoria Scarlett, and the Reverends Louis Delhommeau, Pierre Bizeau, Henri Bremond, and Philippe Ploix. Among my many supportive colleagues at the University of Washington, I would like to single out Tom Hankins, who offered comments and encouragement at a critical moment. Special thanks to Jacques Benoist for his cordial friendship; the late David Pinkney, for cultivating my interest in Paris; Jean-Clément Martin, for showing me the Vendée; Frank Bowman, for not letting on, at least at first, how much work the Sacred Heart would be; and Lynn Hunt, a constant source of inspiration and encouragement.

A book so much about the uses of memory has generated a few fond memories of its own. Thanks to funding awarded to me as a Fulbright Senior Scholar, my family and I lived in a village in the Vendée. On weekends and holidays we made site visits throughout the west of France. Sometimes research was a combination of serendipity and good training—my daughter Elizabeth, then just ten years old, discovered a framed souvenir of an 1865 diocesan consecration to the Sacré-Coeur among a stack of prints in a second-hand shop in Machecoul. Her discovery alerted me to the importance of diocesan consecrations to the cultivation of a popular piety. Anthony and Katherine had their share of discoveries of Sacred Heart artifacts and stained glass, too. My wife, Patricia, sustained me with thoughtful questions and (apparently) unfeigned interest in the visionaries and lunatics, relics and reliquaries, heroes and scoundrels, builders and iconoclasts, persecutors and martyrs who have populated my imagination for the duration of this project. This book is for her.

AN EPIC TALE FOR MODERN TIMES

An Introduction

On one of my first visits to Paris, a solicitous friend—who also happens to be a distinguished historian of modern France—graciously took me on a tour of historic sites around the city. Montmartre was on our itinerary and we reached it as most tourists do, by leaving the Métro at Anvers, walking northward to the Place Saint-Pierre, then ascending the steep stairway to the basilica of the Sacré-Coeur. As we ascended Montmartre, the basilica and its domes gradually appeared, rising above the crest of the hill, their details taking shape through the brown haze of a Parisian summer day. Toward the top of our climb, we encountered clutches of tourists who had installed themselves on the steps, making the most of the deep August sun. We had to pick our path through the bodies and backpacks and vendors.

When we reached the basilica my friend stopped and sat down on the steps. I stopped beside him, puzzled. Ours had been no easy ascent, but this was not a matter of fatigue. He simply refused to enter. I asked my friend why we weren't going to join the hundreds of tourists milling through the front doors of the basilica. He responded with a brief history of the Sacré-Coeur. I listened attentively. He told me that the revolutionary Commune of Paris had begun on Montmartre in March of 1871, and the church had been built as a kind of monumental reappropriation of the terrain, the result of a vow taken by a chastened and devout bourgeoisie. My friend's reluctance to enter was a principled statement, a refusal to set foot within a structure that celebrated the defeat of the people of Paris. I admired my friend's moral conviction, but his story only increased my curiosity. With an earnest tone and dialogue worthy of an American G. I. movie, I looked reassuringly at my friend and said, "Wait here. I'm going in."

I left Montmartre that day moved by the power of the place and the legends constructed around it. My friend's attempt to turn our visit to Montmartre into a "teachable moment" raised more questions than it answered. What had begun as a simple tourist visit turned into something much more. I "made a vow" to return to the basilica and explore its history. But when I began work on the project I soon became convinced that the story that I wanted to tell could not be neatly organized around the basilica of the Sacré-Coeur. It certainly could not be confined to the history of Paris, much less that of the Commune. The basilica could not be understood outside of the context of the devotion to the Sacred Heart of Jesus, itself deeply implicated in the history of modern France.

The key episodes in the saga of France and the Sacré-Coeur played out at sites throughout France and over an expanse of some two hundred years. In the seventeenth and eighteenth centuries, visionaries reported that Jesus had appeared to them and displayed his heart as a source of grace and love but also as the recipient of the wounds of human disdain and indifference. The most important of these visionaries, Marguerite-Marie Alacoque, described numerous visions and conversations with Jesus in the 1680s. The central message of these communications was that France was elect among nations, that the French were a chosen people, and that to seal this alliance the king of France—it happened to be Louis XIV—need only consecrate France to the Sacred Heart of Jesus, build a chapel in honor of the Sacred Heart, and put the image of the heart of Jesus on the royal colors.

It's hardly surprising that Louis did not fulfill this request—if, indeed, he ever heard of it. Louis had plenty of lively interests and appetites, but the imaginings, threats, and demands of cloistered nuns from the Charollais were not among them. The more eccentric features of the Sacred Heart devotion would fall away in years to come, except among a minority of Catholics who looked upon Louis's failure as a sin of pride and a missed opportunity for national greatness. This notion would be revived as an explanation for every subsequent national setback, notably after 1789. Outside of these circles, however, what endured in the eighteenth century was the image of the heart of Jesus as a devotional object of enormous popularity.

The Jesuit order, largely with the support of the hierarchy of the Catholic Church, promoted the image of the Sacred Heart of Jesus as a symbol of divine love for humanity. Lay Catholics, with the approval of Catholic clergy and hierarchy, wore the emblem as a talisman for protection against danger, illness, and evil. Images of a heart with the inscription "Arrête! Le Coeur de Jesus est là!" were credited with halting catastrophic plague in Marseille in 1720. In 1789 and after, as Catholics became increasingly troubled by the course of the Revolution, they again wore the Sacré-Coeur for protection, a sure sign of their conviction that the Revolution signaled a real demonic presence. In the west of France, in an area known as the Vendée, peasants stitched the Sacré-Coeur to their clothing for protection when they took up arms to fight against the Revolution: little wonder that the Sacré-Coeur soon became the dominant symbol of royal and Catholic counter-revolution.

The entry of the Sacred Heart of Jesus into French political culture thus coincided with the Revolution. Prior to 1789, the Sacred Heart addressed anxieties about apostasy, error, and schism; afterward, it challenged a revolution held to be hostile to Catholic belief, public order, and the essentially Catholic nature and vocation of France. Henceforth the Sacred Heart related to republican political culture as a symbol of opposition and as a Christian patriotic alternative to the idealized Republic. Historians including Maurice Agulhon, Frank Bowman, Lynn Hunt, James Leith, Mona Ozouf, and Michel Vovelle have shown how after 1789 the French Left developed a secular, republican political culture—sometimes through republican parody of Catholic ritual (the cult of Marianne for the cult of Mary, the devotion to the Sacré-Coeur de Marat), sometimes through iconoclasm (de-Christianization, vandalism, and anti-clericalism), but always in a self-conscious rejection of royalist and Catholic rituals and symbols. This book is about how French Catholics responded with a bitter condemnation of the Revolution and the secular republican ideal and a promise of national redemption through the re-Christianization of public life, notably via a national consecration to the Sacré-Coeur. Whenever Marianne went into combat, she encountered the Sacré-Coeur.

Sustaining the critical discourse of the Sacré-Coeur in nineteenth-century France was a task assumed by Catholic clergy and relayed by Catholic laity. Diocesan consecrations to the Sacré-Coeur served as local rehearsals for the national consecration so ardently sought; some dioceses were actually *re*-consecrated to the Sacré-Coeur after a respectable interval. Catholic families were encouraged to consecrate themselves to the Sacré-Coeur in lieu of a national consecration; in devout villages, municipal leaders were urged to consecrate their municipalities—many obliged. Large-scale pilgrimages, one of the characteristic features of nineteenth-century popular culture as well as one of its most neglected, became occasions for ritualized revival of a tale of post-revolutionary French decline and the promise of regeneration through the Sacré-Coeur. Clergy distributed Sacré-Coeur emblems to pilgrims with instructions to pin them to their chests, a gesture whose seditious significance was lost on no one. At a time when strikes were still relatively small and infrequent, pilgrimage eclipsed all other forms of popular mobilization. And no strike or demonstration could mobilize on a national scale in the way that pilgrimage shrines and rituals could. Moreover, from Béziers (where pilgrims waved Bourbon-white kerchiefs and sang "Give us a king in the name of the Sacred Heart!") to Paray-le-Monial (where, in 1873, more than a hundred deputies from the National Assembly participated in a ceremony dedicating France to the Sacré-Coeur) pilgrimages blended the sacred and the profane, prayer and politics. The anthropologist Victor Turner's classic works on pilgrimage argue that pilgrimage was essentially "anarchical" and "anticlerical"—a kind of Mardi Gras masquerading as piety. Turner was wrong. The French episcopate effectively disciplined and channeled the practice of pilgrimage in pursuit of their vision of the moral and political regeneration of France. Pilgrimages were penitential plebiscites.

Pilgrimage linked communities to a network of sites. Throughout France, stained-glass windows, chapels, and entire churches served as landmarks on the Sacré-Coeur landscape. They could serve as mnemonic devices, evoking memories of victims of the Revolution and the heroic resistance of those who opposed it in the name of the Sacré-Coeur. Many of these sites, including the Sacré-Coeur de Montmartre, were destination shrines. They also fulfilled a didactic purpose, going beyond instructing the faithful about Jesus, the lives of the saints, and the basic tenets of Catholic faith and morals: they explicitly addressed questions of French identity. Using familiar historical allusions and self-consciously medievalized artistic style, these sites conferred on certain responses to the challenges of the present a holy and heroic pedigree. Stained-glass windows are the Bible of the people. A window representing the Vendéen general Jacques Cathelineau (known colloquially as the "Saint of the Anjou") within a series of windows featuring saints from Biblical antiquity to the recent past conferred an aura of sanctity on acts of resistance to the Republic. Such sacred art linked the past to the present (the France of the Third Republic) in morally and politically prescriptive ways. In effect, these sites were centers of cultural production, generating and sustaining a counter-discourse that challenged a still-fragile republican hegemony. These sites also contextualize that most famous votive church in the Sacré-Coeur network—the basilica on Montmartre.

The construction of the Sacré-Coeur de Montmartre reveals an astonishing capacity on the part of the Catholic hierarchy for innovation in the techniques of mass-marketing. French defeat in the war with Germany in 1870–71 inspired the Montmartre project, but ingenious marketing techniques raised the money to build it. Newsletters, site visits, "shareholder" certification, souvenir sales, "naming opportunities," fund-raising pitches playing on the vanities of donors large and small—in full-fledged or incipient form, all of these were employed to build the church on Montmartre. When the church was finished on the eve of World War I, decades late and tens of millions of francs over budget, it gave Paris its most prominent monument to a deeply conservative vision of France. It had been financed, ironically, thanks to some of the most daringly creative promotions of modern times.

The devotion to the Sacré-Coeur in nineteenth-century France represents a campaign of cultural politics of breathtaking skill and sophistication. It thrived on monuments, memories, rituals, and the cultivation of millennial expectations. While republican France defended the "universal ideas of 1789 and the imprescriptible Rights of Man," advocates of the Sacré-Coeur spoke of the restoration of the Rights of God and described a Christian utopia attendant upon the reunion of God, King, and France. The devotion began to break free of its association with the campaign for Christian monarchy in the late 1870s, once the political ineptitude of the Bourbon pretender-in-exile became apparent, and in the 1880s when Pope Leo XIII, the successor to the bitterly counter-revolutionary pope Pius IX, advised French Catholics to reconcile with their republic. But memory is long in France. Although the Catholic rank and file moved away from monarchist politics, as much by force of circumstance as by anything else, they had a much harder time pulling away from the deeply ingrained conviction that the Republic, descendant of a despised Revolution, incarnated values that were anti-Catholic and therefore, by partisan definition, anti-French.[1] This was the political residue of ritualized politics of memory: if they were no longer sure of what they were for, they remembered reflexively what they were against.

In the late twentieth century, the Sacred Heart emblem retains some of its former symbolic power. Even in the United States, the Sacred Heart resonates thanks not only to the ubiquity of the Sacred Heart emblem as a devotional image, but also to its kitsch status in American popular culture, featured notably on television (*The X-Files*), in film (*William Shakespeare's Tragedy of Romeo and Juliet*), and at Los Angeles dance clubs. The Sacred Heart emblem is not as banal as the stop sign, but it is a fairly common and readily recognizable icon. It by no means evokes the same meanings in the United States as it once did in France, nor did it ever. Within France, Sacred Heart devotional literature and imagery of the nineteenth century regularly referred to France's "special status" or to the French as the chosen people of the New Testament. Outside of France, Sacred Heart literature and imagery almost never made such claims. Indeed, with rare exceptions, by the second half of the twentieth century such assertions had vanished from religious rhetoric even in France. Today in France the Sacred Heart as a seditious emblem occupies a place somewhat analogous to that of the Confederate "stars and bars" flag in American popular culture—a symbol thriving on a mix of resentment and nostalgia, most often found on chrome bumpers of vehicles well past their prime.[2] It would be a mistake to read seditious intent into the continued presence of the Sacred Heart in churches and in sacred art in France; there as elsewhere laity and clergy perceive the Sacred Heart today as little different from other religious images. The Sacred Heart has its place alongside the Virgin Mary and the saints.

This book thus represents a kind of "return of the repressed"—an encounter between history and memory. The basilica of the Sacré-Coeur de Montmartre remains one of the top five destinations of international visitors to the city of Paris.[3] As such, the Sacré-Coeur remains, along with the Eiffel Tower and the Arc de Triomphe, one of the signature monuments of the French capital. But few, if any, who visit Montmartre are aware of the basilica's once-contentious status. This book can be read as the "secret history" of the Sacred Heart by readers already familiar with the Sacred Heart as an object of devotion (or the Sacré-Coeur of Montmartre as a landmark) but unaware of the Sacred Heart's former status as an icon of resistance.

This book has a story to tell to readers who have been to Montmartre; readers interested in Paris and its monumental architecture; readers interested in saints and visionaries and body rituals and devotions like the Sacred Heart; readers interested in the mythic beliefs of the French Right from the Vendée to Vichy. The book also serves as a rapid introduction to the millenarian beliefs and historical vision of the Catholic Right in France, a field badly and wrongly neglected by scholars and teachers here and abroad. For the nineteenth century and much of the twentieth, the Sacred Heart defined "Frenchness" for French Catholicism; it was an integral nationalism, and as such its history also belongs to those "others" it defined and excluded.

THE SACRED HEART VISITS THE CHAROLLAIS

And Moses hid his face; for he was afraid to look upon God.

Exodus 3 : 6

Those unsearchable riches of your glory, Lord, were hidden in your
secret place in heaven until the soldier's spear opened the side of your
Son our Lord and Savior on the cross, and from it flowed the mysteries
of our redemption.

GUILLAUME, ABBOT OF SAINT-THIERRY,
ca. 1085–1148, trans. Sister Penelope

To monopolize the Sacred Heart for France, that's not Catholicism:
that's particularism.

CARDINAL BILLOT,
French Jesuit, quoted in Le Figaro, *4 May 1918*

DEEP IN THE CHAROLLAIS at Paray-le-Monial, west of Lyon and not far
from Cluny, a ceremony was about to begin. A saintly body was to undergo
final preparations for public display and veneration. This was France of the
Second Empire, the year was 1865, but the ceremonial dressing of the body
manifested an attention to ritual detail worthy of the Middle Ages.

Monsignor Bouange, vicar general of the diocese of Autun, carried out an
inventory of the remains. Beside and behind him, officers of the Catholic
Church looked on with the attentiveness of medical students in a surgical
theater. Bouange's task was to reconstruct a body for display, working from

a likeness, using bones and wax. He began with the parts of the body to be visible, adding wax components and filler to the skeletal framework of a woman's body. He built up the shoulders, neck, forearms, and face with soft wax, working first for bulk in proper proportions. Then he modeled the wax, giving proper contour and detail so that the figure would resemble the living person.

When Bouange had completed the waxen portion of the effigy, he took the remaining parts of the body—that is to say, the bones making up the trunk and legs—and wrapped them in cotton batting for bulk. The cotton batting, in turn, was wrapped in white silk. Bouange folded the edges of the wrappings and fastened them tightly. Then he fixed the edges with wax and added the episcopal seal so that the wrappings could not be disturbed without damaging the seal. Bouange then carefully positioned a waxen mask over the skull of the holy woman. He adjusted the ersatz face, then pressed it into place. When he was satisfied with the appearance he added several episcopal seals at the margins to secure the visage to the skull.[1] Finally, Bouange stepped back from the effigy, genuflected, and blessed the ensemble.

When the pieces were satisfactorily assembled and arranged, each in its place, the reconstituted body was dressed in the habit of a member of the Visitationist order. The cushion on which it rested, made of fabric embroidered with silver thread, set off the flesh tones and the black-and-white garments of the recumbent effigy. The effect was stunning. The body appeared to be in a restful sleep.

Those present agreed that the figure bore a striking resemblance to Marguerite-Marie Alacoque, beatified only months earlier, in 1864. Since this was a reconstruction, her age was a matter of discretion, so the face chosen for Blessed Marguerite-Marie was that of the young adult, not that of the fifty-year-old woman who had died in 1690. The Sacred Heart of Jesus was placed in her right hand. The gaze of her prosthetic eyes was fixed upon it. In her left hand was a white lily, symbol of virginal purity.[2]

Once the body had been ritually prepared, it was ready for ceremonial veneration. As the assembly knelt, the reconstituted body of the Blessed was placed on a decorated table. Censers were lighted and made to swing from their chains as the priest circled the body solemnly, leaving a trail of incense to drift, swirl, and surround it. When the priest returned to kneel before the body, he led the singing of a Latin hymn, "Corpora sanctorum." Those pres-

Figure 1. The effigy of Marguerite-Marie Alacoque.

The remains of Marguerite-Marie Alacoque, transformed into an effigy shortly after her beatification, are displayed to this day in a reliquary in the Chapel of Apparitions at Paray-le-Monial. Paray-le-Monial became an important pilgrimage site, especially after the disasters of the Terrible Year of 1870–71.

ent approached the body; one by one they kissed the hand. Finally, as the choir sang "Come, O Bride of Christ" (*Veni sponsa Christi*), Bouange placed a diadem on the waxen head.

As this was to be the last human contact with the body of the Blessed for some time, the bishop of Autun arrived in time to preside over the final disposition of the body. As the bishop looked on, the reconstituted body of Marguerite-Marie Alacoque was gently lowered into a splendid reliquary of glass and gilded silver (fig. 1). With her blessed body safely wrapped, sealed, and enclosed—yet visible through the reliquary glass—Marguerite-Marie was now ready to leave the security of the convent.

Paray-le-Monial's most celebrated inhabitant would serve as the focus of a ceremony at once civic and sacred. Porters took their positions beside the reliquary, raised it, and carried it in solemn procession to the town square where it was placed upon an elaborately decorated *reposoir,* an open-air altar. This was merely the first station in a procession similar to that of the annual celebration of Corpus Christi in which the body of Christ, represented by the host enclosed in a monstrance, moves in procession through the town from station to station. Like the Corpus Christi procession that celebrated human redemption through the body of Christ but also reinforced the relationship between town and God, the procession of the corpus of Marguerite-Marie through the neighborhoods of Paray-le-Monial sealed a symbolic union of the patron and her town.[3] It would yet promise national redemption.

This extravagant attention to the body of the holy dead—the wrappings, modelings, and sealings—highlights the persistence of baroque piety well into the nineteenth century.[4] The late twentieth century, like the late nineteenth, is obsessed with bodies, but the bodies of our times are sources of sensual delight—living, hard bodies to look upon, with sculpted contours to aspire to or to seek pleasure in; dead bodies have no use except as inconvenient reminders of mortality in an age fixated on youth. In the European nineteenth century, a saintly body served as a reminder of mortality and an exhortation to piety—a spur to efforts leading to salvation. Marguerite-Marie's body revealed her enduring power, a power accumulated over a lifetime of meditation and prayer. Marguerite-Marie's body validated the claim that through faith one could triumph over death itself.

But not without paying a certain price. The meticulous care with which Marguerite-Marie's body was prepared owes much to the significance of the devotion she helped to popularize and the enormous political significance it had acquired in France. Indeed, the ceremonial wrappings just described in the context of her beatification by the Roman Catholic Church were not the first time after her death that her body was subject to manipulation. In July of 1830, during the twilight days and hours of the Restoration monarchy, the body of Marguerite-Marie had undergone a meticulous inspection. The process of consideration for beatification had just gotten underway and with the hope, if not presumption, of eventual beatification, her body became of matter of special concern.[5] Not only was the body then potentially an object of veneration—indeed, some smaller bones were removed as relics—its very state of preservation might reveal clues about her spiritual worthiness.[6] Well-preserved bodies, or at least those spared significant decomposition, were routinely interpreted as indicating divine favor, and this kind of information could strengthen the case for beatification and canonization.

In fact, it's hard to imagine how the alternative, the natural corruption of the flesh, could be read favorably, so powerfully embedded was the implication of divine favor in the uncannily preserved corpse. The French expression that a person died *en odeur de sainteté,* literally "in the odor of holiness," is generally interpreted more in the sense of "aura," that is, that a person had lived out her days in an extraordinarily Christian and saintly way and thus had generated an aura of saintliness. But the expression could be interpreted literally, and great significance is attached, in the Christian tradition, to the odors emitted by bodies at the moment of death or at the time of exhumation. Élisabeth de France, the famously devout sister of the unfortunate Louis XVI guillotined by the Revolution in 1793, was herself guillotined months after her brother at the Place de la Révolution, later renamed the Place de la Concorde. Witnesses would later claim that at the moment the blade severed her neck, the entire square was filled with the smell of roses.[7] In the nineteenth century, the remains of a courageous and deeply devout army officer generated a minor controversy when his tomb was opened. Partisans of beatification insisted that his body seemed hardly decomposed at all, even remarkably preserved. Impartial observers then felt obliged to set the record straight and reported that the body emitted a cadaveresque odor powerful enough "to bowl one over."[8]

Although Marguerite-Marie died in the odor of holiness in the metaphorical sense, there seems to have been little about the state of her body in 1830 from which one could adduce additional evidence in favor of beatification. Her exhumation and inspection were likely prompted by the declining prospects of the restored Bourbon monarchy. No one could be sure what the future held in July of 1830 when the regime entered its terminal crisis, but it would have been hard to imagine the ostentatiously devout Charles X being replaced by someone more sympathetic to religion. Marguerite-Marie's tomb was opened on 22 July 1830, the week before the three "Glorious Days" that ended with the abdication of Charles X and the end of the Restoration monarchy. Mere days before workers and shopkeepers would gather to erect barricades in the streets of Paris, sixty priests gathered at Paray-le-Monial for the exhumation of Marguerite-Marie.[9]

These preoccupations with the body of Marguerite-Marie, in 1830 and in 1865, relate to her body both as an index of her saintliness in life and as an object that in death could generate and inspire spiritual sentiments. The 1830 inspection yielded clues of divine favor; the 1865 dressings and venerations validated her designation as "blessed," the final stage before canonization and official recognition as a saint by the Catholic Church. All this attention to a lifeless body—what more fitting tribute to a woman who had given her life to contemplation of the attributes of the body of Christ?

And yet, Marguerite-Marie had not "invented" the idea of spiritual practice organized around the Sacré-Coeur, or Sacred Heart of Jesus. Years before

Marguerite-Marie Alacoque, Jean Eudes had worked to spread the devotion to the heart of Jesus first around Normandy and later, through his advocates and missionaries, throughout France.[10] The fact that the work and career of Marguerite-Marie eclipsed his own has to do with certain features specific to her vision, which we will explore shortly. The fact that his saintly career overlaps with that of Marguerite-Marie—he died in 1680, ten years before Marguerite-Marie—does not suggest that she "borrowed" this devotion from him; it merely underlines how both Eudes and Alacoque built upon the contemporary and enduring vogue for the human heart in sacred and popular culture. Anne de Bretagne was buried beside her spouse, Louis XII, but she asked that her heart be returned to Brittany as a token of her attachment.[11] Henri IV and Louis XIV both gave their hearts to the Jesuits. The Visitationists of Lyon kept the heart of François de Sales, cofounder of their religious order.[12] These hearts were not spiritual objects, of course, but they reveal a broader, secular fascination with the heart as the seat of the emotional or spiritual life of the person. The devotion to the Sacré-Coeur, in its Eudist and Alacoquist variants, built upon this.

What set apart Marguerite-Marie Alacoque was not her fascination with the heart of Jesus, a fascination shared by many others—by many before her. What made Marguerite-Marie different were the visions she claimed to have had in the 1680s and later, visions in which Jesus recommended the devotion of the Sacred Heart to her and commanded her to make it widely known (fig. 2). These visions attracted wide attention, in part because they offered specific advantages to individuals if they faithfully observed the devotion to the Sacred Heart. For example, one vision held out the promise of a "good death"—a good death being a death that is not sudden, allowing the dying person time to confess, to make amends, and to prepare the soul for judgment. Facing divine judgment in an unprepared state was one of the great anxieties of believers everywhere for whom the promise of a "good death" was therefore not to be scoffed at. At the level of popular religion, this is what drove the success of the Sacré-Coeur long after the death of Marguerite-Marie Alacoque.

But the message of the Sacré-Coeur operated on many levels, and other visions addressed not the individual believer but France as a whole. France in the time of Marguerite-Marie Alacoque was one of the leading Catholic powers of Europe, but its security was threatened by frequent wars and powerful neighbors over the Pyrenees, beyond the Rhine, and across the

Figure 2. The Sacred Heart appears to Marguerite-Marie Alacoque.
*Instructions, pratiques, et prières pour la dévotion au Sacré-Coeur de Jésus:
L'Office, vespres et messe de cette dévotion* (Paris, 1752).

Marguerite-Marie Alacoque, in an early engraving, kneels before a
vision of Jesus, who presents his heart.

Channel. There was also the internal threat of religious civil war.[13] Marguerite-Marie's visions began almost a century after the Saint Bartholomew's Day Massacre (1572), in which tens of thousands of Huguenots (French Protestants) had lost their lives at Catholic hands. And the Edict of Nantes (1598) had granted certain rights of religious toleration to Protestants, but these had been weakened after 1629 and would be withdrawn in 1685, raising the specter of a renewal of religious violence.[14] This was the context in which the Sacred Heart appeared to Marguerite-Marie and offered a kind of alliance with the king of France against his enemies. In effect, the visions of Marguerite-Marie offered victory to Louis XIV under the sign of the Sacré-Coeur, much as Constantine, that other Christian king, had once been promised victory under the sign of the cross.

The solicitude later shown the body of Marguerite-Marie Alacoque thus had to do with much more than respect due to the body of a holy woman. It had to do with the extraordinary significance of her visions, not only for individual Catholics in pursuit of salvation thanks to the promise of a "good death," but also for a uniquely Catholic vision of the status and future of France. In the century following Marguerite-Marie's visions, between the 1680s and the 1780s, the status of a specifically Catholic France became more precarious, not less. The appeal of a divine alliance grew accordingly. Marguerite-Marie's visions thus constitute the founding event in the epic tale of France and the Sacré-Coeur. For that reason, they merit closer inspection.

A DIVINE PASSION

The career of the heart as a religious icon in the modern period owes much to the efforts of Jeanne de Chantal and François de Sales, founders of the religious order that Marguerite-Marie Alacoque would join. François and Jeanne shared an intense spirituality that fed upon an inspired union with heart of Jesus. Their correspondence revealed a casual intimacy based upon a metaphorical union with Jesus—and through Jesus with each other. "I don't know where you will be during Lent, at least in body," François wrote to Jeanne early in 1610. "But I hope that in spirit you will be in the cavern of the turtledove in the pierced side of our dear Savior. I'll do my best to be there often with you."[15]

Salesian and Chantalian spirituality celebrated such visions of chaste intimacy—turtledoves being, then as now, a common symbol for lovers—in which the heart of Jesus served as love nest. Their style of intense, intimate, person-to-person spirituality was preserved and institutionalized through the founding of the Visitationist order in 1610.[16] Baroness de Chantal (she entered the religious life following the death of her husband, the Baron de Chantal) had wealth and nobility in addition to her considerable spiritual assets, and she put them all to work in setting up the Visitationist order. The order grew rapidly with new convents and new vocations in the generations to follow, among them Marguerite-Marie Alacoque. Marguerite-Marie was born in 1648 to Philiberte Lamyn and Claude Alacoque. In 1671, at the age of 23, she entered the Visitationist convent at Paray-le-Monial, not far from her hometown in the Charollais.[17] She completed her vows shortly thereafter.

The spiritual development of members of religious orders, especially new vocations, is a matter of paramount importance and very much in the Salesian-Chantalian tradition.[18] So was spiritual development by means of dialogue, whether in person or by means of letters, and the letters of Jeanne de Chantal and François de Sales trace a kind of trail map for their *via spiritualis.* Reflection, conversation, and transcription enhanced and chronicled the spiritual development of the soul. Accordingly, new vocations were encouraged to verbalize their religious faith, ecstasies, and anxieties. Mother Saumaise was the superior at the Paray convent during Marguerite-Marie's earliest years there, and she enjoined Marguerite-Marie to write down the significant details of her spiritual life.[19] At first, Marguerite-Marie reported difficulty in obeying this request of her spiritual director, but in time it was evident that writing had become central to her spiritual and personal growth. Soon, in note after note, Marguerite-Marie began to report the most startling things—presentiments, divine voices, visions. Marguerite-Marie had established with Jesus the richest and most regular form of contact. "Divine revelations" would be one way of describing these, but "revelation" suggests such a monologic, rather than dialogic, relationship that the term falls short of what Marguerite-Marie's notes, letters, and transcripts describe.

Marguerite-Marie had entered into a personal relationship with Jesus, whose utterances and messages touched upon many parts of the private as well as spiritual life of Marguerite-Marie. In fact, it is difficult to resist the conclusion that Marguerite-Marie had learned how to use her spiritual life to work through some of the challenges of her personal life in the convent—to recruit Jesus as an ally in convent politics. "One evening Jesus [mon Bien-Aimé] reproached me," Marguerite-Marie explained in a note to Mother Saumaise about her visions and some of her friendships at the convent. "He did not want to share my heart." Jesus advised her to break contact with some of her more troublesome convent sisters and leveled an ultimatum to the effect that if she "did not withdraw from these creatures, he would withdraw from me."[20] Mother Saumaise rightly had doubts about some aspects of Marguerite-Marie's divine communion, doubts presumably shared by some of Marguerite-Marie's sisters at the convent. Indeed, it is not difficult to discern in Marguerite-Marie's visions a ploy to imagine a world in which her will prevailed, a fantasy world that allowed her to shun those she found vexatious and to do so with divine sanction.

One can well imagine the hesitations of Mother Saumaise and others, because the personality of Jesus, as revealed by Marguerite-Marie, sometimes had more in common with the God of the Old Testament and less in common with the warm, loving God of Jeanne de Chantal and François de Sales. There are no turtledoves in the spiritual rhetoric of Marguerite-Marie. Her Sacré-Coeur could be a jealous God, insisting upon mortification of the flesh and unswerving loyalty as often as charity and selfless acts of kindness. Once, when Marguerite-Marie balked at an act of mortification, Jesus prodded her on and reproached her by pointing out the many wounds on his body, wounds endured for her sake. Jesus wondered at her ingratitude.[21]

Marguerite-Marie was driven by strong emotions. Little about her inner spiritual life seems calibrated or modulated. Women who take religious vows are said to have become brides of Christ; sometimes Marguerite-Marie's relationship with the Sacré-Coeur took on tones of great sensitivity and intimacy. "I was favored with the loving caresses of my heavenly Spouse," she once wrote.[22] In these moments, Marguerite-Marie could be as blissfully engaged as one who has found a life-long companion. In other moments, she might display the shattered feelings of one who discovers that her generous love is returned with a love that is possessive, suspicious, and demanding. At these times, Jesus spoke to Marguerite-Marie as a jealous lover or controlling spouse. "My Jesus," she wrote, "asked me often if I loved him. These words gave very great pain."[23] "He told me that I must renounce all pleasures, that He alone sufficed. In all my actions, I saw only infidelities and ingratitudes."[24]

Despite such episodes, Marguerite-Marie remained utterly committed; her engagement was unconditional, and the tormented and conflicted episodes in her relationship with the Jesus of her visions typically gave way to moments of sweet ecstasy. Her fascination with the Divine was most acute when it focused on the body of Jesus. The rewards of her spiritual life were rich, including the most inspired moments of contact and emotional release. Who would dare to imagine such familiarities, when even Moses had been afraid to gaze upon a mere representation of God?

Marguerite-Marie not only had visions of Jesus: her visions invited contact and resulted in keen experience of physical union with God. In this she was like Saint Catherine of Siena, who had been blessed by visions or experiences of actual contact with the body of Jesus (fig. 3). In fact, such experiences of divine reverie were not uncommon within the Salesian and Chantalian spiritual tradition. Anne-Marie Rosset, mother superior at the Visitationist convent at Marseille, entered an ecstatic state when she leaned forward to kiss the feet on a crucifix: "It seemed that the crucifix leaned toward her, and she found herself with her lips stuck to the wound in the side of Our Savior, with such a great loss of self and such a raising of her own heart into the heart of Jesus, that she fainted and was blessed with a rapture like she had never experienced." [25] These women achieved intense spiritual states that delighted the body and consumed the soul.

Marguerite-Marie also yielded to such divine transports. The peaks in her spiritual life consisted of blissful, ecstatic contact or union with the body of Jesus. On one occasion, she described how a beam of light flowed from the wound in the side of Jesus and flowed directly into her heart, producing indescribable feelings. [26] Her intense feelings involved other intimacies. Once she described how Jesus pressed her "mouth to the wound in his side, holding me tightly there for three or four hours, yielding delights I cannot express." All the while that she was held there, she heard repeated continually, "Now you see that nothing is lost . . . and everything is found in my pleasure [*jouissance*]." To which she replied, "O my Love! I would gladly give up this extreme pleasure just to love you for the love of you, my God!" She repeated this phrase, "for as long as he repeated his divine caresses." [27]

One can well imagine how an irresistible spiritual urge for union with God might lead to such encounters. And yet the image of lips pressed to gaping wounds, the inexpressible pleasures, the intense warmth of prolonged embraces, the stimulating caresses, the gasped and rhythmic utterances—in

Figure 3. Léon Bénouville, *The Mystical Communion of Saint Catherine of Siena* (1856). Musée du Louvre, Paris. © RMN—Arnaudet.

"He placed my mouth to the wound in his side, holding me tightly there . . . , yielding delights I cannot express." Marguerite-Marie Alacoque, *Vie et Oeuvres*, 2:69. The devotion to the Sacré-Coeur potentiated a chaste but intensely intimate relationship with the divine and easily lends itself to erotic interpretation; these elements of Marguerite-Marie's vision were prefigured in Catherine of Siena's mystical union with Jesus.

the late twentieth century it is impossible to read such things without seeing in them a (barely) repressed or deflected erotic desire. Indeed, the simile all but breaks down. It's not *as if* spiritual union induces states of ecstasy *like* carnal union—as described by Marguerite-Marie, it simply *is*. Does it have to be? Caroline Bynum has warned against missing the distinction between sexual intimacies and the caring, comforting intimacies of a loving (and divine) parent. Jesus the loving Mother is a common enough trope in medieval spirituality.[28] Why shouldn't it be at home in the seventeenth century? Conversely, an age more at ease with sexuality is perhaps more sympathetic to a woman who, in the austere surroundings of the convent, enjoyed such a rich and intensely pleasurable spiritual life. Why not admire one whose prayerful meditations climaxed in reveries and in visions of a profound union with God? Why not admit the possibility of a spiritual ecstasy distinct from sexual ecstasy?

And yet not only the twentieth century wonders at Marguerite-Marie's intimate visions. They have been the target of withering criticisms from some of the sharpest critics of earlier times. Henri Grégoire, priest and politician during the Revolution and implacable enemy of the Jesuits, wrote openly of his contempt for what he called the *cordicoles* and their idolatry of the heart, their *cordiolatrie*. He wondered about the touching of body against body and the nighttime "colloques amoureux" reported by Marguerite-Marie.[29] Jules Michelet, historian and defender of the Republic, saw Marguerite-Marie as merely an extreme example of a blatant attempt to impart an erotic charge to Christianity—to make belief sexy in an age of religious skepticism and carnal self-indulgence.

Michelet had little regard for the intellectual capacities of women. He saw the devotion to the heart of Jesus as part of a priestly plot diabolically constructed to play upon the presumed sentimentality and weak character of women. "With women," he wrote, "the life of the heart is everything. This organ, passageway of blood, is strongly influenced by the circulation of blood. [In women, the heart] is no less dominant than their sexuality."[30] For Michelet, part of the appeal of the devotion to the Sacré-Coeur is that it validates the use of intimate language about a bodily organ, precisely because the heart is not a sexual organ. It makes intimate language safe by placing it in a spiritual context. "The heart is a nobler organ than the sexual organ, so it has the advantage of permitting many expressions of dubious but decent meaning, a range of equivocal tender expressions that don't make one blush."[31]

The Sacred Heart is an aim-inhibited object, a displaced object of desire. It breaks down the binary opposition between virtue and desire; it potentiates intimacy without shame.

At times, Marguerite-Marie's voices and visions suggest that she was struggling with power relations and personal conflicts in her immediate surroundings. What did Mother Saumaise think when she learned that Marguerite-Marie's visions included a dream of a deceased member of the convent? This deceased appeared to Marguerite-Marie in a dream and spoke of the torments of Purgatory: she'd witnessed one of her parents being cast into Hell and the deceased herself suffered from an ulcerated mouth ("for my lack of silence") and experienced her tongue eaten by vermin ("for my uncharitable words"). She reproached Marguerite-Marie for her comforts: "There you are at ease in your bed; look at me lying in a bed of flames."[32]

Marguerite-Marie claimed that such incidents inspired her to persist in her mortifications in hopes of easing the suffering of those who had passed on. However, it was also true that her privileged access to the dead and the divine presented a unique challenge to those with power over her. Her visions and voices threatened the very authority of Mother Saumaise when they involved the conduct of women entrusted to her care. Bad enough that Marguerite-Marie's visions exacted posthumous revenge on her sisters by revealing their fate once they had passed on; it was worse when her visions touched on the transgressions of those still alive. In one of her visions, Marguerite-Marie saw Jesus bearing a rough crown of thorns. Marguerite-Marie remarked that the crown consisted of nineteen very sharp thorns that pierced the flesh of Jesus' head. "He told me," Marguerite-Marie later recounted, "that he had sought me out to remove the thorns that had been driven in by an unfaithful spouse."[33] Marguerite-Marie related this vision to her superior, along with the advice that acts of humility on behalf of the members of the convent would remove the thorns. She noted that this was pleasing and efficacious because Jesus, in a vision five days later, had relief from three of the thorns.[34] With such immediate results, Marguerite-Marie effectively operated as middleman in an economy of grace and intercession, with corresponding benefits of status and prestige.

22   THE SACRED HEART VISITS THE CHAROLLAIS

Not only did Marguerite-Marie's visions provide privileged access to the prideful acts and transgressions of the other members of her order, they also linked her to the saintly founders of the Visitationist order, Jeanne de Chantal and François de Sales. "On the feast day of François de Sales, when I was kneeling before the Holy Sacrament, I distinctly heard this blessed Father, accompanied by our most worthy Mother de Chantal, say to me, 'God has ordered me to visit all the convents of our order and all those I recognize for my true daughters will be received by Him as his true spouses'; to fulfill this request I only had to visit the hearts of our Superiors [such as Mother Saumaise] in which the hearts of all of the daughters of the Visitation are enclosed." [35]

Not only is Marguerite-Marie in contact with the founders of her order, but her vision reveals that they continue to make the rounds of their convents. They know the hearts of the mothers superior and, through them, the identities of their true daughters. Moreover, they bypass channels and circumvent hierarchies by communicating directly with Marguerite-Marie. A generous reading of this vision would have it that the founders continued to watch over their successors; another reading suggests that this was convent politics by other means. [36] Indeed, a later vision seemed to hold out to Mother Saumaise not a threat but a promise of divine gratitude. "Another time," wrote Marguerite-Marie, "he told me that he would make a crown of twelve of his most beloved, those who brought him the greatest glory on earth; they would be rendered as twelve bright stars surrounding his Sacred Heart. It seemed to me that you were in this number. . . ." [37] Marguerite-Marie's visions empowered her to rearrange relationships and hierarchies within the convent world. She did not directly challenge the authority of her superior, but her superior became her client in the sense that she depended on Marguerite-Marie for reassurance of her salvation.

Marguerite-Marie's visions, like those of all visionaries, threatened institutions and hierarchies through disintermediation. She possessed unmediated access to the Sacred. Visionaries pose a challenge to the revealed religions and their institutions because one of the functions of religious institutions is to protect orthodoxy and thus safeguard revealed truth once the source of revealed Truth has passed on. Visionaries challenge this function in the sense that revelation continues thanks to their direct communion with God. And, after all, who can gainsay a visionary? Of course Marguerite-Marie would not have been the first mystic to challenge Church authority, but her challenges to authority were local—her visions were, in effect, brilliant maneuvers in convent politics. Her visions allowed her to circumvent her superior, pull rank, and appeal directly to the founders of her religious order and her religion.

Validation for Marguerite-Marie came through the intervention of an outsider. A young member of the Jesuit order, Claude de la Colombière, was posted to Paray-le-Monial in 1675. He became Marguerite-Marie's confessor and, as her confessor, he became another privileged interlocutor.[38] She described her revelations to him. Soon he experienced his own revelations, revelations that confirmed for him the divine origins of Marguerite-Marie's communications. Colombière helped to interpret her visions to the larger world, to shape her message or, if not "her" message, then the message she was chosen to convey. Colombière became one of Marguerite-Marie's most ardent advocates. Her cause became his. He relayed her message to his superiors. The Sacré-Coeur became a Jesuit cause.[39]

Colombière's validation of Marguerite-Marie and her visions gave her extraordinary new power. Her visions, by themselves, were important. But Jesuit sponsorship, which followed Colombière's endorsement, gave the power that comes from recognition by an established authority—and a male authority at that. The fact that this recognition came from outside the Visitationist convent at Paray-le-Monial helped Mother Saumaise and others within the Visitationist hierarchy to suspend their disbelief. The visions of Marguerite-Marie Alacoque were no longer strictly a Visitationist matter. Indeed, Marguerite-Marie's visions became more elaborate and worldly as time went on. At first they had were largely limited to her world at the Visitationist convent, her sisters there, her mother superior, and Jesus. Soon, her visions manifested a new set of preoccupations involving the king and the fate of France itself.

DIVINE ALLY FOR A CHOSEN PEOPLE

One of Marguerite-Marie's earliest visions related to concerns well beyond the confines of the Visitationist convent at Paray-le-Monial. "My Jesus made me see that his justice was disturbed," Marguerite-Marie told Mother Saumaise, "because his chosen people were in revolt against him."[40] His chosen people were the people of France; their apostasy left Jesus feeling deeply aggrieved. In earlier visions, Marguerite-Marie had established the fact that bodies were an index of other things. When a deceased nun appeared to her from Purgatory, her body bore wounds and sores in places where she had sinned—her lips, her tongue. Jesus' body, too, bore wounds and sores not from his sins, of course, but from those who had sinned against him. A crown of nineteen thorns had symbolized the pride and infidelities of a spouse (a Visitationist nun). Now, in another vision, the body of Jesus revealed the injuries and insults of an entire people. "He presented himself to me," Marguerite-Marie wrote, "covered with wounds and His Body all bloody, his Heart torn by wounds and all worn out. In fear, I lay face down before him. I dared say nothing, and he said to me, 'Here is the state to which my chosen people have reduced me.'"[41] This vision, and others like it, opened up a vastly enlarged political domain for Marguerite-Marie. Now the body of Jesus revealed the transgressions of a nation. France had the blood of Jesus on its hands.

In the 1680s, Marguerite-Marie's visions entered a directly political phase, demanding recognition at the royal court. "He desires," wrote Marguerite-Marie, "to enter with pomp and magnificence into the palaces of princes and kings. He wants to be honored there as much as he was scorned and humiliated during his Passion. He receives . . . pleasure in seeing the mighty of the earth brought low and humiliated before him. . . ."[42] The veneration of the Sacred Heart in the palace of the king would compensate for the injuries of apostasy. The Sacré-Coeur was to become an official devotion.

Marguerite-Marie's visions revealed the ambitions of the Sacred Heart. The Sacré-Coeur demanded recognition from the Sun King. In her vision, Marguerite-Marie was to deliver a message to "the eldest son of my Sacred Heart." (France was frequently referred to as "the Eldest Daughter of the Church"; the king would be "the eldest son.") The Sacré-Coeur "wants to reign in his palace, to be painted on his standards and engraved on his arms, in order to render them victorious over his enemies" as well as those of the Holy Church. The king was to receive grace and eternal glory by means of a consecration to the Sacré-Coeur. In effect, the king and the Sacré-Coeur were to become partners in a world still divided by heresy and political discord. In return for a consecration to the Sacré-Coeur, the king of France would reign in triumph over his enemies and those of the Church. It was an alliance made in heaven to ensure the earthly triumph of the chosen people.

Later commentators would take exception to some parts of this language, especially the reference to the king's "arms" or weapons, complaining that this must be understood in the sense of *armoiries,* or ensigns, since, as a 1915 commentator put it, "Our Lord would never ask that the image of his Heart, symbol of his love, be engraved on engines of destruction."[43] The rest of the message was treated as authentic, however, and the very nature of the message assured a certain amount of attention. After all, this was a divine request, a direct message from God to the king of France. It contained explicit demands with clearly assigned responsibility for fulfillment. The yield was certain. Never since the time of Moses or, arguably, Paul's journey on the road to Damascus, had divine will seemed so unambiguous. The Sacred Heart was offering a new covenant to a new chosen people.

Subsequent communications fleshed out the details. In August of 1689, Marguerite-Marie described another vision in which it was clear that these demands on the part of the Sacré-Coeur were made by, as Marguerite-Marie put it, "the Eternal Father" who wished to repair the bitterness and anguish suffered by "the heart of his divine Son," as well as the humiliation and outrage inflicted upon Jesus during the Passion.[44] The Sacré-Coeur was "to establish his empire in the court of our great monarch," and there was to be "an edifice where this divine Heart was to receive the consecration and homage of the king and the entire court." In return, the Sacré-Coeur would become the protector and defender of the king over all of his enemies, dispense grace and bounty throughout the realm, and bring success to all of the king's enterprises. Louis XIV would become the new Constantine, the very model of the Christian monarch. France would triumph through the Sacré-Coeur.

Marguerite-Marie's visions expressed ambitions that surpassed the limits of the Visitationist convent. Indeed, they exceeded the limits of the spiritual realm. On the personal level, they sought to establish Marguerite-Marie of Paray-le-Monial as the interlocutor between God and king. Marguerite-Marie's visions put her at a privileged position between the court of Louis and the heavenly court of the Sacré-Coeur. On another level, her visions served the purposes of her Jesuit sponsors, locked in mortal combat with their rivals, the "protestantizing" Jansenists, for the soul of France.[45] Finally, her visions showed how divine will united the destinies of France and the Sacred Heart. The designs of the Sacred Heart now touched upon the very destiny of France and the French, God's chosen people. Over time, the political message of the Sacred Heart would be reduced to three points: France, through its king, should be consecrated to the Sacré-Coeur; an edifice should be built for this purpose; this historic compact should be recorded on the royal insignia—the fleur-de-lis would have to make room for the Sacred Heart.

A consecration, a building, an insignia. But how was such an important request to be made known? Surely the king took no interest in the writings of modest convent nuns, however grand and ambitious their visions. Yet all those who knew of the miraculous visions of Marguerite-Marie and believed in them shared the conviction that the king must be told. These visions touched on matters of state. The responsibility for pursuing this initiative with Louis XIV passed to his confessor, Père La Chaise. Nothing is known about the fate of this initiative except that the king never acted on these demands—if he ever learned of them. Perhaps Marguerite-Marie's message and request surpassed the credulity of Père La Chaise and the message was never conveyed to Louis XIV. It's also possible that the substance of the request *was* conveyed to the king and it surpassed *his* credulity. As one commentator blithely put it, "It's God's secret!"[46]

And so it remains, for the truth died with the Sun King and his confessor. The story of France and the Sacré-Coeur might have ended there, a missed opportunity for national redemption or a splendid minor farce. However, no divine plan could remain contingent on the will and action of a mere mortal, even if that mortal were a king. Moreover, Marguerite-Marie's spiritualized will to power, driven by faith and imagination, was too strong to accept early defeat. Her visions continued to guide the prodigious growth of this devotion and to secure her place within it. Claude de la Colombière had endorsed her at a crucial moment, when her Visitationist sisters and superior still harbored doubts; Colombière offered confidence and the support of the most powerful religious order of the day. After his death, her visions guided Marguerite-Marie back to the Jesuits. With or without the king, they would take the lead in the propagation of the Sacred Heart devotion.

AN ECONOMY OF GRACE

At the same time that she was envisioning a royal consecration to the Sacré-Coeur, Marguerite-Marie also recruited mortal and saintly allies on behalf of a popular devotion to the Sacré-Coeur. In 1688 she described seeing the Sacred Heart on a throne of flames. Beside the throne were the Blessed Virgin, François de Sales, and the recently deceased Colombière—an extraordinary team of advocates. The appearance of Colombière in such company must have astounded those who had known him in life. Saints tended to be shadowy, remote figures removed in time and known only through legends of sanctity or triumph over persecution. Within the space of a lifetime, Colombière had moved from the status of an ordinary mortal with ordinary human failings to a prominent place in a heavenly inner circle. This was an unparalleled triumph.

Marguerite-Marie could only be strengthened by a vision featuring her former confessor and advocate raised to the rank of heavenly companion and adviser. Colombière's rapid promotion was an implicit rebuke to those who had doubted her, and the cameo appearance by François de Sales served as an endorsement of the Sacred Heart devotion within the Visitationist order that he had founded. The Virgin herself reminded the Jesuits of their obligation to popularize the devotion to the Sacré-Coeur when, in Marguerite-Marie's vision, she addressed Colombière: "For you, faithful servant of my Divine Son, you have a great part in this precious treasure . . . for it is reserved to the Fathers of your Company [the Jesuit order was also known as the Company of Jesus] to make known the utility and value of this devotion."[47] In a later vision, it was the Sacré-Coeur who called upon the Jesuits to sponsor the devotion: "He wishes that the Reverend Jesuit Fathers make known the utility and value" of the devotion to the Sacré-Coeur.[48] The popular appeal of the devotion was enhanced by other pronouncements. Domestic shrines to the Sacré-Coeur became common in devout households thanks to the promise of protection and grace wherever the image of the Sacré-Coeur was displayed.[49]

Marguerite-Marie sketched one popular image of the heart of Jesus, which she distributed to novices to the Visitationist order for display and veneration (fig. 4). Marguerite-Marie also encouraged novices to wear the Sacré-Coeur emblem close to their hearts, that is, pinned to their garments.[50] Early emblems were handmade, but reproduction in quantity soon followed. Marguerite-Marie encouraged Mother Saumaise to have the image engraved, so that it could be distributed widely and popularized as part of the devotion. In the economy of grace in which she was now a major intercessor,

Figure 4. Marguerite-Marie Alacoque and the image of the Sacred Heart of Jesus. In Victor Alet, *La France et le Sacré-Coeur* (Paris, 1871).

Marguerite-Marie Alacoque holds a sketch of the Sacré-Coeur— a wounded heart surrounded by a crown of thorns.

Marguerite-Marie promised Mother Saumaise that "if you will procure Him this honor, He will not fail to compensate you."[51]

Two centuries later, at the end of the nineteenth century, such practices would be worked into a standard set of recommendations associated with the Sacred Heart devotion. "Display the Sacred Heart image in a place of honor in the home, decorate with it, kiss it piously, wear it on your person in the form of a scapular."[52] And even if there would be no royal chapel or royal consecration in honor of the Sacré-Coeur in her time, Marguerite-Marie's family organized a scaled-down version. One brother, Chrysostome Alacoque, was mayor of the village of Bois-Sainte-Marie; the other, Jacques, was the pastor of the parish church in the same village. In a demonstration of what connections can do in small-town France, Mayor Alacoque proposed to erect a chapel in honor of the Sacré-Coeur in the Bois-Sainte-Marie parish church.[53] In their respective roles, the Alacoque brothers—one the mayor, the other the pastor—promoted a devotion and consecration to the Sacré-Coeur organized at the level of the municipality; they were, in effect, stand-ins for Louis XIV. Their local gesture demonstrated good will and compensated, in some small way, for the failure of the king.

Such acts, in lieu of a royal fulfillment of the demands of the Sacré-Coeur, would have many imitators. They hinted at a popularization, even a democratization, of Marguerite-Marie's vision. Marguerite-Marie's visions built upon the assumption that God concludes agreements with kings, in the manner of Constantine, Clovis, and Louis XIII. Failing that, Marguerite-Marie and her agents had to rethink their strategy. Until a royal consecration could be secured, they would have to make do with a grassroots campaign: private, domestic, and municipal gestures of confidence in the Sacred Heart of Jesus.

THE SACRED HEART OF JESUS, FONT OF NATIONAL GRANDEUR

Marguerite-Marie Alacoque did not invent the devotion to the heart of Jesus. For centuries Christians had pondered the mysteries of the corporeality of the Son of God. Surely Jesus had had a heart in the same way that he had had a human head to bear the crown of thorns and limbs by which to be fastened to the cross. What had that heart felt? What pain, what suffering, what love would a divine heart feel? Would a divine heart bleed? And how much more would a divine heart ache? What nurturing warmth would a divine heart exude? For generations, such questions had stimulated the imagination of the faithful fascinated by the humanity of the God-Man of Nazareth.

Marguerite-Marie's specific contributions were more in the category of extensions, rather than inventions, of the devotion. No one before her had quite imagined and expressed as she had the intense desire one might feel for the actual body of Jesus. Marguerite-Marie eroticized the body of Jesus, not as a source of sexual pleasure, but as a source of grace, of plenitude, of comfort yielding intense satisfaction. To want Jesus was a banal ambition in Christendom. To want Jesus with the intensity of a bride, to express spiritual needs not *as* sexual desire but using metaphors of sexual desire—these were innovations in the vocabulary of spiritual yearning. Few of Marguerite-Marie's predecessors surpassed her in this regard.

Marguerite-Marie's fascination with the corporeal Jesus extended to other parts of the body and their meanings too. If Jesus had died to redeem a fallen humanity, his wounds were the outcome of sin, hence their special fascination. Few before her had described with such compelling interest the actual wounds—extensions of the crucifixion—that the body of Jesus might receive as the result of human sin. Marguerite-Marie thought visually and symbolically. Her fascination with the wounded body of Jesus was her way of thinking through the conundrum of the persistence of evil after the redemptive act of Jesus. Jesus died so that man might conquer sin, yet man still sins and the body of Jesus must reveal the traces of those sins too.

Finally, there is the ambition of Marguerite-Marie, for nothing impresses us more than her obvious will to win others over, her drive to conquer others for the Sacré-Coeur and for herself through the Sacré-Coeur. Marguerite-Marie's visions focused on Jesus; hers were Christian visions. But only Marguerite-Marie had these visions, and they put her at the center of an economy of spiritual knowledge, of grace, of revelation. Marguerite-Marie's visions, especially when they touched on the inner life of her colleagues, eventually either won over the skeptics or silenced her enemies. Her visions generated curiosity, anxiety, dread. What might she see next? What will she reveal? What more does she know? It's my word against hers and her word comes from God. Who will dare to doubt her? And what if she is right? What then is the fate of my soul?

The personal immediacy of her visions stimulated her political expansiveness. For just as Jesus had spoken directly to her, Jesus was also speaking to

Figure 5. "The Hearts of Jesus and Mary Presented to France as Her Supreme Hope." *Messager du Sacré-Coeur* 40 (August 1881): 161.

In the late nineteenth century, Marguerite-Marie Alacoque's visions of the Sacré-Coeur validated France's special status among nations, especially for French Catholics anxious about their nation's decline. In the right foreground, allegorical representations of the four continents (Asia, Africa, Europe, and the Americas) look on in wonder as France receives grace from on high.

her times and to France through her. Revelation continues: Jesus has not redeemed humanity only to abandon it; he speaks and calls for action. There is a new chosen people and they have sinned. God calls upon his people to return to the ways of faith and proclaim publicly their divine vocation. The French realm must be consecrated to the Sacré-Coeur, there must be a chapel constructed for this purpose, and the banners and ensigns of the Crown must bear witness to the union of France and the Sacred Heart of Jesus (fig. 5). Once this pact could be concluded, abundant grace would shower down on France and the king of France would triumph over his enemies in an astonishing demonstration of the power of the Christian God. Until then, the people are called upon to honor the Sacred Heart of Jesus through their own public acts of piety. They are to attach its image to their persons, display it prominently in their homes, and honor it in their churches.

Marguerite-Marie's visions made her a prophet of a nation's destiny. Even if the Sun King remained ignorant or indifferent to her vision of a formally Christianized realm, a realm consecrated to the Sacré-Coeur, her vision had nonetheless attracted the attention of powerful Jesuit sponsors. As news of her wondrous and troubling visions spread, thanks to Jesuit efforts, her story captured the imaginations of devout Catholics everywhere. Just as the bits and pieces of Marguerite-Marie's body were wrapped in cloth or fleshed out with wax and assembled for display at Paray-le-Monial after her beatification, the bits and pieces of her visions were fashioned into a coherent whole, to present a picture of a divinely favored people called to fulfill a historic task. It was a script for the life of a nation, a saga well adapted to a people inclined by habit and the undisputed facts of the seventeenth-century world to see their own experience as normative, as divinely ordained. How could a great power not be blessed by God? And how could a great power, when it stumbled, not be prey to the idea that it fell because it had answered divine favor with arrogance—that it had turned its back on God?

PREFIGURATION:
MARSEILLE AND THE SACRED HEART

You shall be counted and delivered to the sword,
because I called you and you did not answer.

Isaiah 65:12

God said that all those who pray and adore his divine Sacred Heart
would obtain everything they seek; as soon as they invoked the
Sacred Heart to stop the plague in Marseille, it stopped.

Instructions, pratiques, et prières
pour la dévotion au Sacré-Coeur de Jésus, 1752

Why drew Marseille's good Bishop purer breath,
When nature sickened, and each gale was death?
. . . .
God sends not Ill, 'tis Nature lets it fall
Or chance escape, and Man improves it all.

ALEXANDER POPE,
"An Essay on Man," 1734

THE MERCHANT VESSEL *Grand Saint-Antoine* slipped into the harbor of
Marseille in June of 1720. The *Saint-Antoine* had made ports of call throughout the eastern Mediterranean. It carried a rich cargo of cotton and silk, but
its most important passenger was the plague.

Plague was no stranger to the city of Marseille. In *Satyricon,* Petronius states that even in the days before the arrival of Caesar, the people of Marseille had a well-established procedure for warding off the plague. It began with the selection of a "volunteer"—a young male, a boy—from among the poor of the city. For a year the boy would be treated to the very best the city had to offer. He was doted upon and fed fine food, including meat, fruit, and delicacies. At the end of the year, the suitably fattened surrogate would be dressed in sacred garments, adorned with verbena, then paraded through the streets of the city. As he walked, the people would gather around and shout imprecations at the chubby boy. They heaped scorn upon him, making him the bearer of the evils of the city. As the boy continued his tour of Marseille, people fell in behind him. Then they marched him to a high place and threw him to his death. The sacrificial boy took with him the woes of the city.[1]

Such practices had long since been abandoned in Marseille, in favor of a far more effective procedure—the careful control of arriving ships. Vessels from suspect ports were routinely submitted to certain precautions against plague; indeed, the *Saint-Antoine* had been subjected to them. The ship had sailed from Sidon with a *patente nette,* a declaration from the port of origin to the effect that no contagious illness prevailed locally on the date of departure. After leaving Sidon, the *Saint-Antoine* had a stopover in Tripoli, then made for Cyprus, arriving on 18 April. But it was soon evident that something was quite wrong aboard the *Saint-Antoine.* Three sailors and the ship's surgeon died at Cyprus; three others were dead by the time the *Saint-Antoine* made port at Livorno in Italy. Normally a ship with seven dead would be quarantined upon arrival at Marseille, denied port and sent to Jarre Island, an uninhabited piece of earth close to Marseille. There, barracks and apartments housed crew and officers while warehouses protected merchandise. Although the *Saint-Antoine* was denied port initially, a full quarantine was not imposed. After a brief delay in which the deaths were explained away, the *Saint-Antoine* was allowed to make port and unload.[2] Carried by crew and then by porters and longshoremen, plague made its way through the old quarters of Marseille, nearest the port. Its first victims were the aged and the infirm. By August, the loss of life had extended to children and adults and had taken on the proportions of a disaster. Silence fell over Marseille, a silence broken only by sobbing and the sound of the carts that hauled away the mounded bodies of the dead. By December, the plague had taken 50,000. Marseille was devastated; half its population was gone.[3]

Plague brought disaster to Marseille, Toulon, and inland cities of Provence in the 1720s. And while a similarly catastrophic natural disaster—earthquake—on All Saints' Day in Lisbon in 1755 prompted reflections on the inscrutability of God and the unknowability of God's plans, plague in Marseille inspired certitude: God was displeased. Such was the power of the rival religious and secular cultures of the age that what was opaque to one was transparent to another and that what mattered was not so much what had happened as who could provide the most plausible commentary on it. On such commentary turned the perception that either God still watched over his creation, or that God, having completed the work of creation, had long since turned his attention elsewhere.

Voltaire used Lisbon to problematize evil and senseless tragedy and to question the assertion of God's involvement in human affairs. Catholic commentary would turn Marseille into an exemplary case of divine solicitude. The city would overcome natural disaster by turning to God. Marseille would show secular and religious leaders struggling together to rescue a city in need of salvation. Marseille would demonstrate how the Sacré-Coeur provided protection against evil. Finally, the story of Marseille was fully scaleable—to talk about Marseille was to talk about France in reduced but correct proportions. The story of Marseille and the Sacré-Coeur prefigured that of France.

HOLY MEN AND WOMEN OF MARSEILLE

The bishop of Marseille, Henri François Xavier de Belsunce de Castelmoron, was an energetic man whose episcopate was defined, in part, by his manifest preference for baroque piety and spectacular public manifestations of faith. After his installation as bishop of Marseille but prior to the onset of plague, Belsunce established his authority via pastoral visits to the religious orders of his diocese. He also reorganized the existing network of lay penitential confraternities, bringing them firmly under clerical control and joining them to broader pastoral efforts. Souls may be won singly, but Belsunce believed that faith defined a community and that a community's faith should be manifested collectively and publicly. Belsunce promoted a Catholicism that was publicly demonstrative, including large-scale pilgrimages and public processions; he used these to work the population of Marseille with the relentless effort of a missionary. The mission of 1718, his first, was typical of Belsunce's pastoral style. The mission lasted a month, involved dozens of members of local religious orders as well as the lay confraternities, featured an immense public procession, and culminated in the planting of a monumental missionary cross on the Esplanade de la Tourette.[4]

Belsunce's appetite for ostentatious devotional acts may be attributed both to the struggle against the protestant faith of the Jansenist enclaves in his diocese and to a reaction against his own French Protestant origins.[5] Belsunce's Huguenot parents had decided that it would be best for him, as the second son of a noble family, to be raised a Catholic, even though he had been baptized a Protestant. They had him educated at Louis-le-Grand in Paris, the premier Jesuit lycée in France.[6] There were, after all, pragmatic concessions to be made to a Catholic status quo. Pragmatic considerations were doubtless paramount for Belsunce's parents, but under the guidance of the Jesuits at Louis-le-Grand, Belsunce embraced the Catholic religion with a zeal that was sincere, not opportunistic, and cut across the austere faith of his Huguenot origins. Given that the Jesuit order had assumed the special obligation, conveyed via Marguerite-Marie Alacoque and the Jesuit priest Claude de la Colombière, to propagate the devotion to the Sacred Heart of Jesus, it is certain that Belsunce encountered the devotion to the Sacré-Coeur at Louis-le-Grand. And he surely encountered the Sacré-Coeur at Marseille, where Anne-Madeleine Rémuzat (fig. 6), a nun of the Visitationist order, was pursuing sanctity and the Sacré-Coeur with the persistence and ardor of Marguerite-Marie herself.

Anne-Madeleine had visions of the Sacré-Coeur. These led not only to the ecstatic unions with the body of Christ of the kind treasured by Marguerite-Marie, but also to bodily manifestations of divine favor. In one episode, Jesus appeared to Anne-Madeleine, removed her heart and placed it within his own, which she described as a "flaming furnace" that turned her heart into fire for an instant. When her heart was returned she felt "the same pain one feels when fire touches the body, with this difference—the pain was accompanied by sweet feelings I cannot describe." Later, a heart-shaped blemish appeared on her chest. This mark of divine favor, red and swollen, remained until her death.[7] In another episode, Anne-Madeleine received the stigmata —the marks of the crucifixion on hand and foot.

Anne-Madeleine had a penchant for acts of bodily control as a means to self-mastery and spiritual development. Her superior consulted with Bel-

Figure 6. Anne-Madeleine Rémuzat. *La Vénérable Anne-Madeleine Rémuzat* (Lyon, 1894).

Anne-Madeleine Rémuzat was in some respects the successor of Marguerite-Marie Alacoque, not as the privileged recipient of divine revelations but as the tireless advocate of the devotion to the Sacré-Coeur. The epic tale of the Sacré-Coeur was bound up in visions of French grandeur.

sunce regarding Anne-Madeleine's appetite for acts of corporal discipline. Belsunce was already familiar with Anne-Madeleine because she had encouraged Belsunce's interest in the Sacré-Coeur; Anne-Madeleine convinced him to create a diocesan Association de l'Adoration perpétuelle du Sacré-Coeur de Notre-Seigneur Jésus-Christ in March of 1718.[8] As for her personal spiritual practices, Belsunce authorized Anne-Madeleine to do whatever she felt was consistent with the wishes of the Heart of Jesus. With the bishop's approval, her daily routine consisted of fifteen minutes of "cruelty against herself" which often left her body bloodied.[9] At one point Anne-Madeleine inscribed the letters J-E-S-U-S on her chest.[10] She habitually wore irritants, such as a hair shirt, close to her body, and she induced periodic suffering through the use of bracelets and belts studded with metal barbs; one such device consisted of a heart textured with iron points.[11] For Anne-Madeleine, these acts were not masochistic acts but acts of mortification—part of a program of spiritual development. One masters the body by disciplining it, and these disciplinary acts were part of a daily routine of spiritual perfection.

Bishop Belsunce and Anne-Madeleine Rémuzat apparently shared the conviction that faith should mark the body as well as the spirit, whether the body in question was a single body or a body of believers. Anne-Madeleine's penchant for a body bearing the signs of faith—stigmata, welts, the name of Jesus—had its analogue in Belsunce's conviction that the faith of a body of believers should be visible, be demonstrative. The body of the believer must be consonant with the spirit. Hence his preference for pilgrimages, public ceremonies, and processions by a community of believers.

The body also served as an instrument of atonement, and the atoning body of Bishop Belsunce featured in initial attempts to halt the plague (fig. 7). So did the idea of plague as a metaphor for spiritual sickness within a community. Charles Borromeo, bishop of Milan in the sixteenth century, owed his reputation and his sainthood to the public zeal he showed when Milan was threatened by plague and by the pernicious ideas of the Reformation. Mindful of Borromeo's example, on 1 November (All Saints' Day, the day before All Souls'), Belsunce stepped out of his episcopal residence not in episcopal regalia, but in the garb of a penitent.[12] Church bells throughout Marseille had been ringing since dawn by his order, and at ten o'clock the bishop and proud nobleman stepped barefoot into the cold streets of plague-ridden Marseille. Crowds gathered to witness this spectacular act of atonement as well as of personal courage; they then followed in procession as Belsunce walked solemnly up the Canebière to where it meets the Grand Cours, the main axis in the city of Marseille. Belsunce had a cord around his neck and he carried a crucifix before him. At the Grand Cours (subsequently rebaptized the Cours Belsunce and known by that name today) he approached an altar that had been erected for the purpose. He kneeled down before it and offered penance. He uttered penitential words, an *amende honorable,* and concluded with a consecration, "O Venerable Heart of the Savior of all men, I consecrate myself to you."[13]

Belsunce repeated the procession and ceremony in November and December as if each iteration pushed back the poisonous miasma. The plague slowly, perceptibly, gave way. These ceremonies also afforded pastoral opportunities. On these and on other occasions he inferred divine intentions

Figure 7. Nicolas-André Monsiau, *The Devotion of Monsignor de Belsunce during the Plague of 1720,* Salon of 1819, Musée du Louvre, Paris. © RMN—Arnaudet.

The last major outbreak of plague in France took place at Marseille in 1720. By the time it was over, it had taken some fifty thousand souls. Churches were closed down to limit the risk of contagion, but the clergy of Marseille, including Bishop Henri de Belsunce, went into the streets at great personal risk to minister to the dying.

from disastrous consequences. The plague was an invitation to penitence sent by an angry God whose patience with crime, heresy, and sin had been tested and exceeded. The Sacred Heart of Jesus was the best recourse, according to Belsunce, and his consecration of the city of Marseille to the Sacred Heart was the correct spiritual initiative to take in the face of the plague. The Sacré-Coeur had driven the plague from Marseille.

Mostly. Despite Belsunce's claims of divine succor, the churches of Marseille remained closed through June of the following year because of the ongoing risk of contagion. Undaunted, Bishop Belsunce went forward with preparations for the ceremony of thanks to the Sacred Heart.[14] The miraculous intervention had begun in November, but the feast of the Sacred

Heart fell in June, the week following Corpus Christi, and Belsunce was determined that commemoration of the protection of Marseille should take place on the feast of the Sacred Heart in 1721. This configuration would reinforce both the Sacré-Coeur devotion and the memory of divine intercession. A letter-circular distributed throughout the diocese announced and promoted the event.

The sound of hammering punctuated the air around the Old Harbor at the foot of the Canebière. In the days leading up to the June consecration, men and women labored to prepare the massive *reposoir*—literally, a resting place, but in ceremonial terms, a station and altar. On days of religious procession such as Rogations or Corpus Christi there were often several *reposoirs,* at least one in each neighborhood. For the June consecration, there would be one station, and it would be built on the esplanade at the foot of the Canebière, at the port, where Marseille meets the sea. After the frame of the *reposoir* had been hammered and lashed together, planks for a ceremonial stairway and platform were affixed. Then the entire structure was wrapped in fabric and decorated with flowers and accents of colored cloth and paper. Like any temporary structure of such singularity, the station commanded the attention of passersby. The *reposoir* at the Canebière, the heart of Marseille, would serve as the dais and ceremonial center for the consecration of the city to the Sacred Heart of Jesus.

The dedicatory procession and ceremony on the 20 June 1721 reproduced the pomp and dignity of the events of the preceding autumn and spring, but on a much grander scale. The June procession was larger as it circulated through the squares and along the streets of the city. Catholic Marseille was rich in penitent confraternities—lay devotional groups for men—and they lent color and movement to the procession.[15] Confraternities distinguished themselves by their distinctive dress and signature colors—gray for the Penitents Gris du Nom de Jésus, white for the Penitents Blancs de Notre Dame, blue for the Penitents Bleus de Notre Dame, red for the Penitents Rouges de la Sainte Croix. They processed in robes of heavy fabric. Barefoot or shod in leather sandals, they wore rope around the waist, gloves over the hands, and pointed hoods into which two holes had been cut for the eyes. Their depersonalized appearance emphasized their penitential commitment to anonymity and their desire to avoid the sin of pride; it also added solemnity and an air of mystery. Some carried statues and reliquaries affixed like sedan chairs to pairs of poles hoisted at either end. Some prayed; others chanted.[16] An embroidered banner preceded each confraternity, and these swayed with the slow cadence of the procession itself. The scene must have been fascinating and horrifying at the same time.

Like the elaborate Corpus Christi processions celebrated throughout France well into the twentieth century, this procession manifested the Christian beliefs of the community while it reinforced precedence within the ecclesiastical hierarchy. In Marseille, behind the gray-, white-, blue-, and red-hooded penitents, came the religious orders, the diocesan clergy, chaplains of various institutions, deacons in white surplice, and the altar boys. After making its way through town, the procession halted at the large *reposoir* set up at the Canebière. At the top of the stairs stood the altar, decked out with starched linens and illuminated with candles in glistening candelabra. Belsunce mounted the stairs and there, high above the crowd, he kneeled before the altar on which stood a gleaming monstrance. At the center of the monstrance was a consecrated host, the Eucharist—the Divine brought within reach through the miracle of consecration. The bishop rose from his knees. He took the monstrance into his hands; then, holding it high and before him, he slowly turned to face the crowd. With his arms still holding the monstrance high, he turned from side to side so that all could see the glistening vessel.[17] Heads bowed. This visual communion of people with the Divine represented the climax of the ceremony. Marseille was reunited with God. Plague was gone.

This was baroque piety in all of its splendor, designed to lend pomp and dignity to a celebration of divine deliverance. But it also put on display the decimation in the ranks of clergy and laity; it was a somber occasion that allowed Catholic Marseille to take stock of the devastation wrought by the plague. The ceremony conjured away fear. Did it also dispel doubt? Everyone in Marseille knew that plagues arrived by the sea, and, as it turned out, the owner-outfitter of the *Saint-Antoine,* the vessel that had brought plague, was owned by one of the *échevins* of Marseille, a city magistrate. The well-established practice of quarantining vessels suspected of carrying disease had been set aside for the *Saint-Antoine,* and that lapse—perhaps the result of official pressure—had exposed Marseille to devastation.[18] It would later be remarked that Belsunce's June 1721 Sacré-Coeur spectacular served to mask the criminal negligence of the owner of the *Saint-Antoine,* but such a reading is too simplistic to be completely satisfying. In the vision of Bishop Belsunce, the Sacré-Coeur devotion transcended the greed, the influence, and the parochial concerns of Marseille and its lay leaders.

Belsunce persisted in using the plague and the corruption of the body as a metaphor for moral failure, a discursive gambit potentiated by the return of the plague in 1722. In other circumstances and with less capable opinion management, the return of plague would have raised doubts about the efficacy of Belsunce's 1720 invocation of the Sacré-Coeur. Instead, it became the occasion for more profound reflection on the moral status of Marseille. If plague returned to Marseille, it was because the piety of the Marseillais was shallow; the passing of the plague and the revival of city life had led directly to the revival of the practices that had brought shame and divine reproach in 1720.[19] The Jesuit historian Auguste Hamon, writing in the twentieth century, emphasized the struggle against the plague as parallel to the struggle against errors and Jansenist heresies, but he also conceded that the matter went beyond theological disputations and included the combat against "libertines and courtesans."[20]

Belsunce seized upon the 1722 relapse as an opportunity to initiate a broader lay initiative. In what might well have been an oblique reference to the criminal negligence of the owners of the *Saint-Antoine,* Belsunce chastised Marseille's civic and business leaders for their failure to participate in his 1720 ceremonies. In effect, the return of the plague was the consequence of moral failings and the shortcomings of municipal leadership. Belsunce reproached the city leaders with the observation that they did not "take part in any of the holy ceremonies . . . performed in honor of Jesus Christ our liberator. In reparation of this, gentlemen, I . . . propose . . . a perpetual vow to the Divine Heart."[21] Every year, on the feast of the Sacred Heart of Jesus, the leaders of Marseille were to make a votive offering "in reparation of the crimes of this town." Belsunce emphasized that this vow would "cost the town nothing" but had great chances of success, for it would "cause our evils to cease, or at least that they would be very considerably lessened."[22]

AN OFFICIAL CONSECRATION TO THE SACRED HEART

For Jean-Pierre Moustier, Balthazar Dieudé, Pierre Remusat, and Jean-Baptiste Saint-Michel, Belsunce's logic was compelling. On 28 May 1722, these "Officers, Protectors, and Defenders of the Privileges, Franchises, and

Liberties of this Town of Marseilles" gathered in the Marseille Hôtel de Ville in the presence of the marquis de Pilles, King's Lieutenant in the Government of Provence. There, they made a solemn vow to consecrate the city to the Sacred Heart of Jesus and to engage their successors to honor their vow in perpetuity. Jean-Pierre Moustier, the chief officer, explicitly accepted Belsunce's theologized account of the plague and its meaning. "The scourge of God's wrath," he remarked, "can only be arrested by acts of religion." And in a remark reflecting his weariness and despair, but also his faith, he asked, "Where then can we fly to, but to the Sacred Heart of Jesus?"[23]

The promise was kept. The following month, Moustier, Dieudé, Remusat, and Saint-Michel dressed themselves in the red robes of office and marched in solemn procession to Notre-Dame de la Major, the cathedral of Marseille. Once within, they approached the altar and dropped to their knees. As Belsunce looked on, Moustier read the text of the vow on behalf of the city of Marseille. A few weeks later, on 12 June, Belsunce celebrated the feast of the Sacré-Coeur and sealed the bond uniting city and divine patron. Church faithful had erected a temporary platform decorated with flowers and bunting in the plaza next to the Accoules church.[24] From the heights one could survey nearly the entire city of Marseille, and as Belsunce mounted the steps to the platform the church bell rang as a signal for Marseille to join in a prayer of consecration to the Sacred Heart of Jesus. People crowded the streets and rooftops. Belsunce gave a brief address and offered a prayer of reparation, after which church bells rang out throughout the city. The sound of cannon at the citadel and on vessels in the harbor joined the chorus. As Belsunce raised the gleaming monstrance containing the Eucharist, the air of Marseille was filled with prayer and the tumult of bells and cannon, as if to drive the plague before them.[25]

By September, the remaining traces of the plague had passed. Belsunce ordered the singing of the Te Deum, a hymn of praise and thanks to God. At nightfall, Belsunce led a procession from the cathedral. The city magistrates in their red robes were with him, followed by dozens of religious in vestments, carrying white candles. Behind them walked hundreds of children adorned with white sashes.[26]

Walking together in procession through the streets must have felt like a joyful liberation. Plague killed; it had also poisoned the social life of Marseille. Through months of shuttered windows, locked doors, and restricted human contact, the people of the city had turned one another into fearful specters—sources of contagion, disease, and death. Besides its ostensible purpose, Belsunce's procession banished that fearful vision and celebrated the recovery of the social promiscuity and vigor of the city of Marseille. As the procession entered the Canebière, candles appeared in the windows along the way. Marseille was illuminated in celebration. Fireworks flew over the port, pushing back the darkness and marking the end of the long night of disease.

MARSEILLE AS EXEMPLARY NARRATIVE

The saga of the city and diocese of Marseille contains the principal elements of the Sacré-Coeur story. Over the next two hundred years, the actors would change and the credulity of participants and spectators would vary, but the lessons and main story elements would not. The first of these lessons was that of divine immanence. Calamity, war, or natural disasters are acts of God—these things don't "just happen." They happen because God wills them to happen. God wills them because of divine dissatisfaction with a willful or sinful community. Within a month of the arrival of the *Saint-Antoine,* Belsunce had ordered his diocesan clergy to call the people to penitence in hopes of halting the menacing hand of an angry God.[27] After the plague had passed, Belsunce told the people of Marseille that they must "forever renounce all disorders; be henceforth pure, chaste, mild, charitable; be enemies to slander, injustice, and usury; be humble, attached to truth, submissive to the Church."[28] Disaster had befallen the community because of the evil men do.

If God had wreaked vengeance, God could also offer succor; the second lesson of Marseille was the promise of divine solicitude. "The scourge of God's wrath can only be arrested by acts of religion," was how Jean-Pierre Moustier expressed it.[29] God had turned his face from a community; the community must learn how to appeal to God for relief through the Sacred Heart of Jesus. Belsunce had shown how this could be done in the aggregate—a community appeals to God via collective ritual, prayer, and ceremony. The Sacré-Coeur would play a mediating role. Belsunce demonstrated this most dramatically through the numerous processions he organized through the streets of Marseille, in effect, posing as the city's main interlocutor. In November 1720, he led penitent Marseille to the monumental altar constructed at the intersection of the Grand Cours and the

Canebière. He closed the catastrophic year 1720 with a procession outside the city's perimeter wall, tracing the boundaries of the city from the Porte de Rome to the Porte de Notre-Dame du Monde. He tacitly recognized the dead as well as the living as his route along the wall passed the mass graves of the year's dead, parts of their hastily buried bodies—arms, legs, heads—emerging from the soil in silent, pleaful gesture. In June of 1721, he made the most of the esplanade where the Canebière descends to the port and the sea. In November of 1721, he led a procession across the city beginning at one of its most sacred sites—the historic cathedral of Notre-Dame de la Major—and ending at the other—the heights of Notre-Dame de la Garde. At every opportunity, Belsunce used rituals and ceremonies to trace the community's symbolic boundaries, to exploit its symbolic centers, to organize a collective appeal on the part of the community, and to represent the city before the face of heaven.[30]

Anne-Madeleine Rémuzat, meanwhile, had continued the privileged status of the Sacred Heart visionary. The plague at Marseille and Anne-Madeleine's visions of the Sacré-Coeur occurred within one generation of the death of Marguerite-Marie Alacoque. Anne-Madeleine's vision, along with the spectacular story of the plague at Marseille, guaranteed the continuation of the saga of France and the Sacré-Coeur. She positioned herself as Marguerite-Marie's successor such that in Sacré-Coeur lore, Anne-Madeleine's visions were interpreted as a renewed attempt on the part of the Sacré-Coeur to communicate a set of divine desiderata, as yet unfulfilled, including the desire for a royal consecration of France to the Sacred Heart.[31]

In after-the-fact readings of the plague, Anne-Madeleine became a kind of Jeremiah, the emissary of God for her times, chosen to convey a divine message to bring the people back to faithful observance. In the reconstructed scenario of pre-plague events, witnesses recalled a 1718 miracle (that is, two years before the onset of plague) in which the face of Jesus appeared in a Host on display in a monstrance at the Church of the Cordeliers. The face was "both tender and severe." Although Anne-Madeleine had not witnessed the miracle, she experienced a divine revelation about its meaning: the tender expression was a sign of divine compassion, but the severe expression was a warning that the city would be chastised if the people did not return to God.[32] The warning was ignored. Instead, as later accounts put it, the people hardened their hearts; the plague set in two years later.

Anne-Madeleine's contribution had been decisive after the onset of the plague; she deserves the credit for putting the Sacré-Coeur at the center of Belsunce's holy response to the threat of plague. Indeed, Belsunce had at first been tempted by an older practice—the use of relics to counter a threat to a community—and there was no shortage of suggestions about how such spiritual weapons should be deployed. A deeply devout nun under the spiritual direction of Father Rainier had had a vision of the Virgin shortly before she died.[33] The Virgin Mary announced that God would end the scourge of plague under certain conditions: the relics and reliquaries from two of Marseille's churches were to be carried in procession through the streets of the city. When the two processions met, the plague would end and the sick would be made well.

A simple prescription. Given the stakes, one would think that the required ceremony would have been organized quickly. However, the program soon became mired in questions of personality and precedence. Belsunce backed the proposal, seeing in the scenario of a meeting of relics a symbolic representation of the reconciliation of God and sinners.[34] However, the abbé of Saint-Victor, who controlled some of the necessary relics, would agree to the procession of reliquaries only if, at the end of the procession, the relics were placed on altars that were absolutely identical and positioned side-by-side in the public square in front of the Hôtel de Ville. Moreover, masses were to be offered simultaneously on the two altars—a scheme designed to humiliate Belsunce by putting him on the same level as the abbot of Saint-Victor.[35] Perhaps it was a matter of a simple struggle with the episcopal hierarchy. Perhaps it was a scheme of crypto-Jansenists eager for revenge on Belsunce.[36] In any event, Belsunce backed away in favor of Anne-Madeleine's appeals on behalf of the Sacré-Coeur.

Within the relative safety of the Visitationist convent, Anne-Madeleine and her sisters had already adopted anti-plague prophylactic procedures that blended science, religion, and folk remedies. Given that the Visitationists were a cloistered order, their best protection was to observe convent regulations strictly. But even cloistered religious have a certain number of unavoidable transactions with the larger world; in these cases, special procedures were imposed. The nuns sprinkled vinegar on letters and coins that entered the convent. Meat entering the convent was boiled just inside the convent door. Then there was the power of relics. All members drank daily from water in which the relics of the founders, Jeanne de Chantal and François de Sales, had been dipped—a kind of holy tea. Since the water the Visitationists prepared in this way drew upon the power of the founders themselves, to drink it was to invoke the protection of Jeanne and François.[37]

But Anne-Madeleine's great practical innovation was an emblem that could be worn by individuals as a protection against threats of all kinds. In 1611, François de Sales had described the Sacred Heart symbol that he wanted to become the signature of the Visitationist order: a single heart enclosed in a crown of thorns, surmounted by a cross and pierced by arrows.[38] Later, Marguerite-Marie Alacoque had drawn stylized representations of the heart of Jesus based upon her visions; she had distributed these as devotional images to novices at Paray-le-Monial. During the plague Anne-Madeleine and her Visitationist sisters popularized the practice of conspicuous placement of the Sacré-Coeur—over doorways, in the foyer, or at other strategic points around a residence. These Sacred Heart "safeguards" consisted of images drawn on paper or of patches of wool or linen fabric on which a heart was embroidered or affixed by appliqué. Around the perimeter one could read the expression, "Arrête! le Coeur de Jésus est avec moi!" or "Arrête! le Coeur de Jésus est là!"

The practical significance of the Sacred Heart talisman was that when it was affixed to clothing it kept the plague at bay.[39] It was as if the events at Marseille were a recapitulation of the plagues sent against Pharaoh during the Egyptian captivity. The plague might seem to attack indiscriminately, but the Sacred Heart marked the community of faithful and protected them. This was a subtle but important shift. After Marseille, the Sacred Heart performed not only as a safeguard but also as an insignia. The Sacred Heart defined a community whose persons and homes were marked by the heart of Jesus. In the context of a plague sent as punishment for sin, the Sacred Heart became the sign by which the righteous distinguished themselves before God; it set them apart from the wicked and the indifferent.

Marseille also laid the groundwork for public acts of consecration. The Sacred Heart identified individuals who had marked themselves as members of a self-defined community. Public consecrations put the seal on such communities and made them official through the involvement of lay and religious leadership. Belsunce's 1720 consecration of the town and diocese of Marseille drove back the plague, but only temporarily. When it returned, he insisted that his consecration be renewed, with the participation of lay authorities. It was their obligation, he claimed, "to endeavor to appease the anger of the Lord, and obtain a cessation of the contagion that has begun again in this town." The result was a religious devotion but with an official public sanction. The politics of Old Regime France notoriously mixed sacred and profane; cities and towns, not to mention guilds and trades, all had their patron saints and founding legends, but Belsunce and his Marseille collaborators innovated in 1722 by making a public consecration of their city.[40] In doing so, they set an example for their own time—Aix, Arles, Avignon, Toulon soon followed the lead of Marseille—and they established a model of a community with a fully integrated political and religious leadership. Marseille became the reference point for an integral vision of a community saved by putting religion at the center of its identity and its public life.

How to keep it there? Marseille's consecration was never monumentalized, which is one of the more obvious and permanent ways of inscribing a moment in local memory. However, Belsunce was aware of the importance of the problem, and he approached it through ritualized practice. He explicitly addressed the issue of memory in 1723, on the occasion of the first anniversary of the consecration of Marseille to the Sacré-Coeur. He called upon the people of Marseille to let "the remembrance of these wonders be forever engraved on your minds and hearts; relate them often to your children that they may repeat it to their children, . . . that the memory of them may pass to future ages." [41]

Belsunce's answer to the problem of memory was to ritualize it, which, after all, was a profoundly Christian, not to say human, thing to do. Memory of the Last Supper was ritualized in the Eucharist. Memory of the consecration of Marseille to the Sacré-Coeur was etched into community memory by means of an anniversary ceremony, an annual recapitulation of the oath and procession.[42]

Later commentators would remark that the experience of Marseille showed again that people do not choose God, but that God chooses people. Divine sovereignty, in this sense, is independent of popular will.[43] But if Marseille showed how God speaks, it also showed how peoples ought to talk back. As the plague moved along the Provençal coast to such places as Toulon, or inland to Aix, Arles, Avignon, and Carpentras, political and religious leaders made symbolic, votive and ritualized gestures modeled after those inspired by Belsunce at Marseille.[44] Across Provence, wherever disaster spread, wherever loss and grief led people to inquire as to the inscrutable designs of God, the example of Marseille and Belsunce found a receptive audience. The question now was whether the story would scale up. If this is how God speaks to peoples in their cities and towns, is it also how God speaks to nations?

The legend spread. Within thirty years, the story of Marseille had become a fixture in devotional guides intended for a national readership. Occasionally the most fantastic claims were made on behalf of the power of the devotion to the Sacré-Coeur, with the example of Marseille as supporting evidence. A work published in 1752 claimed flatly that "God said that all those who pray and adore his divine Sacred Heart would obtain everything they seek; as soon as they invoked the Sacred Heart to stop the plague in Marseille, it stopped."[45]

"Pas très catholique"—"Not very Catholic," as the French say when they encounter something a bit unorthodox. The English poet Alexander Pope, no enemy to Catholicism, attributed the story of Marseille to "nature" and "chance." "God sends not Ill," he complained in his *Essay on Man,* written a mere decade after the events. Such efforts aside, the story of Marseille helped to associate the Sacred Heart with an accessible God, a God who sends punishments to individuals and to peoples but whose vengeful hand can be stayed. A bronze bas-relief on the pedestal of the statue of Bishop Belsunce at Notre-Dame de la Major would later show Belsunce in prayer, consecrating Marseille to the Sacré-Coeur while in the heavens an avenging angel sheaths a drawn sword (fig. 8).

The story of Marseille entered into the commonsense world of eighteenth- and nineteenth-century Catholicism. By the 1820s, Belsunce and Marseille had become part of episcopal efforts to promote the Sacré-Coeur devotion. In Paris, the archbishop touted the "sure gains" that result from this devotion, citing Marseille as a case in point.[46] In 1866, when Amiens suffered from cholera, the city became the scene for the replay of scenes and roles drawn from the story of Marseille.[47] By the 1870s, Marseille was recognized in pilgrimage ceremonial for its signal role in the saga of France and the Sacred Heart. When pilgrims converged at Paray-le-Monial in June of 1873, those from Marseille took precedence in the pilgrimage procession. As one commentator put it, "It's the right of the diocese of Belsunce."[48] Bel-

Figure 8. Bishop Belsunce consecrates Marseille to the Sacred Heart. Bronze bas-relief, Notre-Dame de la Major, Marseille.

Henri Belsunce invokes the Sacré-Coeur and consecrates the city (represented as a woman weakened by plague) to the Sacred Heart, which rains down grace while an avenging angel sheaths its sword and departs.

sunce remained a meaningful referent, a name and association commonly understood among French Catholics 150 years after the plague.

Likewise, Marseille figured prominently in sacred art. One example—the artistic program for the stained glass in the nineteenth-century church of Sainte-Madeleine du Sacré-Coeur in Angers. One of the medallion scenes in the church window depicts "Monsignor de Belsunce leaving his episcopal palace, barefoot, rope about the neck, cross in his arms, surrounded by an immense crowd. He utters the *amende honorable* and the act of consecration to the Sacred Heart. The plague ends immediately" (fig. 9).[49] Marseille and Belsunce rapidly became part of Catholic legend. For later generations, their story would be an article of faith, part of the lore of France, its status as a leading Catholic country, and its special relationship with the Sacré-Coeur.

Figure 9. Bishop Belsunce leads a procession through the streets of Marseille. Jean Clamens, stained-glass medallion, 1894, Sainte-Madeleine du Sacré-Coeur, Angers.

Bishop Belsunce, dressed as a penitent, leads a procession through the streets of Marseille. A victim of the plague lies before him.

Marseillais lore had it that the city was marked for distinction from the very earliest days of the Christian era. According to local legend, shortly after the ascension of the resurrected Jesus, Lazarus, whom Jesus had brought back from the dead, and Mary Magdalene, the reformed public sinner, had departed the Holy Land and sailed the Mediterranean. Lazarus and Magdalene, icons of the power of redemption, ended their journey at Marseille, where they proceeded to proselytize. Marseille had thus gotten its Christianity if not "from the source" then at least from those who had known Jesus and been part of his entourage. Accordingly, Marseille was the first of the cities of Gaul to be Christianized; Lazarus, the man whom Jesus saved from death, has conventionally been regarded as Marseille's first bishop. Seventeen centuries later, this special honor was compounded when the city of Saints Lazarus and Mary Magdalene would become, through the grace of God and the efforts of the city's lay and religious leaders, the city of the Sacred Heart of Jesus.[50] In both instances, the story of Marseille anticipates the story of France itself. The Christianization of France had begun with Marseille; Marseille would lead the way too in the consecration of France to the Sacré-Coeur.

The story of Marseille and its harbinger status served as a fixture in Catholic rhetorical practice, especially the rhetoric of community crisis, well into the twentieth century. Marseille and Belsunce appeared in sermons and print literature before and after the wars of 1870–71 and of 1914–18, by which time "Marseille at the time of the plague" could serve as an analogy for France in peril. The episodes of 1720 and 1722 were cited not only as examples of remarkable faith in desperate times but also as part of a pattern of divine appeals to France as a nation. "France turns to the Heart of Jesus in all of its moments of grave peril," wrote one Catholic monthly, citing Marseille as example.[51] For a Catholic orator in 1919, the story of Belsunce and Marseille had entered the lore of Catholic France alongside the stories of Clovis at Tolbiac, and Joan of Arc at Orléans.[52] Marseille had become a defining moment, an episode in the epic tale of France and the Sacré-Coeur. The rhetorical strategy of those who transmitted and built upon the Marseille legend was to link the Sacré-Coeur with a Catholic idea of *la patrie en danger,* the nation at risk. This meant "scaling up" the story of Marseille and transposing certain terms such that for "Marseille" one must read "France"; for "plague" one must read "the current crisis"; for "Belsunce" and "the city fathers of Marseille"—well, as we shall see, the answer varied.

THE FRENCH REVOLUTION, CATHOLIC
ANXIETIES, AND THE SACRED HEART

Long live Christ, who loves the Franks!

Prologue to the Salic Law

May God remember his covenant, and may he not forsake you
in times of evil.

FRANÇOIS PIE,
bishop of Poitiers (paraphrasing 2 Maccabees 1 : 2, 5)

May the holy lives around us appease the anger of heaven.

PIERRE-JOSEPH PICOT DE CLORIVIÈRE,
11 July 1791

IN MARCH OF 1793, the fourth year of the French Revolution, some five thousand peasants assembled and marched on the town of la Roche-Bernard, near Vannes on the Vilaine River. They were armed, though poorly. Some carried muskets or pistols. Most carried simpler weapons, including pikes and farm implements. They shared the conviction that after nearly four years, it was time to face the fact that the Revolution of 1789 had gone badly wrong. It was pointless to think of marching on Paris, which was days away from them in any case. They had before them a handier target and a much more personal cause. The French Republic had called upon the nation to take up arms and fight against an invading army intent on ending the Revolution and restoring the monarchy; each city, town, and village had the responsibility of supplying its quota of men for the armies of the Republic.

The insurgents massing outside of la Roche-Bernard preferred to fight than submit to conscription.[1] Within the town, fewer than 200 men were willing to offer resistance against the peasant army. They were led by the mayor and district officials who sought to impose their will by putting on the blue, white, and red tricolor sashes that were a mark of their status as agents of the Republic. When they went out to meet the peasants, they could see that their position was hopeless. The peasants refused to submit. They would continue their march on the town and show that they, and not the revolutionary officials within, possessed local authority. Finally, town officials decided not to defend the city in exchange for assurances of safety for persons and property. But as officials and insurgents met in what looked as though it would turn into a peaceful understanding, a shot rang out. More shots were exchanged and some twenty-two defenders of la Roche-Bernard fell. The wounded were executed, and the crowd invaded the town.

La Roche-Bernard was a county seat, and the insurgents knew enough about political administration to know that paper is the medium of political power. Accordingly, they destroyed every piece of administrative paper they could find. They also seized two district administrators, by the names of Sauveur and Le Floch. Unsure of how to dispose of them, they put them into prison and held them overnight.

The next morning, the insurgents swarmed noisily outside the jail. The crowd parted to make a pathway as the two prisoners were led from the prison. From the outset, their deaths seemed certain, but what must have begun as a simple execution degenerated into a politically inspired death ritual. According to accounts, one of the men—Le Floch—attempted to address his captors; he was immediately shot. The other prisoner, President Sauveur, the leading revolutionary official in the district, was also shot. However, his wound was not mortal, and what happened next took on the aspect of a pageant of death. Sauveur's hands were bound and he was paraded through the streets of la Roche-Bernard; as he passed, he was spat upon and taunted and kicked and beaten until he was bloody. Once knocked to the ground, he was told to cry, "Long live the King!" He refused and cried instead, "Long live the Republic!"

Sauveur's route took him past a religious shrine, a calvary of the kind one still finds in villages and at rural crossroads in France. He was ordered to kneel and plead for forgiveness, to make an *amende honorable.* Instead he raised his eyes to the crucifix and cried out, "Long live the Nation!" He was then dealt a blow to the face. Rising, he was led on, stumbling through the streets, falling, rising, falling again. According to accounts, he was told to ask forgiveness and plead for the salvation of his soul; instead, he pressed his lips to the medal of office he wore around his neck. There was another shot. Sauveur dragged himself to the edge of a pit, raised himself to his knees, turned to his tormentors and said, "My friends, finish me off. Don't let me languish. Long live the Nation."

Obviously, this was no ordinary execution. Sauveur could have been executed immediately, as his companion was, at the exit from the prison. Or he might have been led directly to the gallows. However, killing Sauveur was not the only point of the events of that morning, for there are far more efficient ways of disposing of a life. Whether Sauveur's death occurred exactly as sources describe it, we will never know, but his Rasputin-like ability to survive the wounds he received helped to draw out his death and give it a ritualistic quality it would otherwise have lacked. Moreover, the evident prolongation of his death justifies the supposition that the blows of his captors were intended not to kill except cumulatively. The crowd wanted Sauveur to die, but it wanted him to suffer first.

Civil wars are not like other wars, as our twentieth century has amply shown: among the first casualties are the distinction between civilian and soldier and the respect for legal procedure. Civil wars of the eighteenth century were little different in this respect. Indeed the counter-revolutionary wars of the French Revolution add the complexity of religious conflict. For there was something ritualistic, even carnavalesque, in the treatment of Sauveur, his procession through the streets, combined with a sense that his suffering was a form of atonement. Sauveur was invited to eradicate the evil he had brought into the world by recanting—either by shouting, "Long live the King!" or by making an act of contrition before the cross.

Sauveur's incapacity for betrayal of the cause of the Revolution both confirmed his evil nature in the eyes of his tormentors and ensured his death. This fidelity, combined with his desire to forgive his tormentors, allowed him to secure a kind of posthumous revenge. His death provided a momentary satisfaction for those who killed him; they had eradicated evil. But the manner of his death made his reputation. In those horrible final moments of his life, Sauveur earned a martyr's wreath. As the account of his death was repeated and spread and (undoubtedly) embellished, the outlines of a heroic tale of patriotic triumph over death began to take shape.[2] His parade through the streets became a Christ-like stations of the cross, a posthumous mockery of the Christian beliefs of his tormentors. His *Via Dolorosa* and his suffering after receiving several serious wounds at the hands of the rebels allow us to understand that this was no mere mortal. Add to that his name— Sauveur means "Savior" in French—and the fact that he died during Holy Week and we realize that the Revolution had in Sauveur a patriotic model, a man whose love for the Republic was so great that he would lay down his life for it. Apprised of Sauveur's fate and deeply moved by the manner of his death, the National Convention rebaptized the town of la Roche-Bernard. In 1793, la Roche-Bernard became la Roche-Sauveur.[3]

The Revolution had not begun this way. The events of 1789, at least at first, had not been a war between transcendent values, between the Roman Catholic God and the French idea of the Republic. By 1793, the French Revolution was bitterly contested. Its partisans and its detractors, as the Roche-Bernard / Roche-Sauveur episode reveals, had gone beyond mere partisan differences. These were not differences of degree. These combatants were driven by competing transcendent visions. The same utter commitment to the cause of the Republic manifested by Sauveur became for his tormentors proof of his very wickedness. Revolutionary and counter-revolutionary values were simply incommensurate. By 1793, Revolution and Counter-Revolution had their rival ambitions for France. Each threatened the future happiness sought by the other. Competing themes and symbols marked their intransigent positions. For revolutionary France the symbols were the tricolor flag and cockade, the *sans-culotte* (prototype of the modern political militant), and the key ideas of liberty and equality. For the counter-revolution, the defense of "God and King" was paramount, the devout peasant was the agent, and the symbol was the Sacred Heart of Jesus.

A REVOLUTION GONE ASTRAY?

When the representatives of France's Three Estates met at Versailles in May of 1789, it was not their ambition to destroy Catholicism in France. The financial crisis of the French monarchy, brought about by the insolvency of the royal treasury, had created an opening for significant reform. At the same time that the clergy (the First Estate), the nobility (the Second Estate), and everyone else (the Third Estate) were invited to select their representatives for the meeting at Versailles, they were asked to draft a list of grievances and proposed reforms. Once these representatives met at the Estates General at Versailles, these grievances and reforms, known as *cahiers des doléances,* were to have served as the basis for a thoroughgoing reform of the realm, not only of its finances, but in many other areas as well, including religion. Many appeals for reform called for the termination of "abuses," including abuses benefiting the Catholic Church and its privileged position as the established church within France.[4] But none of these amounted to a frontal attack on Catholicism. And even if they had, it's hard to see how such an attack could have succeeded—fully one-quarter of the Estates General—the members of the First Estate—consisted of Catholic clergy. In this sense, the Estates General was as much a corporate body designed to represent institutional interests as it was a fledgling representative body in the modern democratic constitutional sense. The financial crisis had created a breach in state authority; a good portion of French public opinion sensed and desired that this crisis would become the occasion for what was called the "regeneration" of France, a broad refashioning of the French state and public life. Just the same, the corporate nature of the Estates General seemed to insure that this regeneration would not threaten fundamental interests.

Events soon overtook the Estates General. The deputies of the Third Estate, representing the overwhelming mass of the French population, refused to respect the distinctions of privilege and hierarchy that set the clergy and nobility off from the Third Estate. What mattered in the new era was the French *nation,* including all of its members irrespective of birth or social rank. The nation should be the measure of law. Faced with the resolute insistence of the Third Estate, King Louis XVI relented. In June of 1789, he ordered the representatives of the first two estates of clergy and nobility to join in deliberations with the representatives of the Third Estate, undermining the political significance of birth and rank. The Estates General became the National Assembly. An important political and social revolution had been won.

The cultural revolution over the place of the Catholic Church in public life was only beginning. The seizure of the Bastille in Paris in July 1789 was followed by weeks of rioting in provincial France, as peasants, mobilized by fears that brigands would destroy crops in the fields and undermine the Revolution, took over chateaux and burned manorial records. These impromptu peasant insurrections alarmed representatives in the National Assembly. The Assembly sought to address peasant demands and anxieties on 4 August 1789 by voting to abolish the remaining privileges of the institutions of the prior regime, including the privileged status of the Catholic Church and some sources of church income, notably the tithe, associated with privilege or seigniorial rights.[5] The Declaration of the Rights of Man and Citizen was completed and approved in the same month. Its many articles expressed the guiding ideas of revolutionary France. Article 10, regarding freedom of opinion, implicitly challenged Catholicism's privileged and protected status in France by guaranteeing the free practice of minority religions.

Although such changes weakened the powerful position of the Catholic Church in France, the majority of Catholic clergy in the National Assembly supported these measures in the summer of 1789. Many of them also supported much of what was to follow. Indeed, it was a member of the clergy, albeit hardly an exemplary one, who proposed the nationalization of the property of the Catholic Church as a solution to the problem of teetering state finances. Charles Maurice de Talleyrand, bishop of Autun, proposed such a decree to the National Assembly in a speech on 10 October 1789.[6] The financial logic behind such a move was unassailable. The church owned a significant amount of wealth in land, by common understanding about ten percent of the real estate in France—in certain cities such as Paris, as much as twenty-five percent. Nationalizing this property, then selling it, would bring a clean and rapid end to the vexing problem of the insolvency of the French treasury.

The political logic was somewhat more complicated. "What appears certain to me," Talleyrand stated, "is that the clergy is not a proprietor like other proprietors, because the property it holds . . . has been given . . . for the service of functions."[7] Those functions included the performance of religious services, the work of charity, basic education, and the operation of hospitals. Talleyrand also recognized the importance of the maintenance of church buildings and the support of the clergy. There could be no harm in taking the Catholic Church's property, the logic went, as long as the state also funded or took over the services the property was intended to support. As for the religious men and women who performed these services, they would go on the public payroll and become state functionaries.

Talleyrand glossed over the issue of property donated by private parties rather than by the crown. The origins of church property are ancient and sometimes just as obscure, but private estates were a significant ongoing source of property accumulation for the Catholic Church. It was not uncommon for pious men and women to make large donations at their death, especially if they had no immediate heirs.[8] Talleyrand had little to say about how his logic could incorporate church property of such origin, but he was implacable in his utilitarian logic with respect to contemplative orders whose main products were meditation and prayer rather than education or comfort for the sick and dying. The nation has the right to "destroy" certain orders "if it judges them harmful or simply without purpose."[9] Moreover, the nation has the right to claim "extensive powers over the disposition of their property." Such expropriations were, in an obvious sense, more attractive. Since members of such orders performed no useful service, transfer of their property entailed no corresponding obligation to assume responsibility for their support.[10] According to Timothy Tackett, nearly three-fifths of the body of religious, men and women, simply lost their positions in this manner.[11] Members of dissolved orders were to be given a choice: they could shift to approved "useful" positions and orders, or they could opt for a not terribly generous offer of early retirement.

The National Assembly voted early in November of 1789 to accept a version of Talleyrand's proposal, putting ecclesiastical property "at the disposal of the nation." The measure had its opponents—there were 346 votes against and 568 in favor—but it would have been difficult not to accept the pragmatic argument that some such measure was necessary, given the political impossibility of raising taxes.[12] Administering changes in the status of the clergy was left for another day and another piece of legislation, but making loyal civil servants of the Catholic clergy would become one of the most difficult challenges the revolutionary political leadership would have to face.

The National Assembly hoped to meet this challenge with legislation passed in July of 1790. What would be known as the Civil Constitution of the Clergy regulated the status of the clergy. This legislation put the administration of the Catholic Church in France on a footing similar to that of secular and civil administration: the law redrew the boundaries of the Catholic dioceses, making them coterminous with secular administrative units; the law provided for elections of bishops and pastors according to procedures like those used for corresponding secular officials; the law specified pay steps according to responsibilities and the size of communities served.

There was an admirable rationality about the whole thing. And there were important European precedents for such reform; Joseph II, the Habsburg monarch, had undertaken a similar Enlightenment reform of the church in Habsburg domains. Some of the statements (*cahiers*) drafted leading up to the Estates General, especially *cahiers* from lower clergy, had called for church reforms. One could plainly see that this legislation meant that the revolutionary regeneration of France would extend to every aspect of existence, including religion. Moreover, these reforms were in keeping with the growing Gallicanism of both clergy and laity in eighteenth-century France. The pope had his role as spiritual head of the Catholic Church, and he held authority by virtue of apostolic succession. His was the "chair of Saint Peter." But many French Catholic clergy and laity were ready to concede, if not heartily advocate, the strict limitation of the authority of Rome in the operations of the French church. Elected bishops, elected pastors, redrawn dioceses, suppressed orders—these and other unilateral reforms put Rome on notice that, except in matters of faith, papal authority could operate only according to guidelines laid down in Paris.

This was one approach to the modernization of church/state relations. An alternative path, that of separation of church and state as in the American republic, was perhaps less compelling because of the absence of religious pluralism in France—some 99 percent of French were at least nominally Catholic—and the sense of obligation following upon the nationalization of church lands. One could not simultaneously strip the church of much of its wealth and set it free to fend for itself. The Civil Constitution of the Clergy was in this sense overdetermined: if it was possible to advocate doing it differently, it was very difficult to imagine doing without. It was, however, the most important blunder of French revolutionary leadership in that it created an opening for the expression of sentiments of disaffection with the Revolution. This, in turn, prepared the way for schism and civil war.

And yet nothing in the Civil Constitution had not been proposed before. According to Timothy Tackett what impressed contemporaries, lay and clerical, were the accumulated effects of these proposals.[13] The proposals were generally in line with the Gallican or populist religious impulses of the age, but taken together, they amounted to a wholesale reform of church/state and lay/clerical relations. This reinforced the impression that these reforms were not inspired by a desire for enlightened reform but were part of a broader attack on religion.

THE OATH AND OPPOSITION TO THE REVOLUTION IN THE WEST OF FRANCE

Given that priests were now functionaries, the imposition of an oath of loyalty was but a small step. A decree passed in August of 1790 required bishops and pastors to take a loyalty oath as a condition for receiving pay.[14] Would the clergy submit? In October of 1790, some thirty National Assembly representatives who also happened to be bishops or archbishops signed a lengthy statement critical of the legislation and implicitly declining the oath.[15] Nationwide, the majority of clergy took the oath, but it was a narrow majority according to Timothy Tackett, the scholar who has examined the issue most closely. There were wide variations among regions, and in the west, where Catholic and royalist counter-revolution would later break out, most clergy refused the oath (see fig. 10). In the city of Nantes, a city loyal to the Revolution throughout its duration, just over one-third of parish priests took the oath. Elsewhere in the diocese of Nantes, in rural parishes and small towns, the imbalance was even greater. A mere one in four out of some six hundred clergy had taken the oath by May of 1791. And some of those who took the vow subsequently retracted it.[16]

The formula for the oath was banal. It involved a statement of loyalty to the nation, the law, and the king, and a promise to defend the constitution.[17] It contained little, it would seem, that would provoke a crisis of conscience. What grounded hundreds of decisions to reject the oath was not its language but the sense in which the oath amounted to an endorsement of the Revolution. Clergy who largely identified with the progress of the Revolution took the oath without qualms; clergy whose nights were troubled by mis-

Figure 10. "A Way to Force Aristocratic Bishops and Curates to Take the Oath. . . ." ca. 1791. Musée Carnavalet, Paris. © Photothèque des Musées de la Ville de Paris.

Whether members of the clergy took the oath or not often depended on local community sentiments regarding the Revolution. Here, community sentiment is clearly in favor of the oath.

givings about the Revolution did not. Before the oath, doubts and fears about the Revolution could be overcome by mental reservations and elisions. The oath, however, removed all room for such private maneuvers, mental reservations, and half-measures. One assented to the demand for an oath and all that it implied. Or one did not.

Indeed, some clergy had already made such a decision earlier. François Chevalier had served since 1764 as pastor in the village of Saint-Lumine-de-Coutais, just south of Nantes. In 1789 he was elected to the Estates General as a representative of the clergy of Nantes. He resigned his position in the National Assembly in August 1789—that is, at about the time that the very first nobles, including one of the king's brothers, decided to emigrate rather than stay in revolutionary France. Upon his departure from Paris and the National Assembly, Chevalier made not for the frontier but for his parish of

Saint-Lumine, where he later led the movement to refuse the oath among clergy in the Nantes diocese. When the bishop of Nantes, Charles de la Laurencie, returned from a six-month absence from his diocese, he seconded Chevalier's efforts and became, for a time, a visible public advocate for clerical resistance to the oath and the reforms of the church.[18] Bishop Laurencie's hostility, voiced from Paris, had been clear enough, but his absence from Nantes left the initiative to parish clergy such as Chevalier.[19] Indeed, Chevalier's determined resistance proved to be exemplary. He later went into hiding, to reemerge in 1793 as a chaplain in the royal and Catholic armies of the counter-revolution.[20]

A career such as Chevalier's was atypical. After all, few clergy actually served in the armies of the counter-revolution, but it shows how the oath revealed a fault-line pointing backward toward early misgivings about the Revolution and forward toward rupture and counter-revolution. Although the oath was often refused on grounds that it violated the principle of priestly subordination to the Catholic hierarchy, decisions on the oath were often made without direct episcopal guidance, as in Nantes. Episcopal absenteeism was a common enough problem prior to the Revolution, but it only got worse when bishops suspected of lukewarm patriotism became the target of popular violence and intimidation. Pierre de la Gorce, a Catholic historian sympathetic to the counter-revolution, noted with bitter sarcasm the departure of bishops from their dioceses within weeks of the National Assembly's decree on the oath. Commenting on the apparent episcopal predilection for "truth proclaimed at a distance," Gorce noted how many bishops chose the hardship assignment of self-exile to Nice, in sunny Provence. Indeed, so many bishops chose a Provençal exile that "they could have held a little council down there."[21] Moreover, given that Nice was not yet annexed to France, residence there put them just beyond the reach of French authorities. Ironically, this tended to leave the battle for the respect of church authority and the prerogatives of the Catholic hierarchy in the worthy hands of determined and courageous, but subordinate, parish clergy! Pastors and their assistants became the grunts of religious combat.

And not only priests. Women religious faced similar choices, although their story is more often neglected. The same utilitarian logic that separated "useful" male religious orders and activities (education, charity, etc.) from "non-useful" (monastic prayer and meditation) applied to women. Women in preferred (i.e., useful) occupations, like their male counterparts, became state functionaries. They would go on the state payroll; they were expected to take the oath. Because the religious life of women was organized exclusively through religious orders, there was no feminine equivalent to the choice religious men faced between life in a religious order (Dominican, Benedictine, etc.) and the more independent "secular" existence of the parish priest. Women who were deeply religious either entered the regulated existence and life-in-common of a religious order (Carmelite, Visitationist, etc.) or they tended to their salvation through lay forms of piety.

Given their disciplined form of existence and the lack of a "secular" alternative to the life in a convent, women's decisions about the oath tended to be made collectively. Despite the attempt of revolutionary officials to treat the oath decision as individual rather than collective, women religious tended to reject the oath uniformly.[22] For example, all of the sisters of the Visitationist order at Nantes, save one, refused the oath.[23]

Convents could become local centers of resistance to reform. Women's orders are situated within the Catholic hierarchy under the supervision of the bishop, but women could be implacable when changes in personnel put them under the supervision of bishops who had taken the oath. In Caen, for example, women religious refused a pastoral visit from their bishop, a member of the constitutional (oath-taking) clergy. Asked to explain himself, Bishop Fauchet said simply, "I come in my capacity as your bishop." "Sir, our former bishop is not dead," replied one of the nuns. "We recognize no one other than him." "But then, in what manner do you regard me?" the bishop inquired. "We regard you as the son of Satan," she replied.[24]

Such matter-of-fact rejections could have consequences. When Bishop Laurencie chose exile from his diocese of Nantes because he refused the oath, his departure was interpreted as abdication of his episcopal seat. His replacement, the constitutional Bishop Minée, sought to begin his tenure with pastoral visits to parishes and religious orders. The episcopal equivalent to "showing the flag," pastoral visits projected authority. As an act of resistance, the Carmelite sisters of Couëts refused to see him and in effect refused to recognize his authority. Local patriots treated this affront as an insult to the nation's honor. On 1 June 1791, an angry crowd of women, and some men, forced their way into the courtyard of the Carmelite convent. The women, belonging to the Society of Patriotic Women, wanted an explanation of the Carmelites' decision not to receive Bishop Minée, and they demanded an audience with the convent superior.

The request for an appointment refused, a group of women broke into the convent buildings. They made their way to the chapel, where the nuns had assembled, frightened and huddled in prayer. The crowd of women descended upon the nuns, shouting insults and demanding explanations. Then they grabbed the nuns by the necks and pushed their faces toward the ground. With the nuns bent at the waist, the Patriotic Women raised the nuns' gowns and spanked their exposed thighs and buttocks in the convent chapel. As one indignant commentator put it, "the saints of Couëts suffered an indecent flagellation in front of the altars!" The nuns were then herded from their convent with a hail of blows, shoves, and shouts. Outside, one of the nuns was pushed into a pond.[25] A group of women religious working in a Nantes hospital were similarly beaten and humiliated.

A MALEVOLENT PRESENCE

The story of the "Fouetteuses de Couëts"—the whippers of Couëts, as they were known—revealed a bitter animosity. The Revolution of 1789 was the dawn of a new era of enlightenment and liberation. France, the leader of nations, would show the way to a future beyond ignorance and superstition. And yet by the spring of 1790 it was obvious that, instead of participating in this triumphant march forward, some were holding back. Indeed, it seemed more and more evident that the values of the Revolution were increasingly at odds with Christian belief, or at least with the prerogatives of Catholic institutions. From the point of view of groups such as the Society of Patriotic Women, Catholic clergy and religious orders, along with their properties and establishments, were emerging as centers of resistance within a network of opposition to the Revolution.

And they were right, although it wasn't so much the Revolution as what it portended that troubled men and women religious. From the opening months of the Revolution there had been presentiments of disaster—the day following the seizure of the Bastille, the comte d'Artois, brother of King Louis XVI, sensed the political chill and made his way toward the frontier. The religious sentiment of an evil shadow spreading over the land dates from the same conjuncture. In Anjou, at la Chapelle-du-Genêt, the abbé Yves-Michel Marchais, who had a pronounced penchant for providential interpretations of natural calamities, was ready with a providentialist reading of the opening events of the French Revolution. Marchais's sermon to his parishioners showed that politics and weather made a dangerous mix, and how a demonic presence made sense of them. Not yet two weeks after the fall of the Bastille, on 26 July 1789, Marchais drew up an inventory of cataclysms for the faithful of his parish. He noted how weeks of rainfall and a shortage of grain and bread had come "after the frost and bitter cold of an unprecedented winter." Then, politics: "trouble, unrest, and the most violent jolts to the state and the government" which could only be explained by "a demon of discord" who had agitated spirits and poisoned relations between "the best of kings and the most faithful of peoples."[26] These events, these calamities, were not only chastisements for sin and calls to atone, but also signs of powerful evil forces at work.

Marchais mixed political commentary with the reading of signs and portents. Indeed, just weeks after the Declaration of the Rights of Man and Citizen had proclaimed the values of liberty and equality, Marchais warned his flock from the pulpit that liberty and equality were the most dangerous of evils. "God grants you the honor of thinking better, in respecting and honoring the king as the head of the nation whom we cannot refuse to obey," he advised them. As for the nobility, "Respect and honor them also. They hold the first rank after the king and consequently deserve their prerogatives and distinctions." Marchais endorsed the social hierarchy of the Old Regime, including distinctions of birth, and advised only the correction of abuses, not the destruction of privilege.[27]

The thoughts and utterances of the abbé Marchais are among the best documented of the parish clergy of the revolutionary period. They reveal a surprising consistency with the attitudes of well-placed clerical and counterrevolutionary opinion in Paris. The brilliant Catholic polemicist Augustin Barruel, former Jesuit and editor of the *Journal Ecclésiastique,* is best known for his 1797 anti-revolutionary critique *Mémoires pour servir à l'histoire du jacobinisme.* But Barruel had wasted no time in 1789 getting into print a denunciatory pamphlet built from essays he had published earlier in his *Journal Ecclésiastique.* The pamphlet, *le Patriote véridique, ou Discours sur les vraies causes de la Révolution actuelle,* set forth a providentialist discourse on the Revolution similar to that of Marchais.[28] France had sinned; the Revolution was divine chastisement. The near simultaneity of the appearance of condemnations so similar in content in places so remote as Barruel's Paris and Marchais's la Chapelle-du-Genêt is suggestive. It is suggestive not so much of a rapid and well-coordinated network relaying anti-revolutionary critical commentary, although such publications as Royou's *l'Ami du Roi* and Barruel's *Journal Ecclésiastique* constitute the elements of one. More plausibly, it is suggestive of a shared culture, constructed and maintained by a clergy given to "reading" the events of the day in hopes of catching a glimpse of the hand of God. Marchais, for example, had interpreted a 1783 earthquake in Messina, Italy in similar terms: God allowed the event to take place in order to punish some and instruct others.[29] Some priests, especially in rural parishes, welcomed noisy storms for similar reasons: they prompted sinners to seek forgiveness and elicited prudence on the part of those tempted by sin.[30]

Such arguments were a tougher sell in Paris. The abbé Jean-Siffrein Maury, clerical member of the National Assembly and, like Barruel, staunch defender of the king and absolute monarchy, would move the critique of the Revolution beyond a simple providentialist reading.[31] Maury denounced the significant reforms and innovations of the Revolution by emphasizing the anti-Catholic and Protestant origins of key revolutionary ideas.[32] He condemned, notably, the Civil Constitution of the Clergy as the work of the enemies of Christianity. Barruel also joined Maury in condemning the Revolution not only as anti-Christian, but also as the product of a conspiracy. For them and many others, their opponents, the advocates of the Revolution, were not innocent victims of error. The proponents of the Revolution were not merely wrong, they were malevolent schismatics.[33]

Maury would later be rewarded for his efforts by being named to the cardinalate and, for a time in the 1790s, serving as the exiled Louis XVIII's de facto ambassador to the Vatican.[34] His vision, however admired and rewarded, was by no means unique. The "opening out" and popularization of the Catholic critique of the Revolution as an anti-Catholic conspiracy had already taken place. By mid-summer in 1791, it would break into the open.

VOLTAIRE MOVES IN; THE SAINTS MARCH OUT

Voltaire made a posthumous visit to Paris in July of 1791. He never left. The occasion was his admission to an exclusive club, that of the "great men" recognized by the French nation and dignified by the translation of their mortal remains to a place called the Pantheon, a home for gods.

Before his ceremonial entry into the city of Paris, Voltaire, or at least his remains, journeyed from the Scellières abbey in Champagne, where he had been buried at the time of his death in 1778. Given that the archbishop of Paris had forbidden his burial within the city at the time of his death, his return was a triumph. His itinerary within Paris took him to the site of the Bastille, where the slow procession halted in recognition of Voltaire's status as revolutionary progenitor and temporary resident of the fortress. It then proceeded by way of the Louvre / Tuileries complex, seat of the monarchy, past the newly baptized quai Voltaire, then to the Left Bank, past the Odéon, then known as the Théâtre de la Nation, where Voltaire's own *Brutus* was playing, to the Pantheon on Sainte-Geneviève hill.[35] François-Joseph Gossec's "Marche lugubre" provided musical atmosphere, and although there *was* something plaintive and lugubrious in the flourish played by the woodwinds, the crash of the cymbals sounded triumphant. Triumphalism was certainly intended in Gossec's music and in the itinerary of the procession; both suggested Voltaire's vindication and posthumous triumph over his opponents.

For the ardent supporters of the Revolution, the ceremonial relocation of Voltaire provided a convenient means of appropriating a powerful and prestigious predecessor, a way to claim an intellectual lineage for a revolution still insecure in the face of a dynasty measured in generations and centuries. Indeed, historical commentators, following many contemporary observers, have tended to emphasize the unflattering comparison the ceremony drew between Voltaire's heroic triumph and King Louis's cowardly attempt to flee France just weeks earlier. The departure of angry, frightened, and disaffected nobles, begun in July of 1789, had continued apace through 1790. In spring of 1791, Louis XVI's alienation was complete and he, the queen, and their allies began to plan the surreptitious departure of the royal family for June of 1791. The failure of their flight (they were observed and halted near the frontier, at Varennes) gravely compromised the king's authority and prefigured the overthrow and "departure" of the monarchy the following year. Voltaire's veneration as a "great man" in early July contrasted sharply with the king's political failures, including the failure to make a clean escape in June but most of all his failure to fulfill honestly, and with conviction, his role as constitutional monarch and patron of the regeneration of France.

Such an analysis makes eminent sense, in terms of high politics and the symbolic politics guiding public opinion in the reception and assimilation of the news of the royal flight. The king's "flight to Varennes" and the veneration of Voltaire have their place in the desacralization of monarchy. They also have their place in the preparation of public opinion for the substitution of a hierarchy of merit and achievement for a discredited hierarchy of birth—in short, to make room for a republic in the public imagination. However, Voltaire's pantheonization bears other meanings and resonances, notably within a Catholic public opinion increasingly alarmed, even embattled, by revolutionary policy toward religion.

A VOTIVE CHURCH BUILT BY A KING
IN FULFILLMENT OF A VOW

The revolutionary home for great men, the Pantheon, was not built for such mundane purposes. In fact, the structure had been erected as the result of a royal vow made by Louis XV. In 1744, Louis was gravely ill. Faced with his own mortality, he made a conditional vow to build a fine church if he recovered his health; it was not the first and was surely not the last of royal vows to build a church in exchange for—or in expectation of—a divine favor rendered. Louis recovered his health. When it came time to make good on his promise, Louis selected Jacques Soufflot as architect for the project; Soufflot was the brother of the royal mistress Madame de Pompadour—presumably the king's recovery did not hinge upon rectitude in his private behavior.[36]

The church Soufflot was to design and build was to serve as a replacement for an aged church—by the 1740s well into its fifth century—built in honor of Saint Geneviève, the patron saint of the city of Paris. Geneviève, legend had it, was a humble shepherd, the "virgin of Nanterre." Her holiness had allowed her to intercede with God on behalf of the city of Paris. Her prayers saved Paris from the rampaging infidel bands of Attila. Centuries later, under Louis le Gros, Geneviève's relics were credited with the cures of several victims of an internal ailment called *la maladie des ardents* and characterized by a burning sensation in the abdomen. The cure was brought about by means of a procession of Geneviève's relics through the streets of the city of Paris (fig. 11). At the moment that Geneviève's relics crossed the threshold of her church, those who suffered from the *maladie des ardents* were cured.[37]

But it was Geneviève's status as protector that made her a powerful national figure (at least in Catholic circles), as well as a Parisian patron. Geneviève's church was among the properties nationalized according to the terms of the legislation of November 1789, and in the consolidation of parishes and

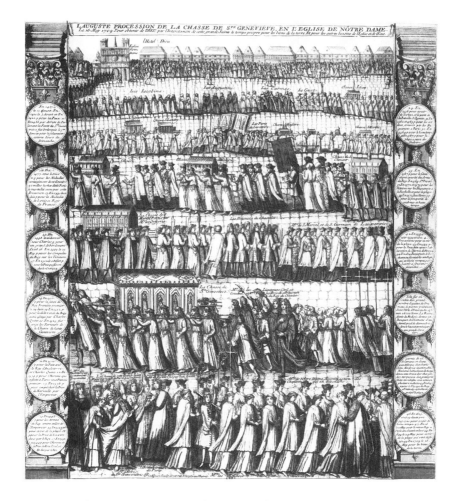

Figure 11. "The Majestic Procession of the Relics of Saint Geneviève to the Church of Notre-Dame, 19 May 1709." Early eighteenth century. Photo: Bibliothèque Nationale, Cabinet des Estampes, Paris.

When Louis XV suffered from a serious illness, he made a vow to rebuild Geneviève's church should he recover. Louis recovered, and the new church of Sainte-Geneviève was designed around her relics. The procession of Geneviève's relics through the city of Paris was a major event, involving the participation of the members of the Parlement of Paris, lay penitential societies, and the representatives of the major religious orders in strict order of precedence.

the sale of church properties, it became available for reassignment. It would soon figure in a major symbolic clash between the Catholic cult of the saints and the new secular religion of revolutionary patriotism. The matter was first raised on the occasion of the death, in March of 1791, of the deputy and revolutionary leader Honoré Mirabeau. Mirabeau was the first of the outstanding figures of the early Revolution to die, so his death prompted reflection on how a revolutionary nation should mourn the loss of its own. Such reflections inspired proposals designed to offer special recognition to this patriotic servant. A petition sponsored by one Parisian neighborhood and seconded by many others called upon the National Assembly to inter Mirabeau under the altar of the fatherland, on the Champ de Mars, then known as the Champ de la Fédération.[38] Another group called upon the National Assembly to honor Mirabeau, Voltaire, and others by converting the Sainte-Geneviève church into a national monument in honor of great men.

The question took on an air of urgency when the National Assembly learned that among the former Catholic properties up for sale was the Scellières abbey, where Voltaire had been buried. The abbey might be for sale, but the remains of such a distinguished figure simply were not; something had to be done. However, the question of the honorable disposition of Voltaire's remains became the occasion for a serious dispute about his legacy and his stature as an undisputed "great man," worthy of treatment heretofore reserved for dead royalty and the holy men and women of the Catholic Church. What followed was inflated rhetoric and insults traded in salvos. When the deputy Jean-Baptiste Treilhard suggested that Voltaire had predicted the Revolution, the abbé Couturier remarked that if Voltaire was such a prophet, his relics should be shipped to Palestine. Couturier's use of the term "relics" in reference to the remains of Voltaire belied his offended religious sensibilities and alluded to the displacement of the relics of Geneviève. His insulting suggestion that Voltaire be sent abroad was countered by Treilhard with the remark that "while alive Voltaire had been torn apart by ignorance and fanaticism: it's not surprising that he is still pursued."[39] "Fanaticism" and "ignorance," frequently accompanied by the word "superstition" were widely understood to be code words for Catholicism, especially in its more intransigent and uncompromising forms. Around the bodies of Voltaire and Geneviève (Geneviève's relics would be burned on the Place de Grève in a fit of iconoclasm in 1793) a discussion was taking shape over the place of Catholicism among the values, ideals, and heroes of post-revolutionary France.

Some objections were headed off by pointing out that Isaac Newton had been honored at his death with burial alongside kings (in Westminster Abbey), overlooking the fact that Westminster, unlike Sainte-Geneviève, remained a church and that Newton, unlike Voltaire, had not made a career of pointing out the failures of the established church and its clergy. Voltaire's heroic indictment of the Catholic Church in the Calas Affair was but the most notorious incident. There were others. In Voltaire's *Candide,* at the end of the tale, Candide finds his teacher grievously afflicted with venereal disease, and as Pangloss recounts the etiology of his illness, the reader learns that it originated with Christopher Columbus's cabin boy and infected Pangloss only after transmission via a litany of male and female religious, including the obligatory Jesuit—funny, but crude and bound to offend. Anyone with such well-developed anti-clerical reflexes was unlikely to reassure Catholics or to make a noncontroversial candidate for a broad and inclusive patriotic sainthood.

Indeed, although historians for years treated revolutionary festivals and cultural policy as peculiar examples of revolutionary taste of little consequence for "real" politics, contemporaries certainly understood that the battle over Voltaire and the Pantheon was essentially a battle about the religious politics of the Revolution. For Madame Roland, Voltaire's pantheonization represented a defeat for Catholicism and a triumph for the anti-clerical and anti-Catholic bent of the Revolution, just as Mirabeau's pantheonization amounted to a public rally for the ideal of liberty.[40] Three days after the triumphal procession of Voltaire's remains across Paris to the Pantheon (fig. 12), she wrote that the event "seemed to foreshadow the complete ruin of superstition."[41] "Superstition," of course, was a code word for Catholicism.

In effect, Voltaire's ceremony was the second in a pair of very important pieces of national theater to debut in the summer of 1791. The first of these was the royal family's attempted flight, which could be interpreted as an unscripted drama on the transitory and ultimately superfluous nature of kingship. The second was Voltaire's pantheonization, which demonstrated the nationalization of Christian virtues—self-abnegation, heroic sacrifice—in secular form in the new revolutionary culture. It also revealed an obvious

Figure 12. "The Sequence of the Cortege to Translate the Remains of Voltaire, Monday, 11 July 1791." Engraving by Berthault after Prier, ca. 1791–92. Musée Carnavalet, Paris. © Photothèque des Musées de la Ville de Paris.

The church of Sainte-Geneviève was one of the properties converted to secular purposes when the National Assembly voted to nationalize the property of the Catholic Church after 1789. The Assembly decided to make the church a "pantheon"—a mausoleum to house the remains of men who had made extraordinary contributions to the life of the nation. Voltaire's remains were transferred to the Pantheon in a magnificent procession. Just as in the procession of the relics of Geneviève, organizers carefully coordinated the participation and precedence of various groups and corporate bodies. Many Catholics were horrified.

co-optation of Catholic ritual. Voltaire's procession neatly aped the Catholic rituals associated with Corpus Christi—the stops at the Bastille and the Louvre resemble the processional pauses at *reposoirs*—and even recalled Geneviève's triumphant procession resulting in the cure of the *maladie des ardents*. No record mentions miraculous cures coinciding with Voltaire's remains crossing the Pantheon threshold, although Madame Roland does mention a salutary pedagogical effect. These symbolic pageants—Varennes, the Pantheon—amounted to a working through of certain fundamental problems posed by the Revolution. It was as if they played out before the public imagination a vision of France without those mainstays of the Old Regime—monarchy and the Catholic Church.[42]

Did peasants and provincials understand what the enshrinement of Voltaire had meant? Most men and women could barely read, much less sit down and work through Voltaire's *Lettres philosophiques.* But over the years the name/word "Voltaire" had become a synonym for skepticism and anti-clericalism, just as surely as "fanaticism" and "superstition" coded Catholicism. "Voltaire" was thus by reputation anathema; his veneration and his displacement of a saint of the Church as august as Geneviève could not be a good thing.[43]

Such events resonated all the more deeply in that they coincided with a spring and summer of local dramas turning on themes of godliness, honor, transparency, the sacred, and the profane. The National Assembly had decreed, in late November 1790, that clergy should take the civic oath. By January of 1791, faced with clerical resistance to the oath, or the adoption of "modified" vows and vows "with reservations," the Assembly initiated discussion of legislation to bring about the prompt replacement of clergy who had not taken the civil oath. By April, the Assembly had adopted similar legislation with respect to women religious employed in schools and hospitals.[44] In most cases, the taking of the oath or the refusal of the oath served as a catalyst to local mobilization for or against the Revolution.

The oath could be an occasion for showing impatience with the Revolution or, as in the case of the Fouetteuses de Couëts, impatience with those who opposed it. Timothy Tackett describes a case near Montpellier where "fanatical" clergy were accused of influencing the politics of their faithful at the same time that those faithful were accused of intimidating their clergy into rejecting the oath.[45] In most of the communities of the department of the Yonne, near Paris, four out of five clergy took the oath, presumably manifesting their parishioners' attitudes as well as their own; those who refused the oath went home, left France, or disappeared as their oath-taking successors arrived to take their places.[46] In Paris, the *Gazette de Paris* engaged in rhetorical volleys with the Assembly majority and the supporters of the reforms, inventing a heated vocabulary of opposition: clergy who resisted the oath were idealized as proto-martyrs while constitutional clergy were "dregs of society," "the vomit of Hell," "heretics," and "supporters of Satan."[47]

In the west of France, oath-takers tended to be in the minority, and among those taking the oath subsequent retraction was fairly common.[48] The schismatic potential of the Civil Constitution and the oath was fully revealed following their condemnation by Pius VI in March of 1791. No one expected the National Assembly to back down on its position under papal pressure; this would have amounted to abdication of sovereignty in the eyes of many patriots. Instead, plans proceeded apace to replace non-juring (non-oathtaking) priests in their parishes with priests who had submitted to the will of the National Assembly and taken the oath. Tensions grew as these oath-taking clergy arrived to assume authority in parishes where clergy had refused the oath. Clergy who resisted the oath would have to vacate their residence and relinquish access to the parish church. But these were only the opening maneuvers in what could become a protracted war of religion.

Establishment in the parish clerical residence and access to the parish church gave oath-taking clergy a considerable advantage. They would dwell where parishioners had expected their priests to dwell. They controlled the sacred places. They would perform religious services in the manner and in the places where parishioners were accustomed to seeing them performed. Presumably, such continuities would be reassuring to the faithful: familiar gestures and sacred phrases would occur in the right places and at the pre-scribed times. To the naive or the uninformed, the oath might amount to this: one priest would leave, another would arrive; their spiritual lives would go on as before. After all, most of them had seen such transitions before, when their priests died or retired.

The difference was that wherever clergy resisted the oath, they made sure that their parishioners understood what was at stake and that they too had a choice to make. Make the wrong choice and their salvation would be jeopardized. This work of propaganda, an energetic information campaign among the faithful, got underway prior to the arrival of the oath-taking suc-cessors. Its success turned upon the credibility of clerical claims that the only efficacious rituals and services were those performed by clergy in good stand-ing with the Roman Catholic Church. The unique power of the clergy de-rives from their ability and authority to perform the sacraments. The im-portance of the sacraments derives from their necessity for salvation. Put simply, according to Catholic teachings, humans are born in sin and are restored to grace by the sacrament of baptism. They maintain their relationship to God by means of the sacrament of penance, wherein they reveal their transgressions, and by receiving communion at least once per year, normally during the Easter season. To fail in these efforts—to forego these sacraments—was to risk dying in a state of sin, which would mean spending eternity in torment, cut off from God and the faithful.

In leaflets and in sermons, clergy who had resisted the oath warned their parishioners of the dangers to salvation posed by the arrival of the replacement oath-taking clergy, now commonly referred to as *intrus*—intruders. The essential message was this: the *intrus* may possess the presbytery and offer services in the parish church, but unless they retract their oath they risk condemnation and excommunication from the Catholic Church; moreover the sacraments they perform are null.[49] The first task was to make sure that Catholics knew that there was a choice, by setting up a clear alternative to the services performed by the *intrus,* the constitutional clergy. This was achieved by setting up parallel parishes alongside those to be operated by the constitutional clergy, an arrangement that confronted the faithful with a clear choice. Thus, by early June of 1791, André Brumauld de Beauregard, vicar general acting on behalf of the bishop of Luçon (in the Vendée) produced a letter-circular in which he described what amounted to political and ecclesiastical "rules of engagement." Brumauld de Beauregard advised parish clergy to "secure as soon as possible a place where they might . . . gather their faithful and carry out the functions of their office as soon as their would-be successors seize control of their churches." In some parishes, alternative places of worship might include a private chapel, such as many chateaux, convents, monasteries, and large estates possessed, or even a barn. The vicar general also drew up an inventory of priestly paraphernalia reduced to essentials—a portable altar, a chasuble of printed fabric or any ordinary cloth, a pewter chalice and ciborium—with an eye toward mobility and ease of operation in clandestinity.[50] Brumauld de Beauregard emphasized the gravity of the situation and the potential risk without actually using the word "martyr." Instead, he invoked the memory of the persecutions of the early Christians, speaking of the necessity of gathering secretively in barns and "caves and tombs."

In addition to offering alternative sites for Catholic rituals, it was also necessary to explain why this alternative was important—to show as clearly as possible how the *intrus* differed from the Catholic clergy who had resisted the oath. This was essentially a question of catechism, and "dialogues" between a priest and a sincere believer were printed and distributed—a technique commonly used in missions.[51] In the spring of 1791, that is, shortly after the papal condemnation of the Civil Constitution had been announced, copies of a catechism pamphlet were already in circulation in the west of France. The catechism provided instructions for the faithful in the face of the imminent arrival of the *intrus*. One passage read as follows:

LE FIDÈLE: What should one do if there is no Mass other than that offered by the *intrus?*

LE PRÊTRE: You must do without, even on Easter.

LE FIDÈLE: But the Church commands us to go to Mass on Sundays and holy days?

LE PRÊTRE: Yes, when possible; but Mass from priests such as that, it's as if you hadn't gone at all.[52]

Similar documents warned of marriages performed by constitutional clergy. Since the marriages aren't genuine, offspring will be illegitimate.[53] The only valid sacraments were those performed by clergy who remained loyal to Rome and resisted the demand for the oath. In communities where Catholics could not or would not transfer their confidence to the constitutional clergy, the arrival of the *intrus*—and the departure of clergy who refused the oath—prompted profound anxieties. And what security was there in a world where the validity of a religious act could turn on an oath or its retraction? When a guilt-ridden Michel Pierre of Nantes retracted his oath in August of 1791, he felt compelled to announce that "all absolutions I have given since [my oath], all marriages I have celebrated [are null], and the infants issuing from those marriages are illegitimate before God."[54] For those who accepted the Roman Catholic insistence that the efficacy of the sacraments depended upon a priest's acceptance of the authority of Rome, the schism in the Catholic Church placed in jeopardy the sanctity of marriages and the salvation of souls.

Little wonder, then, that the constitutional clergy were sometimes greeted in their parishes not as holy men but as wicked and profane intruders whose liturgical gestures amounted to mockery and sacrilege. At the village of May, near Angers, villagers subjected the new priest to all manner of vexations. Children dogged his steps on his arrival, shouting "Heretic!" and "Thief of sacraments!" as he made his way toward the center of town. When he visited the parish church, he dipped his fingers in the font of holy water and made the sign of the cross, a ritual sign of cleansing before entering a chapel or church. Upon observing this gesture, a group of women immediately and noisily washed the font, as if he had contaminated it by his unholy touch.[55] When he stopped into an *auberge* for dinner he was served poorly and over-charged. When he later walked the village on foot, he noticed women gathering stones, as if preparing to stone him—a chilling preliminary.[56] As he well knew, since Biblical times stoning had been a form of popular execution commonly imposed upon those whose conduct had defiled the community; its power as a form of collective punishment derives from the fact that it brings death from an accumulation of blows, death by collectivity.[57]

Such blatant forms of intimidation could only be practiced in communities where public opinion was overwhelmingly hostile to the constitutional clergy. Elsewhere, especially in larger towns and cities, opinions tended to be split or favorable to the new revolutionary clergy. This called for more discreet and prudent tactics. In Bordeaux, for example, opponents of the new clergy dropped printed sheets of anti-*intrus* poems and lyrics in public ways where passersby might pick them up and read them. On the reverse of the sheet, a message advised the reader to drop the sheet to the ground after reading it, so that it could be picked up by yet another reader. One read: "If you tear me up, you are an oaf. Toss me back to the ground."[58]

Acts of resistance, whether anonymous or openly defiant, took their toll on the confidence and sense of purpose of constitutional clergy. In several areas, and not only the areas of future insurgency, members of the constitutional clergy concluded that pursuing their mission was not worth the effort—or the risk. In Normandy, at Coutances, in September of 1791, administrators of the revolutionary government petitioned the National Assembly for legislation to protect constitutional clergy against various forms of "persecution." Some priests had been hanged in effigy, others had barely escaped death, still others had been obliged to flee.[59] By the end of 1791, the stakes in the game of religious warfare had gone up sharply. In November, officials in Anjou wrote a letter to the National Assembly warning them that unless something was done "you will not find a single constitutional public functionary in office."[60] The "public constitutional functionary" intended here is the constitutional priest.

Even so, in most places the constitutional clergy benefited from two strategic advantages: they had the active support of revolutionary public authorities and they had the power of place—they controlled the churches. However, as oath-resistant clergy lost control of places of worship, they not only developed alternative sites, they also cultivated alternative faith practices. They even tolerated practices that they might previously have scorned. Eighteenth-century clergy merely tolerated certain practices seen as driven by superstition or as tending toward idolatry. These included pilgrimage, certain devotions to the saints, and the tendency to see certain places as "holy" and offering privileged or unmediated access to the sacred. Clerical attitudes on these matters were driven partly by sensitivity to Protestant and Jansenist criticisms—it wasn't hard to see how veneration of the saints could blend into idolatry—but also out of concern about religious devotions practiced by the laity without priestly guidance. Priests were concerned and sometimes alarmed by the emotional and spiritual investment the faithful would make in practices, such as pilgrimages, entirely unsupervised by priests or other trained religious. Clergy were naturally worried about the dubious orthodoxy and potentially seditious nature of devotions carried out without the guidance and intervention of clerical authority.

Now that the official constitutional clergy were in place, such devotions functioned effectively as counter-practices with enhanced value as tools of sedition, precisely because they challenged clerical prerogatives, albeit those of the *intrus,* the constitutional clergy. Displaced clergy, those who refused the oath, now actively encouraged devotions they once regarded as suspect, even vaguely heathen. What had once seemed threatening because of its populism and implicit anti-clericalism now offered significant potential for those very reasons.

In early August of 1791, Yves-Michel Marchais, the displaced pastor of la Chapelle-du-Genêt, devoted an entire sermon to the hearty endorsement of pilgrimages. Marchais had not always supported pilgrimage but for two months he had been encouraging pilgrimages to a local shrine at Belle-fontaine; his parishioners had responded enthusiastically. He felt compelled to explain and defend his prior objections to pilgrimage. "Sometimes [in the past] I appeared aloof and even opposed to such pilgrimages," he noted, "because I feared they led to levity and dissipation. . . ." Happily, that was not the case; instead Marchais observed "fervor, spirituality, and solid devotion."[61]

Marchais wanted to contextualize his remarks not only in terms of his prior positions on pilgrimage, but also in terms of the problems of the day. "Holy pilgrimages" and "devotional voyages" suited well the challenges of a time of religious persecution, comparable to those of "the early times of the Christian church." They offered hope and protection against "the evils that afflict us," including "the evils one fears in matters of religion and in the commerce of everyday life."[62] Marchais validated pilgrimage as a means of defining a Christian community (to the exclusion of the *intrus*), as a response to religious and political anxieties, and as a form of reparation for acts committed against God and the Christian faith.

For these reasons, the number, scale, color, and vitality of pilgrimages and non-sanctioned services served as a barometer of the anxieties and resentments of a Catholic *peuple.* In the summer of 1791, processions, pilgrimages, and clandestine services presented striking tableaux in hidden valleys and along rural byways. Jacques Bougler was an early witness; Bougler was posted to Angers as a member of a mounted gendarme brigade. As he made his way from Trémentines toward Cholet about an hour after nightfall on a warm August night, he observed from a distance an eerie pattern of lights moving along a path. As he approached, he could discern a lantern attached to a pole and a number of torches lighting the way for of a large crowd of people in a religious procession.[63] Bougler did not try to approach the procession and he never learned its purpose or destination. It could have had a strictly local purpose: a mass, a visit to a local shrine, a stations-of-the-cross *en pleine air.* It's possible that he had happened upon a pilgrimage of abbé Marchais's parishioners or some other parish on their way to a chapel at Bellefontaine.

Even more popular was the shrine of Notre-Dame-de-Charité, near Saint-Laurent-sur-la-Plaine, a few kilometers downstream from Angers and south of the Loire. Whatever the destination of the nocturnal procession, the eerie glow of lanterns, candles, and torches in the summer night illuminated the faces of men and women whose allegiance to the new regime was in doubt. It was undoubtedly why revolutionary authorities sought to limit access to devotional sites and looked askance at processions and other apparently uncoordinated religious activities. By the early autumn of 1791, such manifestations had become so alarming that revolutionary authorities in Angers ordered the demolition of the Notre-Dame-de-Charité chapel. Troops were sent in to do the job. After a few hours of work tearing off the roof and pulling stone from stone, the chapel of Our Lady was gone. Only the altar remained, standing alone in the open air.

But in their eagerness thereby to end the seditious procession they were, in fact, forced into the role of sorcerer's apprentice because there where the chapel had stood, the Virgin Mary appeared. Sometimes she appeared on the altar of the former chapel, the only part of it to remain after the demolition. Other times she appeared among the branches of a nearby oak. But as news of the apparition spread, the pilgrims returned in numbers greater than ever. Entire parishes made journeys of as much as fifteen leagues in hopes of a glimpse of the Virgin whose very appearance served as a divine rebuke to revolutionary authorities. An ominous sign: local authorities reported a shift in the demeanor of the pilgrims. Before the destruction of the chapel and the Virgin's apparition, pilgrims carried rosaries and one heard prayers of *Ora pro nobis;* after, they carried clubs and stones and murmured threats to revolutionary authorities.[64]

Pilgrimage is a penitential act. From the earliest Christian times through medieval times (when pilgrimage in some places was an extension of what moderns would call the criminal justice system), pilgrims sought to atone. Although many of the pilgrims of 1791 surely had private concerns and intentions, their processions and prayers evidently conveyed a public message too. They exposed the fragile status of the constitutional clergy and, through them, of the Revolution itself. They also revealed popular anxieties about the consequences of what were regarded as profanations—acts of which Voltaire's displacement of Sainte Geneviève in Paris was only the most obvious example. The closing of monasteries and convents, the consolidation of parishes (and consequent closing and sale of parish churches), the election of pastors and bishops: what seemed like the inevitable outcome of necessary reforms proved to be deeply troubling. The overarching fear: profanations and acts of sacrilege would invite the punishment of God. The obligation of the holy: ward off divine wrath through acts of reparation, including prayer and pilgrimage. Thus the processions to holy places not only measured popular alienation from the Revolution, they also served as a barometer of popular anxiety.

THE MARK OF GOD'S PEOPLE
(NEW VISIONS OF THE SACRÉ-COEUR)

"May the holy lives around us appease the anger of heaven," wrote Pierre-Joseph Picot de Clorivière on 11 July 1791, the date of the translation of the relics of Voltaire to the Pantheon.[65] "The new church of Sainte-Geneviève has been turned into a heathen temple," lamented Picot. "Christ is trampled underfoot and wickedness is exalted." Profanation was on the mind of Alexandre Lenfant, another former Jesuit, when he complained that the heavy rains that followed the procession of Voltaire's remains failed to wash away such an outrageous public impiety.[66] In his royalist newspaper, *l'Ami du roi,* the abbé Royou had likewise described Voltaire's pantheonization as a "scandalous profanation."[67]

Profanation of the sacred, exaltation of the wicked, reparation by the holy few: these were the preoccupations of Picot and Lenfant, preoccupations they shared with a widening circle of Catholics. For some, the religious policy of the Revolution was sure to bring down divine chastisement, for others, the Revolution was *itself* a chastisement. In either case, profanations and wicked exaltations were the signs by which they recognized in the Revolution an evil of terrifying and unsurpassed strength.

What was to be done? In the past, devout men and women faced such systemic threats by marking themselves, just as the Hebrew people had marked their homes to protect themselves against the scourges sent against Egypt. In Marseille, during the plague, individuals protected themselves and identified themselves as members of the community of the faithful by wearing the image of the Sacré-Coeur. After Marseille, and throughout the eighteenth century, the distribution of Sacred Heart emblems, along with rosaries and medals, had been a regular feature of internal missions in France, especially in Brittany, Anjou, and Poitou.[68]

By the 1780s, such gestures had become reflex, not only in religious communities such as the Visitationists for whom the Sacré-Coeur, thanks to Marguerite-Marie Alacoque, was a central devotion, but also among the laity. Marseille and the legends and tales of salvation it inspired helped make the Sacré-Coeur emblem—with its aggressive motto "Arrête! Le coeur de Jésus est là!"—part of a popular arsenal, to be used in times of sickness and anxiety.

There were some 167 Visitationist convents scattered across the French realm. Through their regular exchange of correspondence and letters-circular they constituted a de facto network by means of which the message of the Sacré-Coeur devotion and its emblem remained in circulation. Indeed, in 1787 correspondence between Visitationist convents fairly buzzed with extraordinary news. A Visitationist sister had been blessed with visions of the Sacré-Coeur.[69] With her, the present generation, like the generations of the time of Marguerite-Marie Alacoque and Anne-Madeleine Rémuzat, would have its divine interlocutor. The new visionary had requested anonymity; it was known only that she was a member of the Visitationist convent of Nantes.[70] However, the command conveyed through her was clear: revive the faith of the "chosen people" (the people of France) through the devotion to the Sacred Heart.

The visions continued. With the onset of the Revolution, the messages took on a greater sense of urgency. They enhanced the sense, through portentous signs, that these were extraordinary times. Jesus appeared to the Nantes visionary and promised that all who wore the image of the Sacré-Coeur "would come to no harm in the present revolution."[71] Inspired by this message, the Nantes Visitationists began to produce Sacré-Coeur emblems. The sisters of the Ursuline order at Nantes asked for a model image from the Visitationists, which they copied and reproduced by the hundreds.[72] As the news spread, convents across France ramped up production of Sacred Heart images and "safeguards." In 1790, Troyes, Meaux, and Langres asked for images and began to reproduce them, as did la Rochelle, Tulle, Bordeaux, Cahors, Auch, Avignon, Marseille, Lyon, and Moulins (fig. 13).[73] Visitationists, Ursulines, Filles de Sagesse—the religious order mattered little; what mattered was that their convents served as production and communication nodes in a national network of the Sacred Heart.

The use of convent labor to fabricate religious objects did not set this period apart. Two things did: the sheer volume of production and the belief that the production of Sacred Hearts was the most potent spiritual counter to a growing ambient revolutionary evil. Variation there was, to be sure. But it was in the area of materials and minor variations in words, initials and phrases, and subtle modification of motifs: hearts of wool, of silk, and of flannel, embroidered hearts, asymmetrical hearts, red hearts, brown hearts, black hearts, hearts of red and green, hearts of silver, lead, and pewter, hearts affixed by appliqué, hearts to be stitched on, hearts to be pinned, hearts to

Figure 13. Hand-painted Sacred Heart emblem. Bibliothèque Municipale de Nantes.

As Catholic alarm at the Revolution grew, the Sacré-Coeur emblem became more popular. Lay and religious Catholics reproduced it by the thousands, in homes and in convents. The Sacré-Coeur would soon become the insignia of counter-revolutionary sedition.

be worn around the neck, hearts worn as rings, hearts with bleeding wounds, hearts pierced by lances, hearts pierced by arrows, hearts surmounted by crosses, hearts spewing flames, hearts ringed by thorns, hearts conjoined, hearts with the names of Jesus and Mary, hearts crowned.[74] The possibilities seemed endless, but stitched to the inside of one's vest or suspended around one's neck, the Sacred Heart motif expressed the overwhelming sense that the Revolution was no mere political difference of opinion; the Revolution was a conflict between good and evil. Indeed, at the time of Voltaire's pantheonization, the abbé Royou had referred to Voltaire as "a plague"—a significant rhetorical elision.[75] The heart offered protection after 1789, just as it had in Marseille. Safeguard and insignia, the Sacré-Coeur answered compelling needs: the need to make choices, the need to seek protection, the need to break out of a sense of embattled isolation. Pinning on the Sacré-Coeur expressed conviction, secured comfort, identified allies. The People of God would recognize one another by the sign of the Sacred Heart of Jesus.

As production of the Sacré-Coeur emblems increased, so did the number of stories of miraculous interventions and inexplicable events associated with it. In December of 1791, sisters at the Avignon Visitationist convent reported an extraordinary grace associated with the Sacré-Coeur. Three "brigands" had descended upon their house during a period of political violence. The convent had taken the precaution of placing Sacré-Coeur images on their doors; the convent was spared.[76] Claude-Marie de Bruc, mother superior of the Nantes Visitationists, tirelessly promoted the Sacré-Coeur "safeguard." Her correspondence with other convents shows that she attributed to the Sacré-Coeur emblem the security of several chateaux in the Nantes region during the Great Fear, when peasants in many areas seized estates and ransacked them.[77] Along with convents spared and chateaux saved, Claude-Marie de Bruc also credited the Sacré-Coeur with more personal protections. "Not a single accident has befallen persons who possess these safeguards," she reported to fellow Visitationists at Nancy.[78] "Protection" could be relative, however, according to at least one account. Robbers attacked a man, stabbed him several times, beat him with an iron rod, then tried to finish him off with a musket fired at close range. Left for dead, the mere fact of his survival was attributed to his safeguard.[79] In anxious times, full of evil portent, mere survival passed for a sign of divine favor.

In the tumult of revolutionary change and fears of violence, disorder, and anarchy, demand for Sacré-Coeur safeguards surged. Mother de Bruc, by example and by exhortation, had fostered this devotion. She now professed herself astonished at the extraordinary network of producers of Sacred Heart safeguards. Three convents in Paris had turned out thousands; a center in the faubourg Saint-Antoine alone turned out as many as all of Nantes. Visitationists at Tulle had produced a million images of the Sacred Heart of Jesus and claimed a corresponding yield of miracles, numbered to the "infinite."[80] Rumor enhanced the sense among supporters of the Revolution that a formidable grassroots spiritual movement in favor of the Sacré-Coeur was concealed behind convent walls and behind feigned or merely public conformity to the new revolutionary ethos. Indeed, there were rumors that the "Poor Claires" of Nantes operated a clandestine press behind their high convent walls.[81]

As convents closed, former religious occupied themselves sketching and coloring emblems by hand. A veritable cottage industry in Sacré-Coeur paraphernalia arose. A man identified only as "Monsieur le chevalier de ————" painted a dozen Sacred Hearts on a piece of paper and sent them to a friend in one of his letters.[82] At the time of her arrest in 1793, Catherine de Joussemet, a former sister of Notre-Dame, had hundreds of hand-painted Sacred Hearts in her possession.[83] By 1791, the infrastructure of a spiritual economy was in place; it turned on the power of the image of the heart of Jesus and its effectiveness in the face of a Revolution deemed threatening, even demonic. The number of Sacred Heart images in circulation best measured the power of the image. The demand for Sacred Heart safeguards seemed limitless; the emblem's appeal united the most humble traveler with the occupants of the innermost circles of the royal court. After 1789, the Sacred Heart could be found wherever the future inspired not hope but fear.

While female religious assumed the greatest responsibility for advocacy and production, male religious were active too. Pierre-Joseph Picot de Clorivière was by no means the "typical" Roman Catholic clergyman at the time of the French Revolution, but he was surely typical of the kind of obsessed, driven individual needed to elaborate a vision and pursue it relentlessly. Picot was already in his fifties when the Revolution of 1789 broke out. Indeed, he was old enough to have begun his training for entry into the Jesuit order a few years before the Jesuits were proscribed in France, then suppressed—an event that undoubtedly reinforced his skepticism of secular authorities and prepared him for a life in semi-clandestinity.[84] Rather than forsake his vocation, Picot chose exile in Liège, where he completed his Jesuit training and took his vows. Picot's exile came to an end when the Jesuit order was suppressed by papal edict (*Dominus ac Redemptor*) in 1773. With the Jesuit order officially disbanded, Picot's life in exile lost its purpose. Forced to give up his life as a Jesuit, he chose the life of a simple parish priest at Saint-Malo, in his native Brittany.[85]

Picot became one of the Revolution's most ardent opponents. As the religious policy of the Revolution took shape, Picot felt a kind of holy rage. He became, in effect, a metaphysician of counter-revolution, endowed with the power to discern behind the appearances of politics and policy the actual supernatural forces at work, guiding men, shaping law, compromising fatally the spiritual health of France. He expressed forcefully his conviction that the Revolution was not just wrong, but evil—Satanic.[86] He could express only contempt for clergy who took the oath of loyalty and became agents of evil thereby: "What can be expected from men who have openly delivered themselves to Satan, [who] work for him by destroying the Church of God?"[87] Picot was convinced that combating the Revolution would take new resources and a new organization. Given the corruption of the secular Catholic hierarchy by the revolutionary reforms, what better than the revival of the Jesuit order—independent, militant, and, best of all, free of the constraints of a hopelessly compromised episcopate? At the same time that revolutionary legislation weakened the ties between Rome and French Catholicism in the name of national sovereignty and revolutionary Gallicanism, Picot felt the need to revive a priestly order independent of local and episcopal constraints and fiercely devoted to the defense of papal authority.

On 2 February 1791, six men made their way northward out of the city of Paris toward the high ground of Montmartre. Picot was the obvious leader in the group. He led the men to the small chapel built on the place where, as legend had it, Saint Denis had been beheaded. It was also the chapel Ignatius Loyola had chosen in 1534 for the founding of the Society of Jesus, the Jesuit Order.[88] There, Picot celebrated Mass and each of the five took a vow linking them as members of a new association, to be called the Society of the Heart of Jesus.[89] Elsewhere in Paris, four women consecrated themselves to a new order that would eventually be known as the Society of the Heart of

Mary. In parallel services in Dinan, Saint-Malo, and Paramé other women formally committed themselves to the new order.[90] That these religious saw their vocation as involving a struggle with Revolution for the soul of France was made plain enough by their respective fates. Within three years of taking their vows on Montmartre, four of the six men would die violent deaths —victims of popular violence; a fifth would be guillotined.[91] Alone among the original six, Picot would survive the Revolution to see to it that the Society of the Heart of Jesus would become the kernel of a revived Jesuit order in post-revolutionary France.

In a parallel initiative within the émigré community beyond the frontier, another group of men sought to establish a men's order committed to an aggressive defense of Catholicism in the face of the challenge of the Revolution. The career path of one of the original members, Joseph Varin d'Ainvelle, is instructive. Varin was the son of a powerful noble family of Besançon. In 1788, at the age of nineteen, he decided on a priestly vocation and joined the seminary of Saint-Sulpice in Paris. Varin persisted in his seminary training, even though his energetic and restless nature suggested a less than perfect match of personality and vocation. With the onset of the Revolution and the debates on the place of Catholicism in public life, the status of the clergy and, by extension, seminarians became problematic. Soon Varin abandoned the seminary and followed other nobles and clergy into exile. Once abroad, he found his way into the ranks of the counter-revolutionary army of Condé and fought against the Revolution in 1792 and 1793, apparently with valor and distinction.

Varin was still receptive to the call of the priesthood when, while still abroad, he encountered two acquaintances from his seminary days. Éléonor de Tournély and Charles de Broglie shared with Varin noble birth, émigré status, counter-revolutionary convictions, religious zeal, and the energy of youth.[92] What set them apart was that Varin had abandoned the religious life in order to fight the Revolution with force of arms, while Tournély and Broglie had remained committed to the religious life. Indeed, their religious engagement revealed an awareness of the broader cultural implications of 1789. In exile, Tournély and Broglie had formed a new men's order explicitly modeled on the Jesuit order. Its members were zealous, well educated, free of the obligations of parish clergy, independent of the episcopal hierarchy, and fiercely loyal to the pope. It was called the Society of the Sacred Heart,[93] and it was a perfect match for Varin's personality in that it combined piety and an appetite for combat. In a tearful ceremony in 1794, Varin decided to fulfill his priestly ambition and join the new order. His greatest concern was that his new vocation emphasize action over the contemplative life. "Do whatever you want with me," he pleaded with Tournély. "Just don't make me a monk." "Relax," Tournély told him. "You will still be a soldier. Nearly all of your comrades come from the army too, and we fully expect to serve God militarily."[94]

Tournély, Broglie, and Varin, like Picot in Paris, had grasped something essential about the Revolution. For the Revolution and its values to prevail, it would have to drive Catholicism and *its* values from their leading position in public life. By implication, Catholicism in France would have to be defended from outside the reformed Catholic hierarchy that the Revolution had set out to create. The Revolution would tolerate parish clergy and other "useful" religious; as civil servants they would minister to the spiritual needs of the people, and they would be clearly subordinated to episcopal and secular authorities. But there would be no place in France for such engaged and militant orders as the Jesuits, whose training and elite status put them in a position to influence the values and culture in which the nation as a whole operated. Indeed it was the common culture of militant engagement of both of these new priestly organizations—the Society of the Sacred Heart abroad and the Society of the Heart of Jesus within France—that marked them as the nucleus of a restored Jesuit order in France in 1814.[95] Until then, they would stand, with the Sacré-Coeur as their insignia, as defenders of Catholic France. They would combat the manifest evil of 1789 and bring about the regeneration of France through a consecration to the Sacred Heart of Jesus. Between the emblems being churned out by the tens of thousands in convents and in private homes and the new militant priestly orders named for the Sacred Heart, the Sacré-Coeur emerged as the devotion and the image of Catholic resistance to the scourge of Revolution.

THE SACRED HEART AND THE
COUNTER-REVOLUTION IN THE VENDÉE

It is better for us to die in battle than to see the ruin of our country
and the destruction of our altars.

1 Maccabees 3 : 59

I heard a story about a famous naturalist who said, "If anyone were to ask
me what is the missing link in the chain of being linking monkeys and
men, I would respond that it is the native of Bas-Poitou."

JEAN-BAPTISTE LECLERC, *1797*

And almost all things are by the law purged with blood;
and without shedding of blood is no remission.

Hebrews 9 : 22

IMAGINE A CHILLY FEBRUARY day in Paris. The king of France, Louis XVI, and the queen, Marie-Antoinette, have planned a visit to Notre-Dame cathedral. The year is 1790. The French Revolution is not yet a year old, but since October of 1789 the royal family has lived at the Tuileries Palace in Paris, not at Versailles. Indeed, the family had been forcibly moved from Versailles by an enraged crowd of market women from the city of Paris. Ever since, and despite public protestations to the contrary, the king and queen have felt trapped, forced to live in a city that is the center of a Revolution they see as hostile to them and the interests of France.

The king and queen are accompanied by their children, the king's deeply devout sister Madame Élisabeth, and several pious women of the court, including Madame de Carcado, Madame de Lastic, and Madame de Saisseval. Once within Notre-Dame cathedral, the king approaches the sanctuary with a deliberate step. His wife and children accompany him. He kneels before the statue of the Virgin Mary and quietly consecrates himself, his family, and his kingdom to the Sacred Heart of Jesus.[1]

Nice story. Should we believe it? Perhaps. Here's another.

It's two years later, late spring in 1792 in the city of Paris. Things are worse, not better. In fact, the king and queen have few remaining political options. A year earlier, in June of 1791, they and their family had sought to flee Paris and France by making a dash for the eastern frontier. They had traveled in disguise and under assumed identities, but the king was easily recognized and apprehended because his distinctive profile perfectly matched that found on the coin of the realm. To make matters worse, Louis had left behind a candid political testament. It revealed the king's profound reservations about the Revolution, contrary to previous public pronouncements.

For many, the failed royal escape of 1791 had shattered any remaining illusions that the old regime and the new could be reconciled in a constitutional monarchy with Louis at its head. Yet Louis retained his throne, and the new constitution granted him a powerful weapon—the veto—which he put to use protecting his counter-revolutionary allies. When the Legislative Assembly decreed the confiscation of the property of political émigrés from France, Louis vetoed the measure. When the Assembly authorized the deportation of Catholic clergy who refused the loyalty oath, Louis again vetoed the decree.

These gestures made plain Louis's political sympathies, and they strained relations with his Girondin ministers, whom he dismissed on 10 June 1792. Revolutionary politics were at an impasse. Only a miracle would save Louis and his throne. That is precisely what he sought five days later. On 15 June, Louis gathered his family around him.[2] The fifteenth of June was the feast of the Sacred Heart and with the help of his confessor, Père Hébert, Louis promised a solemn and public act of consecration of "my person, my family, and my realm to the Sacred Heart of Jesus" if he recovered his freedom of action.[3] He never did. On 20 June, a Parisian crowd, exasperated by the king's obstructionist politics, invaded the Tuileries Palace. The king held fast to his vetoes and his throne, but the day was merely a dress rehearsal for the overthrow of the monarchy. Seven weeks later, on 10 August, another crowd, larger and armed, returned to the Tuileries and finished the job. The king was tried and executed a few months later, in January of 1793.

These Rashomon-like thought experiments, constructed from accounts of the king's spiritual life in the final years of the monarchy, are not dead certainties.[4] They are imaginative recreations of what might have taken place and what some sources assert *did* take place. And although neither account can be proven conclusively, these consecrations, which amount to desperate appeals for divine rescue, not only appeal to the imagination but also fit well with the known facts.

That is because the vocation to promote religious revival in the name of the Sacré-Coeur, like the feverish production of Sacré-Coeur talismans in convents and cottages, was part of a broader cultural rejection of the Revolution. The Sacred Heart was by no means the exclusive symbol of rejection of the French Revolution, but it was undoubtedly the most common. In fact, at about the same time that Edmund Burke's *Reflections on the Revolution in France,* with its condemnation of the revolutionaries' arrogant and imprudent rejection of inherited institutions, reached the European public, Catholic elites were condemning the Revolution for its impiety and upholding the devotion to the Sacré-Coeur as an alternative.[5] In Paris, the royalist newspaper *l'Ami du Roi* was among those leading the attack on the Revolution as "a conspiracy formed against altar and throne."[6] Similar convictions drove Pierre-Joseph Picot de Clorivière to revive the Jesuit order under the name of the Society of the Sacred Heart in Paris.[7] Early in 1790, repentance and consecration to the Sacré-Coeur were the aims of the *Association de quarante jours.* Crapart, the publisher of the *Association de quarante jours,* was also the publisher of *l'Ami du Roi,* widely believed to be subsidized by the king. A pamphlet published by the *Association de quarante jours* recommended forty days of penance culminating in a prayer of consecration to the Sacred Heart on the feast of the Sacré-Coeur in June of 1790.[8] Later that year, *l'Ami du Roi* carried advertisements for a new pamphlet on similar themes titled *la Dévotion aux Mystères de Jésus Christ et de Marie.*[9]

Part of what drove the popularity of the Sacred Heart devotion in Catholic and royalist circles was the conviction that the king and queen were themselves

Figure 14. Élisabeth de France, devotee of the Sacred Heart. Alcide de Beauchesne, *La Vie de Madame Élisabeth, soeur de Louis XVI* (Paris, 1869).

Philippine-Marie-Hélène Élisabeth de France, better known simply as Madame Élisabeth, was the sister of Louis XVI, king of France. She was an advocate of the Sacré-Coeur at court and remained the very image of piety until her death by guillotine in 1794.

deeply committed to the new devotion. The devotion to the Sacré-Coeur as a vehicle for the expression of misgivings about the Revolution was at least as strong at court as it was within the broader, popular culture of counter-revolution. Like the king himself, the king's sister, Madame Élisabeth (fig. 14), was famous for her piety. She was deeply attached to the devotion to the Sacré-Coeur, an attachment owing, in part, to the influence of Marie Leszcszynska, wife of Louis XV and grandmother to Élisabeth and Louis XVI.[10] Élisabeth was also known to be fond of the bishop of Amiens, Monsignor d'Orléans de la Motte. Orléans de la Motte had witnessed the plague at Marseille and wondered at Belsunce's energetic and grand response. The episode made such an impression on him that he made the devotion to the Sacré-Coeur the focus of his own Christian spirituality.[11]

Although Élisabeth was ultimately a victim of the Revolution—she was guillotined on 10 May 1794—she left testimonial evidence of her passion for the Sacré-Coeur. In 1790, Élisabeth sent an ex-voto, a votive gift, to the cathedral at Chartres.[12] The purpose of an ex-voto is to serve as the physical aspect of a wish, prayer, or intention. The pilgrim carries the ex-voto to the pilgrimage destination and leaves it there; when the pilgrim is unable to make the journey, as was the case with Élisabeth, the ex-voto serves as proxy. It symbolizes the request for intercession, the hope that the pilgrim's prayer and penitence will serve to bring about the fulfillment of a wish. The intention accompanying Élisabeth's ex-voto has not survived, if indeed it was ever written down, but plausible inferences can be made from its design. Élisabeth's ex-voto consisted of two hearts cast as one. A crown of thorns ringed one heart; on top of the heart was a cross, in the manner of the Sacré-Coeur. A sword pierced the second heart, a trope common to the iconography of the heart of Mary but also a signifier of a soul identifying with the sorrows of Mary; a fleur-de-lis, symbol of the Bourbon dynasty, rested on top.[13]

Political despair heightened Élisabeth's fervor for the Sacré-Coeur. Élisabeth felt ready to confide such despair in the weeks following the sending of the ex-voto. By early January 1791, that is, after the Civil Constitution of the Clergy, Élisabeth had given up hope for a political recovery of royal authority, short of divine intercession.[14] She actively promoted the Sacred Heart devotion at court where her brother the king shared her religious faith and conviction. "You are right to put all of your confidence in God, who alone can save us," she wrote to her friend Madame de Raigecourt. "We are beginning a novena to the Sacré-Coeur."[15]

The king's confessor, Père Hébert, was also an ardent supporter of the Sacred Heart devotion. Besides serving as the person most responsible for the state of the king's soul, Hébert was *supérieur général* of the Eudists, a male religious order that took its name from its founder, Saint Jean Eudes, a man deeply committed to the propagation of the devotion to the Sacré-Coeur. Eudes's passion for the Sacré-Coeur antedated, in fact, the visions of Marguerite-Marie Alacoque, and his devotion differed from hers in that it emphasized the contemplation of divine love for humanity, whereas Alacoquist spirituality tended to dwell upon human indifference to divine love—but these are differences of degree.[16] No matter. Hébert's vocation as a member of the Eudist order would have been predicated on a commitment to the Sacred Heart devotion. Whether as an Eudist he would have shared a sense of urgency about fulfilling the demands expressed to Marguerite-

Marie, including a consecration to the Sacré-Coeur, is an interesting question. However, there can be no doubt about the importance of the Sacred Heart devotion to him, nor about his hostility to revolutionary religious policy—Hébert had refused the oath. Hébert's principled intransigence would soon cost him his life. Rounded up along with other refractory priests after the overthrow of the monarchy on 10 August, Hébert was among the clergy to lose their lives in the September Massacres of 1792.

Nor can there be any doubt that Hébert had the confidence of the king. By June of 1792, Louis recognized that he no longer had any credible political options. His preoccupation with spiritual matters deepened; he seemed reconciled to the fact that only spiritual initiatives remained open to him.[17] When the hostile crowd invaded the Tuileries Palace on 20 June, they occupied the quarters of the royal family for hours, haranguing and insulting the king, the queen, and the king's sister Élisabeth. The king was incapable of doing anything to end the torment. "Come see me," he wrote afterward to Hébert. "I have finished with men. I need only occupy myself with heaven."[18]

Finally, there is the matter of the proliferation of Sacred Heart emblems at court. Madame Élisabeth remained deeply devoted to the Sacré-Coeur up to the very end of her life.[19] She was a likely source for many of the emblems. So was Jacques-Henri-Louis de Bruc, cousin of Claude-Marie de Bruc, the mother superior at the Nantes Visitationist convent. At the same time that his cousin Claude-Marie governed one of the most productive "nodes" in the production network of Sacré-Coeur emblems, Jacques de Bruc was preparing to take part in the defense of the Tuileries on 10 August 1792. Jacques would later serve as an officer in the armies of the counter-revolution; his brother would serve as army chaplain.[20]

Whatever the origin of the Sacré-Coeur emblems at court, it is also known that the queen, Marie-Antoinette, possessed one. The mere fact that such things could be found among her personal effects was to be introduced as evidence against her at her trial.[21] A Sacred Heart emblem in the possession of the dauphin was introduced as evidence that the queen and Madame Élisabeth sought to influence and corrupt the boy who was in line to succeed to the throne of France. That was the contention of the ultra-revolutionary René Hébert when he testified that a Sacred Heart emblem had been discovered in the possession of the dauphin. The queen disputed portions of this testimony but acknowledged that the dauphin possessed a Sacré-Coeur emblem, saying "the heart he mentions was given to my son by his sister."[22]

Clergy who served as contacts in the distribution network of Sacré-Coeur images claimed as early as July 1791 that the king himself possessed a Sacré-Coeur insignia and that the king's confessor was also a likely source of Sacré-Coeur paraphernalia at court. Alexandre Lenfant, former Jesuit, chaplain, and sometime confessor at court assured his correspondent that not only was the Sacré-Coeur efficacious, the king himself wore it. "Wear one at all times and place one in your home. It provides special protection," wrote Lenfant in July of 1791. "The king himself [ce qu'il y a de plus grand en France] possesses one."[23] Endorsements such as this helped to set up a strategic alignment of forces among those opposed to the Revolution, with the Sacré-Coeur as its center.[24] Ordinary men and women, religious men and women in convents, in presbyteries, and at court could begin to discern a pattern.[25] Inspired by accounts of visions in Nantes and Paray-le-Monial, or by the dramatic cessation of the plague at Marseille, they had learned to turn to the Sacré-Coeur in times of danger.[26] For those to whom the Revolution was disturbing, threatening, or frightening, there was comfort and reassurance in the image of the suffering heart of Jesus. They stitched hearts to the inside of their blouses and vests. They displayed Sacred Hearts inside their homes. These hearts protected them on journeys and reassured them that they were not alone in their convictions. When they heard that the king and queen secretly felt and did as they did, they no longer felt so insignificant and powerless. The Revolution had its symbols and insignia; now those who felt threatened and embattled had theirs.

From the remotest village to the very court itself, the Sacred Heart provided the symbolic link uniting those opposed to the Revolution. As the Jesuit Lenfant put it early in June of 1791, "the devotion to the divine heart of Jesus is the salvation of the kingdom. The most illustrious persons, even crowned heads, are outfitted with this precious shield."[27] In fact, Lenfant would die with Père Hébert in the September Massacres, giving the lie spectacularly to the claim that the Sacred Heart guaranteed any special protection. But this was manifestly a situation where belief mattered as much as results. Even when partisans of the Sacré-Coeur died violent deaths, their martyrdom reaffirmed belief in the religious nature of the present conflict, the persecutorial intentions of the regime, and the need for a religious response. The king's vow and the bloody deaths of the devout only strengthened the conviction that this was a struggle for the soul of a nation (fig. 15). If we wish to understand persons who defined themselves in terms of belief

Figure 15. Jean-Jacques Hauer, *The Vow of Louis XVI,* before 1829.
Musée Lambinet, Versailles. © Photographie Bulloz.

As the political position of Louis XVI became increasingly precarious,
he received repeated encouragement to interpret the Revolution in spiritual terms. Sources assert that he made a solemn promise to consecrate
France to the Sacré-Coeur if he recovered his freedom and political
power.

and who were searching for a higher moral ground for their politics, historical belief is what matters. That they *believed* in the king's vow renders it historically significant. *Si non è vero, è ben trovato.*

Belief in the king's vow validated resistance to the Revolution in the name of the Sacred Heart. That resistance was both royal and sacred, just as the vow had been, and it revealed how the king's authority could only be enhanced by his death, not diminished. From the conventional perspective of high politics, Louis XVI was a laughable figure by the end of 1792. Louis was a cipher in national politics, a figure to be held in contempt, a person whose remaining political utility consisted of undergoing execution in order to mark the passage from monarchy to republic. And yet, within a paradoxical logic defined by royal martyrdom, every effort to diminish the king's authority, every political blunder Louis committed, enhanced his stature. As his setbacks weakened him and humiliated him, they contributed to the desacralization of royal authority and facilitated his political elimination and execution. But this same desacralization also built up the king's sacred status as a martyr for a holy cause.

From a religiously inspired counter-revolutionary point of view, Louis's weakness was his power. Indeed, never before has a personality so perfectly matched a person's fate. Unlike the queen, who answered insult with insult and injury with injury—whose remarks show real spirit and real venom— the king often answered his enemies with silence. In the face of this christic composure, every insult increased the king's stature among his admirers. Every humiliation enhanced his moral authority. By the end, events had overtaken Louis's ability to comprehend his fate, except in spiritual terms. Spirituality was the only means by which he could achieve an advantage over his opponents. His faithful reading of Thomas à Kempis's *Imitation of Christ* defined his strategy. He would prevail in death, if not in life.[28] His death confirmed his sacred status as martyr. When Louis was guillotined and his blood flowed onto the stone pavement of the Place de la Révolution, witnesses rushed forward to dip pieces of cloth in it. They took home relics.

The drama and tragedy of the king's trial and execution brought the nation to the brink of open civil war. At his trial, those who argued for Louis's conviction and death outlined a compelling political logic: either Louis was guilty of treason or those who overthrew him were. If Louis was right, the Revolution was wrong. To put Louis on trial was thus to put the Revolution on trial. Little wonder, then, at the outcome: Louis must die. A less obvious point was that as long as Louis lived, he would embody a political goal: recovery of his liberty and his throne would be synonymous with defeat for the Revolution.

Louis was worth more to the counter-revolution in death than in life. Alive, his politics consisted of little more than a temporizing retreat—Fabian tactics adapted to politics, poorly executed at that. In death, Louis's vow to the Sacré-Coeur served as a yoke to the popular counter-revolutionary will. The tension between the piety of the vow's sentiments and the torment of his imprisonment, trial, and execution generated a sacred aura about the king and his political testament. For those who believed in the vow and believed in its vision of national redemption, the vow to the Sacré-Coeur united their personal political convictions with a larger, nobler cause, one defined by their convergence with divine will and royal will. To oppose the Revolution was no longer a mere political sentiment or the result of a vague disquietude, but a righteous stand in the face of evil. Counter-revolution was a duty. The Sacré-Coeur served as the icon in a discourse of Christian populism, defining the people as a Christian people and linking the anxieties of a people to a transcendent struggle to safeguard the soul and destiny of a nation. The promise of the Sacré-Coeur assimilated the will of a Catholic people, by way of their king, to the very will of God.

Handwritten copies of the text of the vow of Louis XVI were in circulation by late 1792. Benjamin Fillon, writing in the 1840s, puts the date of "fabrication" of the vow around November 1792, that is, after the overthrow of the monarchy. The date is not substantiated and is probably a guess.[29] Fillon's assertion of the vow's fabrication underlines the place of partisanship in belief in the vow. Supporters of the Revolution and their descendants, such as Benjamin Fillon, cast doubt on the authenticity of the vow; defenders of the counter-revolution asserted its authenticity. In fact, Fillon's date matches that of many nineteenth-century royalist commentators, who tended to refer to the vow as "the vow of Louis XVI in the Temple," the Temple being the name of the prison in which Louis was held with his family after his overthrow. Other sources, as we have seen, would place the vow in June of 1792, or even early in 1790.

Real or fake, by 1792, it was widely believed in royalist circles that Louis had consecrated his realm to the Sacré-Coeur, in effect fulfilling at least one of the demands made through Marguerite-Marie.[30] Real or fake, the end of 1792 seems to be when copies of the vow became widely available, leading

Figure 16. Pierre Bouillon, *The Trial of Marie-Antoinette,* 1794. Musée Carnavalet, Paris.

In October of 1793, the Revolutionary Tribunal tried Marie-Antoinette, the former queen. Evidence presented against her at the trial included a Sacred Heart— devotional object and damning proof of her counter-revolutionary sympathies.

one to wonder whether publicity surrounding the vow was intended to generate sympathy for the king during his trial. Coincidence or partisan strategy, copies of the vow to the Sacré-Coeur did not cease to circulate after the king's execution in January of 1793. As Élisabeth and Marie-Antoinette were to discover, mere possession of Sacré-Coeur paraphernalia was enough to draw suspicion (see fig. 16), hence the need to conceal the text of the vow. Copies were distributed only among members of reliable communities of belief and to individuals whose allegiances were unquestioned. Lapses were inevitable. In the spring of 1793, Laurent Gennéteau, a herdsman, and René Sochard, a weaver, produced a copy of the vow of Louis XVI as evidence when appearing before a surveillance committee to testify on counter-revolutionary activity near Angers.[31] The widow Bertho, arrested for making uncomplimentary remarks about a revolutionary emblem, was found to have a packet of Sacré-Coeur paraphernalia, including the king's vow. Under interrogation, when asked about how she learned of the vow, she made the unlikely claim to have "read it in the papers."[32] In Paris, Adelaide de Cicé kept her copy of the king's vow, "one of the first," hidden in a crack in the wall. She pulled it out from time to time in order to share it with friends because of its intrinsic spiritual value and as a promise of better times to come.[33] In Bordeaux, Sacré-Coeur prayer-houses were set up at various points in the city: the rue Hugla, the rue du Grand-Cancera, rue Sainte-Eulalie, rue Beaurepaire, rue des Ayres. Sacré-Coeur paraphernalia moved from house to house: prayer cards, devotional images, the text of the king's consecration—anything related to the Sacré-Coeur and the project of national reparation. Some found their way into criminal dossiers.[34] Possessing a copy of the vow was dangerous, obviously, but by no means necessary in a society heavily dependent upon oral transmission. In the eighteenth century, most people still got their news from the pulpit. Yves-Michel Marchais, a priest operating in clandestinity, made the vow the topic of a sermon in the summer of 1793.[35] Doubtless dozens of other priests, if not hundreds, did likewise.

THE SACRED HEART INTO BATTLE

Martyrdom is a sublime act, best observed from a distance. The execution of the king was a fine example to contemplate, but, thanks to the Sacré-Coeur, it was possible to identify with the king's political testament in sentimental or purely symbolic form. The king's vow to the Sacré-Coeur helped secure the status of the Sacré-Coeur as the preferred form of ritualized and symbolic resistance to the Revolution. Over time, however, merely symbolic resistance to the Revolution became increasingly difficult to sustain, especially as the Revolution began to make demands for more than passive support.

Early in 1793, revolutionary France was besieged. A coalition of European monarchies organized armies that threatened virtually all of its frontiers: in Flanders, in Alsace, at the borders with Italy and Spain. The British fleet threatened along the Channel, Atlantic, and Mediterranean coasts. In the face of such potentially overwhelming military challenges, the National Convention sought to mobilize the nation's military resources.

Able-bodied men were sought as volunteers, military conscription being both reminiscent of the Old Regime and inconsistent with expectations of patriotic ardor. A new decree, in February of 1793, called for three hundred thousand new men under arms. Each of the eighty-some departments was to supply its quota of volunteers. Where the number of volunteers fell short, the local administration would have to develop a suitable mechanism for selecting those to be conscripted.

In most cases, the young men to be taken were selected by drawing lots, a *tirage au sort*. Local revolutionary officials called on eligible men to assemble on Sunday. In many parts of France, young men resisted this procedure, or they complied but in unexpected ways; that is, they would mobilize not for the drawing of lots, but in order to resist conscription. Young men would gather, agree to resist, then overwhelm revolutionary officials, seize weapons, and destroy papers. In some cases, they put to death anyone associated with the Revolution, notably administrative officials and constitutional priests. In the west of France, widespread resistance of this kind led to open revolt against the Revolution. The area in question incorporated most of four departments—Loire Infèrieure, Maine-et-Loire, Deux-Sèvres, Vendée—but very soon the revolt was known simply as "the Vendée," a name that would henceforth be associated with armed and violent counter-revolution in the west of France.

Jacques Cathelineau lived in le Pin-en-Mauges, a village in the Anjou just south of the Loire River near the town of Saint-Florent. As a father of five and an itinerant wool merchant, Cathelineau was a significant figure in le Pin-en-Mauges and the surrounding villages and towns; it would have been his business to get to know other people and to stay on good terms with them, to maintain a network of clients. Cathelineau was better educated than many of his compatriots. When Cathelineau was a boy his parish priest, the abbé Quesneau, selected him to go away to receive an education. Quesneau sent Cathelineau to live and work with Yves-Michel Marchais, then the pastor at la Chapelle-du-Genêt.[36] In effect, Cathelineau was a scholarship student, selected no doubt because of his intelligence, but also because he was perceived as good material for a religious vocation.

For whatever reason, after five years in the care of Marchais, Cathelineau chose not to enter the priesthood. He remained deeply devout. Indeed, as a *colporteur,* an itinerant merchant, it would not have been unusual for Cathelineau to market items other than fabric: religious objects, sacred articles, emblems, even copies of the king's dedicatory vow surely traveled by such means. Traveling merchants were one of the better unofficial sources of information, especially in remote rural areas. Their movements were difficult to follow; their activities were difficult to police. As such, they were not only purveyors of goods but also purveyors of subversive ideas, rumors, and disavowed perspectives. What they had to say carried weight with a public opinion that was *frondeur,* convinced that the truth was out there, but that it rarely originated with official sources. Men such as Cathelineau sustained and relayed counter-discourses for the consumption of those suspicious of information originating with revolutionary government officials in Paris and in provincial capitals.

Cathelineau's emergence as one of the leaders of the Vendée revolt owed a great deal to his commercial contacts. Men and women like him served as living links within a rural information relay in the west of France. But his stature also was more than a function of contacts; it also owed something to his religious commitments. When news broke about the appearance of the Virgin at the shrine of Notre-Dame-de-Charité, near Saint-Laurent-sur-la-Plaine, Cathelineau was among those to spread the news and to organize pilgrimages to the site.[37] And when the day for the requisition of "volunteers" for the army came to le Pin-en-Mauges, Cathelineau led the resistance. Rather than be compelled to defend a revolution they regarded as suspect and perhaps even diabolical in origin, Cathelineau and his fellow resisters chose to take up arms against it. They attached Sacré-Coeurs to their lapels and put rosaries around their necks as signs of their devotion and common bond.[38] Men in neighboring towns and villages, such as Jallais and Chemillé, did likewise. By the end of the day, 13 March 1793, some twelve hundred insurgents had joined the counter-revolution under the sign of the Sacred Heart of Jesus.

The following day, rebels from neighboring towns, including Bressuire and Mortagne-sur-Sèvre, joined the army of insurgents. Some five thousand strong, the insurgents marched upon the administrative center for the region, the town of Cholet. Cholet had a special importance because of its administrative significance, but also as a center of revolutionary patriotism—the National Guardsmen who demolished the chapel at Notre-Dame-de-Charité were from Cholet. When Cholet fell on 14 March, it was but one of several small cities and towns to fall under counter-revolutionary control. Near the Atlantic coast and just south of the city of Nantes, insurgencies at Challans, Legé, Saint-Philbert, Saint-Etienne, and Touvois culminated in the collapse of republican authority at Machecoul.[39] On the nineteenth, at Pont-Charrault, insurgents scattered a contingent of some three thousand regular troops under the command of General Louis de Marcé.[40]

The accumulated effect of these actions was devastating for the Revolution. Not only had the rebels succeeded in disrupting the military conscription, they had seized de facto control over parts of four departments. A mere "conscription riot" had turned into the opening campaign of a civil war. It would be weeks before effective fighting forces would be sent to attempt again to crush the treasonous resistance. In the meantime, the insurgents had time to choose leaders and establish a rudimentary government. In a speech before the assembly in Paris, Bertrand Barère gave an electrifying speech about the revolt he called simply "the Vendée," taking the name of one of the four departments under rebel control, the Vendée, and applying it to the revolt as a whole.[41] Thus the Vendée was born.

François Athanase de Charette, Henri de La Rochejaquelein, Maurice d'Elbée, Louis de Lescure, and Charles Artus de Bonchamps soon joined Jacques Cathelineau and Jean-Nicolas Stofflet as officers and generals in the Royal and Catholic Army of the Vendée. The selection of the itinerant merchant and plainly non-noble Jacques Cathelineau as commander-in-chief underlines one of the great ironies of the Vendéen war: the insurgents and their leaders implicitly accepted the new revolutionary ideal of equality. A "Conseil Supérieur," the Vendée's "political wing," was created in late March; it was as close as the Vendée ever came to a central political authority, and it incorporated a surprising number of clergymen, including the returned émigré abbé Bernier of Angers, the former Benedictine Pierre Jagault, and the abbé Guyot de Folleville.[42] The overwhelming presence of former nobles among Vendéen military leadership and the presence of members of the clergy in leading political positions gave rise to republican caricatures of the Vendéen insurgents as little more than priest-ridden dupes of the nobility.

The intensity of interest in the role of nobles and clergy in the insurrection derives from the embarrassing fact that the Vendée revolt was undeniably a *popular* revolt. For a revolution and a regime deriving their legitimacy, in part, from their claim to represent the people in their struggle against the discredited elites of the Old Regime, the Vendéen insurrection was a horrible embarrassment. The involvement of the popular classes in counter-revolution in such numbers could only be reconciled with the image of a people's revolution if one ascribed to the clergy and nobility a great and nefarious influence. The incomprehension of revolutionary leadership was palpable in a June 1793 story in the *Journal de la Montagne,* a radical Parisian newspaper. "Thousands of French, deliberately confused and mislead by bloody priests and proud nobles, march against their brothers and friends, the very ones who had won for them their liberty."[43] What revolutionaries of the twentieth century would call "false consciousness," the revolutionaries of the eighteenth century would attribute to superstition and fanaticism.

The situation was more complicated than that. Fighting under a religious sign, such as the Sacré-Coeur, implies a level of religious engagement, the belief that one's action is consistent with divine law. But the charge of "fanaticism" implies something more—that clergy used the promise of divine reward to induce peasants to fight, in effect, telling them that if they lost their lives fighting for a just cause, their salvation was assured. In fact, there were eyewitness accounts of priests using such inducements: lose your life, but save your soul. The marquise de La Rochejaquelein reported witnessing one such incident, but only one.[44] And it became harder to persuade the insurgents that God was on their side after they had experienced some serious setbacks.[45] At bottom, they were defending their lives and livelihoods and those of their households and they were keeping the Revolution at bay. Some possessed the zeal to die for God and King. For others those were convenient higher causes with which to embellish their more local concerns. It came down to this: they would prefer not to fight and risk their lives, but conscription gave them no choice. Since they must fight, they would fight to defeat a revolution they could not support, let alone defend.

As for the prevalence of former nobles within the Vendéen leadership, it should be pointed out that nobles had not led the initial revolt. The insurgents, having established de facto authority over a significant piece of the territory of the French Republic, found themselves in a situation they almost surely had not anticipated. They knew that reprisals and counter-attacks were inevitable. In turning to the nobility for leadership, they were turning toward the only persons in their midst who had had experience in leading men in battle.

Moreover, the insurgents were hardly the docile and submissive soldiers the caricature would suggest. Jean-Clément Martin, one of the leading French specialists of the revolt, is correct, I believe, to insist upon the origins of the revolt in any assessment of the motive behind the revolt.[46] The insurgency began with resistance to conscription, not in defense of the king or the nobility. Once the war of the Vendée was underway, the behavior of the Vendéen insurgents was more like that of minutemen or a citizens' militia than like that of fanatics, dupes, or even disciplined and obedient foot-soldiers.

Their range of military action extended little beyond their homes and a landscape they could recognize and they tended to remain mobilized only so long as necessary to repulse the enemy. Far from being reckless fanatics, the Vendéen insurgents were sometimes such diffident warriors that they had to be directed into battle not by orders from the rear but through the heedlessly courageous example of officers in front. Casualties among Vendéen generals were correspondingly high. And Vendéen officers were continually frustrated by the tendency of their men to vanish at the conclusion of significant engagements.[47] When a battle ended and the enemy had been driven off, most insurgents simply started home; there was little that anyone, priest or noble, could do to stop them. When the fortress city of Angers fell to the Vendéens in the summer of 1793 and the road to Paris lay open before them, it proved impossible to retain enough men to hold Angers, much less lead a march upon the capital.

And yet the influence of the nobility should not be minimized either. It was surely not an accident that certain members of the nobility ended up as leaders of the insurgency. Many of them had been deeply involved in counter-revolutionary activity long before the "conscription riots" of March 1793. Henri de La Rochejaquelein (fig. 17) and Charles d'Autichamp were members of the *garde constitutionnelle du Roi*—in effect, the king's security staff—prior to the overthrow of the monarchy on 10 August 1792. Lescure, Marigny, and Charette were *chevaliers du poignard*—literally, "knights of the dagger"—a term applied to members of the nobility committed to the defense of the crown in the days leading up to the assault on the Tuileries.[48] It would be absurd to assume that these men stopped their counter-revolutionary efforts when they returned to their provincial homes in the west of France after the overthrow of the monarchy. Seven months after their failed defense of the king and the Tuileries Palace, these same deeply committed defenders of the cause of royalism reemerged as leaders of the Royal and Catholic Army of the Vendée.

Marie-Louise de La Rochejaquelein was always careful to put the insurgents and their leaders in the best possible light. But her memoirs provide one of the better examples of how the peasants of the Vendée willingly

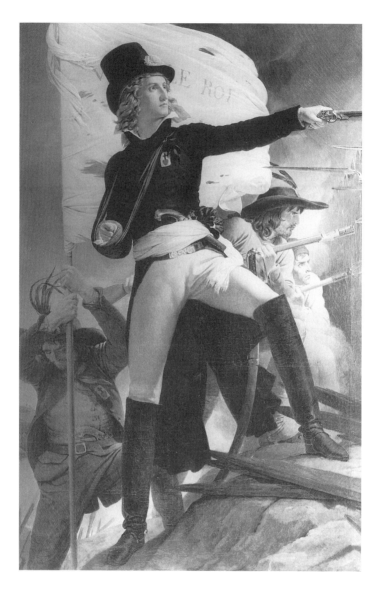

Figure 17. Pierre-Narcisse Guérin, *Henri de La Rochejaquelein,* Salon of 1817. Musée d'Histoire et des Guerres de Vendée, Cholet (Maine-et-Loire).

Many of those who had vowed to defend Louis XVI before his overthrow on 10 August 1792 subsequently took up arms against the Revolution under the sign of the Sacré-Coeur. Among them was Henri de La Rochejaquelein, pictured here as a Vendéen general with the Sacré-Coeur on his lapel.

accepted noble and clerical leadership. In one passage she reveals how "Prior to the Revolution, when the time came to hunt for wolf, boar, or stag, the priest would notify the peasants from the pulpit. Each took his rifle and met at the assigned place and time. The hunters [the nobles] set the men in position and they followed orders strictly. Later, [during the wars of Vendée] they were led to combat in the same way and with the same docility."[49] The marquise de La Rochejaquelein's romanticized account of social relations under the Old Regime may test the reader's credulity, but it does provide an insight into how the Vendée revolt relied upon and reproduced certain features of Old Regime social deference.[50] The nobility exercised an unquestioned authority on the ground, while the clergy dispensed cultural cues. The insurgents fought under the leadership of nobles and under the sign of the Sacré-Coeur.

A DEMONIZED ENEMY

At its apogee, between March and October of 1793, the insurgency of the Vendée controlled or disputed control of the greater part of four departments south of the Loire River between Nantes and Angers. The terrain gave significant advantages to defenders, and exposed attackers to considerable risk. To the west of Angers, beyond the river Layon, lay the Mauges. The Mauges constituted the largest part of a transitional area between the orbits of such larger cities of the French west as Nantes, Luçon, Poitiers, and Angers.[51] Viewed from within, the Mauges seems to offer only limited perspectives. Rural roads and pathways follow the contours of the low ground between surrounding hills. Tall hedgerows (*bocage,* in French) line the roads and mark the boundaries of fields and farms; they also obscure the horizon, so that visitors quickly become disoriented. Habitations tend to be scattered rather than agglomerated, so that true roads are few and pathways—little distinguishable one from the next—link one small settlement to another. To the west of the Mauges, near the Atlantic coast, lay the Marais, where the terrain levels out as one approaches the similarly daunting marshlands, with their sloughs and bogs, near the coast.

Historians of the Vendée insurrection have made much of the isolation of these lands, comparing the seeming impenetrability of the landscape with the obscurity and backwardness of its people. Much of the analysis of Charles Tilly and Paul Bois on counter-revolutionary insurrection in the west has turned on the distinction between the isolation of the *bocage,* where counter-revolution prevailed, and the more open adjacent areas, which tended to favor the Revolution.[52] More recently, Jean-Clément Martin and Roger Dupuy, without denying the importance of the conclusions of Tilly and Bois, have emphasized the importance of the social geography of the west not so much for the *fact* of the Vendée but for its survival. The Vendée was a creation of the insurrection itself, not of preexisting factors. Its success depended upon the failure of repression both initially and over the longer term. There were conscription riots like those in the Vendée elsewhere in France. What prevented them from becoming full-blown counter-revolutionary insurrections was an early and efficacious repression. This is where geography was obviously a factor. Early repression failed, and subsequent efforts to restore order foundered on the impenetrability of the Vendéen terrain.

The tenacity of the Vendéens also owed much to the tactics they employed, which anticipated the guerrilla tactics that would be used with such success against the French in Spain. The very tendency of the Vendéen soldiers to mobilize for combat, then disband, made the destruction of Vendéen forces all the more difficult. One cannot fight an army one cannot see. Moreover, when an enemy army disappears by melting into a civilian population, opposing soldiers tend to treat all they encounter as combatants. This led, as it almost always does when regular troops face civilian armies, to the commission of atrocities.

Joseph-Marie Lequinio described all manner of brutal acts committed by republican soldiers against civilians, including women, children, and the aged, in the insurgent areas.[53] Although Lequinio wrote after 9 Thermidor (the fall of Robespierre in July 1794) and his intentions were largely exculpatory, his account provides important insights into the motivations of the insurgents. Lequinio had a lot to lose. With the Terror winding down, the French public was looking for people to blame for the extraordinary bloodshed and brutality of the Terror and the Vendée. Lequinio had headed a *commission militaire* at Fontenay-le-Comte at the end of 1793. His task was to see to the completion of the work of repression after the main fighting in the Vendée was over. In effect, Lequinio converted justice into a batch process, trying dozens and dispatching hundreds of prisoners in a day.[54] When he wrote about it later, his aim was to suggest that there was nothing very extraordinary about what he had done, that the Vendée was a dirty war and atrocities had been committed on both sides.

So Lequinio recounted what he had seen. The result is a vision of the war of the Vendée as a conflict leading to extraordinary acts of cruelty, underpinned by competing redemptive visions: one Catholic, the other republican.[55] What he has to say about the violence of the Vendéens is of particular interest, because it lays bare the religious, even sacred, dimension of the struggle. Lequinio tells how atrocities committed by republican troops helped to validate priestly claims that the Republic was not just wrong, the result of political error, but demonic and evil: "Priests, taking advantage of the misconduct of our republican generals and soldiers . . . painted all of us as true demons, the republican government as a diabolical establishment, and the Republic itself as a glimpse of hell." [56]

As for the insurgents themselves, according to Lequinio they were driven either by the prospect of booty — that is, they truly were brigands — or they were driven by a kind of holy fury. By far, most fell into the latter category, believing "in good faith that they fought for God." Accordingly, they felt little concern for their own lives and looked upon their opponents "as demons escaped from hell." Engaged in a just and holy war, the Vendéens believed that when they killed, they did something pleasing in the eyes of God.[57]

Indeed, a discourse of profanation and purification was part of what made the war in the Vendée as much a replay of the Wars of Religion as a civil war about politics. The discourse was generated, as we have seen, in the opening months of 1791, when the Civil Constitution of the Clergy and its rejection by the pope created a schism in French Catholicism. The proscription of priests and other religious who refused the oath, and their replacement by "constitutional" priests who had taken the oath, fed anxieties about the profanation of churches and the efficacy of sacraments necessary to salvation. Constitutional "bad priests," condemned by the pope, lacked the power to perform sacraments. Without papal authorization, their sacramental gestures amounted to mockery and sacrilege. Moreover, their arrival at their new parishes, where they were to replace clergy refusing the oath, coincided with the "pantheonization" of Voltaire and the displacement of Sainte-Geneviève. Such an extraordinary and, for some, scandalous national act mirrored events in local communities surrounding the arrival and status of the *intrus,* whose presence profaned local holy places. Coming at a time when the Revolution had not yet fully broken with religion, these events lent substance to claims that the Revolution was a conspiracy of the enemies of God and his Church.[58] When anxieties about the Revolution erupted in violence in March of 1793, this discourse became the basis for the torture and ritualized deaths of constitutional priests and revolutionary officials. The language of abomination and profanation had prepared the just and righteous for the destruction of these "demons escaped from hell."

TERROR, TORTURE, AND THE RITUALS OF DEATH

On the morning of 11 March 1793 a thick fog lay over the fields outside the town of Machecoul. Machecoul lies in a marshy plain just a few kilometers from the Atlantic coast, so fog is by no means unusual. But this fog was different. It murmured. And the murmuring grew louder. Witnesses within the town later recounted that at times the fog gave forth a noise "like the sea churned by a storm." As the fog gave way to the morning sun, one could begin to make out shapes and discern the source of the murmured noises—compact masses of peasants armed with scythes, pikes, rakes, and forks. After a failed peace initiative led by local officials and backed by the local National Guard, the insurgents—including women and children—moved into the town and rang the tocsin from the church tower. A massacre began.[59]

Although the word "massacre" sometimes conjures up images of indiscriminate violence, the massacre at Machecoul followed a consistent pattern, a logic of violence. In effect, those who personified the Revolution by virtue of their function or their status made obvious targets. National Guardsmen were among the first to die, along with several prominent townsmen known to have supported the Revolution. The constitutional priest was bayoneted to death. According to one source, a veritable hunt through the streets ensued; one of the insurgents identified and pursued his prey through the streets with the aid of a hunting horn. He sounded *la vue* when he sighted a victim and returned to sound the *hallali* at the victim's death.[60] If true, it was particularly grisly and literal corroboration of the marquise de La Rochejaquelein's observation that the insurgents took some of their combat cues from tactics learned at the hunt.[61] So was the taking of hunting trophies—the bodies of some of the dead were mutilated.[62]

But the dominant metaphors were not feral but sacred, and the acts recalled nothing so clearly as the civil violence of the wars of religion. The Saint Bartholomew Massacres of 1572 drew upon a desire to purge the world of heretics by putting them to death and to use the spectacle of death to persuade others to abjure their faith. In the massacres at Machecoul, as at la

Roche-Bernard, the insurgents were given the opportunity to abjure their revolutionary patriotic convictions by renouncing the nation or crying "Vive le Roi!" Few did, of course, but the insistence on a salvific recantation is significant, and it surely provided an edifying lesson to others.

It's also important to bear in mind that the onset of the Vendée revolt co-incided with the beginning of Lent, traditionally a time of penitence and purification. During Lent, the faithful typically follow a self-imposed regime of prayer and fasting, usually accompanied by vows to abstain from certain foods and activities. Weddings are not celebrated during Lent. One also seeks to avoid extravagance and excess. However, in some Catholic commu-nities, the long, somber period of abstinence is broken halfway between the onset of Lent and its conclusion at Easter. This halfway Lenten festival, the *mi-carême,* is still celebrated in some communities of the west of France, no-tably in and around Nantes, where the *mi-carême* festival rivals Mardi Gras itself in color and gaiety. Although the violent behavior of the insurgents was not in keeping with orthodox Lenten practices, Lenten considerations and carnavalesque eruptions were not absent from their thinking. At the con-clusion of a day of executions of revolutionary sympathizers, one insurgent is reported to have remarked, "Nous nous sommes bien décarèmés aujour-d'hui!" Roughly, "We sure broke our Lenten vows today!"[63]

Preoccupations with the profanation of sacred places also figured in the March insurrection at Machecoul. When the violence had ended, some of the insurgents invited the former pastor of Machecoul, François Priou, to celebrate Mass in the liberated parish church. Priou, who had been displaced when he refused the oath, refused to say Mass in the parish church on the grounds that the schismatic constitutional priest had profaned it. "No. The church has not been purified," he remarked. Instead, he offered Mass out-doors on a makeshift altar.[64]

The horror of profanation and abomination under the leadership of the Revolution and the constitutional clergy induced anxiety as well as exculpa-tory remarks. The abuse of sacred places, by some accounts, explained the wrath of the people. When François Chevalier, counter-revolutionary pas-tor of Saint-Lumine-de-Coutais, wrote about the events at Machecoul, he suggested that libertinism, totemic worship, and profanation had enraged a just and pious people, driving them to massacre. Chevalier related that when the insurgents entered one of the churches of Machecoul, they were horrified to discover upon the altar an effigy of a calf, made from calfskin stuffed with straw. Alongside it was an effigy of a horse carved from wood. The insurgents were certain that they had before them irrefutable proof of "mysterious and nocturnal bacchanals" involving both sexes. Later it was suggested that the items were part of a pastoral scene celebrating the birth of the Jesus. "This is more probable," Chevalier conceded, "but it excuses nothing. The altar must never be used for profane purposes."[65]

Moreover, Chevalier persisted in asserting that this incident furnished proof that "this infamous Revolution" was the occasion for "an infamous substitution of paganism for Catholic principles." The Revolution was, for Chevalier, fundamentally a spiritual struggle for the future of France. There were no "impieties" that these "libertines" would not permit themselves—and not only in private homes. They had polluted sacred and public places with their heathen rituals.

The violence of the insurgents at Machecoul, like that of the insurgents at la Roche-Bernard, reveals aims that go beyond the instrumental. After all, the killing continued long after the town had been secured for the insurrection. The brutality perpetrated on the still-living bodies of the defeated—and the scope of the killing itself—far exceeded any rational assessment of appropriate levels of violence, the violence necessary to achieve a military or political goal. At Machecoul and elsewhere, other gratifications and symbolic aims drove violence well beyond any obvious rational objective.[66]

In writing about violence during the wars of religion, Denis Crouzet explored the varieties and meanings of the deaths to which Protestants and "heretics" were put, especially when the manner of death seemed to defy principles of efficiency, expediency, or instrumentality. Crouzet noted how the violence practiced on the bodies of Protestants was assimilated with the punishments of Hell. The Huguenots were damned; their apostasy guaranteed it. The mutilation of their bodies, according to Crouzet, anticipated the infernal torments their apostasy merited.[67] Moreover, violence was not itself sinful and could be a means of affirming one's loyalty to God. The knowledge that their acts only anticipated the torments to follow death and divine judgment reassured Catholics that their acts were both just and consistent with divine will.

More than two centuries after the wars of religion and the defeat of the Reformation in France, similar arguments went to work to explain the violence of the Vendéens. The certainty of the damnation of their enemies reassured Vendéens who might otherwise have recoiled at the murders they committed. Horrified by what they had done or seen done in the name of God, the insurgents associated their judgment with that of God; they were only instruments of divine will. As the abbé Chevalier put it, "Is it so shocking that God finally avenged his cause by delivering the wicked . . . to an avenging people?"[68] Indeed, in one account of the death of Sauveur at la Roche-Bernard, the insurgents had not only beaten Sauveur and increased his suffering with deliberately nonlethal pistol shots, they also cut off his fingers and then tossed him still alive onto a burning pyre.[69] It was as if the very manner of his death should anticipate the torments of Hell.

Later in the war of the Vendée, the violence did not end. Far from it. But the extent of cruel, casual, and arbitrary violence certainly declined. Vendéen soldiers defeated republican troops (and republican soldiers defeated Vendéens), but it was rare for such battles to be followed by massacres and tortures on the scale of the opening days of the revolt in March of 1793. This was a consequence almost certainly of the imposition of a semblance of order and discipline by the officers of the insurgency. Lucas de la Championnière noted, correctly, that the brutal massacres of the opening episodes of the revolt did not recur after leaders assumed authority within the revolt. In this sense, these massacres were more on the order of riots, like the September massacres in Paris in 1792, and should be seen as distinct from the military skirmishes and engagements characteristic of the Vendée revolt later on.

The decline in arbitrary, cruel, and brutal violence also depended upon a discursive shift in religious rhetoric: Vendéen officers insisted upon the ennobling power of forgiveness rather than the purifying power of blood. Indeed, the history of the Vendée carries more than its share of anecdotes involving officers who restrain insurgents who are about to massacre soldiers they have just defeated. In two celebrated cases Vendéen officers reminded their troops that the God of the Vendée may be an avenging god, but he also taught how to pardon. In October of 1793, the mortally wounded Charles Bonchamps saved thousands of captured republican soldiers from massacre when he uttered, as a dying request, "Grâce aux prisonniers!" At Chemillé, Maurice d'Elbée stopped Vendéens intent on massacre by ordering them to recite the Lord's Prayer, "Pardonnez-nous nos offenses comme nous pardonnons à ceux qui nous ont offensés." Forgive us our sins as we forgive those who trespass against us.

Republican troops sent to suppress the revolt in the Vendée also committed atrocities. For them, however, the motives were different. It was not a

Figure 18. "Madame and Mademoiselles de la Billais, Martyrs of the Sacred Heart, Nantes, 1794." In Victor Alet, *La France et le Sacré-Coeur* (Paris, 1871).

In March of 1794, a revolutionary court in Nantes convicted Madame de La Billais and her daughters of distributing Sacré-Coeur emblems "and other counter-revolutionary signs." They were executed at the Place Bouffay in Nantes. In the heavens above the scene, a figure beckons them upward. The incident reveals the extent to which Catholics saw the Revolution as the incarnation of Evil—opposition to it was thus a moral obligation.

matter of carrying out divine will, but of imposing a national will on a treasonous and recalcitrant people who had proven themselves unworthy of liberty (fig. 18). That the people of the Vendée simply could not be made to live peacefully within the Republic came to be taken as a truth revealed by the revolt itself. Indeed, Jean-Baptiste Leclerc would set the Vendéens not only outside of the Republic but also outside of humanity, characterizing them as "missing links." A systematic answer to the problem of the "inexplicable Vendée" was conceivable, but impractical. "If the population numbered only thirty or forty thousand souls, the simplest solution, without a doubt, would be to cut their throats," noted Lequinio matter-of-factly. "But this population is immense."[70]

Instead, the defeat of the main Vendéen force at Savenay in December of 1793 made intimidation and repression the logistically soundest plan for the Vendée. This was accompanied by a scorched-earth policy conceived as a means to weaken an incipient maquisard effort and to intimidate potential sympathizers. There was also a relentless hunt of surviving Vendéen officers. D'Elbée was captured and executed in January of 1794. Henri de La Rochejaquelein was shot shortly thereafter. François Athanase de Charette and Jean-Nicolas Stofflet were executed in 1796. Effectively, however, the Vendée had died at Savenay, where the main Vendéen army had been defeated and crushed. Many of those who escaped that day, including many noncombatant women, children, and elderly, were subsequently hunted down, imprisoned, tried, and executed. Among those executed was Catherine Joussemet, a former nun, who had followed the Vendéen soldiers and fled after their defeat at Savenay. The most incriminating evidence in the Joussemet dossier? Some two hundred and fifty Sacré-Coeur emblems she had crafted by hand.[71]

THE SACRED HEART AND
THE RETURN OF KINGS

It was a plague of the body that ravaged Marseille.
The Revolution was a plague of hearts and minds.

. . .

The time is coming when the Sacred Heart will receive the solemn
and public devotion owed to him by men . . . and he will pour out
his treasures of mercy upon the earth. Cities and provinces will
erect altars in his honor.

JEAN NICOLAS LORIQUET,
le Salut de la France, 1816

There is reason to hope that His Majesty Louis XVIII . . . will accomplish
the vow of Louis XVI, that he will place his realm under the special
protection of the Sacré-Coeur.

SOPHIE BARAT,
founder of the Sisters of the Sacred Heart, 1814

WHEN THE BROTHER OF Louis XVI returned to France as Louis XVIII
and head of the restored Bourbon monarchy, he knew that his monarchy
must be founded on reconciliation, not revenge. By April of 1814, his
brother's death by execution, while still a signal event in the nation's history
and a matter of living memory for thousands, took its place among other
spectacular moments in twenty-five years of revolutionary and Napoleonic
rule. The Charter of 1814, which would provide the written basis for royal
authority over the next thirty-four years, recognized basic civil liberties and

created a bicameral legislature. It also emphasized a policy of *oubli*, of forgetfulness, which made collective amnesia about specific acts committed during the Revolution a constitutional recommendation. Given that a good many of those who had voted for the conviction and execution of the king's brother were still alive, it was as if Louis was making his own willingness to forgive an example for an entire people. The Restoration would stand for civil peace, not revenge and civil war.

And yet, for the king *oubli* did not rule out commemoration and respect for the dead. Among the king's first official acts was an order to seek to identify the remains of his brother and his sister-in-law, Louis XVI and Marie-Antoinette, among the bodies buried in mass graves in the cemetery of the Madeleine parish. Once the remains were identified, they were translated to Saint-Denis, where they would take their places in the royal mausoleum in the crypt of the basilica. The anniversaries of the deaths of the deceased relatives, 21 January and 16 October, were proclaimed national days of mourning and atonement.

Throughout these ceremonial and symbolic openings to the Restoration era, the Sacré-Coeur, once so central a symbol to the cause of the restoration of royal and Catholic France, appeared hardly at all—at least at official state commemorations. The reasons were mostly political. Although *oubli* was clearly the prudent political position for the Bourbons to take, it was not so clearly the most popular or widely shared among longstanding friends and defenders of Christian monarchy in France, many of whom expected purge for their enemies and recognition (if not reward) for themselves. However, Louis XVIII was determined not to become the hostage of the ultraroyalists whose exaggerated devotion to throne and altar threatened to make them more royalist than the king himself. In Restoration France as much as anywhere else political power lay at the center, which meant that Louis needed to focus on cultivating the more moderate constitutional monarchists and the repentant supporters of Napoleon Bonaparte, for whom the Sacré-Coeur was not a compelling political goal. Indeed, Vendéen veterans and other ultraroyalists needed the Bourbons far more than the Bourbons needed them; a too-close association with them, their emblems, and their heroes could only make it appear as though the Bourbons had learned nothing from the Revolution. Thus was born the legend of the "ungrateful Bourbons," a family that turned its back on those who had sacrificed everything for God and King under the sign of the Sacré-Coeur.

This political configuration changed briefly in 1815, when Napoleon Bonaparte escaped from his island exile on Elba, to return to Paris and power for a hundred days. The revival of civil violence in the Vendée in defense of the fleeing Louis XVIII is one of the most overlooked features of domestic politics during the Hundred Days; indeed Louis de La Rochejaquelein, brother of Henri, lost his life defending the Bourbons in 1815. The net military effect of these efforts was to force Bonaparte to commit troops to the Vendée, troops that might have made the difference at Waterloo had they been available.[1] The net local effect was to give a new generation of Vendéens a chance to associate themselves with the dramatic episodes of what was increasingly called *la grande guerre,* the great war, that is, the Vendée.

Even so, the newly restored Bourbon dynasty pursued an aggressive cultural program and even the "ungrateful" Bourbons did not fail to find ways to recognize the loyalty of the Vendée although, characteristically, they did so by recognizing the efforts of the Vendéen elite. The Bourbons revived the idea of an official portrait gallery of distinguished military servants of the crown. Such a gallery had existed under the Old Regime. This idea was combined with the notion that the Vendéen generals were, in effect, in the service of Louis XVIII. The gallery would be brought back and portraits of the Vendéen generals would be added, suggesting continuity between those who had served the crown during the trials of the Revolution and those who had served prior to 1789. The comte de Pradel proposed the portraits in June of 1816. Louis accepted the idea.[2] The result was a series of monumental canvases in honor of the "giants" of the Vendée, featured at some of the early public art exhibitions (salons) of the Restoration period.

RESTORATION FRANCE LOOKS AT THE VENDÉE

The first set of portraits was ready for display at the Salon of 1817, the first salon of the Restoration. These included portraits of Louis and Henri de La Rochejaquelein and Pierre Constant de Suzannet. Portraits of Louis de Lescure and François-Athanase de Charette were displayed at the Salon of 1819; those of Bonchamps, Cathelineau, and others were not ready until later still.

For most of those viewing the portraits, these would likely be the first Vendéen rebels they had ever seen. These salons presented, therefore, a unique opportunity to shape the image of the Vendéen insurgency. The sheer scale of the portraits reinforces the monumental aspect of the figures and the events they commemorate. These men truly are "giants" in the sense that they are rendered larger than life. The portraits dwarf the viewer.

However, the biennial salons were by no means the only points of public access to these images. A marketing campaign for lithographs based on the portraits began in 1824 and ran for at least five years.[3] Its aim was not so much profit as politics; it fit well with the efforts of "ultra" royalists whose vision of a closer pairing of monarchy and Catholicism—and a more definitive rejection of the revolutionary legacy—remained to be realized. Thus, while the original portraits were removed from public display when they were transferred to the royal residence at Saint-Cloud, thousands of lithographs made their way into private residences, to take their place alongside portraits of the royal family, or the "martyred" Louis XVI and Marie-Antoinette. The salon is where one could expect to influence elite, Parisian "public opinion"—the public opinion that counted most in the still-narrow world of nineteenth-century French politics. From the mass production of lithographed portraits, one may infer that ultraroyalists had grasped the importance of propaganda in the dawning age of mass politics.

Given such an ambitious distribution plan, the portraits bear closer examination for what they tell us about royalist values and symbols. The artists took care to minimize the fact of civil war, the fact that these men had fought and killed other Frenchmen. Although many of the portraits show the Vendéen officers in battle poses, the artists have scrupulously avoided the representation of their opponents, the soldiers of the Republic. Only in the portrait of Henri de La Rochejaquelein (see fig. 17) does one get even a hint of an enemy, and then only by virtue of the line of bayonets facing La Rochejaquelein and his soldiers. Even then, the bayonets jut into the portrait frame from the right, but the soldiers bearing them are only implied—there are no faces, nor even hands.

What were the central values portrayed? Given that most of the men represented in these portraits are dressed as they fought, *en bourgeois,* and that the peasant/wool merchant/peddler Cathelineau has a portrait alongside his noble colleagues, one may infer that royalism accepted the new hierarchy of merit over an outmoded hierarchy of birth. The portraits also offer a range of idealized male virtues: the courage implied by the steely gaze of Henri de La Rochejaquelein, the piety expressed in the heavenward glance of Louis de Lescure (fig. 19), the rugged, spirited manliness of Charette (fig. 20), the simple heroism of the peasant Cathelineau, the noble pride of D'Elbée.

Figure 19. Robert Lefevre, *Louis de Lescure,* Salon of 1819. Musée
d'Histoire et des Guerres de Vendée, Cholet (Maine-et-Loire).

After their restoration in 1814, the Bourbons were accused of ingratitude toward the Vendée by François René de Chateaubriand and
others. The accusation is not entirely accurate. One way the Bourbons
expressed their gratitude was by commissioning monumental portraits
of Vendéen generals, which were to hang among other portraits of
officers who had served Bourbon France under the Old Regime. These
portraits, distributed in cheap reproductions, served as icons in the
ongoing saga of France and the Sacré-Coeur. Here, loyal and devout
Vendéens rally around their equally loyal and devout leader, Louis de
Lescure; a huge missionary cross evokes the pre-revolutionary missionary activities of Louis Grignion de Montfort and his followers.

Figure 20. Jean-Baptiste Paulin-Guérin, *François-Athanase de Charette de la Contrie,* Salon of 1819. Musée d'Histoire et des Guerres de Vendée, Cholet (Maine-et-Loire).

This monumental, larger-than-life portrait of François-Athanase de Charette was displayed at one of the first official salons of the Restoration. Charette had led large formations of Vendéen insurgents during 1793. In years following, he led smaller formations in skirmishes and guerrilla attacks on republican troops. Here, with the Sacré-Coeur stitched to his jacket and Bourbon-white feather and sash, he poses as a leader of men, the model of the Catholic and royalist patriot.

This gallery of manly Christian men would provide a store of images to be deployed throughout the nineteenth century in hopes of reinvigorating Catholic manhood. As the attendance of men at church services declined over the century, the Catholic Church struggled with the resulting progressive feminization of religious practice. The portraits of the Vendéen generals asserted the compatibility of key values—loyalty, faith, and manly vigor. They also furnished a selection of battle-tested icons for nineteenth-century royalist politics. A commitment to monarchy doesn't go without saying, even in the Vendée. A white flag with the motto "Vive le Roi!" embroidered in gold thread provides a dynamic, rippling background to the portrait of Henri de La Rochejaquelein. Louis de Lescure has a Bourbon-white sash wrapped around his waist. As for religion, the oversized rosary draped around the neck of Jacques Cathelineau is at least as impressive as the two muskets secured by a white sash around his waist. Some portraits show military medals and decorations. Others show red and white, or red, blue, and yellow *mouchoirs* (handkerchiefs), one of the signature products of the textile industry of Cholet and a divisional emblem of the men who fought alongside Henri de La Rochejaquelein. The one universal icon? All of the men show stitched to their lapels various versions of the icon of a heart surmounted by a cross: the Sacred Heart of Jesus.

FRANCE: A MISSIONARY COUNTRY?

The Sacred Heart also figured in one of the most ambitious itinerant propaganda campaigns ever undertaken in the history of France. Religious practice had been one of the casualties of the Revolution, a fact by no means entirely due to the de-Christianization campaign of 1793–94 during which belief was ridiculed, ritual mocked, and believers persecuted. The phenomenon also owes something to the confusion generated by the reforms of Catholicism associated with the Civil Constitution of the Clergy. Finally, as Ernest Sevrin and Michel Vovelle have argued, the Revolution revealed (rather than caused) a decline in belief, a decline already underway prior to the Revolution. Given social inducements and pressures to conform in pre-revolutionary France, decline in religious belief was not always accompanied by corresponding declines in practice. In many communities of pre-revolutionary France, nonattendance at Mass had a stigmatizing effect; some individuals thus went to church even when they no longer believed simply because the neighbors were watching. What remained observable was the *habit* of Christian practice and not always the stuff of Christian faith. Thus, the contribution of the Revolution was to accelerate the creation of a social climate in which religious practice was no longer normative. The power of habit and conformity in religious matters had fallen away after 1789. Religious practice became of matter of personal choice.

As a result, France had become a virtual "missionary country"—that is, a country ripe for Christianizing activity. Under the circumstances, the re-Christianization of France could not be a matter of winning back souls one by one. It had to involve the reconstruction of a cultural climate that could sustain and reinforce Catholic practice as a social norm because *that* is what the Revolution had destroyed. This challenge, combined with the sense that the Revolution had been the scene of numerous collective affronts to the will of God—affronts calling for reparation—demanded a new strategy for religious politics under the Restoration. The work of reparation and the regeneration of the tissue of Catholic public culture required something much more ambitious.

The grand strategy of religious politics of the Restoration was to be a large-scale public enterprise. Its architect was Jean-Baptiste Rauzan, chaplain to the king. His proposal involved the creation of a domestic missionary campaign called the Société des Missions. Its aim? To restore a Catholic dimension to French public culture via the evangelization or *re*-evangelization of post-revolutionary France. Louis XVIII embraced the idea and a royal *ordonnance* dated 26 September 1816 authorized the creation of the Société des Prêtres de la Miséricorde—the Society of the Priests of Mercy—better known as the Missions of France.[4]

The Missions were not dominated by a single religious order. The Montfortains returned to their work, emphasizing rural towns and villages of the French west.[5] Their efforts were seconded in the Midi by the Prêtres des Sacrés Coeurs (la Congrégation des Sacré Coeurs de Jésus et de Marie), founded in 1800 by Father Coudrin and Henriette Aymer de la Chevalerie.[6] The Jesuit order had been newly reauthorized by papal decree—significantly, at the moment of the restoration of the European old order in 1814—and the Jesuits took the lead in missionizing the cities. Indeed, the crypto-Jesuit Pères de la Foi had pioneered missionary activities within pre-Restoration France in such cities as Amiens, Beauvais, Abbeville, Lyon, Grenoble, Tours, Poitiers, and Bordeaux. This was obviously not what

Bonaparte had in mind when he signed the Concordat with Pope Pius VII in 1801—Catholic clergy were supposed to support the reign of Napoleon Bonaparte, not announce the coming of the social reign of Jesus. Bonaparte suppressed the Pères de la Foi in 1807, prior to the prohibition of domestic missionary activities generally in 1809.[7]

What these missionaries had in common was a love of the Sacré-Coeur matched only by their suspicion of the Revolution. The Montfortains were credited with cultivating the devotion to the Sacré-Coeur in the Vendée prior to the Revolution. Father Coudrin, cofounder of the Prêtres des Sacrés Coeurs, had been arrested in Poitiers in 1797 for leading a clandestine procession in honor of the Sacré-Coeur in a garden on the rue des Basses-Treilles. His collaborator in that incident, the abbé Soyer, would later be named bishop of Luçon in the diocese of the Vendée.[8] As for the Jesuits and the Fathers of the Sacred Heart founded during the Revolution—their devotion to the Sacré-Coeur goes without saying. Many of the "crypto-Jesuits" who had operated in clandestinity during the Revolution emerged publicly for the first time as agents of the missions. These included Joseph Varin, the nobleman soldier turned Jesuit militant; Louis Barat who, prior to his imprisonment during the Terror, had cultivated the Sacré-Coeur devotion among those who attended his clandestine services on the rue de Touraine in Paris; and the abbé Lambert, whose 1814 pamphlet *le Salut de la France* set forth the idea of a consecration to the Sacré-Coeur as the centerpiece in a strategy for national renewal.[9] For all of these priests-on-mission, the Revolution had been the formative experience of their lives. The Revolution over, they made their mission the annunciation of the return of the reign of God.

To say that the missions were the French equivalent of the religious revival meeting would be to indulge not only in an anachronism but also in an Americanism, yet the large-scale and public nature of the Restoration missions lend themselves to such comparisons. They were planned and choreographed in such a way as to lure individuals to lose themselves in the crowd, to join in a collective response to the dread of sin and the promise of salvation (fig. 21). Prayers, confessions, and communions had their place in the mission, but sermons were the central event. Missionary sermons touched on such themes as the necessity of conversion, the importance of forgiveness, the obligation of reparation, the dangers of dance.[10] Ernest Sevrin, historian of the missions, has noted that the missions were intended to bring France

Figure 21. "Solemn Benediction of a Mission Cross," 1826. Bibliothèque Nationale, Cabinet des Estampes, Paris.

Re-Christianization, after the dislocations of the Revolution, was central to the religious restoration after 1814. Evocations of the Sacré-Coeur and the "martyr king" Louis XVI were standard features in the repertoire of the itinerant missions of France. Here, a mission cross is blessed while the faithful adopt positions expressing penitence and grief.

to God, but also to bring God to France, with all that that implies for a broad, public, even officially endorsed effort.[11]

The missions were to be public spectacles and "popular" in the sense of "accessible to the people." Parish priests prepared their parishioners for the missions weeks in advance and the response was often huge—it was not unusual for speakers and attendees to be forced out of doors in order to accommodate the crowd. Once outside, the setting lent itself to all manner of improvisation. There were processions through the streets of the town or city. There were visits to cemeteries that encouraged reflections on the insignificance of a lifetime compared to the vast stretches of eternity open before the immortal soul. There were halts before places rich in memories of the Revolution, public places where the guillotine had stood, churches profaned by constitutional priests and the revolutionary Cult of Reason, makeshift prisons where members of religious orders had been held and executed. An imaginative speaker could exploit a landscape rich in such memories— memories still accessible to those in the audience who had witnessed the original events—to sharpen the contrast between the depravity of the revolutionary past and the order of the Restoration present. Speakers prompted reflection upon the foolishness of the Rights of Man and the inviolability of the Rights of God.

If a mission coincided with a major anniversary from the revolutionary period—21 January (the execution of Louis XVI), 16 October (the execution of the queen)—missionaries would make the most of the occasion. Bonfires could also be used to dramatic effect, whether to burn relics of the Revolution (phrygian bonnets, tricolor sashes) or to burn books bearing the suspect secular ideas of the eighteenth century (Voltaire, Rousseau). Local dissidents fought back as best they could—mounting a production of Molière's *Tartuffe* was a favorite tactic ("the theater's answer to the pulpit")—but even in some major cities liberal and democratic elements were hugely outnumbered.[12] Missions were such effectively orchestrated spectacles that they drew crowds of curious to augment the crowds of faithful. Missions ended with a spectacular not to be missed, a bonfire (sometimes at a site where religious objects or relics had been shattered or burned during the Revolution), adult first communions (for those unable to make a first communion as children because of the Revolution), the planting of a monumental missionary cross, and consecrations (of persons, parishes, municipalities, dioceses) to the Sacred Heart of Jesus.[13]

These events emphasized a dramatic break with the past. Flames destroyed the remnants of revolutionary apostasy, adult communions (often tearful) symbolized return and a kind of reparation, missionary crosses (like crosses or flags planted on remote shores) symbolized a divine claim on a community. In some cases, as Gerard Cholvy has argued, the missions in general and the devotion to the Sacré-Coeur in particular often slipped into a regrettable kind of "mysticism" emphasizing reparation for the sins of others and a contempt for the modern age.[14] Indeed, much of the history of the Sacré-Coeur devotion pushed it in that direction. The spectacular, pageant-like quality of the missions suggests that they sought to appeal more to the senses than to the intellect.[15] The devotion to the Sacré-Coeur lent itself well to such appeals—it is, after all, the *heart* of Jesus—especially in its emphasis on the pain wrought upon Jesus when the offer of his heart is met with human indifference.

THE SACRED HEART OF MARAT

"High" culture during the Restoration often amplified missionary meditations and reflections on the "excesses" of the Revolution and the consolations of religion. François René de Chateaubriand's *Memoirs from Beyond the Tomb* referenced one of the episodes the Restoration missionaries most loved to hate, one of the most elaborate and celebrated mockeries of the Sacré-Coeur—the cult of the Sacré-Coeur de Jean-Paul Marat. When Charlotte Corday plunged her knife into the chest of the "Friend of the People" in July of 1793, she created one of the Revolution's most powerful martyr heroes. Marat's assassination coincided with the apogee of the revolt in the Vendée, and although Corday was not a royalist, she *was* associated with a broader revolt of moderate republicans, known as the Federalist revolt, against Jacobin control of the Revolution and its legislature, the National Convention.

The National Convention voted the ceremonial pantheonization of Marat, but before any such ceremony could take place, Marat's body was put on public display in the Hall of the Cordeliers (formerly a Franciscan monastery) (fig. 22).[16] Marat's heart was removed and placed in a makeshift reliquary—a bejeweled urn that had once been the property of the king and queen. The urn and the heart served as the symbolic focus of a public ceremony in honor of Marat, held in the Luxembourg gardens. There, a giant *reposoir* had been erected with the urn bearing the heart of Marat on the altar. As Marat's eulogist completed an inventory of Marat's achievements, he pronounced the phrase, "O heart of Jesus! O heart of Marat! Sacred heart of Marat, sacred heart of Jesus, you have equal claim on our praise." The eulogy went on to offer comparisons of Marat with Jesus, of aristocrats with Pharisees, of the Apostles with the revolutionary Jacobins. The eulogist concluded with a phrase subordinating Jesus to Marat: "Jésus est un prophète et Marat est un dieu."[17] Jesus is a prophet; Marat is a god.

Frank Bowman has argued that the cult of the Sacré-Coeur de Marat was not a true religion or even a devotion in the making but an attempt, derivative of the rituals of Catholicism, to honor Marat and the revolutionary

Figure 22. Fougea (attr.), *Funeral Rites for Marat at the Hall of the Cordeliers,* 1794. Musée Carnavalet, Paris. © Photothèque des Musées de la Ville de Paris.

Marat's body was placed on display after his assassination by Charlotte Corday in July of 1793. Eulogistic invocations of his "Sacred Heart" served to confer an aura of sanctity upon Marat but also to mock the beliefs of the Catholic counter-revolution. During the Restoration and long after, critics of the Revolution cited the devotion to the Sacré-Coeur de Marat as an example of the blasphemous excesses of the Revolution and the Republic.

virtues he exemplified. There was no serious attempt, he notes, to perpetuate the devotion to the sacred heart of Marat either as a revolutionary cult or as an extension of Christianity.[18] Indeed, one might go further and note that the point was not to confer sainthood in any conventionally understood sense upon Marat, but to use the occasion of Marat's death to subvert by ridicule one of the central devotions of the counter-revolution, that is, the Sacred Heart of Jesus. Hence the rhetorical flourishes that aped those associated with the Sacré-Coeur; hence the strained attempts to identify similarities between the lives and deaths of Jesus and Marat; hence the fascination with the *plaie,* the dagger wound, which mimicked and mocked intense Catholic fascination with the wound in Jesus' side.[19] Such intentions were also clearly evident in Jacques Louis David's posthumous portrait of Marat, in which the serenely dead Friend of the People lies cradled *Pietà*-like in his bathtub. Such comparisons were also implicit in a separate ceremony over the body of Marat at the Hall of the Cordeliers, where an anonymous orator apostrophized the "bleeding wound" of Marat (a trope borrowed from the Sacré-Coeur devotion), the "enflamed" heart of Marat (the Sacred Heart of Jesus was frequently represented as "ardent" or enflamed), the heart of Marat "which so loved *la patrie*" (whereas the heart of Jesus had "so loved men").[20]

These visual and rhetorical approximations sought to wound the Catholic counter-revolution by mocking its beliefs. They succeeded. One of Pierre-Joseph Picot de Clorivière's young recruits to his Prêtres du Sacré-Coeur, the abbé Cormeaux, was so upset by the sacrilegious Maratist parody of the Sacré-Coeur devotion that for three days he languished in a shattered emotional state. He subsequently organized ceremonial reparation for the following First Friday. Cormeaux, with the penitent's rope around his neck, led his fellow priests of the Sacré-Coeur in a day of prayer, silence, fast, and *amende honorable.*[21] Thus, while on one level the Sacré-Coeur de Marat is simply another example of the sometimes spectacularly bad taste of French revolutionary political culture, on another it helped to sustain a pattern of ritual and counter-ritual. In effect, Cormeaux and his fellow crypto-Jesuits were taking their place in an ongoing dialogue of rituals, like those surrounding the Pantheon, whereby one comments ritualistically on the errors of one's opponents.

SISTERS AND FRIENDS OF THE SACRED HEART

The Restoration was also the setting for the establishment of new religious orders taking their identity, and sometimes their names, from the new devotion to the Sacré-Coeur. Sophie Barat, at the urging of her brother Louis Barat and Joseph Varin, became the cornerstone of a new women's order in the 1790s. She had founded what was to become the order of the Sacred Heart in 1800, but she dared not publicly take the name Sisters of the Sacred Heart because the Sacred Heart name and symbol were still widely perceived as seditious. Until the Restoration, her order was instead known by the more discreet name "Dames de la Foi," constituting her order as the feminine complement to the Pères de la Foi, her brother's crypto-Jesuit order.

Like the Pères de la Foi, Sophie Barat's Sisters of the Sacred Heart were committed to what they saw as the task of the moral reconstruction of France after 1789. Their rules, like those of the Pères de la Foi, were based upon the rules of the Jesuit order.[22] Their novices, like the recruits to the Pères de la Foi, had experienced the Revolution as the formative experience for their generation. For some, counter-revolution and the Sacré-Coeur were a matter of family heritage.[23] Annette, Thérèse, and Julia de La Roche-jaquelein bore the name made famous by their uncle, the Vendéen general Henri de La Rochejaquelein, their mother, Marie-Louise de La Rochejaque-lein, widow of Vendéen general Louis de Lescure, and their father, Louis de La Rochejaquelein, who died defending the monarchy during Napoleon's Hundred Days! For them, taking the vows of the Sacred Heart order combined faith and family honor.[24]

Under Sophie Barat's energetic leadership, Sacred Heart convents were established in six cities and towns across France in 1815. Over the next fifteen years, the order expanded from these six original convents to include some forty establishments, an extraordinary rate of growth. With daughters of the nobility making up much of the membership in the order of the Sacred Heart, these convent-schools were destined to serve as centers of education for the women of the Catholic elite. Indeed, the reconstitution and training of an elite Catholic womanhood was the implicit charge of the order. Looking back from a vantage point late in the century, the vicomtesse Marie Verdet d'Adhemar would remark that the Sacred Heart order possessed "a unique character" that was "specifically aristocratic."[25]

Wherever possible, Barat and her associates chose sites consistent with their broad religious and cultural mission but also with their sense of the past. In the city of Nantes, for example, they set up their convent at an estate called "l'Éperonnière," a fourteen-hectare domain better known locally as "le Sacré-Coeur."[26] L'Éperonnière was rich in associations and meanings because revolutionary authorities had used the site as a prison and place of execution for Vendéens guilty, among other things, of bearing the image of the heart of Jesus—talisman, sign of faith, *prima facie* evidence of treasonous revolt—on their chests.[27] The order's Paris residence benefited from a similarly historic symmetry and fitting reappropriation. In 1820, the order took up residence in the stately Hôtel Biron (now the Musée Rodin) on the rue de Varennes. General Biron, executed under the Terror, had commanded republican forces against the Vendéens at Saumur and Angers.[28]

Sophie Barat's sisters of the Sacred Heart used their network of convents and schools to cultivate a new theology, a Sacred Heart theology that emphasized a God who was more a forgiving redeemer than a stern Jehovah. This was the spiritual legacy of Jeanne de Chantal, François de Sales, and Jean Eudes.[29] After 1793, however, the Sacred Heart also served as an object of memory and a rich source of associations about France, its Christian mission, and the post-revolutionary task of renewal. Sophie Barat took upon herself the Sacred Heart theology and legends in all of their richness and complexity, including the vexed matter of the vow of Louis XVI. Within Barat's Sacred Heart order, a mystical aura seems to have surrounded everything about the man some royalists would call the "martyr king." According to Barat's biographer, prior to the order's move to the Hôtel Biron, some of the novices occupied a house on the rue de l'Arbalère once occupied by Joseph Santerre. Santerre had been commander of the Paris National Guard in 1792 and 1793 and was therefore one of the men responsible for the security of the king during his imprisonment in the fortress-prison known as the Temple. The novices reported that the word "Temple" appeared mysteriously in several places on the walls of one of the rooms, as if Santerre and his dwelling had been haunted by the memory of the martyr king. All attempts to remove or paint over these phantom words failed.[30]

Chilling anecdotes about martyred royalty, repentant revolutionaries, and just recompense helped make sense of a tumultuous revolutionary past for members of the Sacred Heart order. They also guided initiatives undertaken in the present. Sophie Barat added her efforts to the campaign to persuade Louis XVIII to recognize publicly the vow of Louis XVI and his clandestine consecration of France to the Sacré-Coeur. Louis's legendary 1792 vow had been conditional; he promised to make a public consecration once he recovered his freedom. Louis never recovered his freedom, so the public consecration never took place. Sophie Barat and her order joined the chorus of voices urging Louis XVIII to honor the vow his brother had made or to consecrate France in an initiative of his own.

Sophie Barat was optimistic that the restored monarchy of Louis XVIII would at last fulfill the demands expressed by the Sacré-Coeur to Marguerite-Marie Alacoque. The failure to fulfill these demands had brought grief to France; it was time now to show that the lesson had been learned—divine patience had its limits. This project, for which she lobbied aggressively, was an integral part of her effort to see to the reconstruction of France through its re-Christianization in the name of the Sacré-Coeur. "We see more and more how much this devotion [to the Sacré-Coeur] appeals to the faithful," she wrote to Father Fontana, a superior of another religious order. "We know how much this devotion is favored by the Holy See and the bishops of a great many dioceses. Finally, there is reason to hope that His Majesty Louis XVIII will accede to the wishes of his most faithful subjects, that he will accomplish the vow of Louis XVI, that he will place his realm under the special protection of the Sacré-Coeur."[31] For Barat, the Sacré-Coeur meant not only personal salvation but also national salvation.

Lobbying took other forms, notably in the provinces, where local initiatives in favor of the Sacré-Coeur served as a substitute for a national consecration. Poitiers, like Nantes, Paris, Bordeaux, and other cities, had had its local resistance network during the Revolution; in Poitiers, as elsewhere, the Sacré-Coeur had provided both solace and insignia.[32] At the Restoration, Jean Nicolas Loriquet, a crypto-Jesuit who had worked alongside Varin, Ronsin, and Barat as Pères de la Foi, spearheaded a local initiative to consecrate the diocese of Poitiers to the Sacré-Coeur. Loriquet hastily drafted a pamphlet titled *le Salut de la France,* which outlined the historical vision of the Sacré-Coeur.[33] In fact, Loriquet's work serves as a concise summary of the Jesuit/Catholic brief against the Revolution.

Loriquet's pamphlet combines French chauvinism ("the first among peoples") with a culpabilization of the *philosophes,* whom he describes as *faux sages* responsible for the social gangrene with which France finds itself afflicted.[34] In a reference to Belsunce and the plague at Marseille, he remarks that the Revolution was "the plague of hearts and minds." Loriquet's indictment is gloomily millenarian but stops short of apocalyptic visions of damnation; he counsels confidence in the "imminent triumph of grace reserved for these endtimes."[35] He foresees difficulties but he advises Poitiers to "take refuge in the heart of Jesus." The city of Poitiers should be consecrated to the Sacré-Coeur, while waiting for a national consecration that will usher in a period of abundant grace.[36]

Loriquet's message and rhetoric were perfectly adapted to the mood of early Restoration France: defeated, occupied, depleted, exhausted, self-critical, contrite.[37] A coalition of inspired local notables in Poitiers organized "a festival of expiation and reparation." The festival included the restoration of the bishop's chapel within the cathedral, which had been "defaced" with daubs of paint in the national colors of blue, white, and red.[38] A tableau featuring the Sacré-Coeur was installed in the chapel as a sign of the conviction that the return of the Bourbons and the devotion to the Sacré-Coeur were linked "like cause and effect."[39] On 31 May 1816, the diocese of Poitiers was consecrated to the Sacré-Coeur, "in reparation for the crimes of the Revolution" in anticipation of a royal consecration soon to come.[40]

The diocesan consecration at Poitiers, like the large-scale internal missions, aimed to build popular support for a national consecration.[41] So did Archbishop de Quelen's 1822 consecration of the diocese of Paris to the Sacré-Coeur as had, presumably, the large canvas by Nicolas-André Monsiau celebrating Belsunce at Marseille, shown at the Salon of 1819 (see fig. 7). Provincial initiatives also sought to influence high culture in favor of a consecration to the Sacré-Coeur and recruited one of the outstanding artists of Restoration France in order to do so. Lay and religious officials in Montauban lobbied Jean-Auguste-Dominique Ingres to accept a commission of a grand historical subject for the Montauban cathedral. Ingres hesitated, but ultimately he was persuaded to take on a difficult artistic challenge—the vow of Louis XIII to the Virgin Mary (fig. 23). Louis made the vow in 1636, at a moment when his throne was threatened because heresy and civil war divided the land. Louis XIII sought the aid of the Virgin; he offered to consecrate his realm to her in exchange for her protection and intercession. Two years later, his prayers answered, Louis made good on his promise, and he decreed a celebration on the feast of the Assumption in perpetuity. The Revolution put an end to these annual commemorations; they were revived under the Restoration and are still observed (15 August), though unofficially.[42]

Art historian Carol Duncan has rightly criticized art historians' too-narrow focus on the technical aspects of Ingres's canvas, when its real interest lies in its political engagements. Although the painting was first displayed at the Salon of 1824, Duncan points out that the work was commissioned in 1820, coinciding with a crisis in the Restoration monarchy brought about by the assassination of the duc de Berry, the last Bourbon in direct line of descent able to father an heir to the throne. Duncan argues that the intent of the work's sponsors was to ingratiate themselves with the regime by sponsoring a canvas designed to "glorify the Bourbons" at a critical moment for the dynasty and the regime.[43]

That Ingres's canvas commemorates one of the great moments in the history of the Bourbon dynasty is beyond dispute; it also serves as a celebration of Bourbon piety and obliquely confirms Legitimist claims of divine right.

Figure 23. Jean-Auguste-Dominique Ingres, *The Vow of Louis XIII,* 1824.
Notre-Dame de Montauban.

Ingres's *Vow of Louis XIII* figured within a complex campaign to induce
Louis XVIII, the restored Bourbon monarch, to consecrate France to
the Sacré-Coeur. The commission of the painting coincided with a municipal consecration to the Sacré-Coeur at Poitiers, the revival of visions
of the Sacré-Coeur, the consideration of the case for beatification of
Marguerite-Marie Alacoque, missionary campaigns within France, and
publicity surrounding the "vow of Louis XVI" during the Revolution.

However, a more precisely hortatory intent is evident if we place Ingres's *Vow of Louis XIII* at the intersection of several converging Restoration discourses, namely, ongoing critical commentary on the heresy and discord of the Revolution, the theme of national reconciliation through public Christian renewal, and persistent claims of restored order and grandeur through a public consecration to the Sacré-Coeur. By reminding Louis XVIII of how his august predecessor had overcome heresy and discord through a vow to the Virgin, the work asks Louis to achieve similar results through a public consecration to the Sacré-Coeur. The "complementary" nature of the two vows—that of Louis XIII and that of Louis XVI—had been a topic of Catholic commentary ever since the first rumors circulated regarding the 1792 vow of Louis XVI. For example, the vows of Louis XIII and Louis XVI are explicitly placed in tandem in Abbé Marchais's sermons to Vendéen troops in 1793.[44] The association between the vows was strong; the prescriptive intent of the painting would not have been beyond the grasp of many who saw it when it was displayed for the first time in 1824. It surely would not have been lost on the Bourbons.[45]

There is some evidence, albeit circumstantial, that the Bourbon family actually considered a gesture in favor of the Sacré-Coeur. But the gestures were not public. In fact, they were so private that they could be seen as aimed more to placate the vocal Sacred Heart constituency than to satisfy the demands of the Sacred Heart. Louis XVIII contributed a down payment of 100,000 francs for the purchase of the Hôtel Biron for Sophie Barat's Dames du Sacré-Coeur; they borrowed the remainder.[46] Then, in 1823, the royal family decided to make contributions "in kind" to the completion of the Sacred Heart chapel under construction at the Hôtel Biron. The king donated the altar for the chapel while his brother, the future Charles X, donated the decorative flourish or *gloire* above the sanctuary.[47] Was this intended as the legendary "chapel" to the Sacré-Coeur demanded in the visions of Marguerite-Marie? If so, it was never represented as such, and in any case it fell far short of the national public consecration expected by the advocates of the Sacred Heart devotion.

LITERARY COMBATS

If the Bourbons didn't give in to these pressures, it was because they understood that if the Restoration was to achieve the desired post-revolutionary reconciliation, it was unlikely to do so under such a freighted, controversial, frankly partisan and confessional sign as the Sacré-Coeur. If they were inclined to forget, there was a powerful anti-Sacré-Coeur lobby available to remind them. It included the opposition newspaper *le Constitutionnel* and some of the most prominent figures of the day, such as Henri Grégoire, former constitutional bishop, and Henri Beyle, better known as Stendhal.[48]

Stendhal refers to the Sacré-Coeur frequently in *The Red and the Black,* a mocking commentary on Restoration society. *The Red and the Black* was published in 1830, that is, too late to have had an impact on the culture wars of Restoration France; 1830 was the year of the overthrow of the Restoration monarchy. Just the same, Stendhal's novel is a precious source on what was at stake in those years. It still serves as a worthy guide to references meaningful within the ambient culture of the 1820s—references Stendhal relies upon to alert, inform, and guide his reader.

For Stendhal, the term "Sacré-Coeur" is used in various ways, but it is always used as a marker of ultraconservative monarchist and Catholic points of view. Stendhal situates the Sacré-Coeur at the very center of the conservative provincial society his novel aims to dissect. The Sacré-Coeur is the preferred schooling for women of the provincial elite, dispensing credentials indispensable for advancement in Restoration society. Stendhal takes pain to note that his feminine protagonists, Madame de Renal, Madame Derville, and Mademoiselle de la Mole, were all products of a Sacred Heart convent school. Renal and Derville became acquaintances there. Monsieur de Pontlevé is advised that it would be prudent to put his daughter in the convent school and the advice pays off; she later succeeds in marrying an officer closely connected to the court of Charles X. Abbé Pirard, Julien Sorel's mentor and the only likable clergyman in the novel, is defined in part by the fact that he had resisted "Marie Alacoque, the Sacred Heart of Jesus, the Jesuits, and his bishop." For Stendhal, the Sacred Heart is equivalent to cultural orthodoxy in Restoration France.

Henri Grégoire needed no introduction in post-revolutionary France. A priest elected to the Estates General in 1789, he had played a leading role in reforming the Catholic Church in France by means of the Civil Constitution of the Clergy. Grégoire took the oath of the clergy and served in many of the major assemblies of revolutionary and Napoleonic France. He also served for a time as the elected constitutional bishop of the diocese of Blois.

Any one of these facts would have been enough to earn him the enmity of oppositional Catholics in the revolutionary period. During the Restoration, he emerged as one of the sharpest critics of the Jesuits and the "Jesuit" devotion to the Sacré-Coeur. His *Histoire des sectes religieuses* contains a chapter-long critique of the devotion to the Sacré-Coeur. The chapter, titled "Cordicoles, ou histoire critique des dévotions nouvelles au Sacré-Coeur de Jésus et au Coeur de Marie," helped to popularize the term *cordicoles* as a pejorative reference to the Sacred Heart devotion. Grégoire's book was first published in 1810, but a new edition was brought out in 1814, just in time to serve as a counter to the Jesuits, the Missions, and the new Sacred Heart women's order which together led the offensive to remake France in the name of the Sacré-Coeur.[49]

Grégoire's position is essentially that of a sincere Christian offended by a heretical devotion: the cult of the Sacré-Coeur cheapens and sentimentalizes Christian faith and makes it a target of ridicule. Grégoire's devotional appetite ran toward a leaner, Jansenist, proto-Bauhaus style of Christianity. He wondered why Christians concerned themselves at all with the organs of Jesus and, in any event, why the heart? Why not a devotion "to the Savior's feet, hands, or head?"[50] Grégoire's answer is that the devotion to the Sacré-Coeur is a vulgar (in the sense of popular) devotion, designed to appeal to those whose spirituality thrives on sentiments and feelings—a bad thing in Grégoire's hierarchy of values—rather than prayerful reflection. Grégoire was horrified by a procession at the newly reconsecrated church of Sainte Geneviève. The procession featured a gilded heart carried on a platform, "followed by the Holy Sacrament."[51] For someone of Grégoire's convictions, this was sheer idolatry.

In defense of devotees of the Sacré-Coeur, one might ask Grégoire why there should not be a greater interest in the body of Jesus. Given the centrality of the "God become man" motif in Christianity, what needs to be explained is why there wasn't a deeper, more precocious fascination with the features of the body of Christ.[52] But Grégoire's concerns go beyond his distaste for vulgar fascination with the corporeality of Jesus. Behind the rich imagery and the excessive devotional sentiments, Grégoire saw something sinister lurking, an old and familiar nemesis—the reconstituted Jesuit order. In this sense, Grégoire's complaint is an extension of pre-revolutionary quarrels between ultra-Montanist Jesuits and the defenders of Gallicanism, notably in the Parlement of Paris. These disputes had led to the suppression of the Jesuit order in France in 1764 and, indirectly, to the suppression of the *parlements* in 1771.[53]

Jesuit promotion of the Sacré-Coeur, Grégoire claimed, masked its place within a "dominating system." The Sacré-Coeur served "to consecrate despotism" and subjugate nations.[54] Grégoire's rhetoric obviously owes something to the rhetoric of the Revolution; its effectiveness relies heavily on the political disposition and the credulity of the audience. But without accepting the more extreme formulations of Jesuit myths and sinister plots involving the shadowy Congregation, Grégoire does understand that the problem of the Sacré-Coeur is not merely one of dubious religious taste.[55] What Grégoire understood better than most of his contemporaries was that there was an inevitable confusion between the simple devotion to the Sacré-Coeur—which, for all of its baroque piety, *pace* Grégoire, was harmless— and the grand historical narrative to which the Sacré-Coeur was linked. The Sacré-Coeur was a soteriology, a salvation narrative with great moral and literary force. It was also just a symbol for Catholics who liked their religion on the syrupy side.

The danger was in the inevitable blending of the two. The kernel of the problem is already evident in the diocesan consecration to the Sacré-Coeur at Poitiers, which had its analogues during the Restoration in other dioceses, including Paris, Troyes, le Mans, and Saint-Brieuc. These consecrations on some level served a collective therapeutic need to shed guilt or to explain some calamity by allocating blame in some broad cosmic sense. Loriquet's pamphlet, which drove the events in Poitiers, was in large part an orgy of self-recrimination and self-hatred: "We, through our excesses and our disbelief, have brought disaster upon ourselves and our nation." Such sentiments, paraphrased here, helped to prepare reconciliation; they were part of a ritualized closure to sad episodes; they took old animosities out of play by consigning them to History.

But only potentially, because these ceremonies also served to identify and incriminate *others,* especially those who had strayed, and to fix their transgression in memory through the community rituals and monuments of expiation. After all, it was rarely those who atoned who also saw themselves as bearing the greatest responsibility for the national predicament. The Sacred Heart devotion promised a Christian utopia, contingent upon fulfillment of divine demands. Those who did not believe, those who believed differently, those conspicuously lacking in righteousness had not only set the nation hurtling toward the disaster of Revolution; their apostasy remained the principal obstacle between a chosen people and its divinely ordained destiny. By their stubbornness they delayed the promised Christian millennium for France.

These ceremonies of expiation set up a wall within communities, setting off those who had erred from those who had remained true to a divine compact. Such public and ceremonial examinations of community conscience established for many French Catholics a powerful association between national crises, threats to public order, the faults of others, and the Sacré-Coeur. They validated political and confessional prejudices and fed persistent anxieties of national decline. For the next 150 years there would not be a revolution or military defeat which was not moralized, internalized, and nationalized in terms of the Sacred Heart of Jesus. The Sacred Heart of Jesus had become the emblem of Catholic France.

THE RESTORATION GETS ITS VISIONARY

What if the vow of Louis XVI were a hoax? What then of this fine weave of saintly vision and national destiny? Outside of his family and his confessor, only a handful of individuals had known of the king's pious gesture. How difficult would it have been to impose such a peculiar tale, through repetition and embellishment, on a population avid for mystery and drama?

Laure, an orphaned seventeen-year-old girl, harbored no such doubts in 1814. Madame Denys was a mattress maker in the Faubourg Saint-Germain. Inspired by both charity and self-interest, Madame Denys had adopted Laure. Laure would have a home and nourishment; she would also learn the meaning of a day's work, stuffing and stitching mattresses beside Madame Denys and other women.

Laure's imagination reached well beyond the confines of Madame Denys's mattress shop. Laure was deeply impressed with the text of Louis XVI's vow and prayer to the Sacré-Coeur. Perhaps, in her youth, she had heard and grown to love the stories of a proud queen and a pious king beset by ideologues and scheming enemies. Perhaps she imagined that in their place she also would have made a grand gesture before God. Perhaps it was the story of how they had risen above their circumstances and triumphed through faith. Laure resolved to recite the text of the king's vow, prayerlike, every day.

Soon she knew it by heart. She felt her efforts seconded by the people of Poitiers when they consecrated their city. "Ah, if only all of France could know the same happiness!" she is reported to have exclaimed.[56]

In 1822, Laure joined an organization of pious lay Catholics, the confraternity of the Sacré-Coeur. Pierre Ronsin, a priest, was appointed to serve as her spiritual director. That Ronsin would accept responsibility for Laure's spiritual development suggests that she already showed considerable promise. Ronsin was 51 in 1822 and a seasoned veteran of the religious wars of the French Revolution. As a young man, Ronsin's intention had been to join the Trappists, a contemplative order, when the challenges of the Revolution called him to a more active religious life. He was ordained in July of 1801 and joined the crypto-Jesuit Pères de la Foi shortly thereafter. He worked to propagate the devotion to the Sacré-Coeur and he supervised the spiritual development of women religious in Belley and Roanne.[57] He was credited with reforming Monsignor Leblanc de Beaulieu, the constitutional bishop of Soissons, and helping him to rid himself of a few troubling traces of Jansenism, a transformation facilitated by the fact that the Concordat had given constitutional clergy little choice if they wished to remain in religious life in France.

At the Restoration, Ronsin joined the reconstituted Jesuit order, one of two in the first class of militant "new" Jesuits of the post-Revolution. (The other was Loriquet, whose *Salut de France* pamphlet had made such an impression and brought about the consecration of Poitiers.) Ronsin became the provincial (chief executive) of the Jesuits in France and played a leading role in organizing the re-Christianization of post-revolutionary France. He was commonly associated with the Chevaliers de la Foi, a group of men from distinguished noble families such as Mathieu de Montmorency and Alexis de Noailles.[58] And he was the guiding light of the *Congrégation,* an organization created in 1801 as a Catholic charities initiative but suppressed by Napoleon in 1809 because he suspected that it served as a front for a nationwide royalist network. Ronsin revived the Congregation at the first opportunity, that is, with the Restoration in 1814. The Congregation met regularly in the third-floor chapel of the *Missions étrangères* on the rue du Bac. There, the oak boiserie and the distinguished family names, along with the urgent task of post-revolutionary moral reconstruction, imparted a sense of purpose to the meetings of the Congregation and a tone of earnest engagement. So did Ronsin's repeated calls for Catholic men to brave public scorn and use their influence by appearing publicly and proudly as Catholic men.[59] Pierre Ronsin was the hub of the Catholic revival in Restoration France. If Ronsin took on the orphan Laure as his spiritual ward, it was because she was being groomed for greatness.

Laure entered the order of the sisters of Notre-Dame, moving to their convent at the Hôtel des Oiseaux, on the Left Bank, early in 1823.[60] She was twenty-six years old. Laure took the name of Marie de Jésus. Like Marguerite-Marie Alacoque at Paray-le-Monial, Anne-Madeleine Rémuzat at Marseille, and Claude-Marie de Bruc at Nantes, Laure was to become the privileged interlocutor of the Sacred Heart for her generation and her time. Like the Virgin Mary, these women were the privileged vessels of a kind of revealed truth, giving the lie to the notion that God no longer spoke to his people. The Sacré-Coeur would speak to Laure and Laure would speak to France.

Indeed, the Sacré-Coeur had spoken to Laure even before she had entered the convent and become Marie de Jésus. In August of 1822, Laure heard a voice as she prayed silently. Once apprised of the content of Laure's visions, Ronsin told Laure that the words were not for her alone. They completed, Ronsin noted, the revelations made to Marguerite-Marie Alacoque, a fact that both confirmed the status of the revelations of Marguerite-Marie and confirmed Laure's status as Marguerite-Marie's worthy successor. Not only was Laure the latest privileged interlocutor in a distinguished lineage of Sacred Heart visionaries; her visions would authenticate the vow of Louis XVI. According to Ronsin, "The divine Savior added that he ardently desired that this vow be carried out, that is, that the King consecrate his family and his realm to the Sacré-Coeur, just as Louis XIII had once done to the Blessed Virgin."[61] Beyond that, the Sacré-Coeur demanded a feast day to be celebrated each year the week after the feast of Corpus Christi and that a chapel or altar be built in honor of the Sacré-Coeur.

These requests amounted to a recapitulation of the original demands articulated via Marguerite-Marie Alacoque—a royal consecration, an edifice, an annual commemoration. None of this was terribly new, and in a sense Laure's story may be treated as one might treat Chateaubriand's *Memoirs,* that is, as part of the ongoing development of discourses on the ungodly Revolution and the worthiness of the restored Bourbon dynasty. These stories appealed to anxious supporters of the monarchy who wanted and needed to be told that the monarchy was not just one form of rule among others but a transcendent form ordained by God. Laure's visions blended with the pursuit of a *re*-sacralized monarchy.

But there were some new twists. Laure went beyond recapitulation of time-tested messages. Laure not only heard voices; she had visions. In one vision Aloysius Gonzaga, Jesuit patriarch, appeared alongside the Sacré-Coeur. In another, the Sacré-Coeur used a colloquial French expression ("Eh quoi!") to emphasize his surprise and dismay that while revolutionary insults to royalty had been publicly repaired, insults to religion had not.[62] The Sacré-Coeur awaited atonement and the colloquial expression conveyed a sense of wounded pride and growing impatience.

Colloquial expressions, special appearances on the part of distinguished Jesuit personages, a keen sense of moral outrage, an urgent sense of the need for action: these features made Laure's visions more than a mere recapitulation. The implied endorsement of Aloysius Gonzaga had a particularly powerful effect on Laure's spiritual director, Pierre Ronsin. Ronsin had been at the forefront of efforts to revive the Jesuit order in France, along with Pierre-Joseph Picot de Clorivière and Jean Nicolas Loriquet. Of the three, Ronsin was surely the best connected with political and social elites in Restoration France, notably through the Congregation. Gonzaga's association with Laure's visions moved Ronsin to act.

Indeed, the Sacré-Coeur directly addressed Ronsin through one of Laure's visions. As if to anticipate objections that the king might not be receptive to overtures in favor of a consecration, the Sacré-Coeur remarked, "Ah! I hold all hearts in my hand and that of the king is disposed to do whatever one asks for the glory of my name. . . . Let [Ronsin] speak and he will see. I prepare all things; France will be consecrated to my divine Heart, and all the earth will see the blessings I rain upon her. Faith and Religion will flourish in France by means of the devotion to my divine Heart."[63] Ronsin was assured of success. Indeed, he was assured of playing a key role mediating the spiritual regeneration of France.

Did Ronsin act? In the absence of evidence that Ronsin did, the Jesuit historian Auguste Hamon states that "apparently he did not." He offers the odd explanation that the bishop of Autun instead called for the renewal of an initiative, dating from 1715, to bring about the canonization of Marguerite-Marie Alacoque.[64] (Autun is the seat of the diocese that includes Paray-le-Monial, the site of Marguerite-Marie's Visitationist convent.)

Perhaps Hamon's point was that clerical efforts were concentrated elsewhere, but this is hardly adequate as support for the contention that Ronsin did not act on Laure's visions. In fact, the revival of Marguerite-Marie's case for canonization fits well with other provincial initiatives, like those of Poitiers and Montauban, aimed at keeping the Sacré-Coeur in the foreground of Restoration political culture. If anything, the Autun initiative on behalf of the canonization of Marguerite-Marie Alacoque supported Laure and Ronsin.

Moreover, Ronsin believed in Laure and in her visions. Neither Hamon nor any other of the religiously engaged chroniclers of the devotion cast doubt on his sincerity or his belief in Laure's sincerity.[65] If there was weakness, it almost surely would not have been on the part of Ronsin, this veteran of the Revolution's wars of religion. A former Père de la Foi, an order that contributed more than its share of victims to the Terror, would not shrink from finding a way to get a message to the king. Given his courage and his religious convictions, it is inconceivable that a man such as Ronsin would not act. He believed that Laure heard the word of God. He knew that Laure's visions had explicitly commanded Ronsin to approach the king. Ronsin's internalized sense of duty must have proven irresistible.

Did the message get through? Louis XVIII surely heard of Laure's visions in some form or another.[66] According to Victor Alet, some of the women of the Bourbon family knew of Marie de Jésus (Laure) and had visited her "more than once."[67] In the doubtful case that Ronsin suffered from lack of access to the king, they did not. The weak link, if one wishes to call it that, was the king himself. Louis was pious, but he was not given to mystical flights of fantasy about divine imperatives and the fate of Christian monarchy. And he was a much better politician than he is sometimes given credit for.[68] A king who self-consciously modeled his constitution after the institutions and practices of the English constitution knew that France's future did not depend on incriminations and reparations for the sacrilegious offenses of the Revolution. Yet, he was under growing pressure from the royalist Right in the early 1820s during a period sometimes called the Second White Terror, following the assassination of the Bourbon duc de Berry.[69] This pressure was mostly symbolic, taking the form of parallel initiatives such as the consecration of the diocese of Paris to the Sacré-Coeur by Archbishop de Quelen in 1822, the Montauban diocesan commission of Ingres's vow, and the reopening of the canonization dossier of Marguerite-Marie Alacoque.[70]

Indeed, Laure's visions could be seen as part of wider cultural manifestations of Catholic anxiety about a return to revolutionary violence, anxieties prompted by the assassination and expressed and contained within the devotion to the Sacred Heart. But Louis also knew better than to alarm and mobilize liberal opposition by appearing to be beholden to an ultraroyalist Right for whom reconciliation with liberals and former revolutionaries was tantamount to betrayal.

Then what did Louis do? In 1823—the same year that the Sacré-Coeur, through Laure's visions, had insisted upon a royal consecration, a commemoration, and an altar—the king made a discreet gesture. Louis and his brother, the future Charles X, along with other members of the royal family, made donations to hasten the completion of Sophie Barat's convent of the Sacré-Coeur at the Hôtel Biron, near what is now the Eiffel Tower. The transformation of this grand *hôtel particulier* into a convent for a women's religious order, begun in 1820, was nearly complete. The most important single improvement was the addition of a convent chapel, the chapel of the Sacré-Coeur. There, sheltered from the public eye by high convent walls, Louis XVIII, King of France and Navarre, made a singular gift. He donated the altar.[71]

ROME, WAR, AND THE ONSET
OF THE TERRIBLE YEAR

The Revolution of 1789 is the original sin of public life.

FRANÇOIS PIE,
Bishop of Poitiers, 1850

The Revolution howls at the gates of Saint Peter.

A FRENCH VOLUNTEER,
fighting in defense of Rome and the pope, 1861

You know nothing at all; you do not understand that it is expedient
for you that one man should die for the people, and that the
whole nation should not perish.

John 11 :49—50

THERE ARE MOMENTS IN THE life of a nation where the hand of God is clearly visible—or so it seems. The years 1870 and 1871 provided many such moments, notably when France went to war against Germany and suffered defeat, invasion, and occupation on a scale surpassed only in 1940. In fact, the period spanning the declaration of war in July 1870 through the repression of the Commune in May 1871 was of such unsurpassed horror that it was immediately identified as the *année terrible,* the Terrible Year.

The *année terrible* initiated a period of intense reflection on France, its past, and its spiritual and moral well-being. Even secular observers grasped at causes they felt must be commensurate with the dimensions of the tragedy.

Hippolyte Taine pointed to a systemic failure of public values.[1] Ernst Renan would cite the failures of education.[2] In a commentary written for the *Revue des Deux Mondes,* Émile Montégut declared flatly that "the bankruptcy of the French Revolution is henceforth a given, irrevocable."[3] Georges Sand was shocked to note that even republican politicians were prepared to conclude that defeat had metaphysical origins. "We are a corrupt nation," she heard one say.[4] Massive collapse must have profound moral causes.

Catholic reflections in the *année terrible* tended to take place within the boundaries of the devotion to the Sacré-Coeur, and by 1870 France and the Sacré-Coeur already had a long history. Catholic clergy and the Catholic episcopate interpreted these cataclysmic events in supernatural terms, as evidence of divine judgment and condemnation of a nation fallen from grace. They invited the French to engage in self-critical reflection, to imagine a different past, a different national story, a different history, one that would have led to a different outcome for France in the crisis of 1870. This same story would be invoked as a prescriptive guide for national reconstruction after 1870.

THE WAR OF 1870–71

The Terrible Year started on a much different register. The Franco-Prussian War had begun in the summer of 1870 with little reflection, much patriotic fervor, and bold predictions of triumph. In Paris, young men sure of easy victory ran through the streets crowing "To Berlin!" Alistair Horne tells us that a parrot had been taught to take up the cry and was paraded about the city for the amusement of passersby.[5] Catholic attitudes differed little initially, sharing in the enthusiasm for war and savoring the promise of victory. Just days after France slipped into war, an item in the weekly diocesan bulletin of Nantes repeated the story of a mother of Sparta who had prepared her son to die heroically, if need be: "Return alive with your shield or dead upon it." The story concluded with an exclamation—"Voilà la nation française!"—a commentary whose irony and prescience were surely unintentional.[6]

Bold confidence and visions of glory vanished with the early and rapid French defeats. By 10 August, German forces surrounded Strasbourg. A week later, the army of General Bazaine was trapped within the fortress at Metz. The defeats at Sedan in early September, the capture of Louis-Napoleon, the proclamation of the Republic on 4 September punctuated the opening weeks of the war and brought the downfall of the regime that had begun it.[7] And this was only a beginning to the *année terrible,* as civil war followed military defeat, creating the impression that France was hurtling unstoppably toward disaster and collapse.

DEFEAT AS A DOMESTIC DRAMA

If the Catholic hierarchy was not alone in suspecting that military defeat for France had moral origins, it was among the first to articulate this view. On 4 September, Monsignor Fournier, bishop of Nantes, delivered a sermon before a packed crowd in the massive Gothic cathedral of Saint-Pierre in Nantes. Fournier's sermon moralized French defeat ("France has been dealt a blow; this can only be because we are guilty") and theologized it ("Sin has attracted the terrible blows of divine justice").[8] Defeat, Fournier told his listeners, was a punishment from God; it was the consequence of moral failure on a national scale.

Two weeks later, Fournier extended his analysis in an episcopal statement that he then had distributed throughout the Nantes region. He repeated his assertions that defeat had to do with failures that were moral in nature rather than military or strategic. He identified the historical origins of France's special relationship with God: the French were a "chosen people"; their special status dated from the baptism of the Frankish king Clovis in 496, which sealed a covenant between God and his people. French prosperity and greatness must be seen as built upon this relationship; neglect of that relationship just as surely brought decay, crisis, and defeat.[9]

Fournier drove home his argument by casting France and God in leading roles within a domestic drama: France was a woman; God was her man. Libertine France had tested the patience of her faithful but long-suffering husband through her relentless pursuit of drink and pleasure. Her drink was from "the impure cups of impiety" and her pleasure was "sensuous self-indulgence": together they explained the righteous indignation of God. Fournier evoked the image of France as a disheveled woman stumbling from drink, a woman "sacrilegiously drunk" and heedless of the consequences. Faced with such a shameful spectacle, a scene he could endure no longer, God became enraged and "raised himself up." God became the picture of righteous anger, a husband who punished his wife in order "to avenge his outraged love."[10]

In short, the current crisis was an episode in domestic politics. And not only in the household sense. The current crisis was about domestic politics because its origins could be found in the political failures of France, past and present. Fournier explicitly linked the present crisis with an ongoing Catholic critique of the French Revolution, an event itself understood as divine punishment. "Eighty years ago," Fournier declared, "God chastised France in a terrible fashion." Defeat was the consequence of decades of decline that began with the French Revolution. The domestic crisis that threw the divine husband into a fit of rage against his spouse was the consequence of an unresolved domestic crisis left over from the French Revolution. Apostasy was a kind of infidelity, an agnosticism of the conjugal bond.

It was as if military defeat had validated, once and for all, the Catholic critique of the French Revolution as a rupture, the moment of fatal departure from France's Christian destiny. Historic and collective moral failures provided Fournier with an explanation for defeat, they also hinted at a way beyond the numbing apathy and sense of powerlessness that defeat engendered. The Revolution was at the origin of France's troubles and, as in 1789, salvation would come through the Sacré-Coeur. Fournier called upon the people of the diocese of Nantes to join him in a consecration of their diocese to the Sacred Heart of Jesus. On the second Sunday of October, driven by the fears and anxieties of war and the promise of security and salvation in the Sacred Heart, the people of the diocese of Nantes joined Monsignor Fournier in the consecration of their diocese to the Sacred Heart of Jesus.[11] That week confessions and communions nearly exceeded those of Easter time.

CONSECRATIONS TO THE SACRÉ-COEUR

Fournier's creative genius was to recast military defeat as a historic opportunity. Defeat was not an inescapable conclusion but a moment in a salvation story leading to national redemption. Fournier's story set forth a France chastened by defeat but fortified by faith. He shaped the effort of moral renewal and defined the decisive moment in his salvation tale in terms of an appeal to the Sacred Heart of Jesus.

Fournier's successful blend of contrition and hope attracted attention from well beyond the limits of Nantes.[12] He demonstrated forcefully the enduring power of the popular religious idea that public crises had providential origins and could be resolved through a public invocation of the Sacré-

Coeur. In the weeks to come, news of Fournier's creative leadership spread throughout the west of France. Fournier was widely emulated; diocese after diocese carried out ceremonial consecrations to the Sacré-Coeur. Among the first to follow Nantes was the diocese of Luçon, coterminous with the department of the Vendée, whose consecration to the Sacré-Coeur was announced in a letter-circular dated 15 October.[13] The bishop of Luçon quoted the Psalms—"Vous êtes juste Seigneur, et votre jugement est plein d'équité" —and later reproached his Vendéen flock with the remark that the present generation had "degenerated" from "the strong and austere virtues of our fathers."[14] In Luçon as in Nantes, the Revolution was implicated in the present crisis and the Sacré-Coeur stood in opposition to it, just as it had eighty years before.

The diocese of Séez followed the examples of Nantes and Luçon, as did the diocese of Angers, with a conditional vow to the Sacré-Coeur. In the weeks and months to come, more than a dozen dioceses across France were consecrated or reconsecrated to the Sacré-Coeur (fig. 24), and there would be more still throughout the decade of the 1870s. Diocesan consecrations to the Sacré-Coeur were thus one of the outstanding features of official Catholic practice of the Terrible Year and one of the most powerful manifestations of a crisis of national self-doubt. Many of these consecrations were made during the darkest moments of the winter of 1870–71 when the dominant mood was one of anxiety. There was also a movement to counter the drift toward despair with a renewal of faith, but even there the overarching theme was not one of personal renewal but national renewal: to use anxieties about the present crisis to give weight to critical inquiries into the nation's past. Put differently, the sacred rhetoric of the Terrible Year sought to frame political debates yet to come.

The Sacred Heart reappeared in the 1870 crisis as an emblem of opposition to the Revolution; it also reappeared as a talisman. The consecrations of the Terrible Year took the form of appeals to the Sacré-Coeur for mercy and protection. Typically, these appeals took the form of conditional vows —contracts with God—to build a church to the Sacred Heart if the diocese were spared invasion or occupation by German troops. Here, too, Fournier led the way with his vow to build a church in honor of the Sacré-Coeur if his diocese were spared.[15] Bishop Freppel in the diocese of Angers, adjacent to Nantes, made a solemn engagement to consecrate his diocese to the Sacré-Coeur if his diocese were protected from "the plague"—meaning the

DIOCÈSE DE LAVAL.

Souvenir de la grande fête religieuse du 25 Juin 1865.

CONSÉCRATION DU DIOCÈSE
AU
SACRÉ CŒUR DE JÉSUS.

Figure 24. Souvenir of the 1865 consecration of the diocese of Laval to the Sacré-Coeur. Private collection.

The 1864 beatification of Marguerite-Marie Alacoque by Pope Pius IX was the occasion for a renewal of diocesan consecrations as proxies for the national consecration demanded in Marguerite-Marie's visions. The consecration of the diocese of Marseille during the plague of 1720 was the first such consecration. Another flurry of consecrations occurred after the Revolution, under the Restoration Monarchy. The diocese of Laval was the first diocese to carry out a consecration after the beatification of Marguerite-Marie in 1865; the consecrations would accelerate during the national disaster of 1870–71.

invasion, but also a reference to Marseille. When the terms of the vow were met later in the year, Freppel consecrated his diocese and then began planning for a commemorative church.

Freppel's consecration and vow, like the others of the Terrible Year, built upon the assertion that the invading army was a scourge sent from God; they also built upon the reputation of the Sacré-Coeur as a safeguard. Here, they were drawing upon the example of the Marseille of Belsunce, where the faithful had protected themselves with Sacré-Coeur emblems on their clothing and outside their homes and where the bishop had propitiated a fearsome God with penitential acts, a procession, and a consecration to the Sacré-Coeur. As Freppel delighted in observing, the German invasion "stopped at the edge of our diocese." [16] If the German army was sent as a scourge to the wicked, the emblem of the Sacred Heart identified God's own; the German armies advanced unimpeded, then veered away at the threshold of the west of France. It was like the Angel of Death passing over the houses of the Hebrews in the Egyptian captivity.

A PARISIAN VOW TO THE SACRÉ-COEUR

In the dizzying swirl of military defeat, fears of occupation, panicked refugees, plaintive consecrations, and bold oratory, Alexandre Legentil, a pious Parisian, resolved to make a gesture of his own. Legentil had recently resettled his family from Paris to Poitiers to wait out the war in prayer and reflection. During a visit to his confessor, Father Gustave Argand, the Jesuit rector at the local Catholic secondary school, Legentil declared his plan for a Parisian vow to the Sacré-Coeur. He turned to Argand's prie-dieu, dropped to his knees, composed his thoughts, and promised to devote himself to a work of reparation: a church dedicated to the Sacred Heart of Jesus to be built in Paris if the city were spared occupation. [17]

Legentil had left Paris with his family as soon as he realized that French defeats on the frontier left an unobstructed path to the capital. He went first to a family property at Saint-Ouen, just outside the capital, then on to Caen, in Normandy, before settling on Poitiers as his place of refuge until the return of peace. Legentil shared the common opinion that French defeat inescapably possessed a spiritual dimension and revealed a collective moral failure. "*Peccavimus,*" he wrote in his journal. "We have sinned." [18]

In Poitiers, Legentil spent much of his time in prayer and in correspondence with friends—different ways of contemplating the enormity of the disaster. He surely was aware of the growing enthusiasm around him, in Nantes, Angers, and elsewhere, for consecrations in the face of the national tragedy. Early in December, shortly before he made his vow, he had heard about a vow made in the city of Lyon. There, a group of pious Christian women approached the archbishop of Lyon, Monsignor de Genouilhac, about making a vow to replace the aging chapel of Notre-Dame de Fourvière with a new edifice if the city and diocese of Lyon were spared invasion.[19] Archbishop Genouilhac took up their cause, and Lyon joined the ranks of dioceses making conditional contracts with God in the midst of the national crisis.

Legentil, then, was in good company. He had staked out a place for Paris amid the general enthusiasm for consecrations during the anxious months of the winter of 1870–71. He also suggested a conditional vow, promising a church to the Sacré-Coeur. Thus, Legentil's idea was in keeping with the sentiment that inspired the people of Lyon, and both were fully in keeping with the popular religious idea that, just as in Marseille, public crises had providential origins and could be countered through a public invocation of the Sacré-Coeur.

His vow differed from these other vows, however, in that Legentil's vow remained without an episcopal sponsor, whereas these other diocesan vows had enjoyed the support of their respective bishops. But this was an inevitable consequence of the fact that Legentil, like the rest of provincial France, was cut off from Paris and its bishop by the presence of the German army. This could not change until hostilities ended and communication with Paris was reestablished. Until then, Legentil could only seek the next-best thing, namely, the endorsement of the local bishop in Poitiers, François Désiré Edouard Pie (fig. 25).

Fate had placed Legentil and his pious idea in the custody of one of the outstanding and most combative prelates of the age. Pie was born into modest circumstances near Chartres in 1815. His life is a textbook case of how an ambitious young man, without title or private wealth, could make a career for himself within the Catholic hierarchy. This was an innovation of the post-revolutionary period when the church hierarchy was no longer the near-preserve of the nobility—not that Pie ever showed any gratitude toward the Revolution! By the 1860s, Pie had made a reputation for himself as

Figure 25.
François Désiré
Edouard Pie,
bishop of Poitiers
from 1849 to
1880. Louis
Baunard, *Histoire
du cardinal Pie,
évêque de Poitiers*
(Poitiers, 1886).

François Pie was
one of the great
orators of the
episcopate of
nineteenth-
century France.
Throughout his
long life, he was
a close adviser to
the comte de
Chambord, the
Bourbon pre-
tender, and an
ardent supporter
of the cause of
France and the
Sacré-Coeur.

one of the sharpest critics of the Revolution and its heritage. He was also an excellent administrator and pastor. Posted to Poitiers as bishop in 1849, by the end of his career he was known as the "second Hilaire"—Hilaire being the outstanding bishop of Poitiers in Gallo-Roman times.[20]

A short, stout man with energy to spare, Pie was a relentless defender of the idea of Catholic France, that is, the idea that there was something inherently Catholic about France and Frenchness. "France will no longer be France the day she is no longer a Christian nation," was how he liked to phrase it. Pie likewise deeply believed in the historical necessity of Christian monarchy; he was a close adviser to Henri, the comte de Chambord and

Bourbon pretender to the throne, and consulted with him regularly.[21] Pie was also a tireless advocate of French military protection for the pope and the pope's temporal authority. When the war broke out, Pie resisted pressure to consecrate his diocese to the Sacré-Coeur, following the example of Nantes and Luçon. Instead, he pointed out that Poitiers had already been consecrated to the Sacré-Coeur in 1815. But he did speak openly about French culpability and national reparation as a condition for renewal. "Make the Sacré-Coeur reign over France" was the idea that summed up and implied all the others.[22]

When Legentil consulted with Monsignor Pie, he found himself in the presence of a powerful personality and a man of conviction. Self-made man that he was, Pie had enormous confidence in himself and his view of the world. Legentil spoke of a Parisian monument to the Sacré-Coeur and Pie approved the idea, as far as it went. But Pie's vision was grander still. Pie expressed the opinion that not only Paris but all of France should be implicated in the vow to the Sacré Coeur because all of France needed to make amends. For Pie the lay tradition of turning to the Sacré-Coeur in moments of public crisis—plague and war—was inadequate to the grander historical vision of an apostate France, chastised by an angry and vengeful God.

As Pie saw it, and as the other partisans of the Sacré-Coeur would eventually see it, the project of the vow to the Sacré-Coeur had to be fitted into a historical narrative in which the Revolution figured as historical rupture, neatly symbolized by the execution of the king, which brought on national decline and a merited chastisement.[23] The French, as a regicide people, had only recapitulated their historical errors when, in the 1860s, they had failed to defend the pope and his temporal authority—lapses Pie had publicly described as a form of deicide.[24] Pie sought to define a perspective on France and its past in which the crushing defeat of 1870–71 brought France full face with the consequences of turning away from the nation's monarchical institutions, its Christian identity, and its historical role as defender of the Church.[25] Pie urged Legentil to recast his initiative in national terms—to go to the root causes of France's predicament.

Legentil's vow thus outgrew the context of diocesan vows. These consecrations, although they mentioned national crimes, sins, and errors, were limited in scope to their dioceses of origin. One by one these dioceses had sought to be spared invasion and occupation, to opt out of divine chastisement, to serve as Lot in attempting to spare their respective Sodoms. Legentil's vow had to be different in part because the situation of Paris was different. There could be no question of shielding Paris from the rigors of war. German troops already encircled Paris by the time Legentil formulated his vow; they laid siege to the city and sought to starve it into submission. Moreover, Paris is rarely simply Paris, and from the beginning Legentil was tempted to make his Parisian vow to speak for all of France, to become a *national* vow. With the encouragement of Pie and others, he would. In effect, Pie helped to link Legentil's monumental project with ongoing efforts to associate the Revolution with national decline. The proposed church to the Sacré-Coeur would take its place within a grand salvation story as the heroic turning point in the epic saga of French decadence and renewal.[26]

Pie's grand historical vision ultimately prevailed when, at a meeting between Pie, Legentil, and Dom Guéranger, Legentil announced his decision to go beyond a Parisian vow and pursue a fully national vow, centered on Paris.[27] Pie wisely remarked that such a matter must ultimately be reserved for the judgment of the archbishop of Paris. The best that Bishop Pie could do was to publicize Legentil's vow and print its text in his diocesan bulletin, *la Semaine liturgique,* which he did on 29 January 1871.[28] In the weeks and months after his prayerful resolution in Poitiers, Legentil's intentions would undergo some modification, especially as he took advice from clergy.[29] Until he could confer with the archbishop of Paris, the final terms of Legentil's compact with God would remain unfixed.

SONS OF GIANTS

While Fournier, Freppel, Legentil, Pie, and the rest of Catholic France brooded over France's fate, partisans of Italian unity seized the occasion to shape Italy's destiny. The presence of the papal domains across the center of the Italian peninsula meant that papal interests and the cause of Italian unity would inevitably collide. They collided in a spectacular way in September of 1870 when Italian troops attacked the city of Rome, capital of papal Italy. They forced a breach in defenses at the Porta Pia on 20 September and occupied the Eternal City on the same day. Rome, like France, had fallen.

Through the eyes of faith, such a pairing of events could only result from divine agency. If Rome had fallen, it was because France, eldest daughter of the Catholic Church, had neglected its historical responsibility to defend it. If nothing could halt the German advance, it was because God had abandoned his people just as they had abandoned his Church. Never was the hand of God so clearly visible as in the autumn of 1870.

France and Austria, the two great Catholic powers in Europe, had long assumed responsibility for the security of the pope and the earthly domains then believed necessary to his spiritual independence and authority. France, for example, maintained a garrison of troops in Rome for much of the nineteenth century; French diplomatic pressure and French troops had played a decisive role in bringing down the fledgling "Roman Republic" that had threatened papal authority in Rome in 1848. But that changed in the 1850s and 1860s. Under the revived imperial leadership of Napoleon III, the nephew of Napoleon Bonaparte, France gradually relinquished its traditional role as papal sentry. In fact, Napoleon III engaged in diplomatic horsetrading with Italian political leadership in the 1850s, in effect agreeing to "look the other way" in Italian affairs, allowing Italian unification to proceed at the expense of the pope in exchange for territorial compensation. Rome would become Italian; Nice and Savoy would become French.

When the outlines of the bargain became public, the French Catholic establishment was outraged. Some, including those who had once gushingly praised Napoleon III as "the new Charlemagne," now compared his indifference to the fate of the papacy to the pusillanimity of Pontius Pilate.[30] One bishop publicly rebuked Napoleon III with the remark, "Wash your hands, O Pilate!"[31]

In fact France had not abandoned the defense of the Church. Or, at least, as the resolve of official France faded, the anxiety of Catholic France increased. In the years leading up to the debacle of 1870, the attention of French Catholics was focused not upon the increasing power of Germany, but upon the increasingly precarious status of the pope.

As the drive to Italian unification resumed in the 1850s, and accelerated in the 1860s, an appeal went out from Rome for volunteers to join an independent papal military force. Catholics from around the world responded to the appeal—*French* Catholics responded in great numbers, encouraged by bishops who made the recruitment a priority. They heaped scorn on the Italian policy of Napoleon III, while they encouraged young men to fight the good fight, to join what some would call "the ninth crusade."[32] These volunteers for the pope's army were organized into a military force known as the Papal Zouaves. The Zouaves took their name and style of dress from the

Figure 26. Athanase de Charette in the uniform of the Papal Zouaves. Georges Cerbelaud-Salagnac, *Les Zouaves pontificaux* (Paris 1963). Photo by Garreau.

Probably more than any other figure, Colonel Charette embodied the masculine patriotic ideal of Catholic France. The nephew of the famous General de Charette, who had fought the Republic during the Vendée, this Charette led a new generation of Vendéens against the Revolution, this time in Italy. In his later years he served on Archbishop Guibert's Committee of the National Vow, the lay committee responsible for fundraising and oversight of the Sacré-Coeur de Montmartre.

soldiers of North Africa, famous for their loose-fitting outfits so well adapted to the Mediterranean climate—short vests, gray billowy pants, red scarf tied around the waist (fig. 26).[33] They were equipped by generous donors whose contributions to a new collection known as "Peter's Pence" bought uniforms, supplies, and transportation for the papal army and provided a significant war chest for the Vatican.[34]

The funding of the papal army and the encouragement of volunteers serves as an index of Catholic and clerical anxiety about the fate of the pope.

Thousands answered the call. Indeed, if someone had asked Josef Stalin's irreverent question ("How many divisions has the pope?") in the 1860s, the ironic and dismissive thrust of the query would have been missed. Young men rushed to enroll to prove their faith and their enthusiasm for serving the Church, to satisfy their youthful appetite for adventure, and to redeem Catholic France in the eyes of the pope. For many young men from the west of France there was another reason to join—to honor the memory of fathers, grandfathers, and uncles who had fought in defense of God and King in 1793. The revolt of the Vendée had long since become part of local identity in the French west. In the dioceses of Nantes, Luçon, Angers, and Poitiers, where men and women had taken up arms against the Revolution of 1789, counter-revolution was part of the dominant culture.[35] The clergy and episcopate appealed to that culture in order to promote recruitment for the papal army.[36] Service in defense of the pope was situated in local tradition. "The Revolution is on the move," wrote the bishop of Luçon.[37]

The recruitment of the sons of the Vendée showed that the Revolution could not be fixed in time. There had been no closure. The Revolution, or at least some version of it, was still being fought. Indeed, as one of the recruits to the papal army was to write, only the theater had changed. "Nowadays the forces of Hell are known by a name that incorporates them all: the Revolution. Italy is the battleground where the great armies of Christian civilization and barbarism meet."[38] Satan had been secularized in the Revolution. Satan *was* the Revolution, and the Revolution was marching on Rome.

Young men of the west of France affixed the Sacred Heart insignia to their chests just as their fathers, uncles, and grandfathers had done before them (fig. 27).[39] It had become a badge of honor as much as a sign of faith—a sacred obligation. They could do no less. In the same spirit of veneration of the past, the bishop of Nantes wrote a letter of introduction to the pope on behalf of two prize recruits, descendants of a man who had fought "for the cause of religion and legitimacy in our first revolution."[40] They were Athanase and Alain de Charette, great-nephews of François-Athanase de Charette, the Vendéen general. A papal adviser objected that the name "Charette" was potentially compromising because it was like a flag, synonymous with royalism. The pope, Pius IX, reportedly dismissed these misgivings with a grin and the remark that "If he's a good royalist, he'll defend my royalty. If he is like a flag, he'll rally others around him!"[41]

Figure 27. A generation remembers the "giants" of the Vendée. Detail of a Zouave uniform, with a Sacré-Coeur stitched to the vest, ca. 1870. Musée de Loigny-la-Bataille.

When young men in the west of France answered the call to arms to defend the pope and the Papal States, they did so explicitly in the counter-revolutionary traditions of the Vendée and the French West. With the Sacré-Coeur stitched to their uniforms, they became the embodiment of a Christian patriotism and testified to their belief in an ongoing struggle against the Revolution.

With Charette and lesser veteran names under uniform, it was easier than ever to see the defense of Rome as an extension of a familiar struggle. In letters home, their defense of Rome highlighted official French indifference to the Pope's predicament, itself evidence of French decline since the Revolution. In 1866, on the anniversary of the execution of Louis XVI, Henri le Chauff de Kerguenec mourned the passing of a certain idea of France when he wrote to his parents, "Poor France, how could I not think of you, especially on this day of 21 January? For seventy-three years now you have done penance for the assassination of the martyr-king, locked up in the chains of the Revolution. . . ."[42]

After a victory of the papal army at Mentana in 1867, Henri, the Bourbon pretender-in-exile, wrote a letter of congratulations to the Zouave Athanase de Charette. "The Revolution," he wrote, "has been obliged to retreat for the first time in a very long time."[43] For those who could see the defense of the

Figure 28. Beneath the walls of Rome, ca. 1870. Bibliothèque Nationale, Paris.

The Zouaves defended the Papal States throughout the 1860s. In September of 1870, they defended the walls of Rome itself.

Pope as part of an ongoing battle against the Revolution, the defense of Rome was a familiar struggle, a continuation of the counter-revolution, transposed to another setting (fig. 28).

Except that the stakes were higher by the 1860s. Among virtually all Catholics of the nineteenth century, the pope's princely status—his temporal independence—was widely regarded as necessary to the theological independence of the Catholic Church. Many French Catholics, especially in the post-revolutionary era, saw the pope as necessary to social order itself. Louis de Bonald, like Joseph de Maistre, had seen the pope as the keystone to moral order.[44] In 1860, Joseph Guibert, then bishop of Tours, probably expressed the view of most of the French episcopate when, in a pastoral letter on the subject of "the new excesses of the Revolution," he chided European royalty for their indifference to the fate of the pope. Their authority, he warned, was inevitably tied to that of the Pope.[45] It was as if the Revolution, having brought down the Catholic Church's most important secular defender—the French monarchy—in 1789, had now turned its attention to the Church itself, the heart of Christendom and the cornerstone of the European order. On the face of things, the struggles of 1870 were about nations and self-determination, but the metaphysics of 1870 revealed a titanic struggle between good and evil.

Hence the consternation when the defense of Rome failed in September of 1870. With the fighting in Italy thus over, the Zouaves returned to find France in a state of disarray following its spectacular collapse in the face of German invasion. At the moment that the defense of Rome had had to be abandoned, the French government had been forced to abandon Paris under the pressure of the advancing Germans. To those accustomed to seeing the hand of Providence at work in the ordinary affairs of humanity, France's failure to honor its obligation to defend the Church explained God's abandonment of France. Such fateful juxtapositions confirmed for the Zouaves their conviction that the destinies of Rome and France were linked on earth and in heaven.[46] ("France, Rome—même combat.")

And that fight was not yet over, even though Paris was under siege. The national government had abandoned Paris and made the provincial capital of Tours a temporary home for the business of state. With Paris surrounded and large segments of the French army captured or in disarray, the government's main task was to raise more troops and continue the war from the provinces in the desperate hope of liberating Paris and France. If that failed, there would be nothing left but to negotiate a humiliating peace. Colonel Athanase de Charette encouraged a core group of Zouaves to remain together and to fight to defend France. One of the chaplains of the Zouaves, the abbé Daniel, made a *tournée* of diocesan parishes promoting new enlistments.[47] Charette and the Zouaves made their way to the temporary seat of government at Tours.

Was this then the hour of reconciliation, when the sons of the Vendée and the sons of the Republic would finally fight side-by-side animated by the same patriotic ideal? Not at all. Charette's call to arms claimed to extend that of 1793, by honoring the values of the Vendée and by asserting vigorously and by force of arms the superiority of those values over the bankrupt values blamed for the defeat of France. The ranks of the Zouaves had been enlarged thanks to the recruitment campaign of the abbé Daniel. Athanase de Charette, as commander of the Zouaves, offered their services to the French government-in-exile at Tours, the Government of National Defense.[48] Charette pleaded that the Zouaves be allowed to remain together, to fight alongside, but independent of, regular French units.

The Government of National Defense, busy organizing a republican people's war along the lines of 1792, was in no position to reject any serious offer of help, even at the risk of renewing the myths and legends of the Vendéen People's War of 1793. Charette's offer was accepted. He and his men would be allowed to fight and remain in their distinct units. They could even keep their distinctive Zouave uniforms with their Sacred Hearts. But they must change their name. The Papal Zouaves would march and fight under the name "the Volunteers of the West." [49]

THE SACRIFICE OF THE HERO

Charette's Volunteers were assigned to Louis d'Aurelle de Paladine's army of the Loire, where they would be under the command of General Gaston de Sonis. General de Sonis was an energetic young man promoted from the rank of colonel only weeks before. Sonis was delighted when he learned that Charette and his men had been assigned to his command. He knew Charette by reputation and admired him. The great-nephew of the Vendéen general required no introduction, especially to someone like Sonis who came out of a royalist and devoutly Catholic background. Charette's name served as the symbolic link between the Vendée's struggle against the Revolution and the defense of the pope against the Revolution sweeping through the Papal States. Sonis, for his part, had already been featured in the Catholic press as spokesman for patriotic Christian manhood. During the abbé Daniel's recruitment campaign, the weekly bulletin of the diocese of Nantes quoted extensively from a letter that Sonis had written to express a fervent wish that he, Sonis, be allowed to die a Christian soldier's death.[50] In the weeks to come he would nearly get his wish.

General de Sonis contacted Charette and his Volunteers shortly after they joined his forces. As Sonis's troops advanced on 30 November from Villepion toward Loigny to support General Alfred Chanzy, Sonis and Charette walked together in the company of the Zouave's chaplain, Father Doussot. Through conversation, Charette and Sonis discovered that they shared a vision of recovery from cataclysmic defeat by means of a re-Christianized France and a committed Christian military. The enemy was not Germany, but the enemy within. The enemy was the set of values that had become generalized since 1789, values that had led France to betray the pope, values that had undermined France, perhaps fatally, depriving its soldiers of the virtues—Christian patriotic virtues—which had sustained French greatness. Charette and Sonis, by contrast, upheld a vision of True France, built upon the values secular France had abandoned decades earlier. Sonis gestured toward his regimental colors, a white heraldic cross on a blue field. Charette chided him for not having something more religiously pronounced, then said "*Eh bien, mon général,* I have what you need."

Charette then described an embroidered banner that he had received while in Tours. The spiritual descendants of Marguerite-Marie Alacoque, the nuns of Visitationist convent at Paray-le-Monial, had embroidered it and presented it as a gift. The banner bore the image of the Sacred Heart and the invocation "Coeur sacré de Jésus, sauvez la France" (fig. 29).[51] Sonis accepted Charette's banner. However, an aide to Sonis, keenly aware of the irreligion of Sonis's men, advised him to avoid controversy and ridicule by unfurling the banner only when his men were engaged in combat. Sonis agreed. "Wait until the sound of the cannon," he advised, "when no one feels like laughing."[52]

The moment for a dramatic gesture was fast approaching. In November of 1870, the Army of the Loire, of which Sonis and his men were part, was able to make some progress against the German forces, notably at Coulmiers. Victory there had forced the Germans to evacuate Orléans. On 9 November, Aurelle de Paladine's forces marched into Orléans, raising the possibility of a military rescue of Paris to the north.[53] This seemed to set the stage for a breakout of troops trapped in the capital by the siege. If a southward breakout by troops in Paris could be coordinated with a northward push out of Orléans by Aurelle's Army of the Loire, these forces might meet and the siege would be broken. Indeed, on 1 December, Minister of the Interior Léon Gambetta received a message by balloon from Paris—troops had broken out of the capital and taken the village of Epinay.

Gambetta was desperate for good news. For weeks he had been writing and speaking to provincial audiences, with mixed results, about how a reinvigorated republican France would drive the troops of Imperial Germany from French soil. His restless imagination was primed for a dramatic repeat of Valmy where, in 1792, an inspired army of citizen soldiers had turned back a professional Prussian army intent on crushing revolutionary Paris.

Figure 29. The banner of the Sacred Heart at the battle of Loigny, 2 December 1870. *Messager du Sacré-Coeur* 40 (July 1881): 4.

The battle of Loigny was an epochal event in the saga of France and the Sacré-Coeur. As a moment, it had everything: desperation, cowardice, courage, brotherhood, heroism, violence, tragedy, death, redemption. When it was over, Catholic France had its heroes—Charette and Sonis—and proof that True France lived on.

Reading the news dispatch from Paris, he concluded that Parisian forces had reached Epinay-sur-Orge, some twelve miles south of Paris in the direction of Orléans. This would have represented a significant victory and a true breakthrough. In fact, the Epinay in question was Epinay-sur-Seine, a village just north of Paris near Saint-Denis.[54] The action in question was thus little more than an exploratory *sortie.* However, an overeager Gambetta released a pronouncement, ludicrous in retrospect, to the effect that the hour for the final republican sacrifice had at last arrived.[55]

Sonis, too, saw the need for sacrifice and prepared an assault that would reveal the redemptive power of the Sacred Heart. In fact, the situation was grave. The German retreat from Orléans had been tactical and orderly. Having regrouped, they were advancing on a broad front, with considerable success, and threatening to retake the city. On 1 December, Germans drove French forces commanded by Alfred Chanzy out of the village of Loigny. On 2 December, a First Friday, Sonis's troops reinforced Chanzy's men at Villepion, near Loigny, where they were to make a stand and halt the renewed German offensive. Then, inexplicably, Sonis decided to mount a charge in hopes of retaking Loigny.

Perhaps Sonis sensed that the war was irretrievably lost and that the time had come for a grand gesture. Or perhaps he believed that *without* a grand gesture France would be lost. But in ordering the fatal charge at Loigny, Sonis must have foreseen two possible outcomes, both with historical resonances. The first was a stunning victory, carried out by valiant men uncorrupted by the values of the age, fighting behind the bright banner of the Sacré-Coeur. Their triumph would contrast sharply with the moral and military bankruptcy of official France, secular France, Gambetta's France—widely condemned in Catholic circles for the decline and abrupt collapse of France in 1870. Victory behind the banner of the Sacré-Coeur would be like Constantine's vision of the heavenly command "In Hoc Signo Vinces." It would reveal France's celestial mandate. It would answer a divine command, nearly two centuries old, for France to remake itself in the name of the Sacré-Coeur. The alternative outcome for Sonis at Loigny, the one he actually got, was much different. It was not validation through heroic victory, but redemption through bloody sacrifice.

The light was already failing when Sonis ordered his troops to prepare for battle. They were to charge across open fields toward fortified German positions in Loigny. When Sonis's troops hesitated, he berated them. Then he turned to Charette and his Zouaves with the remark, "Those cowards refuse to march. . . . Forward! Let's show them what brave and Christian men are worth!"[56] The chosen standard-bearer, the Zouave Henri de Verthamon, unfurled the banner of the Sacred Heart. Then Sonis and Charette's Zouaves charged the enemy with the cry, "Vive la France! Vive Pie IX!"[57] The Zouave Verthamon, his profile silhouetted against the banner, was cut down almost immediately; another Zouave, Traversay, stopped to retrieve the banner. Traversay led the charge until he was hit and another Zouave took it up. The banner thus passed from hand to hand, in a deadly relay. At least five Zouaves fell bearing the banner through the swarm of bullets. Charette was wounded. Sonis fell from his horse, his leg shattered by German fire. A handful of soldiers survived the charge, overran the German positions, and entered the village of Loigny, but they were badly outnumbered and were forced to withdraw. Of the 300 who joined the charge, 198 fell before Loigny. As night came, snow fell on the dead and dying.

LOIGNY: A BANNER, A BATTLE, AN ALTAR

Sonis's conduct at Loigny has been criticized, sometimes sharply. Military historians, at least implicitly, have rejected the nominal justification for the charge at Loigny, namely, that it was necessary to assure an orderly retreat of the Army of the Loire. They have questioned Sonis's military judgment in undertaking a charge he must have known would lead to such a terrible loss of life. Stéphane Audoin-Rouzeau has described the charge at Loigny as "pointless heroism." Michael Howard wrote that the recently promoted Sonis behaved "like the colonel he was rather than the corps commander he should have been."[58]

But such remarks miss the real significance of Sonis's conduct at Loigny, which rapidly assumed legendary proportions as the story of the battle spread across Catholic France.[59] Eulogies and funeral oratory provided the first occasions to remark the mythic dimension of what had happened at Loigny.[60] In the months and years to come, Sonis and the battle at Loigny would serve as a point of departure for commentaries on France and its fate.[61] Sonis's body itself served as metaphor; indeed, for Bishop Pie of Poitiers, Sonis embodied France. It was only fitting then that Sonis, incarnation of the manly valor of True France, lost his leg in a war which would

leave France mutilated, cut off from its eastern provinces of Alsace and Lor-
raine.[62] The proximity of Loigny to Orléans and to Patay, site of one of Joan
of Arc's victories, invited comparisons. The parallels suggested an irresistible
national destiny, the possibility of regeneration, and the recovery of greatness.[63] Indeed, many commentators reinforced the association with Joan of
Arc by speaking of the Zouaves at Patay instead of Loigny.[64] Patay and
Loigny soon became confused and interchangeable in laudatory rhetoric—
some actually seem to have believed that the battles had taken place
on the same terrain. Others pointed out admiringly that the Zouaves at
Loigny were less like Joan at Patay, where she was victorious, than like Joan
at Rouen, where she was burned at the stake.[65] For them, the point was that
the Zouaves were martyrs. Like Joan at the stake, their immolation was a redemptive act, both spiritual and patriotic, which would bring an end to the
scourge of war. The blood of the innocent would redeem the guilty.[66] All
commentators seemed agreed that Loigny would mark a new beginning for
France and the Sacré-Coeur.

For Sonis himself, Loigny was an act of expiation, a Calvary for himself
and the Zouaves who fell with him. Their blood, "so pure and generous,"
like that of Christ would "purify and regenerate the world."[67] The abbé
Pergeline invoked heroic memory in his remarks at the funeral of three
Zouaves in Nantes. He emphasized the filiation of some Zouaves to the illustrious leaders of the Vendée revolt, the "giants" of '93. He described them
as "covered with the spittle of the Revolution and the blessings of Pope
Pius IX. Oh! How beautiful they are!"[68] Colonel Charette spoke at the in-
terment of the comte de Bouillé, volunteer and grandson of the Vendéen
leader Bonchamps, emphasizing the Sacred Heart as a symbol of love and
expiation and the volunteers as victims whose deaths had appeased the anger
of God and brought mercy upon France. Others would liken the sacrifice at
Loigny to the expiation offered by Louis XVI in 1793—acts necessary for a
new beginning for France.[69]

Remarks evoking unpleasant memories of 1789 and 1793 were less common, however, than commentaries on Loigny as a salutary sacrifice. For later
commentators like the abbé Fonssagrives, Loigny was Golgotha, "a bloody
altar on which the elite of the children of France had to be sacrificed."[70] Situated amid the diocesan consecrations to the Sacré-Coeur that had placed
war within a critique of the French past, Loigny fit neatly within the salvation

Figure 30. Alexandre Legentil (1821–89), lay founder of the basilica of the Sacré-Coeur. Archives historiques du diocèse de Paris.

Legentil, like many others, believed that the disasters of 1870–71 derived from the religious and moral failings of France and the French. Inspired by diocesan consecrations in Nantes and elsewhere, and by reports of Christian heroism at Loigny, Legentil vowed to build a church to the Sacré-Coeur in Paris.

narrative built around the Sacré-Coeur. The sacrifice of the pure—Sonis, Charette, the Zouaves—would redeem a wayward France. Loigny was ritual purification.

Loigny resonated deeply with other historical moments in the French Catholic past. The image of the descendants of the giants of the Vendée running into a hail of bullets with the Sacré-Coeur stitched to their uniforms and the Sacré-Coeur banner fluttering above their heads—little wonder that Loigny captured the imagination of Catholic France. The desire to build upon such a gesture was powerful and immediate. Alexandre Legentil's vow was likely inspired by the story of Loigny, as Jacques Benoist has speculated (fig. 30).[71] Indeed, after Loigny, a number of the Zouaves convalesced at Poitiers, in the very *collège* where Legentil had made his vow. A cascade of consecrations to the Sacré-Coeur, enriched by the Loigny tale, followed in the 1870s and later. The consecrations, the insignia of the Zouaves, the banner, and the battle at Loigny reveal the centrality of the Sacré-Coeur to the spirituality and public religious discourse of the *année terrible.* Thanks to the power of these events, so too would the spirituality of the *après-guerre.* Consecrations, a banner, a vow—together these pointed toward a fulfillment of the demands that the Sacré-Coeur had made of France in a vision to Marguerite-Marie Alacoque.[72] What was missing was a church.

THE TERRIBLE YEAR CONTINUES: CIVIL WAR IN PARIS

In March of 1871, just when it looked as though France's time of trouble was about to come to an end, civil violence erupted in the city of Paris. On 18 March, two French army officers died on Montmartre, victims of summary popular justice rendered by an exasperated Parisian crowd. The manner of their deaths—an autopsy revealed that General Thomas had been shot forty times—suggests the hot anger of their killers.[73] The deaths of generals Thomas and Lecomte marked the opening phase of a deadly French civil war commonly known as the Commune of Paris. These events, and those to follow, dramatically changed the prospects of Alexandre Legentil and his project to build a church in the city of Paris in honor of the Sacré-Coeur. Not that a church to the Sacré-Coeur would not have been built, but the outbreak of the Commune and its bloody, brutal, and tragic conclusion enhanced the sense for many that France was at the mercy of forces it could not comprehend, let alone hope to control.

Negotiations, not force of arms, had finally broken the German siege of Paris. Neither the republican ardor of Gambetta and the Government of National Defense, nor the Christian patriotism of Sonis, Charette, and the Zouaves could change the outcome of the war. An armistice was concluded in January of 1871. Among other things, the armistice allowed for the provisioning of starved and besieged Paris, just as the supply of lame horses, zoo animals, and rats was about to run out. Paris and the Parisians had made their share of sacrifices—burning furniture for heat, hocking personal items for cash, consuming pets and domesticated animals for food—yet the conclusion of the war did not come without misgivings.

Otto von Bismarck, chancellor of Kaiser Wilhelm's victorious and newly united Germany, knew that international public opinion was in his favor. In 1870, France was still considered Europe's great land power and, thanks to

France's expansionist revolution and the ambitions of Napoleon Bonaparte, there were few parts of Europe fully free of lingering resentments traceable to war and French occupation prior to 1815. Moreover, if not exactly the sole aggressor in the 1870 war, France's bellicose attitude had led to war. Finally, France had been defeated militarily. The price for peace would be high and Bismarck intended to extract every ounce of value from it.

Bismarck knew that an enforceable peace required a legitimate negotiating partner. However, the political leadership that had taken France to war, the Empire of Louis-Napoleon Bonaparte, had been one of the first casualties of defeat and was no longer in power. Bismarck insisted on elections for a National Assembly in France, as a prelude to a peace treaty. (Bismarck was also an unabashed monarchist and thought that imposing a representative form of government was the best way to keep France weak and divided for years to come.) The results of the elections, held in February 1871 while German troops still occupied French soil, were astonishing. Paris and many major cities, where republican political sentiments ran high, elected republican representatives. But rural and provincial voters represented the majority of voters, and they gave the Assembly a majority of avowed monarchists. France's future seemed to hold not only a humiliating peace, but also a restoration of monarchy. Republican France shuddered.

Monarchists were gleeful. The elections seemed to prove what many had long asserted: monarchy was not only divinely ordained but also consistent with the will of the majority. Why? Because True France—*la France profonde,* the provincial silent majority—believed in kings. Truth is, it didn't. But as long as republicans like Gambetta talked about resuming a war that provincial France viewed as hopeless, provincial voters would opt for monarchists who, just this once, knew a lost cause when they saw it. The "tactical monarchism" of many provincial voters would only be revealed in time. Meanwhile, republican speakers castigated rural voters and their National Assembly of bumpkins.

They also began to speak openly of a kind of secession, veiled as a federation of French municipalities, which would gain them a degree of independence from a national majority they perceived to be moving resolutely backward. Feelings against the monarchist National Assembly ran especially high among the people of Paris, whose experience of the war had been singular. Unlike Alexandre Legentil and other wealthy Parisians, most working Parisians had remained in the city for the duration of the war and siege. They had suffered severe hardship during the war and now it seemed that they would have little to show for it. Many such Parisians remained suspicious of political leadership, especially monarchist leadership. Many refused to admit the war had been unwinable, subscribing instead to a version of Gambetta's faith in the superiority of the republican form of government, the citizen-soldier, and the possibility of extended guerilla warfare against the foreign occupier.

Secession had been "on the agenda" during the 1860s in the American republic, until the defeat of the Confederacy took it off. Just the same, that didn't necessarily discredit the idea in the French context, especially when Parisians could more easily imagine the advantages than the disadvantages of a loose association with provincial France. Moreover, Paris was far more willing to experiment with some of the new and not-so-new ideas of the age: feminism, worker self-management, municipal autonomy, lay education, civil marriage and divorce, anti-clericalism. A loose federation of municipalities ("*communes*" in French) just might provide the right balance between autonomy and authority, between Paris and France. This was the vision of the Paris Commune.

Things went from bad to worse when the National Assembly, now seated ominously at Versailles, the traditional capital of monarchy, adopted measures perceived as antagonistic toward Paris and the Parisians. Salary payments to national guardsmen, who saw little combat during the war but who relied on the salary payments as a lifeline during the siege, were cut; rent payments, suspended during the war, were declared due and payable, including back rent. And then there was the matter of the Montmartre artillery.

During the siege of Paris, cannon batteries had been organized on Montmartre, a strategic high-ground in the Paris basin with a commanding view of the city and the surrounding plain. The demilitarization of Paris would have to be part of any lasting peace following the armistice. Moreover, Adolphe Thiers, who had negotiated the armistice and was the de facto head of state, knew that his authority in Paris would remain precarious as long as the city was so well armed.[74] The problem was that the removal of the cannon signaled the government's belief that the war against Germany was truly over. And for those who believed that triumph over the invader was still possible, this was tantamount to treason.

Thiers's orders to seize the cannon set up the confrontation that would mark the beginning of the civil war and Parisian insurrection known as the

Commune. Soldiers under the command of General Lecomte had been sent to Montmartre before sun-up on the morning of 18 March to take custody of the cannon in the name of public order in Paris. Partly for proprietary reasons (some of the cannon had been paid for through public donations), partly for what the seizure of the cannons signified (there would be no resumption of the war), a crowd gathered and resisted Lecomte and his soldiers. The crowd fraternized with the soldiers and when Lecomte attempted to reassert his authority, the crowd seized him. Later, a retired officer in civilian dress, General Thomas, was also seized. Before the day was out, Generals Lecomte and Thomas were dead, victims of multiple gunshot wounds but also of Thiers's reckless initiative.

Rather than confront those who killed the generals and risk another humiliating defeat, Thiers resolved to retreat from Paris to Versailles until he could return backed by overwhelming force. Such an enterprise would take weeks. Into the vacuum of authority stepped the proponents of an autonomous Paris: the Paris Commune was born. From the Hôtel de Ville, a proclamation went out to the rest of France. It condemned the failures of the Empire and the presumed intentions of the National Assembly, and it appealed to France's thirty-six thousand *other* communes—villages, towns, cities—to join Paris in a federation of autonomous communes. Sister communes did arise in Lyon and Marseille but failed to generate much enthusiasm and collapsed within days.

Then, in a series of moves apparently not calculated to reassure public opinion in the provinces, the Commune created a Committee of Public Safety (unheard of since the days of Robespierre), shut down several critical opposition newspapers, and finally seized the archbishop of Paris and several members of the clergy as hostages in negotiations with Thiers. A vast right-wing conspiracy could not have concocted a more effective public relations disaster for the Commune of Paris. It was as if the Commune, which had sought to stand as the champion of decentralization and municipal autonomy, had somehow managed to transform itself, in appearance if not in fact, into its opposite—the revival of Jacobin dictatorship of Paris over the rest of France.

Through the first weeks of May, Paris remained fixed in a standoff with the Thiers government and the National Assembly at Versailles. On 21 May, Versailles troops penetrated the walls surrounding Paris, entering at Boulogne, Auteuil, and Passy. The beginning of the end had begun. The western third of the city was barely defended and was rapidly placed under the control of Versailles troops. Then began the much more difficult task of re-taking Paris barricade by barricade, street by street. Fires broke out (as a consequence of the fighting) and fires were set (to impede the advance of the troops). As Paris burned, the Commune executed its hostages, including the archbishop of Paris and a number of Catholic clergy. Casualties on the side of the Commune were far greater. By 28 May, the end of Bloody Week, some twenty thousand insurgents had died in the resistance and the repression. Parts of the city were in ashes and ruins (the Hôtel de Ville, the Tuileries Palace), and unburied bodies could be seen everywhere. Nineteenth-century Europe's greatest civil massacre was over.

THE COMMUNE AND THE SACRÉ-COEUR

The Commune changed nothing of Legentil's plans for a church dedicated to the Sacré-Coeur. Indeed, the Commune aided Legentil in his initiative in some obvious but also surprising ways. The Commune, a civil war rivaled only by the Saint Bartholomew's Day massacres of Protestants and exceeded only by the repression of the Vendée, could only add to the sense of despair and helplessness. Ever since the first reverses of the war in the autumn of 1870, France had been on a headlong flight to destruction; the armistice in January of 1871 had seemed to bring it to a halt. But like the rock climber who slips, recovers, then slips and tumbles, the Commune revealed the armistice to have been only a pause in a cumulative national disaster. As France tumbled from military defeat, to occupation, to civil war, the constituency for Legentil's propitiatory gesture to the Sacré-Coeur grew too, along with a sense of urgency, of helplessness, of despair.

A less obvious link has to do with the practice and rhetoric of the Commune and the history of municipal politics in the city of Paris. Indeed, the last time that the municipality of Paris had pursued a radically independent political program had been in 1792, when Parisian municipal leadership ("the Commune") had collaborated with Parisian militants known as the *sans-culottes* to intimidate provincial moderates and to bring their Jacobin allies to power. The Commune of 1792 had also proven powerless or unwilling to halt prison massacres, including the murder of more than two hundred imprisoned Catholic clergy, in September of 1792. Among Parisian militants and on the French Left, the Commune of 1792 was generally remembered as a good thing, but outside those circles and in the provinces the Revolutionary Commune possessed a vexed image at best. In short, the vocabulary of municipal politics in France was by no means unproblematic. The Commune, by its very name and by the reckless use of Jacobin references (the Committee of Public Safety), lent substance to Catholic claims that it was, in fact, an old and familiar enemy—that the hated Revolution was back again after a limited engagement in the Papal States.

The Commune made an unintended but critical contribution to Legentil's initiative to adorn Paris with a votive church to the Sacré-Coeur. By executing the hostage Georges Darboy, archbishop of Paris, the Commune removed a significant obstacle to the construction of the Sacré-Coeur on a grand, monumental scale. Darboy's approval was vital to the success of Legentil's plan. As provincial bishops in Poitiers and Tours had told Legentil, they could support his pious project, but approval would have to come from Archbishop Darboy. Darboy had been aware of Legentil's project and was known to be cool to it, perhaps because the Sacré-Coeur was perceived to be "a Jesuit devotion" and Darboy was not fond of the Jesuits.[75] Legentil had gone to Paris in early March, after the siege had lifted but before the outbreak of the Commune, in order to make his case to Darboy. Ominously, he was unsuccessful in gaining an audience with the archbishop. When Legentil was finally able to speak to one of Darboy's lieutenants, he learned that the archbishop preferred to rebuild and restore war-damaged churches in the Parisian suburbs.[76] Had he survived the Commune, Darboy's postwar construction projects would have been driven by pastoral rather than monumental considerations. Darboy's death gave Legentil and his project a far more sympathetic patron.

BUILDING THE CHURCH
OF THE NATIONAL VOW

The cross of Constantine is out of fashion in the new Catholic crusade.
[The Sacred Heart] has taken its place.

CAMILLE PELLETAN, *1875*

For which of you, intending to build a tower, does not first sit down
and count the cost, whether he has enough to complete it?
Otherwise, when he has laid a foundation, and is not able to finish,
all who see it begin to mock him, saying, "This man began to build,
and was not able to finish."

Luke 14:28–30

What do these stones mean?

Joshua 4:22

"WHAT DO THESE STONES MEAN?" What indeed? The typical visitor to
Paris in the late twentieth century makes an obligatory visit to Montmartre
and the basilica of Sacré-Coeur. The exotic, white-domed church ranks just
after Notre-Dame, the Louvre, and the Arc de Triomphe among the top five
tourist destinations in the city of Paris. But its meaning to a typical tourist
is by no means clear. Thousands of visitors to the Sacré-Coeur enjoy the
view back toward Paris, but that view does not depend on the church. Most
tourists do venture to enter the church, but probably with little sense for
what they are seeing. They shuffle along the prescribed route, following the

wide side-aisles, glancing right and left through the somber interior. Once outside, the tourists figuratively check off the Sacré-Coeur and redescend to the city below.

High above, stony eyes follow their descent. Decorative busts with human faces, *corbeaux* ("crows") in the French architectural vocabulary, ring the large central dome. None of the characters depicted is likely to be recognized by the casual visitor or even the pilgrim; in fact, they are almost invisible from ground level. But they remain there night and day, gazing out like sentries: Alexandre Legentil, Hubert Rohault de Fleury, Joseph Guibert, and others too—the founding figures of the basilica of Sacré-Coeur. That Montmartre today boasts a monumental church owes much to the monumental vision and efforts of these founders, the "crows" of Montmartre.

When Joseph Hippolyte Guibert succeeded the martyred Georges Darboy as archbishop of Paris late in 1871, he found himself at the head of a diocese in disarray (fig. 31). The city of Paris was partly in ruins and its population was devastated. During the first siege, Parisians had foraged in the streets and parks for food and fuel, leaving the city significantly deforested. During the second siege of Paris, and during Bloody Week, Paris had been caught in the crossfire between Adolphe Thiers's troops and the defenders of the Commune. To take on the task of reconstruction required vision, but it also required personal courage—Guibert's three immediate predecessors had died violent deaths.

Guibert had courage. He also had vision. Guibert could see that although France's problems seemed fundamentally spiritual, they also had a spatial dimension. His predecessor, Archbishop Darboy, had had this insight too, at least in part. Darboy had wanted to restore the war-damaged churches of the Parisian suburbs, and this would probably have only been a prelude to a systematic reconsideration of the distribution of churches across the diocese.

Power always leaves its mark on the land, and the Parisian landscape had been vastly transformed during the 1850s and 1860s under the leadership of Louis-Napoleon and his prefect Baron Haussmann. Guibert understood that the spiritual landscape needed to change with the city but had not. Populations had been displaced; new neighborhoods had grown up on the outskirts of the capital and in the suburbs. Workers, not the middle class, led the way. And it was not a flight *from* the city—who would not prefer to live in Paris? It was more like a herding, a driving away. When old buildings were torn down, residents were forced to move, and as the new buildings had

Figure 31. Joseph Hippolyte Guibert, archbishop
of Paris from 1871 to 1886. Archives historiques du
diocèse de Paris.

Joseph Guibert believed that the campaign to re-
Christianize post-revolutionary France should
visibly transform the landscape. As bishop of Tours
in the 1850s and 1860s he used the project to rebuild
the basilica of Saint Martin as a metaphor for moral
and religious reconstruction. Similar considerations
guided his decision, as archbishop of Paris, to build
the Sacré-Coeur de Montmartre.

gone up, so had rents.[1] There would be no going back. Whole sections of
central Paris had been gentrified. Popular Paris had been displaced.

The popular revolt of the Commune had involved precisely those new
neighborhoods where the displaced had settled, but were underserved by the
diocese of Paris. As Guibert's biographer put it, the popular neighborhoods
had "escaped the vigilance of our archbishops." This had left a gap, a spiritual vacuum, and given free reign to "political adventurers." Impiety had
created an opening for "evil passions, the violent thirst for pleasures, and
hatred of the established order." Guibert moved quickly to redress the imbalance. In 1873, he presided over the consecration of a new parish church
at la Villette, an underserved *quartier*. The church was named for Saint

George, namesake of the executed archbishop Darboy, but also the saint famous for slaying the beast, symbol of evil and disorder.[2]

Darboy had been a "social" archbishop—sensitive to the pastoral mission of his church among the poor; this had made his execution by the populist Commune all the crueler. Guibert was also sensitive to these matters, but his tenure in Tours had revealed a penchant for major projects, *grandes oeuvres.* If asked to choose between the social gospel and monuments to the greater glory of God, he would probably attempt first to reconcile these demands, but there was little doubt where his inclinations led him. When he was working his way toward a decision on the restoration of Saint Martin's basilica at Tours, he had put off the project's lay proponents with a citation from the gospel according to Luke: "For which of you, intending to build a tower, sitteth not down first, and counteth the cost, whether he have sufficient to finish it?" Guibert's reticence forced the project's proponents to redouble their efforts, to deepen their resolve and, of course, to pursue additional resources. Guibert was a master of indirection. He led not by exhortation but by tactical retreat. He knew the arts of political seduction; he knew how to draw people in.

HONING THE VOW

Legentil's vow had gained some powerful supporters since December of 1870. Bishop Pie of Poitiers had published a draft of Legentil's vow in the diocesan bulletin of Poitiers. The Jesuit Henry Ramière, director of the *Messager du Sacré-Coeur de Jésus,* a devotional periodical, and founder of the *Apostolat de la prière,* an international prayer network, had helped to publicize the Legentil vow. Hubert Rohault de Fleury, Legentil's friend and an early collaborator on the vow, wrote about the vow to an acquaintance at Rome, Alexandre Jandel, director general of the Dominican order. Jandel took up the matter with the pope, who expressed some reservations about some of the language, especially as early drafts of the vow expressed some uncomplimentary opinions regarding Germany and its emperor. Once the offending portions were purged, the pope gave the vow his benediction during his meeting with Jandel on 25 February 1871.[3]

Guibert made no secret of his own reservations regarding the vow. It was not the idea of the vow that gave him pause, but its phrasing. The vow as drafted in Poitiers was a conditional vow, like most other vows of the Terrible Year. Legentil had promised to build a "sanctuary" in Paris, a sanctuary dedicated to the Sacré-Coeur, *if* God saved Paris and France and restored the pope's independence. When Legentil and Hubert Rohault de Fleury tried to persuade Guibert to endorse their cause, Guibert made it clear that he cared little for the idea of laying down conditions to God—to withhold a spiritual offering, a church, until God met certain stipulations.

Moreover, Guibert knew that it might be some time before these stipulations were met, and this could be troubling to those expecting a prompt response. How should such a delay be interpreted? What would it mean? Divine indifference to pious gestures? Hostility? Finally, Legentil and Rohault de Fleury relented and dropped the conditional phrasing in a meeting with Guibert toward the end of 1871. "Well enough! Let's give credit to the good God. We will change our vow. Instead of promising that we will fulfill our vow when our prayers are answered, we promise to fulfill it so that they will be answered."

As it turned out, Guibert was right to be wary. The rectification of the status of the pope and the Papal States, which the founders evidently believed would come shortly, was decades away. In fact, the phrase in the vow concerning papal deliverance was not deemed fulfilled until 1929, when the Lateran Accords regularized the status of the Vatican State within Italy.[4] By then, Legentil, Rohault de Fleury, Guibert, Pie—indeed, all those involved in formulating the vow—were dead.

With the wording of the vow sorted out, Legentil pressed Guibert to endorse the project. "Now will you support us?" Ever coy, Guibert responded somewhat ambiguously, "That's fine. I'll think about it. Complete your committee. There should be twelve, like the apostles. And come back and see me in a few days."[5]

Guibert's reservations about the vow had to do with matters of detail, such as the conditionality of the vow, not matters of substance. Guibert revealed his own conception of the purpose of the project in a letter he addressed to the members of the Legentil / Rohault de Fleury committee in January 1872.[6] Preoccupations with the status of the pope were evident in his choice of 18 January for his letter: the feast of the chair of Saint Peter at Rome. Guibert was mindful of anniversaries and feast days and he liked to make every gesture count. The very date amounts to a reaffirmation of the authority of the pope, the bishop of Rome. Guibert's lengthy letter developed more fully than the vow itself an analysis of the origins of the present crisis. He reassures his committee that they are correct in seeing the present misfortunes in France and Rome as the result of infidelities toward God. He expresses a sense of Christians as embattled and the victims of a conspiracy, and he affirms the view that the defense of Rome had been an extension of an ongoing struggle against the French Revolution or, simply, the Revolution: "It was from France that the evil which torments us expanded across Europe." But he also notes the privileged position of France, notably with respect to the revelations of the Sacré-Coeur. "France, birthplace of the devotion to the Sacré-Coeur, will also be the origin of the prayers that will lift us and save us."[7]

Guibert's conception of the proposed church of the Sacred Heart recapitulated many of the features of the Sacred Heart devotion. The church-to-be was fully in keeping with the convention of the Sacred Heart as a talisman; Guibert saw the monument as a safeguard against further acts of divine anger; invasion and civil war had pushed France to the brink. He also envisioned the church as an act of protest against other monuments, secular temples, erected "to the glory of vice and impiety." Finally, Guibert endorsed the idea that the project aimed to bring about the "deliverance" of the pope, captive in his residence and stripped of the temporal authority necessary to his office.[8] In short, Guibert's vision of the purpose of the church combined folk wisdom, Catholic counter-revolutionary political culture, and Catholic anxieties of the Terrible Year.

CHOOSING A SITE

Siting a votive church in the Parisian Babylon posed challenges and created opportunities. By the 1870s, of course, Paris was a city rich in associations, making it easy to relate with existing sites and structures across space, or with historic events and moments over time. For someone with the historical imagination of Joseph Guibert, there would be no shortage of ideas. Thanks to his Committee of the National Vow, newly formed, there were more than enough rival ideas to go around.

Some members of the committee proposed sites in the heart of the city, on the rue de Rivoli, gutted by flames during the defense of the Commune. A deputy in the National Assembly particularly admired the heights of the Trocadéro. For his part, Alexandre Legentil had identified Garnier's unfinished opera house as a site particularly rich in possibilities. He once suggested that it would be only fitting that Garnier's costly and still-unfinished Opéra, symbol of the decadent and despised Second Empire, be dismantled. The temple of the National Vow would be raised on the foundations of what Legentil somewhat excessively called "a scandalous monument to extravagance, indecency, and bad taste."[9] When it was pointed out that the destruction of the Opéra was itself an extravagance, Legentil pondered instead the conversion of the existing structure into a church of the Sacred Heart.

Even though these proposals convey the sense of revulsion some Catholics felt toward a regime they regarded as amoral and sensual (and whose architecture they regarded as correspondingly extravagant and indecent), the sites lacked the religious charge necessary to make them acceptable as a site of pilgrimage, a new sacred center. Only places touched by the sacred retain this quality. They are places apart from the profane and therefore worthy of pilgrimage.[10] Finally, this was a question too important to be left to a lay committee. Guibert himself identified the only possible Parisian terrain with all the requisite features: Montmartre. Guibert visited Montmartre at least twice in October of 1872, once while leading a pilgrimage, again while on a pastoral visit to the pastor of Saint-Pierre-de-Montmartre. As his chief of staff, the abbé Langénieux, recalled it, Guibert chose the Montmartre site after ascending the hill on foot one foggy October morning. Guibert had never seen Paris from this vantage point before when suddenly the sun broke through the clouds and the city appeared, stretched out before him.[11]

In retrospect, the choice seems obvious. Montmartre was steeped in religious history, and the physical attributes of the mountain, towering over the city, must have made the site irresistible. Guibert knew that Montmartre was the site of the martyrdom of Saint Denis, Paris's first bishop, in the third century. For generations, Montmartre had been the site of a chapel dedicated to Saint Denis. The chapel was attributed to Sainte Geneviève, the patron saint of Paris. It marked the hallowed ground where Saint Denis and his companions died until it was razed in 1793, a year after the Benedictine nuns had been driven out by the Revolution.[12] What better place, Guibert must have thought, to initiate the re-Christianization of France than the very place made holy by some of France's first apostles? What better way to repair the revolutionary rupture and the void left by de-Christianization than to return the mountain, after an eighty-year hiatus, to its sacred vocation? What better moment than the present, just months after the eruption of the Commune on Montmartre showed that the Revolution still stalked the land of the Sacré-Coeur?[13]

Montmartre also offered special ritualistic and symbolic possibilities as a sacred location, given its natural features and historical associations. As a site of pilgrimage it possessed the prerequisite of natural relief, like the grottoes and summits of other places of pilgrimage, which set the site apart physically and helped to validate it as distinctive and sacred.[14] As the highest point in the Paris basin, Montmartre seemed destined to serve as a point of contact between heaven and earth. For the pilgrim, as Guibert must have understood on that foggy October morning, the act of climbing served as a metaphor for holy ascent. The journey to the mountaintop implies the pilgrim's passage from the profane to the sacred, the breaking of the ontological plane.[15] As "a place of pious pilgrimage" this sacred center would draw thousands whose every step affirmed the ideal of penitence, renewal, and regeneration through the Sacré-Coeur.

Putting the Sacred Heart church on Montmartre would make the most of the elevation—Guibert would call it "a sacred lightning rod." And then there was the dramatic way that the site addressed the city of Paris: it would not follow the standard east-west orientation for churches. Instead it would align along a north-south axis, allowing the Sacré-Coeur to face the city. Its location would make it the only monument, prior to the erection of the Eiffel Tower, visible from any point in Paris—a temple on a sacred mountain towering above the profane.

THE NATIONAL ASSEMBLY APPROVES ACQUISITION OF THE SITE

Securing the site atop Montmartre, however, would be no mere formality. Several owners held pieces of the site; if any proved obstinate, Guibert faced negotiations that could be time consuming, costly, and might ultimately prove fruitless. The only way to secure the site expeditiously was to persuade the deputies of the National Assembly that the proposed "Church of the National Vow to the Sacred Heart of Jesus" was a matter of national interest, "public utility," what in other contexts would be called "eminent domain." Odds were in Guibert's favor. On 5 May 1873, the archbishop of Paris requested the legal authority he needed in a letter to Jules Simon, Adolphe Thiers's minister of religion.

The monarchist majority in the National Assembly, though divided as to which dynasty to restore, was largely sympathetic. Deputies known as "Legitimists" for their commitment to the Bourbon comte de Chambord and his legitimate claims to the throne according to the rights of succession were clearly in Guibert's camp. Indeed, many of them saw the construction of the basilica as but a prelude to Bourbon restoration and a public, royal consecration to the Sacré-Coeur. The other monarchist camp, known as "Orléanists" for their allegiance to the cadet dynasty of the house of Orléans, obviously had other plans for France. Nor was the devotion to the Sacred Heart particularly admired among them. For some, the Sacré-Coeur was a "Jesuit devotion" (papist, ultra-Montanist, un-French) and suspect on those grounds. For others, the Sacré-Coeur as devotion was simply in bad taste; it was baroque piety—sentimental, smarmy, Saint-Sulpicien—and unbefitting a mature Christian faith. For still others, the Sacré-Coeur was too freighted with partisan political associations—counter-revolution, a martyred Bourbon king, fanatical anti-republicanism, in a word, the "Vendée" —to work as the theme of a "national" monument.

Moreover, one could fairly ask what public utility there was in building another church on Montmartre. Montmartre already had its parish church —the Romanesque Saint-Pierre-de-Montmartre was mere steps away from the site—the neighborhood was not notably devout, and in any event the church envisioned was not destined for the ordinary affairs of a parish. But Orléanists did not wish to alienate their Legitimist allies, some of whom nevertheless brazenly called for a flat-out vote in the Assembly in favor of the dedication of France to the Sacré-Coeur. As long as the proposal was stripped to its essentials, the question of "public utility," it had a chance. The final wording of the legislation as submitted mentioned only the public utility of building a church on Montmartre, an initiative that perhaps even a Voltairean Orléanist could support.[16] It would clear the way for the purchase, forcible if necessary, of the site atop Montmartre.

Legitimists consoled themselves with the knowledge that the church in question would be dedicated to the Sacré-Coeur; Orléanists looked the other way, even while delegations of deputies made their way on pilgrimages to Paray-le-Monial in the weeks before the matter came up for a vote. On 20 June, a massive procession took place at Paray-le-Monial. It featured a parade of lay and Catholic notables, more than a hundred deputies from the National Assembly, a legion of bishops, the heroes of Loigny, and more than thirty thousand other personages bearing some nine hundred and fifty banners evoking the principal cities of France.[17] On 29 June, the bishop of Autun presided over a second mass-pilgrimage to Paray, this one featuring a tearful ceremony in which the Legitimist deputy Baron de Belcastel read a statement consecrating France to the Sacré-Coeur—more than a hundred and fifty deputies would eventually sign the statement. A few weeks later the National Assembly passed legislation, by a margin of 382 to 138, authorizing the archbishop of Paris to purchase the property for what would become the site of the basilica of Sacré-Coeur.[18]

A DESIGN FOR THE CHURCH OF THE NATIONAL VOW

But what kind of church? Legentil's vow had only specified a "sanctuary" dedicated to the Sacré-Coeur. In the visions of Marguerite-Marie Alacoque, the Sacred Heart had merely asked for a "chapel." Both imply rather unassuming structures, at least in their dimensions. A sense of urgency about the project also argued in favor of something rather modest. The point of the Church of the National Vow, as it was now known, was to serve as tangible witness to a national resolve to make amends and renew an ancient covenant. In that case, sooner was better than later; by extension smaller should be better than bigger.

But Guibert's vision of the proposed church was monumental. This was implicit in his choice of the site, but also in the decision to make the vow national. Any structure with pretensions to embody the solemn wishes of the nation raised expectations that would have to be met. So did any structure erected on such prime real estate. And a church on a truly monumental scale would take time. Major additions to the Parisian landscape had taken many years to move from conception to completion, especially those within recent memory. The Arc de Triomphe had taken thirty years. Napoleon's tomb at the Invalides had taken twenty-one. Guibert and his immediate advisers seem at first to have underestimated the enormity of the project they had taken on. In May of 1874, at a meeting at which Guibert presided, committee member Charles Chesnelong predicted that the church could be built "in two or three years."[19]

Unlike most of the great architectural projects of the Old Regime and the early part of the nineteenth century, the design for the Sacré-Coeur would be the outcome of an architectural competition. This was but the first sign of the modernity of the project, because such competitions represented a step away from the practices of patronage still common in sacred and secular architecture. The archdiocese announced the conditions for the open competition; the architects went to work. A public exhibition of the submissions meant that not only was the design competition open to the public but so in a sense was the judging, because the designs went on display weeks before the judges would select and announce the winner. Crowds swarmed into the Palais de l'Industrie on 1 February 1874 to see the seventy-some projects on display. Until the end of the exhibition in June, newspapers and journals took sides as dilettantes, experts, patriots, and politicians debated the merits of the designs.

It was immediately evident that the competitors agreed that the site itself had imposed certain requirements. Even in an age when Eugène Viollet le Duc so ardently propounded the superior rational basis of Gothic architecture, most architects had concluded that Gothic simply would not work on Montmartre—there were only a handful of Gothic designs in the competition. The site atop Montmartre was rather small and squarish, 87 meters by 50, whereas Gothic required a long nave, typically a site at least twice as long as wide.[20]

Gothic, moreover, must be observed up close to be appreciated. Much of the beauty of Gothic is in the details—the abundance of glass, the delicacy of the buttresses, the artistry displayed in carved stone. Most architects in the competition evidently shared the view that what mattered most was how the monument would look from afar, especially from Paris, and that in turn accentuated the importance of profile. The church that would rise above Montmartre needed to look impressive silhouetted against the sky. The Church of the National Vow, as design after design revealed, would be a domed church.

This still left plenty of room for differences and derivative architecture. There were designs reminiscent of Michelangelo's Saint Peter's in Rome; there were designs evoking the churches and baptisteries of Florence and Pisa; there were knock-offs of Baltard's Saint-Augustin. One architect, in a nod to the papal preoccupations of the project's sponsors, proposed a dome that looked for all the world like the papal tiara (fig. 32).

Antoine Étex went in for colossal dimensions and paid far more attention to landscaping than most others. He proposed tree-lined stairways as

Figure 32. An unsuccessful design for the Sacré-Coeur de
Montmartre. Archives historiques du diocèse de Paris.

Entrants in the architectural competition for the church of
the Sacré-Coeur often attempted to express architecturally
some of the anxieties and motivations of Catholic France in the
aftermath of the "Terrible Year." The architect Moyaux sought
to emphasize French Catholic concerns about the fate of the
pope and proposed a church with a dome resembling the papal
tiara; his design was ranked seventh.

approaches to the site and cascades of water. Between the stairs he wanted a "colossal statue of Christ in bronze," while elsewhere he proposed an equally immense low-relief representation of God "whose head alone would measure six meters." Iron serpents would decorate the length of the roofline. Perhaps sensing a more appreciative reception from the general public than from the committee of judges, Étex published and distributed copies of his project.[21] The design competition for the Sacré-Coeur presented a rare opportunity for self-promotion.

Although this was a public competition, the judging was not blind. Each design was identified with the architect's name and the winner would be chosen by a jury of twelve—six determined by a vote of the architects participating in the competition, six appointed by Archbishop Guibert. Moreover, the jury's choice would not be binding: Guibert would reserve the final decision for himself. This measure removed any chance that the winner would be determined largely on the basis of design, always a risk with a committee dominated by architects. Guibert's decision would balance such factors as design, liturgical considerations, the architect's record and, of course, connections. But Guibert was also determined to avoid the embarrassment of an earlier competition for a church design at Notre-Dame de la Treille, near Lille. At that contest, some twenty years before the Sacré-Coeur competition, blind judging had resulted in a profound embarrassment, a "disagreeable surprise" as one source delicately put it. An architect who was neither French nor Catholic had submitted the winning design. It couldn't be denied that the design of English Protestant Henry Clutton admirably expressed the religious sentiments surrounding Our Lady—or at least that could be inferred from the decision in the blind judging. But no one felt comfortable awarding the construction contract to Clutton, a member of a schismatic faith. Fortunately, the terms of the competition had separated the selection of the design from the selection of the general contractor and, in order to mitigate some of the effects of the "disagreeable surprise," it was decided that someone else would build and "enhance" Clutton's design.[22]

Among the architects favored to win the Sacré-Coeur competition was Paul Abadie, a known quantity. Abadie was a Beaux-Arts trained architect who knew and admired Viollet-le-Duc; he had spent much of his career as diocesan architect in the southwest, at Périgueux and Angoulême. There Abadie had restored churches according to the precepts of Viollet-le-Duc, that is, restoring buildings not to their prior state but to an *ideal* state, an

Figure 33. Paul Abadie's design for the Sacré-Coeur de Montmartre. Archives historiques du diocèse de Paris.

The Romano-Byzantine style of sacred architecture found in the southwest of France was the architectural idiom Paul Abadie knew best. His proposal for the Sacré-Coeur architectural competition drew heavily upon his years of work as a diocesan architect in Périgueux and Angoulême. His critics, especially partisans of Gothic architecture, ridiculed his design as more at home in Turkey than France and therefore particularly unsuited to the French Christian patriotic vision of the Sacré-Coeur.

attitude that favored fairly vigorous, even aggressive, interpretation and modification of existing structures. Abadie exercised a fairly light touch on Angoulême's cathedral of Saint-Pierre. Abadie's most famous work, some would say notorious, had been the restoration of Saint-Front, the Romano-Byzantine basilica of Périgueux, whose restored domes and lanternons fairly prefigured those Abadie would propose for the Sacré-Coeur at Montmartre. Abadie was known and respected among practicing architects. His career was a solid one, though not an outstanding one. What his résumé lacked was a Parisian commission, which the Sacré-Coeur would give him.

Abadie was also known to the Church hierarchy. No fewer than three bishops lobbied Guibert through letters in favor of Abadie, apparently at Abadie's urging.[23] For the winner, the Sacré-Coeur would be the commission of a lifetime; Abadie was seeking every advantage. Success would crown his career, mark him out among architects of his generation, give him a major monument in Paris, and might even earn him a spot in the prestigious Institut de France. One critic was so bold as to suggest that this was his primary motivation and that Abadie's protestations of faith served to ingratiate him with the Catholic hierarchy.[24]

Abadie went to work and produced one of the most unusual designs in the competition (fig. 33). His Sacré-Coeur was a blend of Romanesque and Byzantine styles. All openings—windows, doorways, pendentives—were framed by Roman, semicircular arches, not the high, pointed openings characteristic of Gothic. But all of the domed designs had been faithful to Romanesque in this respect. What made his design stand out were its elongated domes, which gave the design a distinctly exotic eastern look. Abadie's design called for one tall central dome bracketed by four smaller domes at the corners in turn topped by and surrounded by several smaller lanternons or cupolas. These domes were sheathed in small stone tiles, giving the surface of the domes a scaly texture. Anyone who had visited, say, Notre-Dame la Grande in Poitiers would know what he was getting at. But this was Paris. Most Parisians hardly knew what to think.

THE SACRÉ-COEUR AND ITS CRITICS

When the jury announced their selection of Abadie's Sacré-Coeur as the winner and Guibert approved their decision, the winning design was immediately subject to intense scrutiny and sharp criticism. Not that it hadn't undergone that already—with the exhibition running five months, there had been ample time for commentary, as well as lobbying that passed as commentary. But now that late nineteenth-century France's most important architectural commission had been awarded, and now that nearly eighty bruised egos were on the loose, and with so much at stake politically, there was bound to be a row. Not surprisingly, some of the sharpest criticisms came from the advocates of Gothic architecture in the tradition of Viollet-le-Duc, for whom Gothic represented the apex of rationality and whose admiration was entirely secular. For them, Romanesque was a transitional form on the path to Gothic. Romanesque was worthy of admiration, to be sure, but hardly worthy of imitation.

Also among advocates of Gothic were Catholics for whom the style embodied the glories of Catholic architecture—that they regarded Gothic as a style perfected in France almost went without saying. Gothic architecture was Catholic and it was French. As a manifestation of a *national* will, only Gothic would do. A group of critics led by Abbé Carle of Nîmes criticized Abadie's design as "drawn from foreign and pagan monuments." [25] They upheld the neo-Gothic style of Jean-Baptiste Lassus—Saint-Nicolas in Nantes is the best example of his work—as an appropriately French ideal. In contrast with the "charming" thirteenth-century architecture of Lassus, Abadie's Sacré-Coeur was alien and derivative. Carle cited the commentary of critics who labeled Abadie's design as "pastiche"—a criticism that Abadie's design has yet fully to shake. [26]

Carle and his Catholic critics were not alone in finding fault with Abadie's design. The trade journal *le Bâtiment* was not partial to Gothic. But while it recognized that the Montmartre site virtually required a domed church, it doubted whether the site required quite as many domes as Abadie proposed to give it. "The main dome is supported by four smaller domes and by a multitude of others arrayed all around; then, all of a sudden, a great tower [the bell-tower] jumps up from who knows where, like a jack-in-the-box," sneered *le Bâtiment.* [27] The archconservative Catholic newspaper *l'Univers* was almost as brutal. "It's not a dome that crowns the edifice but six ovoid cupolas, which are accosted by yet another eighteen smaller ones, which brings the total to twenty-four. That's a lot for a single church." A leading architectural journal, *le Moniteur des architectes,* emphasized the exoticism of the design by remarking dryly that "one would think that one is looking at a Turkish city from which emerges the domes of several minarets." [28]

Critics and journalists competed with one another to coin mocking terms and images: "a jack-in-the-box," "a mosque," "minarets," "a beehive." Soon it was clear that the debate about Abadie's design had gone well beyond matters of architectural merit. It had become a lightning rod for critics of the regime of moral order. One wit, chiding Catholics and playing on the aggressively militant Catholic rhetoric of moral order called for a "crusade" against the "mosque" of Abadie. [29]

What had Abadie intended? The simplest explanation is that Abadie worked within the architectural idiom he knew best and simply adapted it to the requirement of the site. What Abadie knew best was the sacred architecture of the French southwest, where he had served as diocesan architect for much of his career. From Poitiers to Bordeaux one could find many examples of scaly domes and lanternons in sacred architecture. Saint-Front in

Figure 34. Saint-Front de Périgueux, before restoration by Paul Abadie. Félix de Verneilh, *L'Architecture byzantine en France: Saint-Front de Périgueux et les églises à coupoles de l'Aquitaine* (Paris, 1851).

Félix de Verneilh's study of the domed churches of the French southwest, published in 1851, was part of a broader reconsideration of the place of Romanesque and Byzantine styles in sacred architecture in France. In an age obsessed with reading national origins back into everything from architecture to epic tales such as the *Song of Roland,* it was very important to Verneilh that Saint-Front's architecture not be derivative of San Marco in Venice. Verneilh argued that San Marco and Saint-Front might have been contemporary constructions, coincidentally inspired by the church of Hagia Sophia in Constantinople.

Périgueux, which Abadie had labored to restore (some say ruin), was a Romano-Byzantine church of multiple domes; in fact, in its restored form it is the church the Sacré-Coeur most resembles (figs. 34, 35). Most of the competitors agreed that the Montmartre site more or less required a domed church, at least judging by the preponderance of domes among the entries they submitted, and the dimensions of the site favored a squarish, Greek cross plan for the church. It took a certain amount of boldness for Abadie to

Figure 35. Saint-Front de Périgueux, restored by Paul Abadie.

The most obvious source of architectural inspiration for the Sacré-Coeur de Mont-martre, the cathedral of Saint-Front in Périgueux, restored by Paul Abadie, is no less controversial. Abadie's modifications of the twelfth-century cathedral have been cited as a textbook case of how not to restore.

transplant regional architecture from the French southwest to Paris but, given his background and given the constraints of the site, it shouldn't have come as a great surprise.

There is more to the matter than that, of course. In architectural terms, Abadie's Sacré-Coeur can be read as part of a movement away from a hierarchy of styles, notably Viollet-le-Duc's championing of Gothic, the pure and the orthodox. When architects at mid-century had argued over the respective meanings and advantages of Gothic, Romanesque, and Byzantine styles, Léon Vaudoyer had argued that it was by turning toward the East—toward Byzantium—that the early Christians had broken free of Roman examples—then he built the Byzantine Notre-Dame de la Major as a case in point. For Vaudoyer, Romanesque and Romano-Byzantine were better than the more "evolved" Gothic precisely because they were closer than Gothic to Christian origins. Such a preference is implicit in Abadie's design.[30]

But Vaudoyer's Byzantine Notre-Dame de la Major was put up in Marseille. Since Marseille had originally been a Phoenician and Greek settlement, it was an easier fit. Paris was something else altogether. There would have to be more. Again, there is the commonsense argument that it was what Abadie knew, as well as the matter of the associations that Abadie's design brings to mind. The design certainly was exotic for northern Europe, and the reference to Byzantium in Abadie's domes must have been puzzling. One way of reading the design, a blending of Romanesque and Byzantine styles, is as an appeal for a revival of the idea of Christendom. The reference to Hagia Sophia, now a mosque, but originally the Church of the Holy Wisdom in Constantinople, evokes a time when Christendom, for some synonymous with Europe, had not yet been divided by schism. To blend Romanesque and Byzantine architecture suggests the Roman Empire prior to its split between Rome and Byzantium, a time when Christianity knew only one center: Rome. This was a powerful message at a time when Catholic Europe was in retreat and Protestant Europe, notably Germany and England, was on the ascendant. Romano-Byzantine implied an architectural reconciliation of East and West, a reconciliation laden with religious significance.[31]

Finally, there is a hint in Félix de Verneilh's 1851 book on Byzantine architecture, a book that Abadie would certainly have read. Verneilh wrote of San Marco in Venice and of models in Byzantium, but he suggested another important Romano-Byzantine precedent—the dome of the imperial chapel at Aix-la-Chapelle. Was Abadie "quoting" Aix-la-Chapelle? Was Abadie's evocation of Byzantium a reference to the ideal of Christian monarchy in its classical form? Given Catholic appeals for a new Charlemagne, the archetypal Christian king, the idea cannot be ruled out.[32] As for Abadie himself, he made no such claims. The only direct remark he ever made about his design for the Sacré-Coeur of Montmartre was that it was "the style of the Sacred Heart" (fig. 36).[33]

Abadie's design represents a return to early Christian artistic styles and motifs. This was by no means a new idea in the 1870s and did not originate with Abadie. By the 1840s there was a growing conviction that religious art, notably pictorial art, should return to early Christian art as a source of inspiration and renewal.[34] François-Edouard Picot and Hippolyte Flandrin

Figure 36. Cardinal Guibert and the basilica of the Sacré-Coeur as ex-voto, lithograph by Ach[ille] Sirouy, ca. 1880s. Bibliothèque de l'Institut Catholique, Paris.

This image evokes two important dimensions of the Sacré-Coeur project—its expiatory quality and its relation to the city of Paris. Guibert bears a model of the Sacré-Coeur as a pilgrim's ex-voto, token of repentance; the skyline of the city of Paris is visible in the background.

showed the way with their mural decoration of the church of Saint-Vincent-de-Paul, itself a scaled-down knock-off of San Paolo Fuori Muri in Rome. Their work, completed in the 1850s, is a deliberate evocation of the hieratic style of early Christian art. Flandrin's procession of the saints toward the altar drew upon his frescoes at Saint-Germain-des-Prés in the 1840s, also done in hieratic style, albeit somewhat less severe. It would be echoed in the decorative mosaic above the choir in the Sacré-Coeur. The experience of the Terrible Year only enhanced the yearning for sure values and ancient "tried and true" formulas—in art as much as in politics and religion. Abadie's architecture can be seen as an architectural example of the return to early Christian sources, a movement already a generation old by the time of the Sacré-Coeur design competition and deepened by the shattering effect of the Terrible Year.

A MODERN MAGDALENE SEEKS FORGIVENESS

⚜

The Committee of the National Vow, under the direction of
His Eminence Cardinal Guibert, seeks nothing less than the conversion
of France, its consecration to the Sacré-Coeur, and the freedom of the
Church and the Holy Father; isn't this a direct attack on the spirit of evil?

·   ·   ·

We are building the *national temple* demanded by Our Lord through the
Blessed Marguerite-Marie.

Bulletin de l'oeuvre du voeu national au Sacré-Coeur de Jésus, 10 April 1877

Astride the Champ-de-Mars, atop the mount of Martyrs:
Here, the Tower of Iron; there the Sacré-Coeur, a temple of stone,
One, a monument of pride; the other, of repentance.

P. V. DELAPORTE, S.J.,
in Messager du Sacré-Coeur de Jésus, *1889*

No less than medieval Christianity, French Catholicism in the nineteenth century was an intensely visual faith. The devotion to the Sacré-
Coeur added many powerful images to an already rich repertoire. One such
image expressed the penitential and patriotic intentions of the project to
build the Church of the National Vow to the Sacred Heart of Jesus (fig. 37);
it represents France as a penitent, on her knees before Jesus, while Mary con-
soles her. At the feet of the weeping figure are the broken symbols of power:
a sword, a scepter, and a crown. In her hands is a model of the Sacré-Coeur
church. With her eyes downcast, she presents the model to Jesus, who
reaches out to accept. It is tempting to see her as a Marianne, the woman of

Figure 37. "Sacratissimo Cordi Jesu, Gallia poenitens ac devota." *Messager du Sacré-Coeur* 39 (January 1881): 2.

This penitent France, with her unbound hair, recalls the figure of Mary Magdalene, described in the Bible as a prostitute who bathed the feet of Jesus in fine oil and wiped his feet with her hair. Here, France / Magdalene offers the Sacré-Coeur church, on the scale of an ex-voto, in a gesture of repentance.

the people who, since revolutionary times, had been a symbol of republican France. But Catholic France was still far from feeling comfortable with such a controversial figure as Marianne, laden with bitter memories. This France is Mary Magdalene, the prostitute who turns from her dissolute ways and follows Jesus. Although the devotion to the Sacré-Coeur produced many powerful images, and the story of the Sacré-Coeur de Montmartre is a rich and complex tale, this one image most fully evokes the meaning of the basilica of Sacré-Coeur for its founders.

The model in the hands of this Modern Magdalene is what is known as an ex-voto, a votive offering, something a penitent leaves behind at a shrine as witness to the visit. Thus the basilica was to be a massive, national "ex-voto." It would symbolize the rejection of the nation's godless past. It would embody the nation's penitential resolve and prayerful wish that the spiritual union of France with God be restored.

Catholic rhetoric surrounding the Church of the National Vow reinforced and amplified such imagery. In a special appeal to the French episcopate seeking money for the project, Archbishop Guibert included a prayer that asked God to "redeem once again this France that you loved and who, turning from her many errors, wishes to return to her Christian vocation."[1] In their replies to the appeal from the archbishop of Paris, the bishops of provincial France elaborated on the theme of reconciliation and national redemption through the Church of the National Vow. The bishop of Toulon agreed that the Parisian ex-voto would "complete the expiation for the impious acts which have brought upon France the wrath of God."[2] The bishop of Constantine expressed the sentiment that "the day when France will be solemnly consecrated to the Sacred Heart of Jesus will be for her a day of rebirth. We work for the Christian regeneration to which Providence has called our nation."[3]

Other statements allude to events ("impious acts") that are the source of a rupture in France's divine relationship; they also emphasize national, collective culpability, and they lay out before the eyes of the nation the specific ways in which this modern Magdalene had strayed from its vocation. They built upon what by then had become stock ideas in Catholic commentary on the status of modern France: France as a divinely favored nation that had turned its back on God; the Revolution as the moment of rupture and the rupture itself symbolized by the execution of the anointed king; the Second Empire as a political and moral quagmire and the inevitable consequence of the rupture; Protestant Prussia as the sword brandished by a vengeful God; atonement as the only possible means to reconciliation and regeneration.[4] The rhetoric conveys a vision of France's past that recapitulates a salvation story: an original state of harmony → transgression and rupture → decadence and chastisement → atonement and redemption. Within this narrative the Sacré-Coeur would symbolize the work of atonement and the ardent desire for redemption.

The Sacré-Coeur de Montmartre was to serve as a symbol of reconciliation; it was to serve as a vehicle of reconstruction as well. Every act toward the completion of the project would be a pious act. Building the monument would testify to the national will to reestablish its covenant with God. The parade of tragic setbacks for France—war, defeat, civil war—lent a sense of urgency to the undertaking. The bishop of Perpignan expressed this edgy mood of vulnerability when he referred to the proposed church of the Sacré-Coeur as "a lightning rod on the highest point of the capital." The strategic placement of the church on Montmartre would counter the threat of a renewal of plagues and calamities of divine origin; it would "protect us against the lightning bolts of divine anger." [5]

BUILDING THE SACRÉ-COEUR DE MONTMARTRE

If the Sacré-Coeur were to be France's sacred lightning rod, prudence dictated that it be put in place as soon as possible. Donations were coming in, and there were confident predictions that construction of the shell of the church might require only two or three years. Then, disaster struck. Examination of the site revealed problems that threatened to compromise the entire project. Montmartre had been heavily mined over the years, notably for plaster (plaster of Paris). The proposed construction site for the Sacré-Coeur was literally undermined. If they built Abadie's church or anything else of similar mass on the site, they would soon find the earth settling beneath its weight. The foundations would crack and their church, which was to be the mark of French regeneration, would begin to resemble a fractured France, doomed to collapse.

The discovery threw off all of the calculations of Archbishop Guibert and the committee. It might be necessary to abandon Montmartre for another site. Whether they tried to work with the existing site or move to another, delay was inevitable. Likewise, their initial estimate of seven million francs was now in jeopardy.

At first Abadie, who had been commissioned to build his design, thought that a vast platform of concrete four meters thick would be sufficient to stabilize the site. However, it was realized that this too would be subject to

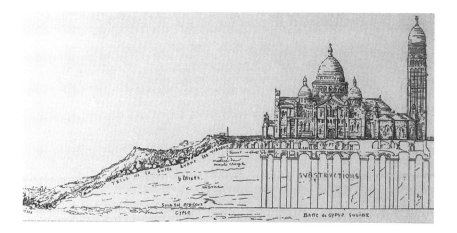

Figure 38. Foundations for the Sacré-Coeur. Bibliothèque de l'Institut Catholique, Paris.

Archbishop Guibert chose the Montmartre site for a variety of symbolic reasons; soil instability at the site nearly forced him to abandon it. The only way to rescue the site was through a major, though invisible, engineering feat—sinking stone pilings down to the gypsum bedrock to create the church's foundations, seen here in cross section.

uneven pressures and would give way and ultimately compromise the church that stood upon it. It soon became evident that the only way to salvage the site would be to lay pilings down through the layers of lime and clay, through the holes and tunnels carved into the mountainside, until they could rest upon bedrock more than thirty meters down (fig. 38).[6] There would be some eighty such pilings in all, made of stone upon stone, rising to the surface at points where they would support the arches of the crypt which, in turn, would support the great mass of Abadie's design. In effect, the foundation of the Sacré-Coeur would rest upon stilts over Montmartre, like a dock set upon pilings over the water. Later, the church's admirers would boast that if a mighty earthquake were to level Montmartre, after the dust settled, the Sacré-Coeur would be seen still standing there in mid-air, as if on stilts, supported by its pilings.

Guibert hesitated. He would literally be burying millions of francs if he continued with the Montmartre site. Finally, in May of 1876 he consented, although he described his decision as like that of a patient with an infected limb, resigned to amputation.[7] If so, it was an amputation Guibert had brought upon himself, given that he had committed himself in every other

Figure 39. Frédéric Théodore Lix, "Paris-Montmartre: Benediction Ceremony for the First Stone of the Church of the Sacred Heart." Musée Carnavalet, Paris. © Photothèque des Musées de la Ville de Paris.

The ceremonial laying of the first stone of the Sacré-Coeur de Montmartre took place on 16 June 1875, although most of the real work was still going on underground. A crowd of dignitaries—including deputies from the National Assembly—looked on as Archbishop Guibert led the ceremony.

way to the Montmartre site long before then. He had already made a considerable symbolic investment in Montmartre, starting with the rhetoric about the "holy mountain" and its rich associations with the history of Catholicism in France—Saint Denis, the foundation of the Jesuit order, etc. Montmartre was part of the mystique surrounding the Sacré-Coeur project. Building it somewhere else, Guibert knew, would drain it of much of its monumental power.

Moreover, almost a year earlier, in June of 1875, Guibert had already officially opened the Montmartre work site with a ceremonial laying of the first stone, an event involving the participation of the papal nuncio, nine bishops, some two hundred deputies from the National Assembly, and General de Charette and a contingent of his Papal Zouaves (fig. 39). In fact, Guibert's original conception for the ceremony was that the laying of the first stone would be accompanied by a consecration of France to the Sacré-Coeur with all of the bishops of France in attendance. However, intemperate remarks by a speaker before a meeting of the *Cercles catholiques* about how the ceremony would mark the burial of the "principles of 1789" forced Guibert to rethink the event.[8] But even without the national consecration, the event had been grand enough to make even the prospect of abandoning the site a matter of considerable embarrassment. Add to that, the *grandeur* of the Montmartre site and Guibert's decision was clear; the Church of the National Vow would not be moved.

MOBILIZING THE MANY FOR THE OEUVRE

The plan to set down stone pilings for the Church of the National Vow gave rise to new punning metaphors about the project. The structure would have "roots" in the national soil; it had "profound" foundations. Thanks to its deep pilings, the Church of the National Vow would also be something of an engineering marvel. But the project would also be seriously delayed and significantly over budget. Had the project stayed within budget, Guibert's steering committee need never have continued its fund-raising efforts beyond the 1870s. But the funds initially raised out of the gloom of the aftermath of the Terrible Year and the enthusiasm for the National Vow would be consumed before anything of the structure would be visible above ground. The organizers of the Oeuvre, as the "work" of the National Vow was commonly known, began to take a long-term perspective. Despite the rhetoric invoking fears of the imminent renewal of acts of divine vengeance against France, the first need of the committee of the Oeuvre was to begin to plan for decades of expensive construction supported by year-round fund-raising.

Moreover, in view of the fact that the church would be ready neither as a place of worship nor as ex-voto any time soon, the work of prayer, reparation, and atonement would be delayed too. From the beginning, the committee envisioned the church of the Sacré-Coeur as no ordinary place of worship. In the instructions distributed to architects planning to participate in the design competition, the committee had advised that the church was to be a place of pilgrimage. Guibert and his organizers imagined thousands of pilgrims making their way to Montmartre and they wanted generous side aisles to accommodate them as they circulated through the church of the

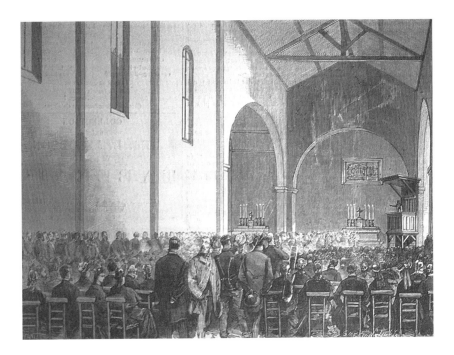

Figure 40. The provisional chapel on Montmartre. Archives historiques du diocèse de Paris.

The provisional chapel was constructed rapidly and consecrated in a ceremony on 3 March 1876, less than a year after the laying of the first stone for the basilica itself. Pilgrimages began almost immediately and constituted a major source of donations to the project.

Sacré-Coeur. But there could be no pilgrims without a destination shrine. The committee sought to make that vision a reality through improvisation. They would initiate the stream of pilgrims. They would begin the work of national reparation by building a provisional chapel on Montmartre.

Given its location outside the old walls of Paris, throughout its history Montmartre had hosted all manner of "marginal" activities and eccentric personalities. By the 1870s, Montmartre had been incorporated into the city of Paris, but habits are hard to break. One purpose for the *chapelle provisoire* was to help people to get accustomed to thinking of Montmartre not as a place of pleasure and self-indulgence but as a place of pilgrimage (fig. 40).

The chapel provided a venue for the offering of prayers of expiation; this, according to one source, was something even Pope Pius IX saw as crucial if

Figure 41. The foundations of the Sacré-Coeur, after the completion of the crypt, ca. 1882. Archives historiques du diocèse de Paris.

Despite an annual income of one million francs, the costly work on foundations meant that for years little of the Church of the National Vow was visible. Here, with the foundations in place and the crypt completed, the church begins to emerge from the soil atop Montmartre.

the Church of the National Vow were to be decades in preparation.[9] Prayer must begin immediately, even if the monumental ex-voto itself would not soon be ready. Equally important was the role of the *chapelle provisoire* as a site of donation, a sustained source of income over the years of costly construction (fig. 41). The enormous cost of the project meant that the conventional patronage model involving appeals to wealthy benefactors would have to be abandoned in favor of appeals to individuals of more modest means. By the early 1880s, the principal source of revenue for the Oeuvre would not come from the gifts of rich patrons directly to the committee or to the archbishop of Paris but from pilgrims to Montmartre and the *chapelle provisoire*. The chapel was designed to accommodate as many as 730 persons at a time; by the end of its first year, a partial year, more than 114,760 pilgrims had made their way to the site.[10] In 1877, the first full year of collections at the *chapelle provisoire,* pilgrims dropped more than 240,000 francs in Montmartre collection boxes, a figure that doubled the following year.[11] For the next thirty years, pilgrims to Montmartre would donate 500,000 to 600,000 francs per year—representing from fifty to sixty percent of all annual donations to the basilica.

FUND-RAISING AND THE NATIONAL AND POPULAR AMBITIONS OF THE SACRÉ-COEUR

The Sacré-Coeur moved people. It not only mobilized Catholics; it persuaded them to contribute. Given the politico-religious nature of the cult, it represents a significant step in the adaptation of the Catholic Church to the demands of modern mass organization. By making the Sacré-Coeur a place of pilgrimage, in addition to a place of symbolic importance, the Church showed that it could take a religious practice of long standing—pilgrimage—and refashion it into a fund-raising vehicle and a modern political ritual (fig. 42).

Mobilizing the faithful in support of a monument of national political and religious significance became one of the outstanding features of the Sacré-Coeur phenomenon. Not only did the long-term financial demands of the project require the mobilization even of modest sums, but the very representation of the Church of the National Vow as a patriotic project of national dimensions demanded it. The idea of a *national* vow, expressing the will of the nation to return to its Christian vocation, suggested the broadest possible involvement. Patronage could not and should not be the work of the wealthy and the nobly born, although only individuals from these privileged strata served on Guibert's committee. Patronage should as much as possible be "popular," in the sense of emanating from the people.

In an effort to draw the support of Catholic workers and peasants, the committee broke new ground in its fund-raising efforts. The first step was to create an investment vehicle in which even the smallest contribution had its place. The *carte du Sacré-Coeur* (fig. 43) was the ideal instrument for the investor of modest means. The "card of the Sacred Heart" consisted of a heavy paper card on which more than a thousand squares were printed in columns and rows. Each time donors set aside ten centimes for the church of the Sacré-Coeur, they filled in a square. Donors picked up the cards or received them in their parishes and homes. Participants were encouraged to share cards among friends or within a family, as a way of hastening the

Figure 42. Pilgrimage procession on Montmartre. Taichon, "The canticle, after the painting by Béraud (Salon of 1887): Construction of the Sacré-Coeur de Montmartre." Musée Carnavalet, Paris. © Photothèque des Musées de la Ville de Paris.

Parishes and dioceses throughout France organized pilgrimages to the construction site on Montmartre. Their presence and their numbers served to validate the popular and national dimension of the project. Religious ritual or public demonstration? Either way, pilgrimages, not strikes or worker demonstrations, were the most important manifestations of collective will in late nineteenth-century France.

completion of the card and also as a way of associating greater numbers with the effort to build the church.[12] The *carte du Sacré-Coeur* reflected the entrepreneurial genius of those leading the Oeuvre, a genius worthy of the Crédit Mobilier and other efforts of the age aimed at mobilizing small investors. Other efforts were more conventional. In the fall of 1883, supporters of the Oeuvre disposed of hundreds of "contributions in kind," such as layettes, hand-knit wool stockings, and bits of royalist bric-a-brac, including images of Marie-Antoinette. The archbishop allowed the ground floor of the archdiocesan office to be used for the sale; this archdiocesan "rummage sale" netted more than 30,000 francs.[13]

Keeping the project before donors and present in their minds was important too. Donors received copies of a monthly publication, the *Bulletin de*

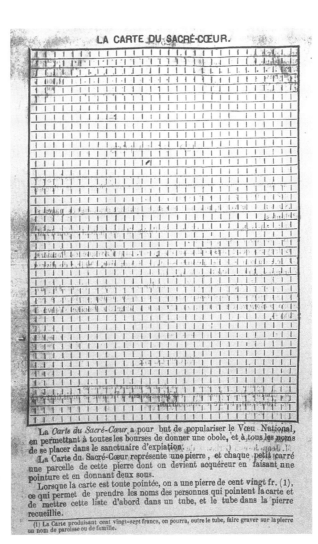

Figure 43. Modern fund-raising: the *carte du Sacré-Coeur*.
Bulletin de l'oeuvre du voeu national au Sacré-Coeur de Jésus 9
(10 February 1884): 126.

A "church of the national vow" worthy of the name should be
democratically funded. Accordingly, sponsors of the basilica
devised means, such as the card of the Sacred Heart, whereby
even those of very modest means could make a significant
donation. Donors checked a box every time they set aside two
sous (ten centimes). When the card was filled, they had saved
enough to donate a stone to the church.

l'oeuvre du voeu national au Sacré-Coeur de Jésus, which served as the official mouthpiece for Guibert, his committee, and their supporters. The *Bulletin* first appeared as part of the weekly bulletin of the diocese of Paris, but soon emerged as an independent monthly publication. As much as anything else, the *Bulletin* defined the aims of the National Vow and described its history, including the history of the Sacred Heart. The illustrated *Bulletin* ran regular features on key events in the history of the devotion to the Sacré-Coeur and the special message of the Sacré-Coeur for France. Anecdotes from the life of Marguerite-Marie Alacoque, the Vendée, the story of Belsunce and the plague at Marseille, the "vow" of Louis XVI, the battle of Loigny, the anniversaries of all of these events—the *Bulletin* kept Catholic France informed of the rich history and heroic tales in the saga of the nation and the Sacré-Coeur.

No one reading it could be unaware of the special relationship between France and the Sacred Heart. It confidently predicted the fulfillment of the special requests communicated to Marguerite-Marie Alacoque—a consecration, an emblem, a chapel—and underlined the critical importance of the Church of the National Vow as a major element in the national compact with the Divine. Like the glossy brochures sent to twentieth-century investors and charitable donors, the *Bulletin* put the best possible face on the project of the National Vow. It told investors how far construction had proceeded and what lay ahead. Quietly, skillfully, persistently, the *Bulletin* let investors know that they were part of a great patriotic and spiritual project and that their support was still needed.

A favorite technique of the editors of the monthly *Bulletin* of the Oeuvre was to place a drawing of the Sacré-Coeur beside a scale drawing of some familiar monument, inviting comparison and a competitive reaction. One such illustration showed the profile of the church next to the profile of one of Paris's other domed monuments, the Panthéon. The comparison was not entirely a flattering one, the graceful lines of Sainte-Geneviève only emphasized Sacré-Coeur's squat profile and its oddly elongated domes—hardly the conventional structure *la France profonde* might like to see and support with hard-earned centimes. The Sacré-Coeur was also shorter than the Panthéon. But the caption reminded the reader that "the soil on which our sanctuary reposes is at the level of the top of the Panthéon's dome."[14] In other words, the Sacré-Coeur begins where the Panthéon ends. This remark suggests how much the project's sponsors saw *their* national shrine, the Sacré-Coeur, as standing in a competitive relationship to the aims embodied by the Panthéon, the erstwhile church, reconsecrated by the Republic as a national temple in the secular cult of republican spirituality.[15]

Advocates for the Sacré-Coeur also stimulated rivalries at the corporate level, between municipalities and dioceses, between professions and affinity groups. The diocese of Chambéry donated the great bell for the basilica, naming it the "Savoyard."[16] Naval officers contributed to one of the small interior chapels of the basilica, the Chapel of the Navy. A Chapel of the Army was similarly funded. Doctors helped fund a Chapel of Medicine; attorneys proposed a Chapel of Justice.[17] Workers were asked to contribute to the chapel of Saint Joseph the carpenter.

Fund-raisers know that donors will contribute larger sums when they derive some incidental benefit from their contribution, a token of their effort and their sacrifice, or when they can see their contributions take tangible form. In order to keep the ultimate goal clearly before the project's backers and to show the progress made to date, the *Bulletin* reported on the progress of construction. An effective technique was to show the Sacré-Coeur church in outline as a kind of vessel. As construction went forward and as donations came in, the Oeuvre's artists could show the Sacré-Coeur "filling up" (fig. 44). This image, more readily than annual reports of donations, gave contributors a clear sense of how much church their money had bought, and how much remained to be redeemed. It also helped donors understand the project in its tangible form and to identify with something larger, grander, and more permanent than themselves.

So did the technique of allowing contributors, individually or collectively, to "buy" pieces of the church, to see their generosity unambiguously associated with a specific item or location within the edifice. Pieces of the church were put up for sale; those who bought them could have their pieces personalized. Their connection with the Sacré-Coeur and its message was thus rendered concrete. Each donor contributed in a tangible way to the work of atonement. Portions of the church available for "purchase" included pillars, decorative columns, and simple stones (fig. 45). Each had its price and could be personalized in some way, typically by affording varying degrees of prominence to the name of the donor. The purchase and personalization of a small decorative pillar required a donation of anywhere between 1,000 and 5,000 francs. Load-bearing columns started at 5,000 and could cost as much as 100,000 francs, especially if they were to display an inscription or coat of

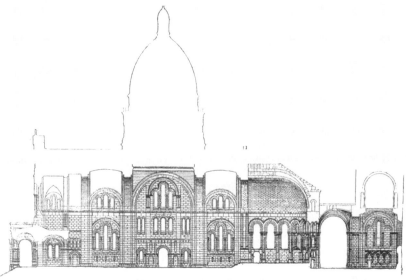

État des travaux en 1888, le remplissage des murs au dessus de la frise ne sera fait que plus tard.

Figure 44. A profile of the church fills as donations come in. *Bulletin de l'oeuvre du voeu national au Sacré-Coeur de Jésus,* 10 July 1888, 391.

Innovative techniques made the campaign for the Church of the National Vow a model of modern fund-raising. The sponsors of the Sacré-Coeur regularly updated a drawing of the church in profile, with the stones "filling up" as donations came in. Reports such as these on the progress of donations helped large and small donors visualize the cumulative effective of their charity and sacrifice.

arms. For donors of more modest means there was always the possibility of purchasing a stone bearing one's initials. Here the price ranged from 300 to 500 francs, according to the placement of the stone and the visibility of the donor's initials or coat of arms. For the more circumspect, 300 francs bought a stone where the initials would not be visible. Those willing to run the risk of a sin of pride could pay larger sums to see their initials etched in stone at eye level. Such "naming opportunities" were available at prices even the most modest investor could afford.

For those whose wishes could not be expressed by a simple motto, the committee would see to it that a prayer or intention was sealed within the walls of the church itself. Donors inscribed their intentions on a small

Figure 45. Lifting stones into place. Archives historiques du diocèse de Paris.

Along with the Eiffel Tower, the Sacré-Coeur was one of the great engineering marvels of late nineteenth-century Paris. Here workers move cut stones into place. Individual stones were attached to chain and pulley by means of a wedge built up by shims; stones were then raised and moved into position.

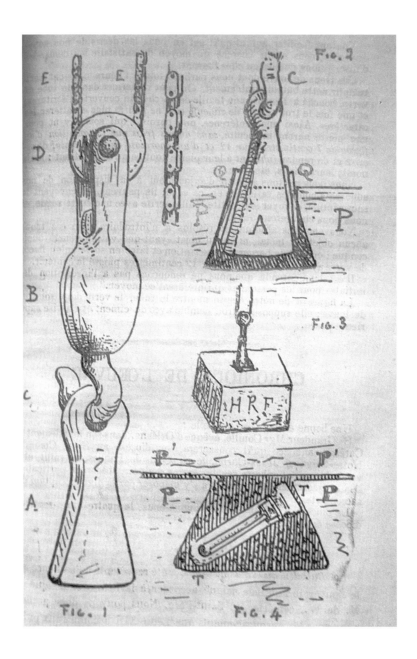

Figure 46. Prayers wrapped in stone. *Bulletin de l'oeuvre du voeu national au Sacré-Coeur de Jésus,* 10 March 1879, 150.

Sponsors realized that the hole used for lifting the stones into position could be filled before being covered with the next stone. Donors were given the opportunity to write their prayers and intentions on slips of paper that were placed in corked glass tubes. The tubes were placed in the hole, then enveloped within the structure when the next stone was put into place. The walls of the Sacré-Coeur incorporate hundreds of such prayers.

parchment scroll that was placed inside a small glass tube and corked like a test tube (fig. 46). After workers lowered the stone into place, they would place the tube and scroll, bearing the donor's wishes and sentiments, in a niche cut into the top of the stone. Mortar and the next row of stones sealed the scroll in place in perpetuity.[18] Sponsors liked to speak of the Sacré-Coeur as a massive ex-voto, the embodiment of a national prayer; thanks to the encapsulation of scrolls, the Sacré-Coeur not only embodied prayer, it incorporated prayer. Donors had the satisfaction of knowing that their prayerful intentions had been deposited within the national ex-voto of the Sacré-Coeur—a prayer within a prayer.

THE TEACHABLE MOMENT:
PILGRIMAGE AND THE SACRÉ-COEUR

The design of the Church of the National Vow revealed the monumental and ritualistic intentions of its sponsors. This was to be no ordinary neighborhood church, a place for weekly and annual rituals along with baptisms, marriages and funerals. Montmartre already had Saint-Pierre for such ordinary events, leaving the Church of the National Vow to assume a distinct role as a place of pilgrimage. Abadie's design revealed that this would be a pilgrim's church, starting with the wide ambulatory (the side aisles) which provided ample space for the circulation of crowds, as well as the chapels around the church and in the crypt for the dozens of priests who would lead the pilgrims. However, it would be more than a decade before the interior of the church would be ready for pilgrims. The hasty construction of the *chapelle provisoire* shows the importance of the ideas of pilgrimage and penitence to the project. Until 1891, when the interior of the still-unfinished church was blessed by Guibert's successor, the wood-and-plaster "provisional chapel" was the official reception point for pilgrims to Montmartre.

Pilgrimage is a voyage to a holy place. Its essential elements are the person of faith, a sacred goal, and the space between. Lesser destinations than Montmartre have succeeded as sacred goals of pilgrimage; indeed obscurity seems to mark some destinations out for greatness. No site in modern times has exceeded the popularity of the grotto at Lourdes where Bernadette Soubirous experienced a vision of the Virgin Mary. Nothing before that day in 1858 marked this village in the Pyrenees as a spiritually lush site. Montmartre had the rich history of the city to draw upon, and the church being built upon it was enriched rhetorically by its sponsors and advocates. The Sacré-Coeur of Montmartre would be likened to a variety of objects: an ex-voto, a sacred lightning rod—even a powerhouse generating "a current of prayers of regeneration." [19] All of these expressed something about the spiritual allure the Sacré-Coeur held for its visitors.

The fact that pilgrims arrived at Montmartre from across France, just as donations did, helped to substantiate the assertion that the National Vow was truly national (fig. 47). The *Bulletin* regularly reported the number of pilgrims and their dioceses of origin as a way of demonstrating the popular and national appeal of their undertaking. These figures reveal the geography of the Sacré-Coeur pilgrimage. The most common dioceses of origin are precisely those known for the faithfulness of their religious practice. The dioceses of the Vendée also sent more than their share of pilgrims, a measure no doubt of the enduring importance of the Sacré-Coeur to local belief and identity.[20] The diocese of Strasbourg was among the better represented among pilgrims to Montmartre, although it is doubtful that many pilgrimages to Paris actually originated there. Strasbourg was no longer a French city after 1871, but the recovery of the "lost provinces," linked to the defeat of 1870–71, were very much a part of the national ambition of the devotion of the Sacré-Coeur. Pilgrimages from "Strasbourg" were probably pilgrimages of Alsatian refugee communities within the new territorial limits of France. Refugees from Alsace, for example, established a sizable colony in Paris's fifteenth arrondissement. In June 1884, two thousand Alsatian pilgrims ascended Montmartre to pray the rosary aloud and in German.[21]

Pilgrimages were also an important source of revenue. Many donations, sizable ones at that, were made directly to the offices of the archbishop of Paris. Many more donations were made to the committee the archbishop of Paris had named responsible for overseeing the construction of the Sacré-Coeur. But within a few years pilgrims at the site itself and the temporary chapel would consistently provide over half of the income for the project. In 1878, the donations of pilgrims exceeded half a million francs for the first time. Donations would remain at or above this figure in subsequent years and beyond the turn of the century. By 1883, the donations of pilgrims exceeded those of wealthy donors solicited by the archbishop or his committee. For the remainder of the century, pilgrims, many of them anonymous, constituted the greatest source of revenue for the project year in, year out.

Figure 47. A Sacré-Coeur souvenir purchased by a pilgrim from the region of Perpignan. Private collection.

Pilgrimage in medieval times was for the most part a solitary activity. The distinguishing characteristic of modern pilgrimage is its scale; in fact, in the 1890s, it blended into a recognizably modern form of organized leisure. The typical pilgrimage to the Sacré-Coeur de Montmartre was an orchestrated event involving dozens of people who benefited from group rates on train travel and lodging. Diocesan and parish priests often served as guides. Pilgrims leave behind their prayers and intentions. They take away souvenirs—literally, memories of their pilgrimage.

Detailed pilgrimage financial records also provide insights into the motives of the pilgrims. When did they make the pilgrimage, and what does this tell us about what drew them to Montmartre? Records were apparently not kept on when pilgrims arrived or how numerous they were, but monthly records of receipts provide some clues. If we assume that income from donations in some rough way reflected the number of pilgrims, these figures give us a useful measure of the annual cycle of pilgrimages. To be sure, the most popular months to make the pilgrimage were the spring and summer months of May through September. Three-fifths of the annual income at the *chapelle provisoire* came during June or in the months immediately preceding or following. Does this mean that pilgrimages to Montmartre were part of larger fine-weather plans? In part. But this should not be surprising: pilgrimage has always been a warm-weather undertaking. And it is worth pointing out that by far the most popular month of pilgrimage was June, the month of the feast of the Sacred Heart.[22]

Pilgrimage to Montmartre also deviated from the pilgrimage paradigm. Indeed the question "Why pilgrimage?" is a perplexing one in this regard because, although the Sacré-Coeur would contain relics, contact with relics never constituted the climax of the pilgrimage experience. Pilgrimages elsewhere typically culminate in the cathartic touching, rubbing, hugging, or kissing of a relic or reliquary. And even where relics are lacking, physical contact with the sacred is assured in other ways: at Lourdes immersion fulfills this function; at Chartres it is "visual communion" with the Virgin's veil and the touching or kissing of the column that supports it. There was no comparable theophanic presence at Montmartre—or at least not one that served as the pilgrim's object of spiritual desire, contact with which served as metaphor for the healing the pilgrim sought. The reason for the absence of the ritualistic contact with the sacred is not clear, but it may have to do with the shift in emphasis from the individual penitent to a collective penitence founded upon a collective responsibility embedded in the nation's past. In the salvation story of the Sacré-Coeur, *history* is theophany and the presence of the Sacred is revealed in time as much as space.

Thus, pilgrimage had a didactic function, explaining the devotion of the Sacré-Coeur and the historical vision of France. Driving home the point was the use of the Sacré-Coeur emblem among pilgrims. The Sacré-Coeur emblem had had its place at crucial moments in France's past—at Marseille during the plague, at the royal court and in the Vendée during the Revolution, on the uniforms of France's papal volunteers in Rome and at Loigny, on the lapels of the deputies at Paray-le-Monial when they tearfully consecrated France to the Sacré-Coeur in 1873. A papal brief of 1861 promised the spiritual reward of a hundred days' indulgence for wearing the Sacré-Coeur image on the chest with the inscription *Adveniat regnum tuum*—thy kingdom come. Additional rewards were offered for openly wearing the image while taking part in public prayers and public processions.[23] In short, the Sacré-Coeur was to become the sign of the Catholic activist in pursuit of the "social reign of the Sacré-Coeur"—shorthand for the re-Christianization of public life.

The clergy who accompanied the pilgrims, and the pilgrimage guides the pilgrims used, drove home these points. The *Bulletin* printed portions of the homilies given before audiences of pilgrims, and these homilies summarized the national historical trajectory, the story of apostasy and national decline followed by the (hoped-for) re-Christianization and regeneration through the Sacré-Coeur.[24] Thus, the climax of the pilgrimage to Montmartre was not the pilgrim's purgative encounter with a relic but the collective experience of holy Mass and homily, a spiritual experience with a didactic component emphasizing the French past and immanence of God in history. Speakers emphasized the importance of developing the private devotion to the Sacré-Coeur as much as possible as a "prelude" to a future national devotion.[25] Songs presented the same ideas in tuneful and easily learned form. One of the most popular songs, dubbed "The Canticle of the National Vow" and, less often, but more tellingly, "The Catholic Marseillaise," summarized the embattled mood of Catholics in a secularized France, especially after the disasters of the Terrible Year. Its refrain ran simply "Merciful God, O Conquering God! Save Rome and France in the name of the Sacré-Coeur!"[26] It was, in effect, the theme-song of the National Vow, and it was heard in pilgrimages from Montmartre, to Paray-le-Monial, to Lourdes throughout the 1870s, 1880s, and 1890s.

In an age of mass politics, crowds in public places at certain moments can be taken to embody "public opinion." Pilgrimage was the most effective way for Catholics to generate such entities and to exercise similar pressures, to pose as a scaled-down version of the nation itself. The number of pilgrims and the distances they traversed witnessed not only to the pilgrims' faith but also to their inner resolve and public engagement. Participation in pilgrimage to Montmartre implied participation in an energetic, collective, public, and patriotic undertaking. Their gestures and insignia signaled their collective assent.[27] Through the practices of monument building, metaphor for moral reconstruction, and holy pilgrimage, metaphor for the re-Christianization of the public realm, the French episcopate and clergy used the Montmartre site not only to foster a new spirituality but also to inculcate Catholic France with a vision of France's heroic Christian past, its decadent, secularized, post-revolutionary present, and a glorious future. The vision of the Sacré-Coeur drew, in part, upon a romanticized, even medievalized and religiously integrated ideal of France, but the techniques of its sponsors were thoroughly innovative and modern. Pilgrimage put masses of people in public places on behalf of France and the Sacred Heart of Jesus.

BUILDING IN FITS AND STARTS

The donations of pilgrims validated the populist claims of the sponsors of the basilica of the Sacré-Coeur. Those same donations also assured the completion of the nation's ex-voto, but the piecemeal nature of that source of funding meant that the construction of the church would take place over decades rather than years. Although the first stone was laid at the Montmartre site in 1875, and the temporary chapel opened early in 1876, it would be 1881 before construction had proceeded to the point that the first of the chapel altars was ready for use. Archbishop Guibert offered Mass in what would be known as the chapel of Saint Martin, a nod to France's Christianizing warrior bishop, Martin of Tours, as well as to Guibert's service as bishop at Tours. The structure was not ready for regular use until 1886, when the practice of round-the-clock prayer was instituted. In 1887, the side chapels—those of the apse and the side aisles—were blessed and made available to visiting clergy. In 1891, the interior of the basilica was ready and solemnly inaugurated by Archbishop François Richard; the temporary chapel was closed. By then, both the church's original architect—Paul Abadie—and Archbishop Guibert had died.

The basilica was far from complete, however. The large central dome was not completed until 1900, when it was inaugurated in June, a full twenty-five years after the laying of the first stone. A ceremonial blessing of the first stone of the campanile did not take place until June of 1905. The visible portions of the campanile were completed in 1912; workers placed the last tread in the staircase to the top of the tower in late summer 1914. At a conference in Lourdes in July of 1914, Archbishop Amette (Richard's successor as archbishop of Paris) had announced the consecration of the completed structure for October of that year. The outbreak of World War I forced the postponement for the duration of the war. In 1919, Amette consecrated the Church of the National Vow before a congregation including nine cardinals, twelve archbishops, and ninety-eight bishops from France and abroad.

Along the way, Abadie's project had undergone some significant revisions. Professor Honoré Daumet of the École des Beaux Arts had succeeded Abadie as architect in 1884; he lasted little more than a year on the job before being edged out following a variety of conflicts. He was succeeded by another Beaux Arts professor (Charles Laisné) in 1886 who was in turn succeeded upon his death in 1891 by Henri Rauline, who had worked with both Abadie and Daumet as general contractor on the site and had in that capacity provided much of the continuity on the project. Daumet, Laisné, and Rauline made some significant changes in Abadie's design, including the raising of the central dome to allow for taller windows, bringing more light to the interior of the church. Lucien Magne served as architect for the campanile. He rejected the elongated dome that Abadie had imagined for the campanile, reckoning that the church already had plenty; he substituted a conical top.[28]

Twenty years into construction at the site, the prominent Catholic politician Albert de Mun could claim some eight million contributors for the Sacré-Coeur. The vigorous pursuit of donors of modest means gave the Church of the National Vow a broad and popular basis. But it was still vulnerable to its critics. There were at least three serious attempts in the National Assembly to abrogate the law of 24 July 1873, which had declared the project a matter of "public utility." Debate was sometimes acrimonious. The republican Left dubbed the church a provocation. In 1882 Georges Clémenceau sharply criticized a monument that signified asking forgiveness "for having fought for the rights of man, to repent for having made the French Revolution."[29] There were similar unsuccessful initiatives undertaken in 1891 and 1897.

Without a doubt, the most persistent and resourceful of opponents was Gustave Téry, a graduate of the elite École Normale Supérieure and a resident of Montmartre. Téry was a positivist skeptic in the tradition of Flaubert's pharmacist Homais. He was also a gadfly, of which Montmartre has produced and harbored more than its share over the years. Téry was a prankster. In one instance, he drafted a letter of complaint to the prime minister, claiming that the basilica, by its sheer weight, was causing the sides of Montmartre to crumble and give way. He cited as evidence the fact that cracks appeared in the paving here and there; that despite every attention lavished on them, young trees refused to grow: they merely withered in the unstable soil. Even worse, a lovely clump of irises planted along the rue Ronsard had shifted by "more than a meter."[30] In another episode, Téry posed as a devout Catholic in order to join the nocturnal prayers, processions, and devotions at the basilica, then wrote a scathing report—an exposé—in a small volume titled *les Cordicoles.* His wildest scheme involved a proposal to expropriate the Sacré-Coeur and convert it into a recreational facility at the disposal of the people. Montmartre's Palais du Peuple would boast a public library, shops, and a theater with seats for an audience of more than a thousand.[31]

Critics of the Sacré-Coeur were, of course, deaf to the religious and Christian patriotic arguments in favor of the project, but there were lay arguments that sometimes made them hesitate. That the construction of the Church of the National Vow provided a steady flow of cash and employment for building workers and decorative trades was undeniable; it constituted one of the best secular arguments the defenders of the Sacré-Coeur could make, and they made it repeatedly. The original legislation for the declaration of "public utility" mentioned jobs for Montmartre construction workers as one of the great benefits of the project.[32] By 1882, at the time of the first serious legislative initiative to undermine the project of the Sacré-Coeur, the project's defenders pointed out that between twelve and fifteen million francs had been spent on the Sacré-Coeur de Montmartre, a rate of well over a million francs per year. By the end of 1896, some twenty years after the laying of the first stone, nearly thirty million francs had been expended.[33] These years were precisely the years of the European "Long Depression" that followed the boom after the Franco-Prussian war and preceded the economic upswing of the Belle Époque at the end of the 1890s. Montmartre and its immediate neighbor Belleville were working-class neighborhoods. The Sacré-Coeur was hocus-pocus or worse for many deputies of the French Left, but the economic benefits of the Sacré-Coeur construction for their working-class constituents were not to be sneered at.

The enemies of the Sacré-Coeur scored a victory of sorts in 1905. General elections in 1902 had given a legislative majority in the National Assembly to a coalition of the republican Left. The leading party, a populist and anti-clerical coalition of republicans known as the Radicals, pushed through legislation mandating the separation of church and state, ending more than a hundred years of public subsidy of religion in France. The new law seemed to validate Catholic fears that the return of the Republic meant a recapitulation of the anti-religious activism of the French Revolution. It unmistakably announced a new phase of strained relations between the Catholic Church and the republican majority. It certainly signaled the end of most lingering Catholic ambitions for the "social reign" of the Sacré-Coeur, Catholic code language for putting Catholic beliefs and values at the center of public life in France.

The 1905 separation law also had consequences for the Church of the National Vow. Church property had been nationalized during the French Revolution. Under the terms of the separation of 1905, places of worship acquired *since* the Revolution—churches, chapels, parish churches—became public property. These properties were municipalized, that is, they became the property of local governments who managed and maintained them and made them available to the clergy for religious services. The archdiocese of Paris disputed the municipalization of the Sacré-Coeur in court. They argued that Joseph Guibert had acquired the property in his capacity as archbishop of Paris in his name and in the name of his successors. In 1908 the ruling went against the archdiocese. It was a devastating setback. Just as the project was entering its final phase, the Church of the National Vow became the property of the city of Paris.

A VISION CAPTURED IN MOSAIC

The Revolution of 1789 was permitted only in order to make possible
an incomparable triumph for the Church.

FRANÇOIS PIE,
bishop of Poitiers, 1860

The Revolution is death. It sullies, it defiles, it shatters, it kills.
Now, in the present hour, the Revolution and the Heart of Jesus
draw closer and closer together.

ALEXANDRE DELAPORTE, *1886*

The Republic has received neither from God nor from history
any promise of immortality.

JOSEPH GUIBERT,
archbishop of Paris, 30 March 1886

HIGH ABOVE THE CHOIR OF the Sacré-Coeur of Montmartre, a triumphant figure of the Sacré-Coeur looks down into the nave of the basilica.
He stands before a throne, his arms outstretched, his heart visible on his
chest. To his right and to his left, phalanxes of figures stand in poses of adoration. It is the apotheosis of the Sacré-Coeur, both of the church and of the
devotion.

At the same time that ownership of the Sacré-Coeur of Montmartre was
passing to the city of Paris, plans were going forward for what would be the

Figure 48. The Sacred Heart in triumph. Mosaic in the Sacré-Coeur de Montmartre. Archives historiques du diocèse de Paris.

Romano-Byzantine architecture called for mosaic decoration inside the basilica, while the "national" nature of the enterprise largely precluded the use of foreign artists. Thus the decoration of the Sacré-Coeur was the occasion for the revival of mosaic art in late nineteenth- and early twentieth-century France.

main work of art within the basilica. Gothic churches rely on light; the sacred art within them typically consists of stained glass. Romanesque churches impress the viewer with their mass; they impose themselves on the viewer with their sheer immensity. The vast interior surfaces of stone within Romanesque churches lend themselves to decoration with frescoes and, where funds allow, mosaics. Paul Abadie had chosen the stones of Château-Landon for the Sacré-Coeur because they whiten with exposure. For the dark interior of the gleaming white church on Montmartre, he wanted the contrast of a church rich in ornamentation, mosaics, gold and silver, in keeping with the decorative traditions of the Romanesque and Byzantine styles.

Although he didn't live to see it, Abadie mostly got what he wanted. His Sacré-Coeur radiated a gleaming whiteness from atop Montmartre. Mosaic would be featured throughout the Sacré-Coeur of Montmartre, in inscriptions, behind and above chapel altars, and on the barrel vault above the choir. By 1911, the basic theme for the mosaic high above the altar had been decided. The painter Luc-Olivier Merson served as artistic director on the project. Merson, Lucien Magne, the architect, his son Henri-Marcel Magne, and Marcel Imbs each contributed to the creation of models and the execution of the actual mosaic. Only Henri-Marcel Magne and Marcel Imbs were alive when the mosaic was completed in 1923.[1]

The monumental mosaic they collaborated to create covers an area of approximately 375 square meters.[2] It recounts in pictures the saga of the Sacré-Coeur. In the center, above the choir (fig. 48), Jesus looks down in triumph from the heavens, his Sacred Heart exposed. To his right and left figures are ranged in two domains, heaven and earth. Above, on the "heavenly" tier stand the saints of the Catholic Church; below them the "earthbound" representatives of the Catholic Church pay homage as do figures representing the peoples and the continents. To the left, the saints of France are shown in heavenly array.

In the earthly scenes below them one finds key scenes from the saga of France and the Sacred Heart. In the first panel, the plague at Marseille (fig. 49): Bishop Belsunce kneels beside a dying man, the bishop's arms open wide in a gesture of supplication to the Sacré-Coeur. Second panel: Louis XVI kneels with his arms outstretched, the dauphin and the dauphine beside him, with Marie-Antoinette and Madame Élisabeth nearby—it is the consecration of his family and his realm to the Sacré-Coeur (fig. 50). Third panel: the National Vow. General de Charette holds the banner from Loigny

Figure 49. Belsunce consecrates Marseille to the Sacred Heart. Mosaic in the Sacré-Coeur de Montmartre. Photo: Emmanuel Michot. © Ville de Paris— C.O.A.R.C.

The monumental mosaic in the Sacré-Coeur takes up the tradition of Byzantine narrative mosaics, showing discrete episodes in distinct frames or spaces.

(fig. 51). In his right hand, he raises his sword in a salute. General de Sonis is beside him. In front of Sonis and Charette are the lay sponsors of the National Vow, including Alexandre Legentil and Rohault de Fleury. Finally come the archbishops of Paris, including Amette, Richard, and Guibert, who holds an ex-voto, a model of the basilica of the Sacré-Coeur.

Almost unobserved in the background of the scenes illustrating the vow of Louis XVI and the heroes of the battle of Loigny, a lone figure, a *sans-culotte,* stands at ease. He leans against the frame, unmoved by the gestures of devotion around him. He has a sullen look on his face. He folds his arms impassively. He alone among this earthly and heavenly multitude is indifferent to the sacred scene before him.

Figure 50. The vow of Louis XVI. Mosaic in the Sacré-Coeur de Montmartre. Photo: Emmanuel Michot. © Ville de Paris—C.O.A.R.C.

Louis XVI, supported by his family and his confessor, consecrates France to the Sacred Heart.

Figure 51. The National Vow. Mosaic in the Sacré-Coeur de Montmartre. Photo: Emmanuel Michot. © Ville de Paris—C.O.A.R.C.

At left, the archbishops of Paris present the Sacré-Coeur; in the center, lay sponsors of the National Vow stand beside a kneeling Alexandre Legentil; at right, Sonis and Charette, the heroes of the battle of Loigny, present their swords and banner. At the far right, a figure in the distinctive dress of the *sans-culotte* crosses his arms in a gesture of indifference.

Within the basilica of the Sacré-Coeur de Montmartre, this figure is the sole representation of the secular France that emerged from the French Revolution. He is, in effect, revolutionary France, taking his place outside of the assembled figures of Catholic France paying homage to the Sacré-Coeur. His posture—indeed, his mere presence—says as much about the carefully cultivated sense of difference among French Catholics as it does about secularized republican France. The devotion to the Sacré-Coeur is a counter-culture, with its own set of sustaining heroic myths set apart from and in conflict with the dominant heroic and transcendent story of revolutionary France. While revolutionary and republican France looks elsewhere, the Sacré-Coeur rivets the attention of Catholic France.

A SINGULAR MONUMENT, A SINGULAR DEVOTION

The basilica of the Sacré-Coeur is the key monument of modern French Catholicism. It is the structure around which one can organize the remarkable salvation story of France and the Sacred Heart, a story which dominated the spiritual and political thinking of French Catholics for more than a century after 1789. The stories of Marguerite-Marie Alacoque, of Anne-Madeleine Rémuzat, of Henri de Belsunce at Marseille—these revealed the power of the devotion and talisman of the Sacré-Coeur at the popular level in the eighteenth century, but the French Revolution introduced the Sacré-Coeur to French political culture as the central symbol of opposition to the Revolution. As Visitationist convents and others churned out Sacred Heart emblems by the tens of thousands during the revolutionary crisis, the kernel of a revived Jesuit Order in France, the Society of the Heart of Jesus, was founded in clandestinity to defend the Catholic Church and work to defeat the Revolution. When Marianne went into combat, she encountered the Sacré-Coeur.

For much of the nineteenth century, the devotion to the Sacré-Coeur had the dual advantages of ritual and memory; the memory of association with counter-revolution and the richness of the devotion meant that one could signal one's opposition by means of the simple rituals of faith. There was something ostensibly innocuous about distributing Sacré-Coeur emblems, as the Catholic clergy did, to pilgrims at Nantes, or Angers, or Paris, or Paray-le-Monial. But could these pilgrims have accepted and pinned on these emblems without thinking of the Vendéen counter-revolutionaries who had

made the same gesture in defiance of the Republic in 1793? One could answer the appeals of the sponsors of the Church of the National Vow, one
could make sacrifices—small economies—and set aside money to contribute a stone to the construction of the Sacré-Coeur. But could anyone do so
without being reminded of Louis XVI, captive of the Revolution, who had
vowed to build such a church if his authority were restored?

The saga of the Sacré-Coeur offered an integral vision of France and the
promise of national renewal upon the fulfillment of the requests expressed
to Marguerite-Marie Alacoque. For a time in the 1870s, it seemed that all of
the elements might come together. The Church of the National Vow would
be built. The people of France, chastened by the disasters of invasion and
civil war, seemed ready to accept the notion that things had somehow gone
radically wrong. For those with a vivid imagination, for those whose minds
could accept the notions of providential designs and chosen people, it was
almost possible to envision a renewal, a restoration of French greatness, following a public consecration of France to the Sacred Heart of Jesus in a ceremony on Montmartre.

Although it was almost never explicitly stated, it was broadly implied that
the return of the would-be Bourbon king—Henri, the comte de Chambord—as the agent of the restoration of Christian monarchy, was part of this
grand design. Cardinal Pie, bishop of Poitiers, was a close adviser to the Bourbon pretender and went to little trouble to hide his conviction that the return
of Chambord was not only desirable for France but necessary to the survival
of their vision of it. Some of the most ardent defenders of the Sacré-Coeur
in the National Assembly, Gabriel de Belcastel and Édouard Cazenove de
Pradines, similarly pushed a program of monarchical restoration, refusing to
make a distinction between their Catholic beliefs and their commitment to
monarchy.

Cazenove de Pradines was a former Papal Volunteer. He was wounded
and lost the use of his arm during the charge at the battle of Loigny. He represented the Nantes region in the National Assembly, whose sessions he
attended dressed in his volunteer's uniform, his arm in a sling, the Sacré-
Coeur stitched to his lapel. Cazenove prided himself on his candor and
made a national reputation for himself by declaring that to postpone a monarchical restoration was "equivalent to postponing the social and religious
restoration" of France.[3] Also known as "chevalier of the Sacré-Coeur," in
1873 Cazenove proposed that the National Assembly *as a body* attend the lay-

ing of the first stone of the Church of the National Vow on Montmartre.[4] The motion failed for lack of votes.

Cazenove de Pradines, with his uniform and his reputation burnished at Loigny, enhanced the image of the Catholic Right. He had the direct speech and manner of a soldier, but he lacked the political polish that Gabriel de Belcastel could bring, so Belcastel spoke more often and more effectively on behalf of the vision of France regenerated through the Sacré-Coeur. Belcastel had served on the Parisian committee of the *Communion Réparatrice,* a devotional community organized by Père Drevon in the 1860s, one of whose goals was to support a national consecration by means of prayer, ritual, and community organization.[5] In 1871, Belcastel was elected to represent Toulouse in the National Assembly, and in the aftermath of the Terrible Year he spoke of a "gigantic war" between the Catholic Church and the Revolution, "which is to say, between social conservation and universal destruction."[6] In June of 1873, he led a delegation of more than a hundred deputies from the National Assembly, Sacred Heart emblems on their chests, on a pilgrimage to Paray-le-Monial, site of Marguerite-Marie Alacoque's original visions. There he read aloud the text of their consecration of France to the Sacré-Coeur, against an background of sobs and cries of "Penitence!"[7] Belcastel promoted Christian monarchy, "the lifeblood and virtue of peoples," as his political program for national renewal.[8] He served on the committee in the National Assembly that hammered out the wording of the declaration of "public utility" that authorized Archbishop Guibert's purchase of the Montmartre site.[9]

French historian Jacques Gadille has argued, and others too, that Archbishop Guibert took care to remove the Sacré-Coeur project "from any counter-revolutionary context."[10] This statement is true in the sense that Joseph Guibert, archbishop of Paris, and his successor François Richard were generally circumspect in their politics and their public pronouncements about the Church of the National Vow. But with advocates such as Belcastel and Cazenove speaking on the "national" importance of the National Vow, they hardly needed to bother. And even so, there were notable lapses in Guibert's vigilance, starting with the invitations extended to Generals de Sonis and de Charette, the heroes of Loigny, to serve on the "Committee of the National Vow" (fig. 52). This blue-ribbon committee was chosen to advise the archbishop of Paris in the construction of the church. The presence of Charette and Sonis on this committee, both notorious Legitimists, was

Figure 52. General de Sonis, hero of the battle of Loigny. Louis Baunard, *Le Général de Sonis d'après ses papiers et sa correspondance* (Paris, 1890).

bound to confuse supporters about the nature and purpose of the Church of the National Vow.

Sonis's inability to distinguish religion from politics was evident in the prayer corner that he kept in his residence. His domestic shrine, lovingly decorated with flowers from his garden, included a statue of Mary, a statue of the Sacré-Coeur, and portraits of Louis XVI and Marie-Antoinette, whom he apparently regarded as as-yet uncanonized saints and martyrs.[11] Sonis declined to serve on Guibert's committee for reasons of health. As for Charette, it would have taken a monumental act of will for Guibert to ignore what Pope Pius IX himself readily recognized — that the Charette name served as a flag for royalism.[12] Moreover, Charette was in regular contact with the Bourbon pretender, the comte de Chambord and his wife; indeed Charette invited them to serve as godparents to his children.[13] In addition to serving Guibert on the Committee of the National Vow, Charette remained openly hostile to the Republic throughout a long and very public life. Even if we concede that the association of Sonis and Charette with the project was a measure not of their politics but of their devotion to the Sacré-Coeur, at the very least their association left the meaning of the project of the National Vow open to misunderstanding.[14]

Moreover, Guibert surely knew that in matters of politics, what one doesn't say often matters as much as what one does. When Guibert's monarchist ally Albert de Mun sought election to the National Assembly, Guibert asked the bishop in de Mun's district to help his friend. Guibert did not ask for an endorsement of de Mun. "We shouldn't get too mixed-up in politics," he wrote. But he did note that the *lack* of support for de Mun's rival would be enough to tip the scales in favor of the monarchist. "All that is necessary is that one knows that you do not support [his rival]."[15] Guibert's icy and silent hostility to the Republic, combined with his warm relations with the monarchist advocates of the Sacré-Coeur, said all that needed to be said about his political preferences.

Little wonder that the death of the comte de Chambord left so many supporters of the National Vow in a state of disarray. Chambord, in exile in Frohsdorf (Austria) for much of his life, had never made a secret of his conviction of the relevance of the Sacré-Coeur saga to the vitality of France. He associated himself in exile with the deputies who had gone to Paray-le-Monial in June of 1873 to consecrate France to the Sacré-Coeur. Every year the ceremony was repeated in exile; the would-be king consecrated himself, his family, and France to the Sacré-Coeur. Had he been able to return to France as king, Henri surely would have made such a consecration formal and official, fulfilling the demand of a royal consecration expressed to Marguerite-Marie Alacoque.[16]

DEATH OF A WOULD-BE KING

Toward the end of August 1883, news reached royalist circles in France that the comte de Chambord was suffering from a grave illness. For Chambord to die without an heir (he had none) and without having recovered his throne and secured an orderly succession would be a disaster. Not only would it signal the end of the Bourbon monarchy, it would undermine the scenario envisioned for the redemption of France through a royal consecration to the Sacré-Coeur. As the news of Chambord's health became increasingly grave, Albert de Mun joined a contingent of Catholic senators and deputies from the National Assembly in a night of prayers at the Sacré-Coeur de Montmartre.[17] Throughout the succeeding days there were fervent prayers at Montmartre for Chambord's recovery. Now only a miracle would save the king and the Sacré-Coeur scenario; for who, without the king, would possess the moral authority to consecrate France to the Sacré-Coeur?

At Frohsdorf, the comte de Chambord's condition worsened. General de Charette was with Chambord, as was Cazenove and several other Papal Volunteers who had fought at Loigny. The dying man took Charette's hand and pulled him close. "I want you to bring me your flag," he whispered in a weakening voice. Charette brought the blood-spattered Sacré-Coeur banner for Chambord to touch a final time. The comte de Chambord died a short while later.

After Henri died, Charette approached the body with his banner and spoke as if the comte de Chambord still lived. "My Lord and my King. You ordered me to bring my flag. Here it is. I place it on your heart!" Then he raised the banner and laid it upon Chambord's body. Then he bowed, leaning forward to kiss Chambord's hand. Each of the Volunteers in attendance did likewise. Then the banner of the Sacred Heart was placed at the head of the bed, alongside the white flag of the Bourbon dynasty.[18]

Monarchist circles were left leaderless by Chambord's death. Some vowed loyalty to the comte de Paris, the Orléanist pretender and rightful heir by the laws of succession. Charette did so, at least initially.[19] But memory is long in France and many Legitimists could not bring themselves to support the comte de Paris because they could not forgive his ancestors. These included Louis-Philippe d'Orléans, who, until his death by guillotine in 1793, was widely suspected of having encouraged the Revolution in order to bring about the downfall of Louis XVI and thus prepare his own succession. And while the comte de Paris provided ample evidence of his piety (unlike his notoriously irreligious ancestor) he lacked credibility as a standard-bearer for the kind of integral Christian monarchy that Chambord, as the descendant of the Martyr King, had possessed.

The apparent disappearance of the Bourbon line with Chambord also revived interest in a longstanding political myth regarding the dauphin, the son of Louis XVI and Marie-Antoinette, known in royalist circles as Louis XVII. This myth had it that the dauphin had not died while imprisoned during the Revolution, but had lived—the French precedent to the Romanov/Anastasia tale. Moreover, the story went, the dauphin had begun a family while in hiding and his descendants (there were several families claiming the honor) had a right to the throne! Others were tempted, after the death of Chambord, by another providential figure—the charismatic General Georges Boulanger. At least one prominent investor in the Church of the National Vow, the duchesse d'Uzès, was also a major backer of Boulanger.[20] Still others were fascinated with the case of Garcia Moreno, president of Ecuador, who had consecrated his country to the Sacred Heart of Jesus in the 1870s.[21]

Rally to the Republic? Unlikely. There was pressure from Rome to do just that after the intransigent Pope Pius IX was replaced by Leo XIII. However, Maurice d'Hulst, who served as adviser to both archbishops of Paris, Guibert and his successor Richard, boldly resisted papal pressure to lead the movement of French Catholics toward the Republic. Presumably his attitude reflected that of his circle.[22] When the bishop of Saint-Paul (Minnesota), John Ireland, visited Paris and gave a speech expressing the American point of view that there was no inherent conflict between Catholicism and republics, his remarks were dismissed as irrelevant in the French context.[23] In fact, the most common denominator among advocates of the Sacré-Coeur was antipathy for the Republic whose genealogy they traced back to the Revolution, still seen as irreligious, persecutorial, even Satanic, and the source of most of France's problems (see figs. 53, 54).

In public this attitude was most effectively expressed by the conviction that the Republic (which in fact would endure until 1940) was ephemeral, inherently weak, and doomed to fail at any moment. Archbishop Guibert expressed this better than most in a letter to Charles de Freycinet, president of the Republic: "Allow an old bishop who has witnessed the political regime of his country change seven times in his lifetime to say one last time what his long experience tells him: The Republic has received neither from God nor

Figure 53. "The Revolution of 1789." *Messager du Sacré-Coeur* 55 (January 1889): 17.

An 1889 Catholic representation of the Revolution shows the goddess Reason and the bust of Marianne at the center of a ceremonial procession. Voltaire pushes the cart and *sans-culottes* pull as it crushes a crucifix beneath its wheels. Banners among the crowd of celebrants tout lay schools, reason, socialism, and the Rights of Man. Heads on pikes are a grim reminder of some of the more repellent forms of revolutionary violence. In the deep background, the profile of the Pantheon is clearly recognizable, the crucifix tumbling down from its dome.

from history any promise of immortality."[24] Given the brevity of the reigns of political institutions in nineteenth-century France, this was not an inaccurate statement. But Guibert's aim is not didactic. Both he and Freycinet knew their recent history. But coming just two years after the death of Chambord, and in the face of Vatican pressure to support the Republic, what comes through is Guibert's profound indifference—not to say antipathy—toward the fate of the Republic. Its collapse would not be unexpected —and it would not be unwelcome.

The problem, then, for Guibert and the Church of the National Vow was not the impossibility of extracting the Sacré-Coeur from a counterrevolutionary context but its unlikelihood given their unwillingness to do so. Indeed, one might ask if *any* reference to the Sacré-Coeur in postrevolutionary France, let alone one on the scale of the Sacré-Coeur de Montmartre, could truly be free of political resonance? The profound and persistent association of the Sacré-Coeur emblem itself with the Royal and Catholic Army of the Vendée is a case in point. The Sacré-Coeur was widely recognized as the insignia of the Vendéens. That the Vendéens stood not

Figure 54. "The Restoration of the Rights of God in 1889." *Messager du Sacré-Coeur* 55 (January 1889): 5.

The Sacré-Coeur in triumph at the centenary of the French Revolution. Jesus as the Sacré-Coeur is borne in triumph on a cart drawn by nuns and pushed by sturdy Gallic types, one bearing the *francisque* strapped to his hip. Also on the cart, a figure of France, wearing a crown, presents the Church of the National Vow to the Sacré-Coeur. In the background and among the onlookers are banners and representations of Christian education, the Catholic press, catechism, and prayer.

only for religious freedom but also for the defense of Legitimism and intransigent opposition to the Republic was well understood. That the Sacré-Coeur could stand for all of these things was certainly understood by Cardinal Richard (fig. 55), who grew up in the Vendée region and for whom the Vendée was not only local history but also family history.[25] The problem with the Sacré-Coeur as the center of a patriotic devotion was its history as a partisan political emblem.

Ironically, the political atmosphere of the early Third Republic in the 1870s, 1880s, and later made the revival of such memories all the easier. The rhetoric of republican politicians, much of it self-consciously in the Jacobin tradition, kept the Catholic Church in France feeling embattled and on the defensive. It easily elicited from Catholics imprudent comparisons between the revolutionary past and the challenges of their own time. Is it any surprise that they would turn to the Sacré-Coeur not only for consolation but also, on occasion, as an object of memory and a symbol of their estrangement and opposition?

Figure 55. François Richard, archbishop of Paris. Archives historiques du diocèse de Paris.

François Richard succeeded Joseph Guibert as archbishop of Paris. His years of service as assistant and heir apparent to Guibert helped to ease the transition at Guibert's death. Richard's understanding of the saga of France and the Sacré-Coeur was rich and deeply personal: he was born in the Vendée, and his father fought as a soldier in the armies of the Vendée rebellion.

In any event, supporters of the National Vow and its *Bulletin,* like most supporters of the devotion to the Sacré-Coeur, saw no reason to discourage such associations, divisive though they might be for Catholics who cherished the Heart of Jesus but felt uneasy about its prior and ongoing association with the cause of Christian monarchy. In the growing enthusiasm for the cult of the Sacré-Coeur during and after the *année terrible,* they regularly gave the wars of the Vendée their chapter in the saga of France and the Sacré-Coeur.[26] At sites throughout France related to the story of France and the Sacré-Coeur—at Paray-le-Monial, at Loigny—visitors would find reminders of the Sacré-Coeur's partisan past and ambiguous present: At the church

Figure 56. "Saint Henri," modeled after the comte de Chambord (Henri V), Bourbon pretender to the throne. Église de Loigny.

The church of Loigny, rebuilt after the battle of 1870, figured prominently in the Sacré-Coeur landscape. Every year on the anniversary of the battle, a speaker would be invited to eulogize the dead and remember the battle while recalling its significance to the epic tale of France and the Sacré-Coeur. The church itself became a museum of the hopes and anxieties of a certain Catholic France. Here, the features of the Bourbon pretender are borrowed for a stained-glass portrait of Saint Henri.

at Loigny, a stained-glass window depicts a number of saints and holy scenes. On first inspection these windows seem no different from windows found in any other provincial church, except that on closer inspection of a window featuring a portrait of Saint Henri, the face of Saint Henri turns out to be that of the comte de Chambord, the would-be Henri V (fig. 56).[27]

Even if Guibert and Richard steered their Church of the National Vow clear of most overt political references, the basilica's sullen mosaic *sans-culotte* guarding Louis XVI as he promises to consecrate his realm to the Sacré-Coeur represents a conspicuous exception. One cannot celebrate a vow that asked for the restoration of Louis's power and *not* take a position against the revolution that had taken that power away. Louis's vow was the counter-revolution masked as prayer. The fact that his political wishes took the form of a private communication with God does not render them apolitical. Try as they might—and the evidence suggests that they didn't try very hard—Guibert and Richard could never disentangle their project from the web of sites, many of them politically compromised, that staked a legitimate claim to a place in the historical landscape of the Sacré-Coeur.[28]

AN AMBIGUOUS LEGACY

Guibert had wanted his monument to be a symbol of national union, of national reconstruction, of a national return to French values, understood as Catholic values. He missed no opportunity to criticize opponents of the Sacré-Coeur who saw it as politically motivated. "Politics has always and will always be far, very far, from our inspiration," he wrote.[29] Guibert could not see, could not imagine, that to embrace a national vow that condemned the secular values of the Revolution and held France responsible for the status of the pope was inevitably to adopt a political position. Like his opponents, who deeply believed in the truth of the values of 1789, Guibert deeply believed in the truth of his belief in France's Christian identity. For Guibert, this was not politics. It was hardly even faith. It was revealed truth.

And yet Guibert persisted in representing the Sacré-Coeur not only as a way to understand and to approach God but also as a way to interpret France's past. In doing so, he missed an opportunity to guide French Catholics toward reconciliation with the Republic. In 1873, Cardinal Guibert offered a view that by then had become part of the standard discourse on France and the Sacré-Coeur since the Revolution: "It is from France that the evil that torments us issued forth over all of Europe; it is also in France that the devotion to the Sacré-Coeur was born. It will raise us up and save us."[30]

Guibert wanted the Sacred Heart to provide the basis for national reconciliation. This was a dubious proposition in any case, given the unlikelihood of religious belief and symbol serving as the basis of consensus within France. Even Guibert's language subverted any conciliatory intent. Guibert's formulation demonizes the Revolution, rejects it *in toto,* and puts the Sacred Heart in direct partisan opposition to it, just as it was after 1789. Any appeal for reconciliation on such terms was bound to sound hollow, especially when pilgrims to Montmartre were, in effect, asked to participate in a penitential plebiscite on the moral status of France since 1789. In their pastoral role as sponsors and promoters of pilgrimage, Guibert and his colleagues asked pilgrims to vote with their feet and demonstrate the vitality of the Catholic Church and its vision in contrast with the spiritual poverty of republican France. Pilgrimage was a sacred instrument in a holy war for the future of France.

Confrontation was built into the very way that the Sacré-Coeur related to the rest of the city of Paris. Guibert envisioned the Sacré-Coeur as a sacred oasis within the city, but also as a monument in dialogic relationship with secular structures. With its profane interlocutors displayed before it, the Sacré-Coeur would stand, in Guibert's words, as "a protest against other monuments . . . built to glorify vice and impiety."[31] Through the nineteenth century, the Revolution, whether represented as salvation, tragedy, or farce, was never very far from the center of debates about power, identity, meaning, and memory.[32] The monumental landscape of Paris participated in this debate: the Restoration had its conciliatory statue of Henri IV on the Pont Neuf; the Bourgeois Monarchy had its orderly but oddly mute July Column; now the architects of Moral Order raised high their contrite Sacré-Coeur.

What the Sacré-Coeur stood for in this dialogue of monuments depended to a great extent on where one stood. What Catholics were asked to hear should be clear enough by now. As the radical Left recovered after the Commune, the Sacré-Coeur came to mean something else. The Commune of Paris had its place in the history of the Church of the National Vow. It added much to the sense, already well established by the events of the preceding months, that France was hurtling toward catastrophe. But the Commune was by no means the catalyst for the church. The initiative was already well advanced before the declaration of the Commune and some version of a votive church to the Sacré-Coeur would likely have been realized anyway. But even though the Commune had not inspired the Sacré-Coeur de Montmartre, the project's sponsors were helpless to prevent the elaboration of a story wherein the Sacré-Coeur was represented as an anti-Communard monument. This ahistorical discourse, sketched out in the early Third Republic and still thriving in some circles today, made of the Sacré-Coeur a handy political target, but as historical analysis it misses the point.[33]

The story of the basilica of Sacré-Coeur as an anti-monument to the Commune has its place in the history of useful fictions of the French Left. For the history of France and the city of Paris, the Sacré-Coeur de Montmartre owes far more to the period of "Moral Order" in the 1870s. Indeed, it is difficult to imagine such a church being built on that site and on such a scale outside of the quite special circumstances of those years. The Church of the National Vow encapsulates a moment in the 1870s when France was overwhelmed with the sense that only massive and collective moral failure could explain its fall. Secularized French had their own ideas, but Catholics, lay and clerical, aggressively advanced their solution. As Bishop Pie put it in 1872, moral renewal was the only possible remedy: "The hour approaches when Jesus Christ will return . . . to the institutions, the social life, and the public life of peoples." The status of France depended on nothing less than national atonement, expiation, contrition in the name of the Sacré-Coeur—in short, the future of France hinged upon the re-Christianization of public life.

Did the rhetoric that defined France as a chosen nation, in turn defined by its Christian mission, express a wish to return to confessional definitions of nation and citizen that antedated 1791? The implicit rejection of Jewish membership in the nation, when juxtaposed with the rhetoric of covenant modeled after that of the Jews of antiquity, amounts to a telling formulation of Catholic self-recrimination. This language paradoxically both defines the "other" and identifies with the "other." Add to that the promise of salvific change delivered by providential men embodying the wishes of the nation and one can identify in the Christian nationalism of the Sacré-Coeur many of the elements that would so trouble the life of the French nation through the collapse of the Third Republic in 1940. The epic tale of the Sacré-Coeur conditioned far too many citizens to think of national politics in transcendent terms. It nurtured the politics of exaltation.

But that is to race ahead. The proper moment to take leave of the Sacré-Coeur of Montmartre is in 1908, when the city of Paris took possession of the Church of the National Vow. Work continued, but at a slower pace. Donations to the Church of the National Vow had trailed off markedly in prior years but the uncertainty surrounding the project generated by the separation of church and state in 1905 was only partly to blame.[34] The work was nearing completion, but the vivid sense of urgency that had driven the project in its early years had long since faded. By the centenary of the French Revolution, *joie de vivre* had displaced Moral Order's *mea culpa* in the ambient culture; at the Universal Exposition of 1889, Eiffel's Tower rivaled the Sacré-Coeur for attention among new Parisian monuments. In the 1890s, economic recovery fueled the Belle Époque—a period of frivolity, self-indulgence, and cultural experimentation even the "decadent" Second Empire might have envied. The contrite mood underpinning the National Vow had eroded.

The political context had changed too. The last Bourbon had died. An anti-clerical majority had assumed power. The Church of the National Vow became the property of Paris, the "modern Babylon." With the Sacré-Coeur thus delivered into the hands of its enemies, it required an extraordinary act of faith to continue to believe in the imminent conversion of France. Who could expect the installation of the "social reign of the Sacré-Coeur" in a political environment that was as hostile as any in recent memory to the ambitions of the Catholic Church in France? The devotion to the Sacred Heart had been built around a contractual idea: the Sacred Heart sets conditions and promises torrents of grace upon their fulfillment. France sought to meet those conditions. The results would be so dramatic that even the enemies of faith would be forced to concede that something extraordinary had happened. Two hundred years after the Sacred Heart had appeared to Marguerite-Marie Alacoque, the "chapel" demanded through her was well underway. But as the basilica of the Sacré-Coeur rose over the Parisian skyline, things were not getting better for the friends of the Sacred Heart. They were getting worse.

NOTES

Translations and photographs, unless otherwise credited, are by the author.

AN EPIC TALE FOR MODERN TIMES: AN INTRODUCTION

1. Ironically, at roughly the same time in U.S. history, to ask whether Catholics could be "good Americans" was a legitimate political question in some quarters.
2. On nostalgia for lost causes in France and the United States, see Raymond Jonas, "La colonne Sherman et la Vendée dans l'imaginaire américaine," in *Guerre et répression: La Vendée et le monde,* ed. Jean-Clément Martin (Nantes, 1993).
3. "Le hit-parade des sites touristiques," *Le Figaro,* 28 April 1998.

THE SACRED HEART VISITS THE CHAROLLAIS

1. Victor Drevon, *Le Coeur de Jésus consolé dans la Sainte Eucharistie,* 2 vols. (Avignon, 1866–68), 1:201.
2. Drevon, *Le Coeur de Jésus,* 202–3.
3. Drevon, *Le Coeur de Jésus,* 209. On Corpus Christi processions, see Miri Rubin, *Corpus Christi: The Eucharist in Late Medieval Culture* (Cambridge, 1991), 245, and Sarah Beckwith, *Christ's Body: Identity, Culture, and Society in Late Medieval Writings* (London, 1993), 33.
4. On corporeal extravagance, see Caroline Bynum, "Why All the Fuss About the Body? A Medievalist's Perspective," *Critical Inquiry* 22 (fall 1995): 1–33 (15).
5. Joseph Burnichon, *Histoire d'un siècle, 1814–1914: La Compagnie de Jésus en France,* 4 vols. (Paris, 1914), 1:475.
6. When Monsignor Bouange prepared the body of Marguerite-Marie in 1865, he observed that several bones were missing, including all of the small bones, the ribs, and

several vertebrae. (*Vie et oeuvres de sainte Marguerite-Marie Alacoque,* 2 vols. [Paris 1991], 2:207 n.)

7. Alcide de Beauchesne, *La Vie de Madame Élisabeth, soeur de Louis XVI,* 2 vols. (Paris, 1869), 2:230–31.

8. Ernest Sevrin, *Le Général de Sonis et la Franc-Maçonnerie* (Chartres, 1952), 28.

9. Letter from P. Debrosse to T. R. P. Roothaan, 29 July 1830, cited in Burnichon, *Histoire d'un Siècle,* 476.

10. Ange Le Doré, *Le Sacré-Coeur de Jésus* (Paris, 1909), 369.

11. Anne de Bretagne's heart-shaped reliquary, minus her heart, is on display in the Musée Dobré in Nantes.

12. Auguste Hamon, *Histoire de la dévotion au Sacré-Coeur de Jésus,* 5 vols. (Paris, 1927), 3:7.

13. On the "partisanship" generated by the wars of religion and its consequences for the lives of women religious, see Elizabeth Rapley, *The Dévotes: Women and Church in Seventeenth-Century France* (Montreal and Kingston, Ontario, 1990), 11.

14. Henry Baird, *History of the Rise of the Huguenots of France* (New York, 1970); Barbara Diefendorf, *Beneath the Cross: Catholics and Huguenots in Sixteenth-Century Paris* (New York, 1991); Robert Kingdon, *Myths About the Saint Bartholomew's Day Massacre* (Cambridge, Mass., 1988).

15. "Lettre de saint François de Sales à sainte Chantal, 25 février 1610," in *Oeuvres,* vol. 14, quoted in Étienne Catta, *La Visitation Sainte-Marie de Nantes, 1630–1792: La Vie d'un monastère sous l'ancien régime* (Paris, 1954), 253.

16. On the Visitationist order and women religious generally, see Jo Ann Kay McNamara, *Sisters in Arms: Catholic Nuns through Two Millennia* (Cambridge, Mass., 1996).

17. Hamon, *Histoire de la dévotion,* 3:248.

18. On the status of women religious and women's religious orders in the seventeeth century, see Rapley, *The Dévotes.*

19. Mgr Gauthey, "Avertissement [1915 edition]" in *Vie et oeuvres,* 2:9.

20. "Écrits," in *Vie et oeuvres,* 2:15.

21. "Écrits," in *Vie et oeuvres,* 2:15–16.

22. "I was favored by the amorous caresses of my heavenly spouse." "Écrits," in *Vie et oeuvres,* 2:52.

23. "Écrits," in *Vie et oeuvres,* 2:20.

24. "Écrits," in *Vie et oeuvres,* 2:21.

25. *La Vénérable Anne-Madeleine Remuzat, la propagatrice de la dévotion au Sacré-Coeur de Jésus, d'après les documents de l'ordre* (Lyon, 1894), xxiv n.

26. "Écrits," in *Vie et oeuvres,* 2:59.

27. "Fragments," in *Vie et oeuvres,* 2:69.

28. Caroline Walker Bynum, *Jesus as Mother: Studies in the Spirituality of the High Middle Ages* (Berkeley and Los Angeles, 1982); Leo Steinberg, *The Sexuality of Christ in Renaissance Art and in Modern Oblivion* (New York, 1983); Caroline Walker Bynum, "The Body of Christ in the Later Middle Ages: A Reply to Leo Steinberg," *Renaissance Quarterly* 39 (1986): 399–439. For a sexually reductionist reading of spiritual ecstasy, see Michael P. Carroll, *Catholic Cults And Devotions: A Psychological Inquiry* (Kingston, Ontario, 1989), 132–53.

29. Henri Grégoire, *Histoire des sectes religieuses* (Paris, 1828), 253.

30. Jules Michelet, *Du Prêtre, de la femme, de la famille* (Paris, 1845), 152.
31. Michelet, *Du Prêtre*, 135.
32. "Écrits," in *Vie et oeuvres*, 2:53–54.
33. "Fragments," in *Vie et oeuvres*, 2:73.
34. Were these visions Marguerite-Marie's way of casting suspicion upon enemies within the convent at Paray-le-Monial? Was she, in effect, conscripting Jesus as an ally against rivals or tormentors? Was Marguerite-Marie too independent or too proud to be able to make allies or supporters within the convent? The vision of the crown of nineteen thorns supports such as view, as do later visions. In one, Marguerite-Marie saw Jesus in deplorable state and heard him say that, "Five souls dedicated to my service have treated me this way." "Fragments," in *Vie et oeuvres*, 2:73–4.
35. "Écrits," in *Vie et oeuvres*, 2:49.
36. Relationships between members of a convent or monastery could sometimes be strained. One of Anne-Madeleine Rémuzat's fellow Visitationists turned a haircut into an act that "bordered on cruelty," thus converting a routine event into an occasion for sacrifice and spiritual improvement through the mortification of the flesh. In a similar episode, Anne-Madeleine endured having her veil pinned to her head instead of her habit. Anne-Madeleine's calm in these circumstances confirmed her saintliness before her observers. See *La Vénérable Anne-Madeleine Rémuzat*, 123–24. See also the discussion of Rémuzat in chapter 2.
37. Letter 86, to Mother Saumaise, May 1688, in *Vie et oeuvres*, 2:296.
38. On the role of confessors and spiritual advisers, see McNamara, *Sisters in Arms*, 508.
39. Malachi Martin, *The Jesuits: The Society of Jesus and the Betrayal of the Roman Catholic Church* (New York, 1987), 208–9.
40. "Écrits," in *Vie et oeuvres*, 2:33.
41. "Écrits," in *Vie et oeuvres*, 2:44.
42. Letter 100, to Mother Saumaise, June 1689, in *Vie et oeuvres*, 2:336–37.
43. See the note of Monsignor Gauthey in the 1915 edition, *Vie et oeuvres*, 2:337.
44. Letter 107, to Mother Saumaise, 28 August 1689, in *Vie et oeuvres*, 2:354–55.
45. On Jesuits and Jansenists and the politics of the Old Regime, see Dale K. Van Kley, *The Religious Origins of the French Revolution: From Calvin to the Civil Constitution, 1560–1791* (New Haven, 1996), 115–18.
46. See editor's notes in 1915 edition of *Vie et oeuvres*, 2:355–57.
47. Letter 89, to Mother Saumaise, July 1688, in *Vie et oeuvres*, 2:305.
48. Letter 107, 28 August 1689, in *Vie et Oeuvres*, 2:356.
49. Letter 131 to Jean Croiset, 10 August 1689, in *Vie et oeuvres*, 2:438.
50. E. Des Buttes, *Le Scapulaire du Sacré-Coeur* (Paris, 1878), 16.
51. Letter 41, to Mother Saumaise, 2 March 1686, in *Vie et oeuvres*, 2:203–4: "Moreover, your name will be written ineffaceably in this Sacred Heart."
52. Xavier de Franciosi, *La Dévotion au Sacré-Coeur de Jésus et au Saint-Coeur de Marie* (Nancy, 1885), 178–79. See also Joseph Hilgers, *Livre d'or du Coeur de Jésus: Pour les prêtres et pour les fidèles. Indulgences et privilèges de la dévotion au coeur de Jésus* (Paris, 1911), 178.
53. Letters 67 (April 1687) and 81 (1688), in *Vie et oeuvres*, 2:255 and 287. Such a chapel to the Sacré-Coeur had been completed and blessed in September 1688. See *La Vénérable Anne-Madeleine Remuzat*, xxv.

1. Paul Gaffarel and the marquis de Duranty, *La Peste de 1720 à Marseille et en France* (Paris, 1911), 2–3. Their account appears to be drawn from the "Fragments" of Petronius's *Satyricon*. See Petronius Arbiter, *Satyricon,* trans. P. G. Walsh (Oxford, 1996), 149. Petronius was a native of Marseille.

2. *La Vénérable Anne-Madeleine Remuzat, la propagatrice de la dévotion au Sacré-Coeur de Jésus, d'après les documents de l'ordre* (Lyon, 1894), 217–18.

3. Edouard Baratier, *Histoire de Marseille* (Paris, 1973), 168–70.

4. On the mission of 1718, see Charles Carrière, Marcel Courdurié, and François Rebuffat, *Marseille, ville morte: La Peste de 1720* (Marseille, 1968), 28.

5. On Jansenism at Marseille and Aix-en-Provence, see Jean-Remy Palanque, *Le Diocèse de Marseille* (Paris, 1967), 166, 168.

6. Andrew Barnes, *The Social Dimension of Piety: Associative Life and Devotional Change in the Penitent Confraternities of Marseille, 1499–1792* (Mahwah, N. J., 1994), 231; Gaffarel and Duranty, *La Peste de 1720,* 161–62; Archives départementales du Bouche du Rhône, 5 G 704, *Livre de raison tenu par l'intendant Goujon, relatant les principaux événements de son passage à l'évêché; Peste de 1720.*

7. *La Vénérable Anne-Madeleine Remuzat,* 332–33, 393.

8. *La Vénérable Anne-Madeleine Remuzat,* 189.

9. *La Vénérable Anne-Madeleine Remuzat,* 171.

10. Letter-circular from Sister Madeleine-Angélique Vincent, 1 September 1730, cited in *La Vénérable Anne-Madeleine Remuzat,* 393.

11. *La Vénérable Anne-Madeleine Remuzat,* 172.

12. Intendant Goujon gives the date as 1 November, All Saints' Day. See Archives départementales du Bouche du Rhône, 5 G 704, "Le vendredi premier du mois de novembre 1720 jour de la Toussaint," in *Livre de raison tenu par l'intendant Goujon, relatant les principaux événements de son passage à l'évêché; Peste de 1720;* Auguste Hamon, *Histoire de la dévotion au Sacré-Coeur de Jésus,* vol. 3, *Paray-le-Monial* (Paris, 1927), 439. On Belsunce and Charles Borromeo, see Carrière, Courdurié, and Rebuffat, *Marseille, ville morte,* 122–23.

13. Hamon, *Histoire de la dévotion,* 3:439.

14. Hamon, *Histoire de la dévotion,* 3:441.

15. On the confraternities, see Michel Vovelle, *Piété baroque et déchristianisation en Provence au XVIIIe siècle* (Paris, 1973); Maurice Agulhon, *Penitents et Francs-maçons de l'ancien Provence* (Paris, 1968); and Barnes, *Social Dimension.*

16. See Barnes, *Social Dimension,* 186–209; Baratier, *Histoire de Marseille,* 244; Hamon, *Histoire de la dévotion,* 3:441.

17. Hamon, *Histoire de la dévotion,* 3:441–43.

18. See Baratier, *Histoire de Marseille,* 169–70.

19. Archives départementales du Bouche du Rhône, 5 G 704, "vendredi 12 juin 1722," in *Livre de raison tenu par l'intendant Goujon, relatant les principaux événements de son passage à l'évêché; Peste de 1720.*

20. Hamon, *Histoire de la dévotion,* 3:455.

21. *Saints and Servants of God,* vol. 2, *The Lives of the Venerable Mother Margaret Mary*

Alacoque, Religious of the Order of the Visitation, and of S. Catherine of Bologna (London, 1850), 251.

22. Gaffarel and Duranty, *La Peste de 1720,* 403–4; *Saints and Servants of God,* 2:252.

23. *Saints and Servants of God,* 2:253.

24. The choice of Accoules for this ceremony may have additional significance in that it was the parish of the abbé Arnaud, a Catholic clergyman of Jansenist tendencies. Carrière, Courdurié, and Rebuffat, *Marseille, ville morte,* 35.

25. Letter from Belsunce to Madame de Camilly, 12 June 1722: "[T]he streets leading up [to the platform] and the rooftops of all the houses were full of people, more attracted by the devotion than by curiosity." Quoted in *La Vénérable Anne-Madeleine Remuzat,* 295; Gaffarel and Duranty, *La Peste de 1720,* 405.

26. Gaffarel and Duranty, *La Peste de 1720,* 331.

27. Episcopal decree of 15 July 1720, in *La Vénérable Anne-Madeleine Remuzat,* 219.

28. *Saints and Servants of God,* 2:264.

29. *Saints and Servants of God,* 2:253.

30. Procession provided the principal means by which the consecration of Marseille would be remembered. See Archives départementales du Bouche du Rhône, 28 V 1, Cultes, Processions. An ix: 1864.

31. See Charles Marcault, *Le Message de 1689 a-t-il été réellement abandonné?* (Chinon, 1918), 62.

32. *La Vénérable Anne-Madeleine Remuzat,* 199–200.

33. There is work to be done on the role of women religious and their (male) spiritual directors. One of the reasons we know more about the spiritual development of women than men is that women religious, unlike men, were routinely assigned spiritual directors who, in turn, urged their wards to write down their thoughts, prayers, and visions. Thanks to these procedures, we have a written record of their development. The important questions seem to be: How did these spiritual directors guide the women they supervised? How much was their own reputation contingent upon the progress of their wards?

34. Jean-Baptiste Bertrand, *A Historical Relation of the Plague at Marseilles in the Year 1720,* trans. Anne Plumptre (London, 1805; reprint 1973), 214.

35. *La Vénérable Anne-Madeleine Remuzat,* 259–60; Gaffarel and Duranty, *La Peste de 1720,* 174–76.

36. It was only a few years earlier that Belsunce had ordered the burning of some three thousand copies of Pasquier Quesnel's *Réflexions morales.* Carrière, Courdurié, and Rebuffat, *Marseille, ville morte,* 35.

37. Letter-circular of 1 May 1721, cited in *Vénérable Anne-Madeleine Remuzat,* 242–43.

38. Letter from François de Sales to Jeanne de Chantal, 10 June 1611, reprinted in *La Vénérable Anne-Madeleine Remuzat,* xiv.

39. Xavier de Franciosi, *La Dévotion au Sacré-Coeur de Jésus et au Saint-Coeur de Marie* (Nancy, 1885), 280.

40. According to Jacques Bainvel, "Dévotion au coeur-sacré de Jésus," *Dictionnaire de Théologie Catholique,* vol. 3 (Paris, 1938), 337.

41. *Saints and Servants of God,* 2:264.

42. This did potentiate future conflicts over whether municipal authorities would fulfill the obligation imposed upon them by their predecessors in 1722. A mayor's refusal 150 years later to renew the vow, and his attempt to ban the procession, provoked a controversy. See *La Semaine religieuse du diocèse de Nantes,* 15 June 1872, 280.

43. "Le Discours du R. P. Janvier," *Bulletin de l'oeuvre du voeu national au Sacré-Coeur de Jésus,* 16 October 1919, 248.

44. Marcault, *Le Message de 1689,* 62; Bainvel, "La Dévotion au coeur-sacré," 337.

45. *Instructions, pratiques, et prières pour la dévotion au Sacré-Coeur de Jésus: L'Office, vespres et messe de cette dévotion* (Paris, 1752), 22.

46. "Mandement de Monseigneur l'archevêque de Paris qui ordonne que la Fête du Sacré-Coeur de Jésus sera célébrée d'obligation dans son Diocèse" (Paris, 1822), in Archives historiques du diocèse de Paris, Basilique du Sacré-Coeur, carton 2. Henri Grégoire was among the most energetic critics of the devotion and the claims made on its behalf. Henri Grégoire, *Histoire des sectes religieuses,* 2 vols. (Paris, 1828), 1:262.

47. Xavier de Franciosi, *La dévotion au Sacré-Coeur,* 280.

48. P. Dugan, *Le Pèlerinage du Sacré-Coeur en 1873: Histoire et documents* (Moulins, 1873), 135.

49. Archives diocésaines d'Angers, OP13, Dossier paroissial, Sainte-Madeleine du Sacré-Coeur, *Notes pour l'histoire de la Paroisse Sainte-Madeleine du Sacré-Coeur d'Angers,* par F. Bouchet, 47.

50. See the introduction to *La Vénérable Anne-Madeleine Remuzat,* 1.

51. *Le Messager du Sacré-Coeur de Jésus: Bulletin mensuel de l'Apostolat de la Prière,* October 1917, 625. See also *La Semaine religieuse du diocèse d'Evreux,* 9 June 1917, 375.

52. "Turn toward Christ: that is the gesture of France in danger." ("Le Discours du R. P. Janvier," *Bulletin de l'oeuvre du voeu national au Sacré-Coeur de Jésus,* 16 October 1919, 248).

THE FRENCH REVOLUTION, CATHOLIC ANXIETIES,
AND THE SACRED HEART

1. Armand Duchâtellier, *Histoire de la Revolution dans l'ancienne Bretagne,* 5 vols. (Paris, 1836), 2:272–80; Charles-Louis Chassin, *La Préparation de la guerre de Vendée, 1789–1793,* 5 vols. (Mayenne, 1892, reprint 1973), 3:376–77.

2. The *Journal de la Montagne,* two months after the event, reported that the insurgents had cut off Sauveur's fingers and burned him alive. See *Journal de la Montagne,* 11 June 1793, 79.

3. Chassin, *La Préparation de la guerre,* 3:377; See also *Archives parlementaires de 1787 à 1860,* vol. 61 (Paris, 1901), 413–14. On some aspects of the early history of counter-revolution in the west, see Emmanuel Vingtrinier, *La Contre-Révolution: La Première période, 1789–1791,* 2 vols. (Paris, 1924), 1:243–54.

4. For an overview of the *cahiers* of the clergy, see Timothy Tackett, *Religion, Revolution, and Regional Culture in Eighteenth-Century France: The Ecclesiastical Oath of 1791* (Princeton, 1986), 146–56; Marcel Reinhard, *Religion, Révolution, et Contre-*

Révolution (Paris, 1985), 42–44. On the *cahiers* generally, see Beatrice Hyslop, *A Guide to the General Cahiers of 1789* (New York, 1936).

5. Tackett, *Religion, Revolution, and Regional Culture,* 11–13. See also Michel Vovelle, *1793: La Révolution contre l'église* (Lausanne, 1988).

6. *Archives parlementaires,* 10 October 1789, 9:398.

7. *Archives parlementaires,* 10 October 1789, 9:398.

8. Michel Vovelle, *Piété baroque et déchristianisation en Provence au XVIIIe siècle: Les Attitudes devant la mort d'après les clauses des testaments* (Paris, 1973). Of course, such donations resumed in the nineteenth century. See, for example, Archives municipales de Nantes, M2 24, Église Saint-Donatien, which describes a large donation by an elderly widow, a Madame Coëffard, in the 1870s. Much of this property again passed into the hands of the French state at the moment of the Separation in 1905.

9. Such views were common among parish clergy of the Old Regime who had embraced Richerism in the battle for a "bottom-up" reorganization of the Catholic Church, as opposed to the "top-down" hierarchy for which the Church is famous. On Richerism, see Timothy Tackett, *Priest and Parish in Eighteenth-Century France* (Princeton, 1977), 242–43.

10. *Archives parlementaires,* 10 October 1789, 9:399.

11. Tackett, *Religion, Revolution, and Regional Culture,* 15.

12. *Archives parlementaires,* 2 November 1789, 9:648–49.

13. Tackett, *Religion, Revolution, and Regional Culture,* 12.

14. Tackett, *Religion, Revolution, and Regional Culture,* 21; *Archives parlementaires,* 11 August 1790, 17:731–33.

15. The bishops objected to the suppression of orders and monastic vows and the prescribed manner of selecting bishops and pastors, among other things. The statement was subsequently endorsed by 104 other bishops. *Archives parlementaires,* 30 October 1790, 20:153–65, and Jean-François Robinet, *Le Mouvement religieux à Paris pendant la Révolution, 1789–1801,* 2 vols. (Paris, 1896–98), 2:361–62.

16. Paul Bois, *Histoire de Nantes* (Toulouse, 1977), 257.

17. Suzanne Desan supplies a translation of the oath in her *Reclaiming the Sacred: Lay Religion and Popular Politics in Revolutionary France* (Ithaca, N. Y., 1990), 231.

18. *Archives parlementaires,* 26 November 1790, 21:1–2.

19. Bishop Laurencie's return to Nantes from Paris was brief. His oath, taken with qualifications, and his resistance to the reduction of parishes in the city of Nantes according to the decrees of the Assembly, made him the focus of patriotic animosity in Nantes. On 26 November 1790, he announced his decision to leave Nantes, "par prudence." See his statement in *Archives parlementaires,* 26 November 1790, 21:21–22.

20. François Chevalier, *Abrégé de l'histoire de la Révolution française* (Nantes, n.d.), excerpted in Chassin, *La Préparation de la guerre,* 3:332. Chevalier returned to his parish under the terms of the 1802 Concordat. He died at Sainte-Lumine in 1813.

21. Pierre de la Gorce, *Histoire religieuse de la Révolution française,* 5 vols. (Paris, 1922), 2:82–83. Of course, at roughly the same time the bishops in the National Assembly issued a statement critical of certain aspects of the reforms, notably the election of pastors by parishes rather than their nomination by the bishops. See *Archives parlementaires,* 30 October 1790, 20:153–65, esp. 159.

22. There is no general study of women religious and the oath comparable to Tackett's study of the male religious in *Religion, Revolution, and Regional Culture*. For the west of France, see Pierre Marie Grégoire, *Les Religieuses nantaises durant la persécution révolutionnaire* (Nantes, 1920), 73, and Étienne Catta, *La Visitation Sainte-Marie de Nantes, 1630–1792: La Vie d'un monastère sous l'ancien régime* (Paris, 1954), 515.

23. A decree of the National Assembly of 20 March 1790 had called for an inventory of the property of religious orders. Municipal officers were also asked to determine whether members of religious orders planned to remain or to leave. This was related to the Assembly's suspension of monastic vows. See *Archives parlementaires*, 28 October 1789, 9:597. For inventories of monastic property, see *Archives parlementaires*, 20 March 1790, 12:267.

24. Anecdote related by Alexandre Charles Anne Lenfant in *Mémoire ou correspondance secrète du Père Lenfant, confesseur du roi pendant trois années de la Révolution, 1790, 1791, 1792*, 2 vols. (Paris, 1834), 2:136.

25. Grégoire, *Les Religieuses nantaises*, 61–64.

26. Sermon of 26 July 1789, "La Tempête la plus furieuse," in François Lebrun, *Parole de Dieu et Révolution: Les Sermons d'un curé angevin avant et pendant la guerre de Vendée* (Paris, 1988), 98–99.

27. Sermon of 27 September 1789, "La liberté et l'égalité, les plus dangereux de tous les maux," in Lebrun, *Parole de Dieu*, 103.

28. See *Mémoires pour servir à l'histoire du jacobinisme*, 2 vols. (Chiré en Montreuil, 1973); Reinhard, *Religion, Révolution, et Contre-Révolution*, 99. See also Paul Beik, "The French Revolution Seen From the Right: Social Theories in Motion," *Transactions of the American Philosophical Society* 46 (1956): 20.

29. Lebrun, *Parole de Dieu*, 22.

30. Louis-Marie Clenet, *Cathelineau, le "saint de l'Anjou"* (Paris, 1991), 19.

31. As a member of the National Assembly, Maury had already made his reputation through his vigorous denunciation of the nationalization of Catholic Church lands as "a disaster." See *Archives parlementaires*, 13 October 1789, 9:425: "France is not yet at the deplorable point of avoiding bankruptcy only through confiscation, which is to say, of having to choose between public disasters." See also Jean Siffrein Maury, *Sur la Constitution civile du clergé* (Paris, 1790).

32. Another energetic member of the Catholic clergy, the abbé Royau used his newspaper *l'Ami du roi* as a forum to defend Catholic and royal interests and to assert the patently Calvinist origins of the individualism of the Revolution.

33. For Maury, see Reinhard, *Religion, Révolution, et Contre-Révolution*, 97–98.

34. Reinhard, *Religion, Révolution, et Contre-Révolution*, 135, 137.

35. Mona Ozouf, "Voltaire," in François Furet and Mona Ozouf, *Dictionnaire critique de la révolution française* (Paris, 1988), 915; Mona Ozouf, *Festivals and the French Revolution*, (Cambridge, Mass., 1988), 77–81; Simon Schama, *Citizens* (New York, 1989), 561–65.

36. Jacques Hillairet, *Dictionnaire historique des rues de Paris*, 2 vols. (Paris, 1966), 2:226–27; Jean Delumeau and Yves Lequin, eds., *Les Malheurs du temps: Histoire des fléaux et des calamités en France* (Paris, 1987): 386–87.

37. On Geneviève, see Raymond Van Dam, *Saints and Their Miracles in Late Antique Gaul* (Princeton, 1993), 24, and Louis de Sivry and M. Champagnac, *Dictionnaire*

des pèlerinages anciens et modernes et des lieux de dévotion les plus célèbres de l'univers,
2 vols. (Paris, 1851), 2:50.

38. See *Archives parlementaires*, 3 April 1791, 24:536.

39. *Archives parlementaires*, 8 May 1791, 25:661.

40. While she admitted that she was "far from sharing the enthusiasm of so many [for Mirabeau]" because she saw Mirabeau (rightly) as venal and corrupt, she nevertheless supported the public homage rendered him not because of what he was but because of what he represented to the public: "This is homage rendered to liberty." Letter of 5 April 1791 to Bancal in London, in *Lettres de Madame Roland,* 2 vols. (Paris, 1902), 2:257.

41. "The afternoon was consecrated to the triumphant procession of Voltaire; the people showed a lively interest in this noble and moving festival, which seemed to presage the complete ruin of superstition." Letter of 15 July 1791 to Bancal, in Roland, *Lettres,* 2:327.

42. Reinhard, *Religion, Révolution, et Contre-Révolution,* 146–47.

43. On clerical attitudes to Voltaire, see Tackett, *Priest and Parish,* 94, 169, 303–5.

44. *Archives parlementaires,* 15 April 1791, 25:107.

45. Tackett, *Religion, Revolution, and Regional Culture,* 181.

46. Desan, *Reclaiming the Sacred,* 82.

47. Laurence Coudart, *La Gazette de Paris: Un Journal royaliste pendant la Révolution française, 1789–1792* (Paris, 1995), 249.

48. On oath-taking in the west of France, see references to Deux-Sèvres, Vienne, Vendée, Loire-Inférieure, in Tackett, *Religion, Revolution, and Regional Culture,* 336, 357–58, 360. See also Charles Tilly, *The Vendée* (Cambridge, 1964), 231–62.

49. Coudart, *La Gazette de Paris,* 250.

50. Letter-circular from André Brumauld de Beauregard, vicar general of the bishop of Luçon, to the priests of the diocese of Luçon, on the organization of clandestine services, Archives nationales, D^{59}15, 123, reproduced in Diocèse de Luçon, *l'Église de Vendée fait mémoire* (Luçon, 1993), 55.

51. On dialogues as teaching tools, see Pierre-François Hacquet, *Mémoire des missions des Montfortains dans l'Ouest, 1740–1779* (Fontenay-le-Comte, 1964), esp. 11; for background on the Montfortains missions in the west of France, see La Gorce, *Histoire religieuse,* 2:349.

52. Célestin Port, *La Vendée angevine: Les Origines, l'insurrection, janvier 1789–31 mars 1793,* 2 vols. (Paris, 1888), 1:385.

53. Port, *La Vendée angevine,* 1:386.

54. Gaétan de Wismes, *Les Loup de la Biliais, martyrs du Sacré-Coeur: D'après des documents inédits* (Vannes, 1898), 31.

55. "A Monsieur le Procureur-général du Département de Maine et Loire, à Angers, 5 novembre 1791," in Port, *La Vendée angevine,* 1:403–4.

56. Port, *La Vendée angevine,* 1:407.

57. Elias Canetti, *Crowds and Power,* trans. Carol Stewart (New York, 1962), 50.

58. Archives départmentales de la Gironde, L 2192, quoted in Henri Lelièvre, *Les Ursulines de Bordeaux pendant la Terreur et sous le Directoire* (Bordeaux, 1896), 37.

59. *Archives parlementaires,* 15 September 1791, 30:646–47.

60. "Lettre du Directoire du Département à l'Assemblée nationale pour réclamer la déportation des réfractaires des Administrateurs composant le Directoire du Dé-

partement de Maine-et-Loire, Angers, 1er novembre 1791," in Port, *La Vendée angevine*, 1:400; see also "Lettre du directoire du département de Maine-et-Loire, et procès-verbaux, au sujet des prêtres non assermentés," *Archives parlementaires*, 25 October 1791, 34:411–12.

61. "La vertu des pèlerinages," 7 August 1791, reproduced in Lebrun, *Parole de Dieu*, 105.

62. Lebrun, *Parole de Dieu*, 106.

63. "Rapport du 25 août 1791," in Port, *La Vendée angevine*, 1:391.

64. "Lettre de Chalonnes à Angers, 24 octobre 1791," in Port, *La Vendée angevine*, 1:397.

65. Quoted in Louis Baunard, *Adelaide de Cicé* (Wetteren, Belgium, n.d.), 97.

66. Lenfant, *Mémoire ou correspondance secrète*, 2:229.

67. *L'Ami du roi*, 1 June 1791, quoted in Edmond Biré, *Paris pendant la Terreur* (Paris, 1890), 35. On blasphemy and profanation in the modern era, see Alain Cabantous, *Histoire du blasphème en Occident, XVIe-XIXe siècle* (Paris, 1998).

68. The most important center, at least retrospectively, was at Saint-Laurent-sur-Sèvre, headquarters of both the Missionnaires de Marie of Grignion de Montfort and the Filles de la sagesse, who turned out a prodigious number of images. See Hacquet, *Mémoire des missions*, 12; La Gorce, *Histoire religieuse*, 2:351–52; "Extrait du Rapport du Procureur-général-syndic, séance du 5 juin (1791)," in Port, *La Vendée angevine*, 1:384. Saint-Laurent-sur-Sèvre was recently the site of a papal visit. See "French Find a Bomb as Pope's Trip Nears," *New York Times*, 4 September 1996.

69. The letter, dated 2 April 1787, was written by Emmanuel-Amédée de Compeys, mother superior of the convent at Annecy. See Auguste Hamon, *Histoire de la dévotion au Sacré-Coeur de Jésus*, 5 vols. (Paris, 1923–39), 4:291.

70. Hamon identifies the visionary as Marie-Anne Galipaud. Etienne Catta argues that the visionary was more likely the superior of the Nantes convent, Claude-Marie de Bruc. See Catta, *La Visitation Sainte-Marie de Nantes*, 482.

71. Letter of 4 October 1791 from Claude-Marie de Bruc, superior of the Nantes Visitationists, to Françoise-Attale de Millenheim, superior of the Visitation at Strasbourg, quoted in Catta, *La Visitation Sainte-Marie de Nantes*, 477.

72. Catta, *La Visitation Sainte-Marie de Nantes*, 294.

73. Catta, *La Visitation Sainte-Marie de Nantes*, 485.

74. See Louis Charbonneau-Lassay, "L'Iconographie du Sacré-Coeur dans les armées contre-révolutionnaires de la Vendée," R*egnabit: Revue universelle du Sacré-Coeur* (April 1922): 448–63. Charbonneau-Lassay produced several articles on this subject in issues published in May, June, and July of 1922 as well as January 1923.

75. *L'Ami du roi*, 1 June 1791, quoted in Biré, *Paris pendant la Terreur*, 36.

76. Letter of 31 December 1791 from sisters at Avignon to the Visitation of Nantes, cited in Catta, *La Visitation Sainte-Marie de Nantes*, 490 n.

77. Letter of 4 October 1791 from Claude-Marie de Bruc to the superior at Strasbourg, cited in Catta, *La Visitation Sainte-Marie de Nantes*, 490.

78. Letter of 15 December 1790 from Claude-Marie de Bruc to the superior at Nancy, quoted in Catta, *La Visitation Sainte-Marie de Nantes*, 490.

79. Letter of 4 October 1791 from Claude-Marie de Bruc to the superior at Strasbourg, cited in Catta, *La Visitation Sainte-Marie de Nantes*, 491 n.

80. Letter of 11 January 1792 from Claude-Marie de Bruc to the superior at Chartres, cited in Catta, *La Visitation Sainte-Marie de Nantes*, 487–88.

81. Grégoire, *Les Religieuses nantaises,* 60.
82. *Mémoires de Madame la Marquise de La Rochejaquelein,* 2 vols. (Paris, 1815), 1:64.
83. Charbonneau-Lassay, "L'Iconographie du Sacré-Coeur," *Regnabit* (April 1922): 459.
84. Joseph Burnichon, *Histoire d'un Siècle, 1814–1914: La Compagnie de Jésus en France,* 4 vols. (Paris, 1914–22), 1:45.
85. Jean Lacouture, *Jésuites: Une Multibiographie,* 2 vols. (Paris, 1992), 2:33.
86. Joseph de Maistre would later give a systematic formulation to the conviction that the Revolution was both providential and satanic in his *Considerations sur la France* (London, 1797).
87. Baunard, *Adelaide de Cicé,* 95.
88. Joseph Grente, *Les Martyrs de septembre 1792 à Paris* (Paris, 1926), 40.
89. Jean Lacouture gives the name as la Société des Pères du Sacré-Coeur de Jésus. See Lacouture, *Jésuites,* 2:33. See also Guillaume de Bertier de Sauvigny, *Le Comte Ferdinand de Bertier, 1782–1864 et l'énigme de la Congrégation* (Paris, 1948), 41, who puts the founding date in 1790, instead of 1791.
90. Baunard, *Adelaide de Cicé,* 81, 94–95.
91. "[The four included] M. Desprez, Olivier Lefebvre, Charles François Legué, [and] M. Lasnier, whose first name is not indicated, [but] by all appearances is J.-M. Lasnier of the Community of Saint-Nicolas du Chardonnet, put to death in Saint-Firmin; another associate was the abbé Cormaux, curé of Plaintel in Bretagne, who died at the guillotine in 1794. The chapel of Saint-Dénis was well chosen . . . to prepare for . . . bloody persecution." Grente, *Les Martyrs de septembre,* 40.
92. Burnichon, *Histoire d'un siècle,* 1:8–9; Louis Baunard, *Histoire de la vénérable mère Madeleine-Sophie Barat, fondatrice de la Société du Sacré-Coeur de Jésus,* 2 vols. (Paris, 1892), 1:356; Lacouture, *Jésuites,* 2:35.
93. As distinct from Picot de Clorivière's Société du Coeur de Jésus.
94. Burnichon, *Histoire d'un siècle,* 1:8–9. Baunard puts it somewhat differently: "You will still be a soldier. We will serve God as soldiers, bearing arms in our hearts and our hands." See Baunard, *Madeleine-Sophie Barat,* 1:35.
95. In *The Red and the Black,* Stendhal uses the Sacré-Coeur as a shorthand for the cultural *revanche* of the Jesuits under the Restoration monarchy.

THE SACRED HEART AND THE COUNTER-REVOLUTION IN THE VENDÉE

1. See "Une oeuvre du Coeur de Jésus: Souvenir du voeu de Louis XVI," *Messager du Coeur de Jésus* 39 (April 1881): 460–63.
2. On Hébert's role, see Joseph Grente, *Les Martyrs de septembre 1792 à Paris* (Paris, 1926), 69; see also Pierre de la Chapelle, "La Prière et le voeu de Louis XVI au Sacré-Coeur inspirèrent-ils l'insurrection vendéenne?" *Revue du souvenir vendéen* 181 (December 1992): 31.
3. The earliest published version of the vow is in *l'Ami de la religion et du roi: Journal ecclésiastique, politique, et litteraire* 3 (1815): 77–80. See also Benjamin Fillon, *Pièces contre-révolutionnaires du commencement de l'insurrection vendéenne* (Fontenay, 1847), 4 ff; *Mois du Sacré-Coeur de Jésus* (Paris, 1850), 286–90; and Félix Parenteau, *Médailles vendéens* (Nantes, 1857), 9.

4. The challenges posed by the reconstruction of the past is an implicit theme of Simon Schama's *Dead Certainties* (New York, 1991). For a survey of many of the sources on the king's vow, see Jacques Benoist, *Le Sacré-Coeur de Montmartre de 1870 à nos jours* (Paris, 1992), 1058–59.

5. French Catholics subsequently appropriated Burke's argument, for although Burke had no particular fondness for the Catholic Church, French Catholics realized that in the French context Burke's brilliant defense of tradition supported Catholicism as well as monarchy. The title of Joseph de Maistre's *Considérations sur la France* (London [Basle], 1797) suggests the extent of his debt to Burke.

6. *L'Ami du roi,* 1 June 1790, no. 1, 1. On *l'Ami du roi,* see Claude Bellanger and others, *Histoire générale de la presse française,* 1: *Des origines à 1814* (Paris, 1969), 483–85. See also Laurence Coudart, *La Gazette de Paris: Un Journal royaliste pendant la Révolution française, 1789–1792* (Paris, 1995), esp. 236–51. On the revolutionary press, see Jeremy D. Popkin, *Revolutionary News: The Press in France, 1789–1799* (Durham, N. C., 1990).

7. Guillaume de Bertier de Sauvigny, *Le Comte Ferdinand de Bertier, 1782–1864, et l'énigme de la Congrégation* (Paris, 1948), 41.

8. *Association de quarante jours* (Paris, 1790).

9. See *l'Ami du roi,* 2 November 1790, no. 155, 642.

10. On Marie Leszczynska, see Paul and Pierrette Girault de Coursac, *Louis XVI et la question religieuse pendant la Révolution* (Paris, 1988), 285. Marie Leszczynska had, according to some, played a key role in securing papal approval in 1765 for a Mass and Office of the Sacred Heart for Poland. Joseph de Guibert, *The Jesuits: Their Spiritual Doctrine and Practice* (Chicago, 1964), 401.

11. Alcide de Beauchesne, *La Vie de Madame Élisabeth, soeur de Louis XVI,* 2 vols. (Paris, 1869), 1:11.

12. A late nineteenth-century source has it that the ex-voto at Chartres was a gift from the king, the queen, and the king's sister. According to this source, Louis made his vow to the Sacré-Coeur in February of 1790 and the ex-voto was sent to Chartres a year later. See "Une oeuvre du Coeur de Jésus: Souvenir du Voeu de Louis XVI," *Le Messager du Sacré-Coeur de Jésus: Bulletin mensuel de l'Apostolat de la Prière* 39 (April 1881): 460–61. If nothing else, the account reveals the ongoing concern with the question of the vow and the enduring belief in its veracity.

13. The ex-voto can be read simply as a gesture honoring the Sacré-Coeur and the heart of Mary. In the context of revolutionary France, it can also be read as the union of will of the Bourbon Élisabeth de France with the Sacré-Coeur, or even as proxies for the hearts of Élisabeth and her brother, the king. The ex-voto is on display in the *trésor* of the cathedral of Chartres.

14. The royal household had sought to leave the Tuileries Palace and spend Easter at Saint-Cloud, where, among others things, they apparently intended to attend Easter services offered by a priest who had refused the civil oath. A crowd, including some National Guard soldiers, perhaps fearing a ruse to cover an attempted flight, refused to let the carriage depart. The king and queen would later be obliged to attend Easter services offered by a constitutional priest at Saint-Germain-l'Auxerrois. Élisabeth remained at the Tuileries. Louise Élisabeth de Tourzel, *Mémoires de Madame la duchesse de Tourzel,* 4 vols. (Paris, 1884), 2:270–74, 284. John Hardman notes that the royal family had been allowed to spend the summer and

early fall of 1790 at Saint-Cloud. Obviously, the public mood in Paris had changed by April 1791. See John Hardman, *Louis XVI* (New Haven, 1993), 183.

15. Beauchesne, *La Vie de Madame Élisabeth,* 1:343.

16. While the Alacoquist tradition emphasizes the suffering heart of Jesus, especially in the face of human indifference, and the need to make reparation, the Eudist tradition emphasizes the contemplation of the internal disposition of the heart of Jesus as a means of reflecting or meditating on the sentiment of divine love. See Guibert, *The Jesuits,* 394–98. Ange Le Doré tends to emphasize the areas of overlap between the Eudist and Alacoquist variants of the devotion in *Le Sacré-Coeur de Jésus: Son Amour d'après la doctrine du Bienheureux Jean Eudes, père, docteur, et auteur de la dévotion au Sacré-Coeur* (Paris, 1909), 394–98. Paul Lesourd would later suggest that the modern devotion to the Sacré-Coeur represents a "synthesis" built from borrowing from the Eudist and Alacoquist traditions. See Paul Lesourd, *Montmartre* (Paris, 1973), 96.

17. Chassin reproduces the text of the vow ("La Prière de Louis XVI") in his *La Préparation de la guerre de Vendée* (1:197–98). While Chassin does not dispute the vow's authenticity, he does situate it in 1791 without offering evidence to support this contention. Some sources suggest a later date—June 1792 being the most likely both for political and devotional reasons. My point is that widespread *belief* in the vow is more important than authenticity. What people believe, even if untrue, is sometimes more important than the truth. See also Jean-François Robinet, *Le Mouvement religieux à Paris pendant la Révolution, 1789–1801,* 2 vols. (Paris: 1896–98), 2:120–22.

18. François Hue, *Dernières années du règne et de la vie de Louis XVI* (Paris, 1816), 247; Hardman, *Louis XVI,* 217; Hamon, *Histoire de la dévotion,* 4:306; Grente, *Les Martyrs de septembre,* 69 n; Beauchesne, *La Vie de Madame Élisabeth,* 1:441.

19. The Sacré-Coeur remained a preoccupation of the king's sister, Élisabeth, up to the very end. She shared the captivity of the royal family in the Temple, and her prayers focused on the Sacré-Coeur. François Hue, the king's personal assistant in the Temple, transcribed one of Madame Élisabeth's prayers while in captivity, an expression of powerlessness and resignation that concludes with an invocation of the Sacré-Coeur: "Here is the prayer of Madame Élisabeth; she permitted me to copy it: 'I know nothing of what might happen to me today, O my God, except that nothing will happen that you have not foreseen for all eternity. That's enough, O my God, for me to remain tranquil. I sacrifice everything to you; I unite my sacrifice with that of your cherished Son, my Savior, asking your patience in the face of our evils, through his Sacred Heart." Hue, *Dernières années,* 355.

20. Étienne Catta, *La Visitation Sainte-Marie de Nantes, 1630–1792: La Vie d'un monastère sous l'ancien régime* (Paris, 1954), 497.

21. *Le Procès de Marie-Antoinette, 23–25 vendémiaire an II (14–16 octobre 1793). Actes du Tribunal Révolutionnaire,* ed. and commentary by Gérard Walter (Paris, 1993), 59, 73–74.

22. *Authentic Trial at Large of Marie-Antoinette, Late Queen of France, before the Revolutionary Tribunal at Paris, on Tuesday, October 15, 1793 . . . .* (London, 1793), 38.

23. See Alexandre Charles Anne Lenfant, *Mémoire ou correspondance secrète du Père Lenfant, confesseur du roi pendant trois années de la Révolution, 1790, 1791, 1792,* 2 vols. (Paris: 1834), 2:230; see also Girault de Coursac, *Louis XVI,* 285.

24. That the king and queen provided protection to refractory priests was fairly widely known. Jean-Sylvain Bailly, once mayor of Paris, claimed to have approached the king on this issue and to have asked the king to send the refractory priests away. See his testimony in *Authentic Trial,* 47.

25. On 13 March 1793, the chevalier de Saint-Laurent de la Cassaigne sent a dozen Sacré-Coeur emblems that he had painted to Marie-Louise de La Rochejaquelein. See *Mémoires de Madame la Marquise de Larochejaquelein,* 2 vols. (Paris, 1815), 1:64.

26. "I join the numerous and faithful flock who, in these days of perversity, redouble their fervor and honor the divine heart of the Man-God," wrote Lenfant. Lenfant, *Mémoire ou correspondance secrète,* 2:229–30.

27. See Letter of 1 June 1791, in Lenfant, *Mémoire ou correspondance secrète,* 2:109; [Baron] Gaétan de Wismes, *Les Loup de la Biliais; Martyrs du Sacré-Coeur d'après des documents inédits* (Vannes 1898), 36 n.

28. Hue, *Dernières années,* v.

29. Fillon, *Pièces contre-révolutionnaires,* 4. A copy of the seven-page "Prière de Louis XVI au Sacré-Coeur de Jésus" can be found in the Bibliothèque Municipale de Nantes, Fonds Dugast-Matifeux, IIe série, no. 36, 14.

30. After the Revolution, when the monarchy had been restored in France, the text of the vow was printed in the royalist periodical *l'Ami de la religion et du roi: Journal ecclésiastique, politique et littéraire* [vol. 3 (1815):77–80], and reprinted in at least one devotional work claiming papal approval: *Exercices de la Dévotion au Sacré-Coeur de Jésus, à l'usage de la Confrérie établie à Semur en Brionnois, et confirmée par N. S. P. le Pape Pie VII* (Lyon, 1818). Representatives of the monarchy and of the Catholic hierarchy were reluctant to engage in a public debate on the matter of the vow of Louis XVI. With the Revolution safely behind them and national reconcil-iation on the agenda, why dwell upon an incident evocative of a time when the na-tion was at war with itself over questions of religion and royalism?

31. Célestin Port, *La Vendée angevine: Les Origines, l'insurrection, janvier 1789–31 mars 1793,* 2 vols. Paris: 1888, 2:115, 129.

32. Archives diocésaines de la Loire Atlantique, L 1.494, quoted in Catta, *La Visitation Sainte-Marie de Nantes,* 494.

33. Louis Baunard, *Adelaide de Cicé* (Belgium, n.d.), 180.

34. Henri Lelièvre, *Les Ursulines de Bordeaux pendant la Terreur et sous le Directoire* (Bordeaux, 1896), 46–49.

35. François Lebrun, *Parole de Dieu et Révolution: Les Sermons d'un curé angevin avant et pendant la guerre de Vendée* (Paris, 1988), 109–12.

36. Louis-Marie Clenet, *Cathelineau, le saint de l'Anjou* (Paris, 1991), 19.

37. According to Pierre de La Gorce, it was the combination of the apparition of the Virgin and the approach of the feast of the Assumption (August 15) in 1791 that inspired the object of the pilgrimages, namely, to reestablish the Catholic reli-gion. See his *Histoire religieuse de la Révolution française,* 5 vols. (Paris, 1922), 2:369, 423. See also Clenet, *Cathelineau,* 74.

38. E. Boisseleau, *Le Sacré-Coeur des Vendéens* (Luçon, 1910), 4 (originally published in *la Semaine Catholique du diocèse de Luçon,* 7 and 14 May 1910); Chassin, *La Préparation de la guerre,* 3:441; Charles Tilly, *The Vendée,* (Cambridge, Mass., 1964), 315.

39. Papiers de Mercier du Rocher, reg. I, n. 66, cited in Chassin, *La Préparation de la guerre,* 3:296–97.

40. Jean-Clément Martin, *La Vendée et la France* (Paris, 1987), 18; Jean-Clément Martin, *Blancs et Bleus dans la Vendée déchirée* (Paris, 1987), 43.

41. Martin, *Blancs et Bleus,* 88.

42. Martin, *La Vendée,* 107; de La Rochejaquelein, *Mémoires,* 1:143.

43. See "Réflexions sur les troubles de la Vendée, leurs causes et leurs remèdes," in *Journal de la Montagne,* 15 June 1793, 105.

44. De La Rochejaquelein, *Mémoires,* 2:73.

45. See the example of the defeat at Fontenay: De La Rochejaquelein, *Mémoires,* 1:71.

46. See the commentary on the work of Jean-Clément Martin and Roger Dupuy in Lebrun, *Parole de Dieu,* viii–x.

47. In writing of the army of the Vendée, Jacques Godechot remarked that "It lacked discipline. The soldiers imposed their will on the leaders." Jacques Godechot, *La Contre-révolution: Doctrine et action, 1789–1804* (Paris, 1961), 236.

48. De La Rochejaquelein, *Mémoires,* 1:27–33; Catta, *La Visitation Sainte-Marie de Nantes,* 497.

49. De La Rochejaquelein *Mémoires,* 1:45.

50. Alexandre Dumas made a similar point in his historical novel *Les Louves de Machecoul* (*She-wolves of Machecoul*) (1859). Dumas had visited the Vendée in the 1830s at the request of General Lafayette.

51. Martin, *La Vendée,* 87–91.

52. See Paul Bois, *Paysans de L'Ouest* (le Mans, 1960), and Tilly, *Vendée.*

53. Joseph-Marie Lequinio, *Guerre de la Vendée et des chouans* (Paris, 1794), esp. 14.

54. Martin, *La Vendée,* 209–10.

55. The best historian of revolutionary transcendence is Mona Ozouf. See her *l'Homme régénéré: Essais sur la révolution française* (Paris, 1989); *Festivals and the French Revolution* (Cambridge, 1988) [Paris, 1976]; *L'École, l'Église et la République, 1871–1914* (Paris, 1963).

56. Lequinio, *Guerre de la Vendée,* 185–86.

57. Lequinio, *Guerre de la Vendée,* 189–90.

58. The claim that the Revolution was the result of a conspiracy of Protestants, Jansenists, Freemasons, *philosophes,* and Jews should be seen in this light. See, for example, Augustin Barruel, *Mémoires pour servir à l'histoire du jacobinisme,* 2 vols. (Vouillé, 1973) [original edition, Paris, 1818].

59. Germain Bethuis, *Massacres de Machecoul* (Nantes, 1873), excerpted in Chassin, *La Préparation de la guerre,* 3:336–37.

60. Pierre Lucas de la Championnière, who operated in the area as a Vendéen officer, claims not to have heard anyone talk of the hunting horn episode and expressed surprise when he learned of it later in life. He did, however, hear of the "rosaries" of Machecoul, whereby the prisoners taken by the insurgents at Machecoul were bound by the wrist, one to the next. Thus tied, the prisoners were made to stand before a trench. One by one they were killed, the dead weight of one pulling the next into the trench, where they were buried. See his *Mémoires sur la Guerre de Vendée, 1793–1796* (Paris, 1904), 10, 182.

61. De La Rochejaquelein, *Mémoires,* 1:45.

62. Some of the grislier details have been summarized by Louis Oury in *Les Chapelets de Machecoul* (Paris, 1993), 32–37.

63. "Rapport des commissaires de la Convention Nationale," excerpted in Chassin, *La Préparation de la guerre,* 3:341.

64. "Rapport des commissaires de la Convention Nationale," excerpted in Chassin, *La Préparation de la guerre,* 3:342.

65. François Chevalier, *Abrégé de l'histoire de la Révolution française,* 3 vols., manuscript, excerpted in Chassin, *La Préparation de la guerre,* 3:334.

66. For an example of such violence in the nineteenth century, see Alain Corbin, *The Village of Cannibals: Rage and Murder in France, 1870,* trans. Arthur Goldhammer (Cambridge, 1992), 39.

67. Denis Crouzet, *Les Guerriers de Dieu: La Violence au temps des troubles de religion,* 2 vols. (Paris, 1990); see also the interview with Crouzet, "La Saint-Barthélemy: Religion et Barbarie," in *L'Histoire* 215 (November 1997): 32–35.

68. Chevalier, *Abrégé,* 3:334.

69. *Journal de la Montagne,* 11 June 1793, 79.

70. Lequinio, *Guerre de la Vendée,* 22–23.

71. E. Des Buttes, *Le Scapulaire du Sacré-Coeur* (Paris, 1878), 20; see also Fillon, *Pièces contre-révolutionnaires.*

THE SACRED HEART AND THE RETURN OF KINGS

1. Jean-Clément Martin, *Blancs et Bleus dans la Vendée déchirée* (Paris, 1987), 126.

2. J. Bottineau, *Les Portraits des généraux Vendéens* (Cholet, 1975), 9.

3. Bottineau, *Les Portraits,* 9.

4. Michel Leroy, *Le Mythe jésuite de Béranger à Michelet,* (Paris, 1992), 30–31.

5. Leroy, *Le Mythe jésuite,* 31.

6. Gérard Cholvy and Yves-Marie Hilaire, *Histoire religieuse de la France contemporaine,* 2 vols. (Paris, 1985), 1:71.

7. Joseph Burnichon, *Histoire d'un siècle, 1814–1914: La Compagnie de Jésus en France,* 4 vols. (Paris, 1914), 1:88–89; Ernest Sevrin, *Les Missions religieuses en France sous la Restauration, 1815–1830* (Saint-Mandé, 1948), 19.

8. *La Semaine liturgique du diocèse de Poitiers,* 24 June 1917, 234.

9. Burnichon, *Histoire d'un siècle,* 1:88; for Varin, see Jacques Crétineau-Joly, *Histoire de la Compagnie de Jésus,* 6 vols. (Paris, 1859), 5:436–37; for Joseph Barat, see Louis Baunard, *Histoire de la vénérable mère Madeleine-Sophie Barat, Fondatrice de la Société du Sacré-Coeur de Jésus,* 2 vols. (Paris, 1892), 1:23.

10. On dance, see Sevrin, *Missions religieuses,* 1:282–87.

11. Sevrin, *Missions religieuses,* 1:ix.

12. The remark is Burnichon's. See *Histoire d'un siècle,* 1:317. On *Tartuffe* and the missions in Nantes see letter of 14 November 1826 (Prefect of the Loire Atlantique to the Minister of the Intérieur) in Archives départementales de la Loire-Atlantique, 2 V 2, Police générale du culte, faits divers, rapports, 1814–69.

13. There were also ceremonial remarriages, given that marriages performed by constitutional priests were regarded as null. Sevrin, *Missions religieuses,* 1:253–55. See also Pierre de la Gorce, *La Restauration* (Paris, 1929), 39–40.

14. Cholvy and Hilaire, *Histoire religieuse,* 1:171.

15. Leroy, *Mythe jésuite,* 31.

16. Jean-François Robinet, *Le Mouvement religieux à Paris pendant la Révolution, 1789–1801,* 2 vols (Paris, 1896–98), 2:525; Auguste Cabanes, *Marat Inconnu: l'Homme privé, le médecin, le savant* (Paris, 1891), 435.

17. Robinet, *Mouvement religieux,* 2:529–30.

18. Frank Paul Bowman, "Le Sacré-Coeur de Marat, 1793," in *Les Fêtes de la révolution,* ed. Jean Ehrard and Paul Viallaneix (Paris, 1977), 155–79, esp. 155–56.

19. Devotees of the Sacré-Coeur loved to speculate and meditate on this wound and the Roman soldier, known as Longinus by tradition, whose lance had caused it. Catholics fascinated by the idea of God become man were intensely interested in the body of Jesus and the organs the wound exposed to view and inspection, in the manner of the disciple Thomas. Gene Vance relates the story whereby French troops hopelessly besieged at Antioch during the Second Crusade were so inspired by the discovery of the lance of Longinus that they were able to fight their way out and defeat the Turks. See Eugene Vance, "'And the Flag was Still There;' Image, Intentionality, and the Semiotics of Flag Burning," in Lawrence Rosen, ed., *Other Intentions: Cultural Contexts and the Attribution of Inner States* (Sante Fe, N. M., 1995*),* 112.

20. *Journal de la Montagne,* 18 July 1793, 276; Cabanes, *Marat Inconnu,* 432.

21. *Vie de M. Cormeaux, curé en Bretagne* (Paris, 1796), 101, cited in Auguste Hamon, *Histoire de la dévotion,* 5 vols. (Paris, 1929–31), 4:310.

22. Baunard, *Sophie Barat,* 1:254.

23. According to Baunard, "nearly all of these first mothers [to join the order] of the Sacred Heart passed through the crucible of the revolution." *Sophie Barat,* 1:97.

24. Baunard, *Sophie Barat,* 2:452. See also François Pie, "Éloge funèbre de Madame la Marquise de la Rochejaquelein, prononcé à la cérémonie de ses obsèques dans l'église de Saint-Aubin de Baubigné, le samedi 28 février 1857," in *Oeuvres de Monseigneur l'évêque de Poitiers,* 6 vols. (Poitiers, 1868–79), 2:636–37.

25. For Marie Verdet d'Adhemar, the Sacred Heart order was the very essence of aristocracy. Better than anything else in post-revolutionary France, it evoked the Old Regime. See *La Femme catholique et la démocratie française* (Paris, 1900), 185. François Mauriac relied on this reputation and image over a generation later in his *Dame de Pharisées.*

26. Baunard, *Sophie Barat,* 1:65.

27. On the founding of the order, see Baunard, *Sophie Barat,* 1:55, 125. On the constitution of the order, see 1:175.

28. Jacques Godechot, *La Contre-révolution: Doctrine et action, 1789–1804* (Paris, 1961), 236–38; Jacques Hillairet, *Dictionnaire historique des rues de Paris* (Paris, 1966), 598–99.

29. On this transition, see Marcel Launay, "Prédication," in G. Mathon and others, eds. *Catholicisme hier, aujourd'hui, demain,* vol. 11 (Paris, 1988), 802.

30. Baunard, *Sophie Barat,* 1:360.

31. Baunard, *Sophie Barat,* 1:266.

32. Hamon, *Histoire de la dévotion,* 4:329.

33. Published by Barbier in 1816, a reprint of an edition in circulation in 1815. It is unclear how this *Salut de la France* relates to the work by the same title and published

in the same years attributed to a Père Lambert by Jacques Benoist in his *Le Sacré-Coeur de Montmartre de 1870 à nos jours* (Paris, 1992), 2:1118. There was a Père Lambert among the post-Restoration Jesuits who participated in the missions. Père Loriquet went on to serve as rector at the Jesuit school at Saint-Acheul and to write other works pertaining to France and its past, including a contentious history of France titled *Histoire de France à l'usage de la jeunesse,* a work Jean Lacouture has called a "caricature obscène d'un enseignement d'histoire." See his *Jésuites: Une Multibiographie,* 2 vols. (Paris, 1992), 2:64.

34. Jean Nicolas Loriquet, *Le Salut de la France* (Poitiers, 1816), 3.

35. Loriquet, *Le Salut de la France,* 6–7, 12.

36. Loriquet, *Le Salut de la France,* 12.

37. See the preface where one reads that "this little work convinced the inhabitants of Poitiers to make the solemn vow it proposes." Loriquet, *Le Salut de la France,* 2.

38. *Les Archives religieuses du Pays Poitevin* 7 (1903), 106.

39. Hamon, *Histoire de la dévotion,* 4:339.

40. *La Semaine religieuse du diocèse de Poitiers,* 24 June 1917, 234.

41. Roger Limouzin-Lamothe, *Monseigneur de Quelen, archevêque de Paris,* 2 vols. (Paris, 1955), 1:139–42.

42. When the Restoration monarchy was overthrown in 1830, the Orléanist regime authorized the continued observance of the feast of the Assumption, including public processions, provided they made no reference to the vow of Louis XIII. See *Moniteur,* 11 August 1831.

43. Carol Duncan, "Ingres's *Vow of Louis XIII* and the Politics of the Restoration," in Henry Millon and Linda Nochlin, eds., *Art and Architecture in the Service of Politics* (Cambridge, Mass., 1978), 84. See, for a more general account, Beth Segal Wright, *Painting and History during the French Restoration: Abandoned by the Past* (Cambridge, 1997).

44. François Lebrun, *Parole de Dieu et Révolution: Les Sermons d'un curé angevin avant et pendant la guerre de Vendée* (Paris, 1988), 35, 108.

45. Ingres's painting remains on display in the cathedral at Montauban, where it decorates one of the transept chapels. To emphasize the point, the chapel on the opposite side of the transept features an equally monumental canvas — of the Sacred Heart appearing to Marguerite-Marie Alacoque.

46. Baunard, *Sophie Barat,* 1:401.

47. Hamon, *Histoire de la dévotion,* 4:348 n.

48. At first, *le Constitutionnel* was subdued in its criticisms of the Sacred Heart devotion and its Jesuit sponsors. By the crisis of the Restoration in 1828, however, the criticisms were overt. For example, when Monsignor de Quelen, archbishop of Paris, opened the 1828 legislative session with an invocation of the Sacré-Coeur, *le Constitutionnel* recognized the need for prayer at such moments, but wondered why it was necessary to mix in the Sacré-Coeur, "which everyone knows belongs to the liturgy of Jesuitism." *Le Constitutionnel,* 3 February 1828.

49. Other editions were published subsequently, and it remained a fundamental work for later critics of the Sacré-Coeur devotion. References here are to the 1828 edition. See Henri Grégoire, *Histoire des sectes religieuses,* 2 vols. (Paris, 1828).

50. Grégoire, *Histoire des sectes,* 2:246.

51. Grégoire, *Histoire des sectes,* 2:280.

52. Along these lines, see Richard Trexler, "Gendering Jesus Crucified," in Brendan Cassidy, ed. *Iconography at the Crossroads* (Princeton 1993), 107–20; Leo Steinberg, *The Sexuality of Christ in Renaissance Art and in Modern Oblivion* (New York, 1983); Caroline Walker Bynum, *Holy Feast and Holy Fast* (Berkeley and Los Angeles, 1987).

53. J. H. Shennan, *The Parlement of Paris* (Ithaca, N. Y., 1968), 314–19. Dale Van Kley takes up these issues in greater depth in *The Religious Origins of the French Revolution: From Calvin to the Civil Constitution, 1560–1791* (New Haven, 1996), esp. 114–19.

54. Grégoire, *Histoire des sectes,* 2:291–92.

55. On the various official and "common-sense" meanings of the term *Congrégation* in Restoration France, see Guillaume de Bertier de Sauvigny, *Le Comte Ferdinand de Bertier, 1782–1864, et l'énigme de la Congrégation* (Paris, 1948), 403.

56. Hamon, *Histoire de la dévotion,* 4:344–45.

57. Burnichon, *Histoire d'un siècle,* 1:124.

58. Lacouture, *Jésuites,* 2:61.

59. Burnichon, *Histoire d'un siècle,* 1:127; Guillaume de Bertier de Sauvigny, *The Bourbon Restoration,* trans. Lynn Case (Philadelphia, 1966), 314–17; de Sauvigny, *Le Comte Ferdinand de Bertier,* 403.

60. Charles Marcault, *Réalisons le message du Sacré-Coeur* (Paris, 1934), 66; Hamon, *Histoire de la dévotion,* 4:344.

61. *Vie de la Révérende Mère Marie-Anne Maria de la Fruglaye* (Clermont-Ferrand, 1868), 345–46.

62. *La Semaine liturgique du diocèse de Poitiers* (27 November 1870), 774; Victor Alet, *La France et le Sacré-Coeur* (Paris, n.d.), 244 (most likely a 1905 reprint of pamphlet originally published in 1871; see Benoist, *Le Sacré-Coeur,* 2:1125).

63. Hamon, *Histoire de la dévotion,* 4:347; Alet, *France et le Sacré-Coeur,* 244.

64. Hamon, *Histoire de la dévotion,* 4:347.

65. The story of Laure (Marie de Jésus) is recounted in most religiously inspired accounts of France and the Sacré-Coeur, including those by Alet, Hamon, Marcault, and Lesourd, as well as by anonymous writers in such Catholic periodicals as the *Semaine liturgique du diocèse de Poitiers* (November 1870), 774, and the *Bulletin de l'oeuvre du voeu national au Sacré-Coeur de Jésus* 54 (September 1919), 211.

66. Louis already had some experience with visionaries bearing urgent messages. In 1816, he met with a certain Martin who promised information about the fate of the Dauphin, son of Louis XVI and nephew of Louis XVIII. The king apparently believed that the best way to rid himself of such supporters and visionaries was to hear them out, then send them away. On Martin, see Evelyne Lever, *Louis XVIII* (Paris, 1988), 473–76.

67. Alet, *France et le Sacré-Coeur,* 241.

68. Some of Louis XVIII's most difficult political battles were fought with ultraroyalists who wanted to carry restoration and revenge far beyond what was prudent. See, for example, Jacques Bonin and Paul Didier, *Louis XVIII, roi de deux peuples, 1814–1816* (Paris, 1978), esp. 118–30.

69. See, for example, Jean Vidalenc, *La Restauration, 1814–1830* (Paris, 1973), 79–82.

70. Archbishop de Quelen continued to promote the Sacré-Coeur as a quasi-official devotion under the Bourbon Restoration. In 1828, he attracted the criticism of the liberal opposition when he opened the legislative session with an invocation of the

protection of the Sacré-Coeur. See "Invocation au Sacré-Coeur, à l'occasion de l'ouverture de la session," in *le Constitutionnel*, 3 February 1828, 2.

71. Hamon, *Histoire de la dévotion*, 4:348 n; Baunard, *Sophie Barat*, 431.

ROME, WAR, AND THE ONSET OF THE TERRIBLE YEAR

1. Hippolyte Taine, *Les Origines de la France contemporaine*, vol. 9: *Le Régime moderne* (Paris, 1899).

2. See Ernst Renan in *La Réforme intellectuelle et morale de la France* (Paris, 1871), excerpted and translated in David Thomson, *France: Empire and Republic, 1850–1940* (New York, 1968), and reprinted in Jan Goldstein and John W. Boyer, eds., *Nineteenth-Century Europe: Liberalism and Its Critics* (Chicago, 1988), 351–55.

3. "Ou en est la Révolution française? Simples notes sur la situation actuelle," *Revue des Deux Mondes* 94 (1871): 875.

4. "Journal d'un voyageur pendant la guerre de 1870," *Revue des Deux Mondes* 92 (1871): 249.

5. Alistair Horne, *The Fall of Paris: The Siege and the Commune, 1870–1871* (New York, 1981), 62.

6. "Le Soldat Français," *La Semaine religieuse du diocèse de Nantes,* 23 July 1870, 354.

7. For a fictionalized account of Sedan, see Emile Zola, *The Debacle [1870–71],* trans. Leonard Tancock (London, 1972).

8. "Allocutions de Mgr Fournier," *La Semaine religieuse du diocèse de Nantes,* 10 September 1870, 441.

9. "Mandement [22 September 1870] de Mgr L'Évêque du diocèse de Nantes à l'occasion de la consécration solennelle de son Diocèse au Sacré Coeur de Jésus," *La Semaine religieuse du diocèse de Nantes,* 1 October 1870, 477–84.

10. "Mandement," *La Semaine religieuse du diocèse de Nantes,* 1 October 1870, 478–89.

11. "Fête de la consécration du diocèse de Nantes au Sacré-Coeur de Jésus," *La Semaine religieuse du diocèse de Nantes,* 15 October 1870, 501–7.

12. "The beautiful message the Monsignor Fournier has published on this subject has had a profound impact, not only in the diocese, but well beyond. . . ." Quoted in "Fête de la consécration du diocèse de Nantes au Sacré-Coeur de Jésus," *La Semaine religieuse du diocèse de Nantes,* 15 October 1870, 501; Jacques Gadille, *La Pensée et l'action politiques des évêques français au début de la IIIe République, 1870–1883,* 2 vols. (Paris, 1967), 1:230; abbé Pothier, *Monseigneur Fournier évêque de Nantes: Sa Vie, ses oeuvres,* 2 vols. (Nantes, 1900), 2:59–60.

13. "Lettre pastorale [15 October 1870] de Mgr l'Évêque de Luçon sur la conduite de la Providence dans les circonstances présentes et mandement pour la consécration de son diocèse au Sacré-Coeur de Jésus," in Archives diocésaines de Luçon, 1 E 7, Actes des évêques.

14. Apparently from Psalms 119:137. See "Lettre pastorale [15 October 1870] de Mgr l'Évêque de Luçon sur la conduite de la Providence dans les circonstances présentes et mandement pour la consécration de son diocèse au Sacré-Coeur de Jésus" and "Lettre circulaire de Monseigneur l'Évêque de Luçon au clergé de son diocèse au sujet des fruits que nous devons retirer des épreuves du temps présent et pour la

célébration d'un service funèbre à l'intention des victimes de la guerre [Luçon, 3 April 1871]," in Archives diocésaines de Luçon, 1 E 7, Actes des évêques.

15. The city of Mâcon also made such a vow. See "Chronique générale," *La Semaine liturgique du diocèse de Poitiers,* 25 December 1870, 842.

16. "Lettre pastorale et mandement de Monseigneur l'Évêque d'Angers annonçant la consécration solennelle de son diocèse au Sacré-Coeur de Jésus et prescrivant un service funèbre pour les soldats morts pendant la guerre," *La Semaine religieuse du diocèse de Angers,* 9 April 1871, 547–48.

17. M. Bony, *Vie et oeuvres de Monsieur Alexandre Legentil* (Paris, 1893), 223; Joseph Burnichon, *Histoire d'un siècle, 1814–1914: La Compagnie de Jésus en France,* 4 vols. (Paris 1922), 4:394 n.

18. Bony, *Alexandre Legentil,* 212.

19. Louis Hautecoeur, *Histoire de l'architecture classique en France,* vol. 7, *La Fin de l'architecture classique, 1848–1900* (Paris, 1957), 956; Gadille, *La Pensée,* 1:231; Bony, *Alexandre Legentil,* 215; Paul Lesourd, *Montmartre* (Paris, 1973), 199; Jacques Benoist, *Le Sacré-Coeur de Montmartre de 1870 à nos jours,* 2 vols. (Paris, 1992), 1:215–16.

20. Raymond Darricau, "Poitiers," in G. Mathon and others, eds. *Catholicisme Hier, aujourd'hui, demain,* vol. 11 (Paris, 1988), 552.

21. Gilberte Larignon and Héliette Proust, *Edouard de Monti de Rezé; L'Inébranlable Certitude: Le Mouvement légitimiste dans l'Ouest* (Laval, 1992), 272.

22. See sermon of 16 October 1870, excerpted in Louis Baunard, *Histoire du cardinal Pie, évêque de Poitiers,* 2 vols. (Poitiers, 1886), 2:410.

23. Here is how Lamennais described the act of regicide: "When Louis climbed the scaffold, it wasn't only a virtuous mortal who died, . . . it was power itself, the living image of God, the principle of order and political existence—it was society itself that perished." "Essai sur l'indifférence en matière de religion," in *Oeuvres complètes de F. de La Mennais,* vol. 1 (Paris, 1836), 336. The image would become a classic. When Monsignor de Cabrières, bishop of Montpellier, spoke on 8 June 1874, he enumerated the three most important dates in the development of the devotion to the Sacré-Coeur. The second was the execution of the king in 1793, a "solemn expiation offered . . . to the outraged heart of Jesus by the broken heart of Louis XVI." Quoted in Gérard Cholvy and Yves-Marie Hilaire, *Histoire religieuse de la France contemporaine,* 3 vols. (Paris, 1985), 1:171–72.

24. Pie had challenged Louis-Napoléon directly and publicly in a pastoral letter when he claimed that he was marked with the "deicide stigmata." In another passage, Pie challenged Louis-Napoleon with the cry "Wash your hands, O Pilate; declare yourself innocent of the death of Christ." See Baunard, *Pie,* 2:568.

25. See Robert R. Locke, *French Legitimists and the Politics of Moral Order in the Early Third Republic* (Princeton, 1974).

26. Pie was by no means alone in expressing these sentiments. In less dramatic terms, another bishop expressed the idea: "We groan under the weight of two great sorrows, the disasters of France, our fatherland, and the trials of the Church, our mother! God has allowed these . . . in order to show us . . . that there is an indestructible solidarity between France and the Church." Letter of 8 November 1870 from La Tour d'Auvergne, archbishop of Bourges, to Ramadié, quoted in Gadille, *La Pensée* (Paris, 1967), 1:212.

27. The sentiment driving Pie was perhaps best expressed by Monsignor de Ségur, who wrote a letter about his vision of "true France" to Pie on 31 January in the following terms: "What a catastrophe! What an annihilation of the ancient glory of France! I know, it's revolutionary France, anti-Christian and anti-Catholic France, the anti-French France that God strikes thus. But do you believe that true France, Catholic and monarchical France will be able to recover from it?" For Ségur, and by all appearances for Pie as well, the defeat of 1870–71 revealed the end-point of a trajectory whose origin was in the tragic rupture of 1793. Baunard, *Pie,* 2:423. On *la vraie France,* see Herman Lebovics, *True France: The Wars over Cultural Identity, 1900–1945.* (Ithaca, 1992). Legentil's vow would receive significant further development under the guidance of Archbishop Guibert of Paris. See Benoist, *Le Sacré Coeur,* 1:243–45.

28. *La Semaine liturgique du diocèse de Poitiers,* 29 January 1871, 72–73; Benoist, *Le Sacré-Coeur,* 1:1032–33.

29. Benoist, *Le Sacré-Coeur,* 1:216–233.

30. Notables such as the journalist Louis Veuillot, the politician/notable Alfred de Falloux, and Bishop Pie of Poitiers were among Louis-Napoleon's most ardent admirers. See Cholvy and Hilaire, *Histoire religieuse,* 1:232; Falloux, *Mémoires d'un royaliste* (Paris, 1888), 287; Baunard, *Pie,* 2:194–95.

31. Baunard, *Pie,* 2:113–14. For the crusade, see Henri Le Chauff de Kerguenec, *Souvenirs des zouaves pontificaux, 1861 et 1862, recueillis par François Le Chauff de Kerguenec [Ancien Zouave Pontifical]* (Poitiers, 1890), 108. See also Marius Faugeras, "Les Fidélités en France au XIXe siècle: Les Zouaves pontificaux, 1860–1870," in Raymond Darricau and others, *Fidélités, Solidarités et Clientèles: Enquêtes et documents* (Nantes, 1986), 280.

32. On the "ninth crusade," see *La Semaine religieuse du diocèse d'Angers,* 17 November 1878, 784; Edgar de Barral, *Les Zouaves pontificaux, 1860–1870* (Paris, 1932), 11.

33. Larignon and Proust, *Edouard de Monti de Rezé,* 250.

34. Collections were organized through a "Comité de Saint-Pierre" in Paris. See Archivio segreto Vaticano, Segretario di Stato 1876, Rubrica 248, fasc. 1, 199–200, 205–9. On the place of Peter's Pence in the raising and funding of the papal army, see Barral, *Zouaves,* 29.

35. Jean-Clément Martin, *La Vendée et la France* (Paris, 1987); Jean-Clément Martin, *La Vendée de la mémoire, 1800–1980* (Paris, 1989); Jean Huguet, *Un Coeur d'étoffe rouge: France et Vendée 1793, le mythe et l'histoire* (Paris, 1985); Claude Petitfrère, *Les Vendéens d'Anjou (1793): Analyse des structures militaires, sociales et mentales* (Paris, 1981).

36. The *Semaines religieuses* of the dioceses of Nantes and Angers, for example, regularly ran items on the Vendée in an effort to promote the memory of the heroic struggle.

37. Archives diocésaines de Luçon, Actes des Évêques, 1 E 6, "Lettre pastorale de Mgr l'évêque de Luçon au clergé et aux fidèles de son diocèse sur la Révolution Italienne à l'occasion de la dernière invasion des États Pontificaux," 4.

38. Letter of Anatole de Ségur, 1861, quoted in Faugeras, "Les Fidélités en France," 283.

39. Marcel Launay, *Le Diocèse de Nantes sous le Second Empire* (Nantes, 1982), 734.

40. Archivio segreto Vaticano, Segretario di Stato, 283–1860, quoted in Launay, *Diocèse de Nantes,* 734.

41. According to Georges Cerbelaud-Salagnac, there were some initial misgivings about Charette among papal advisers, but the pope dismissed them: *Les Zouaves pontificaux* (Paris, 1963), 20 – 21. According to Jacques Crétineau-Joly, the Charette name was already a banner, representing the counter-revolution as a whole, at the time of Charette's capture in 1796: "the blues [the revolutionary republicans] tried to make a spectacle of this soldier whose name was a flag." *Histoire de la Vendée militaire*, 4 vols. (Paris, 1840), 2:422.

42. Le Chauff de Kerguenec, *Souvenirs*, 314, quoted in Faugeras, "Les Fidélités en France au XIXe siècle," 283.

43. Cerbelaud-Salagnac, *Zouaves*, 176 – 77.

44. Cardinal de Bonald, *Essai analytique sur les lois naturelles de l'ordre social ou du pouvoir, du ministre et du sujet dans la société* (Paris, 1836; reprint 1982), 15 – 16, 22 – 24, 60 – 61.

45. "May the princes fool themselves no longer! Would that they understand that it is not only the scepter of a minor Italian sovereign that is broken. The spirit of anarchy is trying to overthrow everything that serves as the basis of the social order!" Joseph Guibert, pastoral letter of 1 October 1860, "Les Nouveaux excès de la révolution contre les États de l'Église," in J. Paguelle de Follenay, *Vie du cardinal Guibert, archevêque de Paris*, 2 vols. (Paris, 1896), 1:306.

46. This view was similar to that held by Fournier. See his letter of 23 October 1870 to the papal nuncio: "We believe that, in this general disturbance of the world, society totters because Rome, which is the cornerstone, is itself shaken." Quoted in Pothier, *Fournier*, 2:58. He would later write (in 1873) that he intended his efforts to lead "to our deliverance from the evils that threatened us at the same time—the Germans and the Revolution!"

47. On the abbé Daniel, see Launay, *Diocèse de Nantes*, 738, and Le Chauff de Kerguenec, *Souvenirs*, 21, 117, 203. On at least one occasion Bishop Fournier had to defend his clergy against the accusation of a public official that a *curé* (in this case the *curé* of Vieillevigne) advised his parishioners to join the Zouaves instead of the regular army. See Pothier, *Fournier*, 2:515.

48. Launay, *Diocèse de Nantes*, 743. One of the prize recruits was Fernand de Bouillé, grandson of the Vendéen general, the marquis de Bonchamp. See Cerbelaud-Salagnac, *Zouaves*, 241 – 42.

49. Cerbelaud-Salagnac, *Zouaves*, 235 – 36.

50. "When God give lessons, he does a masterly job. Nothing is missing from what France is presently undergoing. We ask of God to give us the grace to die as a Christian must die, weapons at the ready, eyes on heaven, the chest toward the enemy, crying: Vive la France!" *La Semaine religieuse du diocèse de Nantes*, 17 December 1870, 617.

51. For the story of the banner, see Cerbelaud-Salagnac, *Zouaves*, 237. On Paray, see Thomas Kselman, *Miracles and Prophecies in Nineteenth-Century France* (New Brunswick, N. J., 1983), 125, and Philippe Boutry and Michel Cinquin, *Deux pèlerinages au XIXe siècle: Ars et Paray-le-Monial*, (Paris, 1980), 208 – 9.

52. Louis Baunard, *Le Général de Sonis d'après ses papiers et sa correspondance* (Paris 1890), 318 – 19.

53. Michael Howard, *The Franco-Prussian War: The German Invasion of France, 1870 – 1871* (London, 1989), 298; Henry M. Hozier, *The Franco-Prussian War* (London,

1872), 164. See also Stephane Audoin-Rouzeau, *1870: La France dans la guerre* (Paris, 1989), 235–37. For a review essay of recent works on the *année terrible,* see Robert Tombs, "L'année terrible, 1870–1871," *Historical Journal* 35 (1992): 713–24.

54. Howard, *Franco-Prussian War,* 310.

55. For Gambetta's statement, see Howard, *Franco-Prussian War,* 510. On Sonis, see Baunard, *Sonis,* 320. Of course, Sonis and the Zouaves were fully aware of the importance of Orléans to Joan of Arc and the liberation of 1429.

56. Baunard, *Sonis,* 325.

57. Baunard, *Sonis,* 327.

58. Audoin-Rouzeau, *1870: La France dans la guerre,* 237; Howard, *The Franco-Prussian War,* 311.

59. Scc *La Semaine religieuse du diocèse d'Angers,* 11 December 1870, 287–88; *La Semaine religieuse du diocèse de Nantes,* 17 December 1870, 617.

60. See Abbé Pergeline, vicaire-général, *Éloge funèbre de Joseph Houdet, Fernand Le Lièvre de la Touche, et Hippolyte de la Brosse, Volontaires de l'Ouest, prononcé dans la chapelle des enfants nantais, le 6 mars 1871* (Nantes, 1871), 11.

61. *La Semaine catholique de Luçon,* 8 June 1879, 717.

62. Baunard, *Sonis,* 381.

63. "[M]ore firmly than ever, we believe in the triumph of France consecrated to the Sacred Heart and brought back to traditional and legitimate monarchy. . . . And what a beautiful day it will be for the regiment of the Sacré-Coeur, the day when we will see its banner flutter like that of Joan of Arc at the coronation of the Most Christian King!" Speech of Alain de Charette, brother and representative of Athanase de Charette, 3 February 1897, in L. Hubineau, *Mgr Pinsonneau, Zouave Pontifical, curé d'Arthon-en-Retz* (Nantes, n.d.), 29–30, quoted in Faugeras, "Les Fidélités en France au XIXe siècle," 286.

64. The deliberate confusion of Loigny with Patay began almost immediately. For an early example, see "La Vraie France," *La Semaine liturgique du diocèse de Poitiers,* 1 January 1871, 9.

65. "What was Joan of Arc's most sublime hour? The hour of the liberation of Orléans? The hour of the coronation of Charles VII at Reims? No. It was the hour that saw her die at the stake in Rouen." Pergeline, *Éloge funèbre,* 15–16, and *La Semaine religieuse du diocèse de Nantes,* 1 April 1871, 148.

66. Monseigneur d'Hulst spoke of the "immolation" of "martyrs" because "they had dreamed of regeneration." Quoted in *Allocution prononcé dans l'église de Loigny par Mgr d'Hulst, Vicaire général de Paris* (Paris, 1876), 7–8; the abbé Fonssagrives remarked that "[p]erhaps never since the sacrifice of Calvary itself has the law of the suffering of the innocent for the benefit of the guilty manifested itself in such stark relief as on the battlefield of Loigny. Perhaps never before have more noble and devoted expiatory victims been chosen." J. Fonssagrives, *Le Sacrifice de Loigny. La Bataille du 2 décembre 1870* (Paris, 1898), 14.

67. Baunard, *Sonis,* 343–44.

68. *La Semaine religieuse du diocèse de Nantes,* 25 March 1871, 134.

69. The speaker is Bishop Cabrières. See *La Semaine religieuse du diocèse de Montpellier* (1874), 758, quoted in Gadille, *La Pensée,* 2:232.

70. Fonssagrives, *Le Sacrifice,* 14.

71. Benoist, *Le Sacré-Coeur,* 2:731 n.

72. Auguste Hamon, *Histoire de la dévotion au Sacré-Coeur de Jésus,* vol. 3: *Paray-le-Monial* (Paris, 1928), 320–21.

73. Stewart Edwards, *The Paris Commune, 1871* (Chicago, 1971), 141.

74. On Thiers's life and political career see J. P. T. Bury and R. P. Tombs, *Thiers, 1797–1877: A Political Life* (London, 1986), and Pierre Guiral, *Adolphe Thiers; Ou, De la nécessité en politique* (Paris, 1986).

75. As a bishop with Gallican tendencies, Darboy was hostile to the Jesuit pretention to answer directly to the pope in Rome, bypassing the domestic French episcopal hierarchy. Indeed, the debut of his episcopacy had been marked by a confrontation with Parisian Jesuits over their accountability to him, their archbishop. Burnichon, *Histoire d'un siècle,* 4:272. Nor did Darboy's take on the war include a retrospective critique of the Revolution. See J. A. Foulon, *Histoire de la vie et des oeuvres de Mgr. Darboy, archevêque de Paris* (Paris, 1889), 500, and "Lettre de l'archevêque de Paris" in *Le Moniteur universel,* 15 December 1870, 345.

76. Lesourd, *Montmartre,* 205; Benoist, *Le Sacré-Coeur,* 1:111–15.

BUILDING THE CHURCH OF THE NATIONAL VOW

1. David Pinkney, *Napoleon III and the Rebuilding of Paris* (Princeton, 1958); David Jordan, *Transforming Paris: The Life and Labors of Baron Haussmann* (New York, 1995).

2. J. Paguelle de Follenay, *Vie du cardinal Guibert, archevêque de Paris,* 2 vols. (Paris 1896), 2:584–85.

3. Auguste Hamon, *Histoire de la dévotion au Sacré-Coeur de Jésus,* 5 vols. (Paris, 1923–1939), 5:44; Jacques Benoist, Le *Sacré-Coeur de Montmartre de 1870 à nos jours,* 2 vols. (Paris 1992), 1:90–91; *Guide officiel du pèlerin au Sacré-Coeur de Montmartre* (Paris, 1892), 30; M. Bony, *Vie et oeuvres de M. Alexandre Legentil* (Paris, 1893), 234–35.

4. Paul Lesourd, *Montmartre* (Paris, 1973), 205.

5. Paguelle de Follenay, *Guibert,* 593–94.

6. Benoist, *Le Sacré-Coeur,* 243–45.

7. Bony, *Legentil,* 255–57; Hamon, *Histoire de la dévotion,* 5:50.

8. Paguelle de Follenay, *Guibert,* 594–95; Lesourd, *Montmartre,* 205.

9. Cited in Lesourd, *Montmartre,* 207. On the other sites, see P. Laligant, *Montmartre: La Basilique du voeu national du Sacré-Coeur* (Grenoble, 1933), 26 n, and Bony, *Legentil,* 266.

10. See Mircea Eliade, *Images and Symbols: Studies in Religious Symbolism,* trans. Philip Mairet (New York, 1961), esp. 39–41; for a comparative perspective, see also Roger Friedland and Richard D. Hecht, "The Politics of the Sacred Place: Jerusalem's Temple Mount," in Jamie Scott and Paul Simpson-Housley, eds., *Sacred Places and Profane Spaces: Essays in the Geographics of Judaism, Christianity, and Islam* (New York, 1991), 24–25.

11. Laligant, *Montmartre,* 26; Hamon, *Histoire de la dévotion,* 5:55.

12. Laligant, *Montmartre,* 9 and 26.

13. On the Sacré-Coeur and the Commune, see David Harvey, "Monument and Myth," *Annals of the Association of American Geographers* 69 (1979): 362–81, and

"Monument and Myth: The Building of the Basilica of the Sacred Heart," *Consciousness and the Urban Experience: Studies in the History and the Theory of Capitalist Urbanization* (Baltimore, 1985), 221–49. On Guibert and the Commune, see Paguelle, *Guibert,* 2:598–99; Benoist, *Le Sacré-Coeur,* 2:828–40.

14. Alphonse Dupront, "Pèlerinages et lieux sacrés," in Raymond Aron and others, *Méthodologie de l'histoire et des sciences humaines* (Toulouse, 1973), 199. See also Dupront's *Du Sacré: Croisades et pèlerinages, images et langages* (Paris, 1987).

15. On ascension and the sacred, see Eliade, *Images and Symbols,* 51. On bodily rituals and memory, see Paul Connerton, *How Societies Remember* (Cambridge, 1989).

16. For minutes of the discussion, see Archives nationales, C 2870, Église de Montmartre: Projet de construction.

17. Charles Seignobos, *Le Déclin de l'Empire et l'établissement de la Troisième République* (Paris, 1921), 364. The figure on the number of pilgrims at the pilgrimage of 20 June is from Louis Baunard, *Le Général de Sonis d'après ses papiers et sa correspondance* (Paris, 1890), 405. Jean-Marie Mayeur puts the number of deputies in the pilgrimage of 29 June at 150. See his *Nouvelle histoire de la France contemporaine,* vol. 9, *Les Débuts de la Troisième République* (Paris 1973), 28. On both pilgrimages, see Benoist, *Le Sacré-Coeur,* 278–99.

18. Thiers resigned on 24 May 1873; the law was passed on 24 July 1873. For the parliamentary debate, see *Journal officiel de la république française,* 22 June 1873, 4084; 24 June 1873, 4149; 25 July 1873, 5012–14. See also Archives nationales, C 2870, Église de Montmartre: Projet de construction.

19. *Bulletin de l'oeuvre du voeu national au Sacré-Coeur de Jésus,* May 1874, 177.

20. [Abbé Carle and others], "Un comité d'archéologues," *L'Église du Sacré-Coeur à Montmartre sera-t-elle de notre style national ou sera-t-elle d'un style étranger?* (Paris, 1875), 12.

21. *Projet pour le concours de l'église du Sacré-Coeur à Montmartre par Antoine Étex* (Paris, 1874).

22. For the Clutton story, see *Bulletin de l'oeuvre du voeu national,* February 1874, 84. Clutton also submitted a highly regarded design for London's new Catholic cathedral in 1867. Clutton's neo-Gothic design was ultimately passed over for a Romano-Byzantine design by John Francis Bentley. See John McIlwain, *Westminster Cathedral* (Andover, 1996), 4.

23. Archives historiques du diocèse de Paris: Basilique du Sacré-Coeur, carton 2: Letters from Bordeaux (2 October 1873), Périgueux (28 September 1873), and Tours (3 September 1873).

24. Léon de Vésly, "Concours de la maison de répression de Nanterre et de l'église du Sacré-Coeur à Montmartre," *Le Moniteur de Architectes* 8 (1874): 114.

25. Carle, *L'Église du Sacré-Coeur,* 12.

26. On Lassus, a student of Henri Labrouste, see the work of Jean-Michel Léniaud, especially *Jean-Baptiste Lassus, 1807–1857, ou le temps retrouvé des cathédrales* (Paris, 1980).

27. "Concours d'architecture pour la construction de l'église du Sacré-Coeur à Paris-Montmartre," in *Le Bâtiment: Journal des travaux publics et particuliers,* 26 July 1874, in Archives historiques du diocèse de Paris, Basilique du Sacré-Coeur, carton 3.

28. De Vésly, "Concours," 114.

29. Carle, *L'Église du Sacré-Coeur,* 11.
30. See Bruno Foucart, "L'Homme du Néo-Roman," in Bruno Foucart, ed., *Paul Abadie, architecte, 1812–1884* (Angoulême, 1984), 22–23; see also Barry Bergdol, "'The Synthesis of All I Have Seen': The Architecture of Edmond Duthoit (1837–1889)," in Robin Middleton, *The Beaux-Arts and 19th-Century French Architecture* (Cambridge, Mass., 1982), esp. 247; Michael Paul Driskell, *Representing Belief: Religion, Art, and Society in Nineteenth-Century France* (University Park, Penn., 1992), esp. 158; Neil Levine, "The Romantic Idea of Architectural Legibility: Henri Labrouste and the Neo-Grec," in A. Drexler, ed., *The Architecture of the Ecole des Beaux-Arts* (New York, 1977), 325–416; David Van Zanten, *Designing Paris: The Architecture of Duban, Labrouste, Duc, and Vaudoyer* (Cambridge, Mass., 1987).
31. In the context of Greek religious nationalism the "Megali Idea" expressed similar hopes, turning on "the romantic dream of a revival of the Byzantine-Greek Empire centered on Constantinople." See Michael L. Smith, *Ionian Vision* (London, 1973), 173–74.
32. Félix de Verneilh, *L'Architecture byzantine en France: Saint-Front de Périgueux et les églises à coupoles de l'Aquitaine* (Paris, 1851), 295.
33. *Bulletin de l'oeuvre du voeu national,* 10 March 1886, 155; Archives historiques du diocèse de Paris, Basilique du Sacré-Coeur, carton 3, "Notes du Comité."
34. Driskell, *Representing Belief,* 145–50.

A MODERN MAGDALENE SEEKS FORGIVENESS

1. *Mandement de son éminence Monseigneur l'archevêque de Paris touchant le projet de construction à Montmartre d'une église votive au Sacré-Coeur de Jésus* (Paris, 1873), in Archives historiques du diocèse de Paris, Basilique du Sacré-Coeur, carton 2.
2. See letter from the bishop of Fréjus and Toulon, 26 September 1873, in Archives historiques du diocèse de Paris, Basilique du Sacré-Coeur, carton 2.
3. Letter from the bishop of Constantine, 6 October 1873, in Archives historiques du diocèse de Paris, Basilique du Sacré-Coeur, carton 2.
4. On violence, sacrifice, and the sacred, see René Girard, *La Violence et le Sacré* (Paris, 1972), 27–52.
5. Letter from the bishop of Perpignan, 19 September 1873, in Archives historiques du diocèse de Paris, Basilique du Sacré-Coeur, carton 2.
6. Jacques Benoist, *Le Sacré-Coeur de Montmartre de 1870 à nos jours,* 2 vols. (Paris, 1992), 1:354–55.
7. Auguste Hamon, *Histoire de la dévotion au Sacré-Coeur de Jésus,* 5 vols. (Paris 1923–39), 5:343.
8. Benoist, *Le Sacré-Coeur,* 1:347–48.
9. According to the *Guide officiel,* Pius IX told Abbé Lagarde, vicar general, "The construction of the basilica will be quite long, prayer should begin before it is finished." See *Guide officiel du pèlerin au Sacré-Coeur de Montmartre* (Paris, 1892), 38–39, in Archives nationales, F19 2371, Église du Sacré-Coeur de Montmartre.
10. The dimensions for the *chapelle provisoire* are from the Cabinet des Estampes of the Bibliothèque nationale (Correspondance et documents divers provenant de Paul Abadie (n.p., n.d.). 1 boite pet. fol.). The figure on the number of pilgrims

represents those who signed the register at the *chapelle provisoire.* Inevitably, the total would be incomplete. See *Guide officiel,* 40.

11. Figures on collections at the *chapelle provisoire* are from Archives historiques du diocèse de Paris, Basilique du Sacré-Coeur, carton 4, Recettes et dépenses de l'église du Sacré-Coeur (1877–1904). The *chapelle* cost 24,000 francs to construct, meaning that its cost had easily been recovered within months of its completion. See *Bulletin de l'oeuvre national au Sacré-Coeur de Jésus* 2 (1876): 3–4.

12. See *Guide officiel,* 801 and *Bulletin de l'oeuvre national* 9 (1884): 126. There is no way to estimate the background of these pilgrims and donors, and although some of them must have been persons of modest means, the costs of participation in a pilgrimage would have prevented many peasants and workers in the provinces from participating. Pilgrims from beyond the Paris basin, then, were more likely to be from well-to-do classes.

13. *Bulletin de l'oeuvre national* 9 (1884): 107–12.

14. *Bulletin de l'oeuvre national* 12 (1887): 245.

15. On the Panthéon as a temple in the tradition of republican spirituality, see Mona Ozouf, "Le Panthéon: L'École Normale des morts," in Pierre Nora, ed., *Les Lieux de mémoire,* vol. 1, *La République* (Paris, 1984), 139–66. On the competitive juxtaposition of the Panthéon and the Sacré-Coeur, see Emmet Kennedy, *A Cultural History of the French Revolution* (New Haven, 1989), 392.

16. Chambéry's archbishop, Monsignor Leuillieux, liked the idea that his diocese would donate the bell that would become "like the voice of France, singing the praises of the Divine Heart high above free-thinking Paris." *Semaine religieuse du diocèse de Nantes,* 5 January 1889, 20. On the installation of the bell, see *le Monde,* 29 February 1896, and Archives nationales, F19 2371, Église du Sacré-Coeur de Montmartre.

17. *Bulletin de l'oeuvre national* 12 (1887): 369–70; Gustave Téry, *Les Cordicoles* (Paris, 1902), 235.

18. See the *Guide officiel,* 80–81, and *Bulletin de l'oeuvre national* 9 (1884): 126. A stone not visible from the exterior or interior of the church was called a *taille cachée.* This is what a person completing a *carte du Sacré-Coeur* could expect.

19. See "Venite Adoremus," *Bulletin de l'oeuvre national* 9 (1884): 947.

20. For important episodes in the political history of Sacré-Coeur, see Jean-Clément Martin, *La Vendée et la France* (Paris, 1987), and Louis Baunard, *Le Général de Sonis* (Paris, 1891).

21. *Bulletin de l'oeuvre national* 9 (1884): 504.

22. The basic seasonal pattern of pilgrimage to the Sacré-Coeur fits the pattern found by Mary Nolan and Sidney Nolan only in the broadest sense. As they put it, "pilgrimage is essentially an outdoor activity, best undertaken in warm weather." *Christian Pilgrimage in Modern Western Europe* (Chapel Hill, N. C., 1989), 56. Using late twentieth-century figures on pilgrimage, they found that August and September were the most popular pilgrimage months by far for the many sites they studied. This differs from the June peak in late nineteenth-century figures for the Sacré-Coeur. One explanation is both social and historical: only in the twentieth century did most workers acquire paid vacations and only then did the preference for August vacations, especially in France, fully manifest itself. In nineteenth-century

France, pilgrimage for many working people would have to have been a strictly local affair.

23. Joseph Hilgers, *Livre d'or du Coeur de Jésus; Pour les prêtres et pour les fidèles: Indulgences et privilèges de la dévotin au coeur de Jésus* (Paris, 1911), 208; E. Des Buttes, *Le Scapulaire du Sacré-Coeur* (Paris 1878), 28. *Adveniat Regnum Tuum* was also the motto of the Assumptionist order, which assumed many publicly activist roles, including the organization of pilgrimages. See Alfred Baudrillart, *Dictionnaire d'histoire et de géographie ecclésiastiques* 4 vols. (Paris, 1930), 4:1142.

24. See, for example, the address of Monsignor Fava on 23 September to the 160 pilgrims from Grenoble, "Pelerinage du diocèse de Grenoble," *Bulletin de l'oeuvre national* 10 (1885): 755, and *Guide officiel du pèlerin au Sacré-Coeur de Montmartre* (Paris 1892).

25. *Bulletin de l'oeuvre national,* 10 April 1877.

26. *Petit Manuel des Adoratrices du Sacré-Coeur* (Paris, 1894), 31; Archives départmentales de la Loire Atlantique (Nantes) 2 V 3, Police générale du culte, faits divers, rapports, 1870–79, Rapport du Commissaire Central [de police] au Préfet, Nantes, 27 June 1881; Archives départementales de la Sâone et Loire (Mâcon) 4 M 158, Police Général; Pèlerinage à Paray-le-Monial, June 1875, Rapport, Commissariat spécial à Paray-le-Monial au Préfet de Saône et Loire, 2 June 1875; Archives nationales F19 5562, Pèlerins, dossier Paray-le-Monial, pèlerinage du diocèse de Bourges à Paray-le-Monial, 15 September 1890; Xavier de Franciosi, *La Dévotion au Sacré-Coeur de Jésus et au Saint-Coeur de Marie* (Nancy, 1885), 303; *Notice sur le Calvaire de Pontchateau* (Nantes, 1873), 55; *La Semaine religieuse du diocèse d'Angers,* 29 June 1873, 757; *La Semaine religieuse du diocèse d'Angers,* 2 October 1875, 630. See also Benoist, *Le Sacré-Coeur,* 2:600–6.

27. The complexity of language can conceal hesitation and mental reservations. The gestures of ritual (the sign of the cross, the genuflexion) are unambiguous signs. See Paul Connerton, *How Societies Remember* (Cambridge 1989), esp. 59.

28. Paul Lesourd, *Montmartre* (Paris 1973), 40, 225–27; Benoist, *Le Sacré-Coeur,* 2:1233.

29. *Annales de la Chambre des Députés* (1882), 771.

30. Archives nationales, F19 2371, Église du Sacré-Coeur de Montmartre, letter of 20 December 1901.

31. Téry, *Les Cordicoles,* 331–32.

32. "Projet de loi tendant à déclarer d'utilité publique la construction d'une Église à Paris (18e arrond.) presenté par M. Thiers, Président de la république française, et par M. de Fourtou Ministre des Cultes," in Archives nationales, F19 2371, Église du Sacré-Coeur de Montmartre.

33. *Annales de la Chambre des Députés* (1882), 698; *Annales de la Chambre des Députés* (1897), 71.

A VISION CAPTURED IN MOSAIC

1. See Hélène Guéné, "L'Éclat triomphant des mosaïques," in Jacques Benoist, ed., *Le Sacré-Coeur de Montmartre: Un Voeu national* (Paris, 1995), 190–91; Jacques

Benoist, *Le Sacré-Coeur de Montmartre de 1870 à nos jours,* 2 vols. (Paris 1992), 2:676–78.

2. *Montmartre: La Basilique du Voeu National au Sacré-Coeur* (Paris, n.d.), 44–45.

3. From *L'Espérance du Peuple,* a Nantes newspaper, reprinted in *Le Télégraphe,* 30 October 1885. See Archives de la Préfecture de Police, Paris, Ba 996, Édouard Cazenove de Pradines.

4. E. des Buttes, *Le Scapulaire du Sacre-Coeur* (Paris, 1878), 24; *Journal Officiel,* 25 July 1873, 5014.

5. Auguste Hamon, *Histoire de la dévotion au Sacré-Coeur de Jésus,* 5 vols. (Paris 1923–1939), 4:236; Philippe Boutry and Michel Cinquin, *Deux pèlerinages au XIXe siècle: Ars et Paray-le Monial* (Paris 1980), 320–21; Gérard Cholvy and Yves-Marie Hilaire, *Histoire religieuse de la France contemporaine,* vol. 1, *1800–1880* (Paris 1985), 171.

6. *Journal Officiel,* 16 January 1873, 295.

7. Albert Delaporte, *L'Année du Sacré-Coeur* (Paris, 1886), 10; Boutry and Cinquin, *Deux pèlerinages,* 209; Adrien Dansette, *Histoire religieuse de la France contemporaine: L'Église catholique dans le mêlée politique et sociale* (Paris, 1965), 455; Hamon, *Histoire de la dévotion,* 5:70.

8. Cited in *l'Univers,* 25 November 1873. See Archives de la Préfecture de Police, Paris, Ba 956, Gabriel de Belcastel.

9. Archives nationales, C 2870, Église de Montmartre, Projet de construction: Séance du 1 juillet 1873; Benoist, *Le Sacré-Coeur* 1:284.

10. Jacques Gadille, *Guide des archives diocésaines françaises* (Lyon 1971), 232.

11. Louis Baunard, *Le Général de Sonis d'après ses papiers et sa correspondance* (Paris, 1890), 445–46.

12. Georges Cerbelaud-Salagnac, *Les Zouaves pontificaux* (Paris, 1963), 20–21.

13. Faugeras, "Les fidélités en France au XIXe siècle: Les Zouaves pontificaux, 1860–1870," in Darricau and others, *Fidélités, solidarités et clientèles: Enquêtes et documents,* vol. 11 (Nantes, 1986), 285.

14. By the 1890s a different committee, but of similar makeup, appointed by Archbishop Guibert's successor, François Richard, attracted the criticism of the papal nuncio in Paris. Ferrata, the nuncio, sharply criticized the composition of the leadership of the "Union de la France chrétienne." Although Ferrata did not doubt that Richard's appointees were men of good faith, he revealed great sensitivity in pointing out that Richard's choice of men so uniformly hostile to the Republic unnecessarily cast doubt upon the good intentions of the Catholic Church. See Maurice Clément, *Vie du Cardinal Richard, archevêque de Paris* (Paris, 1924), 188–93.

15. Letter of 3 March 1876 from Cardinal Guibert to Monsignor Bécel, bishop of Vannes, quoted in Philippe Levillain, *Albert de Mun: Catholicisme français et catholicisme romain du Syllabus au Ralliement* (Rome, 1983), 472.

16. Victor Alet, *La France et le Sacré-Coeur* (Paris 1871, 1903), 322.

17. Levillain, *Albert de Mun,* 744.

18. Albert de Mun, "Les dernières heures du drapeau blanc," *La Revue hebdomadaire* 11 (13 November 1909): 158–59. See also E. Boisseleau, *Le Sacré-Coeur et la France: L'Étendard du Sacré-Coeur à Loigny* (Luçon, 1911), 19–20. On Frohsdorf, see Gilberte Larignon and Héliette Proust, *Edouard de Monti de Rezé. L'Inébranlable certitude: Le Mouvement légitimiste dans l'Ouest* (Laval, 1992).

19. Levillain, *Albert de Mun,* 776.
20. Benoist, *Le Sacré-Coeur,* 2:787.
21. *Messager du Sacré-Coeur,* November 1889, 513–35; Benoist, *Le Sacré-Coeur,* 2:738.
22. In 1884, Leo XIII called Monsignor d'Hulst to Rome. Along with Monsignor Lavigerie, who had been elevated to the rank of cardinal just two years earlier, he wanted to make him the instrument of his policy of rapprochement between the Catholic Church and the French Republic. Monsignor d'Hulst refused. Instead, he undertook a vigorous refutation of all of the arguments that the partisans of this policy had placed before the pope. Alfred Baudrillart, *Vie de Monseigneur d'Hulst,* 2 vols. (Paris, 1912), 1:25; Levillain, *Albert de Mun,* 1000.
23. The abbé Fonssagrives, in the company of Monsignor d'Hulst, told the American bishop that he had "converted all of his Catholic listeners to the Republic . . . the American Republic." Baudrillart, *Monseigneur d'Hulst,* 2:372.
24. Letter of 30 March 1886 from Cardinal Guibert, quoted in Baudrillart, *Monseigneur d'Hulst,* 2:293.
25. Emmanuel de Rorthays, "Le Cardinal Richard en Vendée," *Revue de Bas-Poitou* 21 (1908): 5–17.
26. *Bulletin de l'oeuvre du voeu national au Sacré-Coeur de Jésus* 10 March 1878, 138.
27. For Paray-le-Monial, see "Cantique des pèlerins de l'Anjou," in [Abbé] Dugan, *Le Pèlerinage du Sacré-Coeur en 1873: Histoire et documents* (Moulins, 1873), 454. See also the remarks of Monsignor de Léseleuc, bishop of Autun, at Paray-le-Monial, 26 June 1873: "[B]ien des fois vous avez fait amende honorable au Coeur-Sacré de Jésus pour nos longues ingratitudes accumulées surtout depuis quatre-vingts ans." Quoted in Dugan, *Le Pèlerinage,* 253.
28. Even at Montmartre, there would soon be the mosaic featuring Charette and Sonis, a scene that would plant the seeds of doubt.
29. *Mandement de son éminence le cardinal archevêque de Paris a l'occasion de la bénédiction et de la pose de la première pierre de l'église du Sacré-Coeur a Montmartre* (Paris, 1875), 7–8.
30. *Bulletin de l'oeuvre du voeu national* 1 (1873): 12.
31. *Bulletin de l'oeuvre du voeu national* 1 (1873): 12.
32. See Maurice Halbwachs, *Les Cadres Sociaux de la Mémoire* (Paris, 1952) especially page vi: "[T]here's nothing mysterious about the recovery of memories. There's no need to seek out where they are, where they are stored in my brain, or in which corner of my mind. . . . Memories are recalled from outside, and the groups to which I belong at every moment offer me the means to reconstruct them, on the condition that I orient myself toward them and that I adopt, at least provisionally, their ways of thinking."
33. It is reproduced uncritically in David Harvey, "Monument and Myth: The Building of the Basilica of the Sacred Heart," in David Harvey, ed. *Consciousness and the Urban Experience: Studies in the History and the Theory of Capitalist Urbanization* (Baltimore, 1985), 221–49; François Loyer, "Le Sacré-Coeur de Montmartre," in Pierre Nora, ed., *Les Lieux de mémoire* (Paris, 1984), 3:451–73.
34. Archives historiques du diocèse de Paris, Basilique du Sacré-Coeur, carton 4, "Recettes."

BIBLIOGRAPHY

ARCHIVAL SOURCES

Archives Nationales

Série C, Procès-verbaux des assemblées nationales
  2870 Église de Montmartre; projet de construction.
  3153 Budget des cultes; pièces diverses.
Série F7, Police générale
  13213 Mouvement catholique.
  13214 Mouvement catholique (suite).
  13216 Notes et presse sur l'activité de la ligue patriotique des Françaises, 1910–27.
Série F19, Cultes
  2371 Église du Sacré-Cœur de Montmartre.
  5562 Pèlerinages; établissement "Cœur de Jésus."
  5566 Prières, fêtes, et cérémonies publiques (généralités) 1814–79.
  5583 Honneurs et préséances; affaires générales; tableau des rangs; visites des cardinaux; . . . sacres et obsèques d'évêques et archevêques, an X—1900.
  5609 Police, Guerre franco-allemande: organisation des ambulances; prières publiques, etc., 1870–72.
  5610 Police, Troisième République: rapports et notes sur l'attitude du clergé et particulièrement de l'épiscopat, 1872–1906; prières pour l'Assemblée (1871).
  5636 Police, Troisième République: agissements politiques sous forme religieuse; fêtes de Jeanne d'Arc, 1890–1904; consécration des communes au Sacré-Cœur, 1901–5.
  5639 Police, Troisième République: coupures de journaux, 1897–1907.
  6535 Activité politique du clergé, Troisième République.
  6642 Fiches du personnel catholique, Paris Fl-Le.

6643 Fiches du personnel catholique, Paris Li-R.

7228 Concours.

7229 Dossiers personnels, A et B.

7234 Inspecteurs diocésaines: dossiers personnels. A à C [Paul Abadie].

Archives Départmentales

ARCHIVES DÉPARTEMENTALES DE LA BOUCHE DU RHÔNE
(MARSEILLE)

Série 5G, Clergé séculier

698 Henri-François-Xavier de Belsunce, 1709–55: titres cléricaux.

699 Procédures; nomination et destitution de procureurs; correspondance de l'évêque ou de ses procureurs.

704 Livre de raison tenu par l'intendant Goujon, relatant les principaux événements de son passage a l'évêché; peste de 1720.

763 Carmélites; Miséricorde: offices, quittances, 1627–1721.

860 Assemblées du clergé du diocèse de Marseille, 1606–1727.

Série 1M, Cabinet du Préfet

1427 Royalistes; manifestation lors de la fête du Sacré-Cœur, 1881; fêtes du Sacré-Cœur.

1428 Fêtes du Sacré-Cœur, 1886–77, 1888.

1429 Fêtes du Sacré-Cœur, avec portraits du duc d'Orléans, 1897–98.

1430 Fêtes du Sacré-Cœur, 1904.

Série V, Cultes (24V à 34V, "Police du Culte")

24V 1 Affaires générales; circulaires ministérielles; correspondance, an VIII-1870.

25V 1 Prières publiques.

28V 1 Processions, an IX–1864.

33V 1 Esprit politique du clergé.

ARCHIVES DÉPARTEMENTALES DE LA HAUTE GARONNE
(TOULOUSE)

Série 1M, Cabinet du Préfet

Série 4M, Police

88bis Police générale, 1856–70: soldats de l'armée du pape, 1860.

95 Police générale, 1871–78: mouvement légitimiste, 1878.

96 Police générale, 1879–82: banquet royaliste à Carbonne; enseignement religieux, 1881.

97 Police générale, 1883–84: menées cléricales; activités de l'église et des cléricaux.

98 Police générale, 1885–87: rapports sur les Jésuites qui habitent le château de Mourville-Basses en 1885.

99 Police générale, 1888–89: rapports sur les royalistes réactionnaires.

107 Police: manifestations cléricales, 1899–1900.

15Z 746 Royalistes et nationalistes: surveillance et manifestations, 1901–14.

Série V, Cultes

V48 Séparation: Jésuites, 1902–15.

V53 Congrégations: instructions; coupures de journaux, 1882–1910.

2V Ministère des cultes: culte catholique; personnel; police des cultes.

2V 28 Processions ville de Toulouse; procession de la Fête-Dieu, 1802–1901.

2V 32ter État des nominations; *Semaine religieuse,* 1804–1906.

2V 61 Chant officiel; *Domine salvam;* plaintes, 1878–93.

Archives départementales de la Loire Atlantique (Nantes)

Série V, Cultes

2V 1 Police générale du culte: faits divers; rapports, 1800–14.

2V 2 Police générale du culte: faits divers; rapports, 1814–69.

2V 3 Police générale du culte: faits divers; rapports, 1870–83.

2V 4 Police générale du culte: faits divers; rapports, 1884–1904.

3V 1 Mandements; lettres pastorales; ordonnances épiscopales circulaires, 1801–27.

3V 5 Mandements; lettres pastorales; ordonnances épiscopales circulaires, 1860–70.

Archives départementales de la Maine et Loire (Angers)

Série 1M, Administration générale: Rapports sur l'état de l'opinion publique et la situation générale du département.

1M3 1 Rapports du Préfet au Ministre de l'intérieur, septembre 1865; janvier-février, avril-octobre, décembre 1872; février, avril—juin 1873; 1882; février 1894—juin 1908 à juillet 1910 (avec lacunes).

1M6 58 Fêtes et manifestations publiques organisées par des royalistes, 1881–1914.

1M6 65 Cérémonies et manifestations religieuses: Fête-Dieu, fêtes de Jeanne d'Arc, processions, pèlerinage, missions, visites pastorales, etc., 1873–1913.

1M6 66 Propagande cléricale: Tracts, affiches, catéchisme, soirées, missions, prédications, 1880–1914.

1M6 67 Questions de l'enseignement, 1872–1913.

1M6 68 Questions des congrégations: Conférences, manifestations, incidents divers, placards et affiches à l'occasion des lois sur les congrégations, 1896–1903.

Série O, Biens communaux [classée par ville]

Angers, Église de La Madeleine, Église Saint-Sauveur

Archives départementales de la Saône et Loire (Mâcon)

Série M, Police

158 Police générale: Pèlerinage à Paray-le-Monial, juin 1875.

159 Police générale: Plaintes et rapports du préfet; pèlerinages à Paray-le-Monial, juin 1875.

310 Police: Affaires religieuses; agitations religieuses, congrès, pèlerinages, pétitions en faveur de la reprise des relations avec le Saint-Siège, 1906–17.

312 Pèlerinages, affaires religieuses, mouvements catholiques.

ARCHIVES DÉPARTEMENTALES DE LA VENDÉE
(LA ROCHE-SUR-YON)

Série 1M, Administration générale
> 442 Correspondance, rapports, coupures de presse, tracts, 1871–80.
> 474 Censures de Baudry d'Asson, député; affichage. 1879–80.
> 478 Cultes: Instructions, personnel ecclésiastique, enquêtes, correspondance, an X-1926.
> 536 Prières publiques à l'occasion de la rentrée des chambres, 1872–81.
> 537 Fête du centenaire de la Révolution de 1789 (1889).

Série 4M, Police
> 150 Cultes: Réglementation des sonneries de cloches, bancs des églises, sépultures, processions, 1904–13.
> 165 Évêque de Luçon, 1902–5.
> 178 Royalistes, 1895–1915.
> 405 Troisième République: Réunions, manifestations religieuses, correspondance, rapports, 1879–1939.
> 407 Banquets royalistes, 1879–82.
> 408 Réunions, manifestation et propagande des parties et groupements politiques, 1881–1929.
> 439 Cent jours: Agitation royaliste, rapports, correspondance, 1815.
> 440 Insurrection royaliste: Opérations militaires, rapports, correspondance, etat des réquisitions de l'armée royale, 1815.
> 443 Monarchie de Juillet, 1828–45; chouannerie; rapports des préfets et des sous-préfets, 1830–39.

Série O, Biens Communaux
> 400 Les-Lucs-sur-Boulogne.

ARCHIVES DÉPARTEMENTALES DE LA VIENNE (POITIERS)

Série 4M, Police
> 4M 370 Demandes de renseignements confidentiels, 1914–17.
> 493 Affaires diverses, 1814–1928.

Série R, Guerre et affaires militaires
> 7R Guerre de 1914–18
> 7R 32 Télégrammes, arrêtés, instruction, photographies, censure.
> 37 Circulaires diverses
> 38 Lettres, instructions, télégrammes divers.
> 39 Idem.

Diocesan Archives
ARCHIVES DIOCÉSAINES D'ANGERS

Série A, Relations avec le Saint-Siège
> 4A2 Mgr Angebault: pouvoirs, indults, comptes-rendus sur le diocèse, 1842–62.
> 4A3 Mgr Angebault: pouvoirs, indults, textes pontificaux, 1862–69.

4A4 Vicaire capitulaire: indults, 1869–70; Mgr Freppel, indults, 1870–91.
Série E, Magistère épiscopal: Actes officiels, conseil épiscopal, catéchisme, statuts synodaux, missions.
    2E1 2 Registres du conseil épiscopal, 1846–57, 1857–83.
    9E7 Mgr Angebault proteste contre la surveillance dont le clergé est l'objet de la part des gendarmes, 1860–62.
    9E9 Deux rapports de Mgr Angebault sur l'état du diocèse, 1861–64.
    9E10 Recueil des lettres et pièces administratives, 1849–66.
    9E12–9E15 Mgr Angebault prédicateur.
    9E12 Pendant l'épiscopat: divers, 1861–65.
    9E13 à Cholet
    9E16 Correspondance Mgr Angebault; général de Charette; abbé Cailleaud, aumônier des zouaves pontificaux; général de Lamoricière.
    9E28 Correspondance Mgr Freppel—La Croix; plaintes du gouvernement contre les évêques, 1872, 1873, 1885.
    9E31 Proposition de loi sur la désaffection du Sacré-Cœur de Montmartre.
    9E32 Célébrations religieuses à l'occasion d'événements nationaux. En 1804, puis à la Troisième République.
    9E41 Guerre de 1870–71.
Série 2K9–2K41, Pèlerinages.
    2K9 L'Anjou à Paray-le-Monial, juin 1873; l'Anjou au pèlerinage national à Chartres, mai 1873.
    2K32 Pèlerinages angevins à Lourdes.
    3K5 Propagation de la Foi: fondation Besnarderie, 1877–1904.
    3K7 Quête anti-esclavagiste, 1891.
    4K4 Oeuvres diverses; anciens zouaves pontificaux.
    5K21 Association catholique et royale, 1816–73.
Série OP, Dossiers paroissiaux, église, construction et réparations.
    OP13 Sainte-Madeleine du Sacré-Cœur.
    OP113 Louroux-Béconnais.

ARCHIVES DIOCÉSAINES DE CHARTRES

Loigny-la-Bataille, fonds Provost
    Dossier 4 Général de Sonis.
    Dossier 5 Zouaves pontificaux.
    Dossier 6 Correspondance, 1870–74.
    Dossier 7 Correspondance, 1875–83.
    Dossier 8 Correspondance, 1890–92.
    Dossier 12 Correspondance, 1915–18.
    Dossier 14 Poésies et drames.

ARCHIVES DIOCÉSAINES DE LUÇON

    1E 6 Lettres circulaires, 1866–69.
    1E 7 Lettres circulaires, 1870–71.
    1E 8 Lettres circulaires, 1872–1919.

4L 2 Correspondance après 1905, dossier, la basilique du Sacré-Cœur, la Roche-sur-Yon.

Archives historiques du diocèse de Paris

Basilique du Sacré-Cœur
  Carton 1 Souscriptions, registres, album, plans, gravures.
  Carton 2 La Loi de 1873, brefs et rescrits, mandements et circulaires, liste des chapelains.
  Carton 3 Concours, plans, la décoration des chapelles, notes sur les projets, rapport sur les expropriations, difficultés avec Abadie, difficultés avec Daumet, Rauline architecte.
  Carton 4 Correspondances, affaire du scapulaire, affaire Sandino, recettes et dépenses de l'église du Sacré-Cœur (1877–1904).
  Carton 5 Bénédiction, 1891; Croix lumineuse, 1892; 25ème anniversaire, 1897; consécration 1919, œuvres de dévotion, règlement des chapelains.
  Carton 6 La Ville de Paris, propriétaire de la basilique et des terrains annexes: jugement de 1913.
  Carton 7 Plans divers, vues ariennes, pèlerinage d'action de grâces de l'action catholique à la basilique du Sacré-Cœur (3 juin-24 septembre 1944).
  Carton 8 Album de concours.

Archives diocésaines de Poitiers

M71 Militaires.
M72 Relations avec l'armée.
S1 1 Franc-Maçonnerie.
G3 3 Liturgie, autel privilégiés, dévotions Sacré-Cœur, Notre-Dame de Boulogne.

Archives municipales

Archives municipales de Nantes

Série M, Edifices communaux, monuments et etablissements publics, Églises paroissiales
  M2 24 Église Saint-Donatien, 1791–1889
Série PI, Cultes
  Carton 1, Culte catholique
    dossier 12, "Paroisses et fabriques."
    dossier 15, "Police des cultes, évènements," 1791–1893.
  Carton 2
    dossier 10, Pèlerinages, 1873–91.
  Carton 3, Culte catholique II
    dossier 11, Paroisse Saint-Donatien, an XI–1906
    dossier 20, Dévotions diverses, 1843–
    dossier 21, Plantation des Croix de Saint-Donatien et de Saint-Rogatien, 1816.

Carton 12, Congrégations religieuses
> dossier 12, Dames du Sacré-Coeur de Jésus (1807, 1841, 1857).

Carton 15, Police des cultes—Cérémonies, 1790–1885
> dossier 8, Prédications, 1809–82
>> dossier 15, Rassemblements illicites pour actes superstitieux ou cultes prohibés.

Archives de la Préfecture de Police, Paris

SÉRIE Ba (DOSSIERS PERSONNELS)

870 Charette, (baron) Athanase
874 Veuillot, Louis (journaliste)
910 Richard, archevêque de Paris
943 Aurelles de Paladines. Louis J. B., général
950 Batbie, Anselme Polycarpe, député
956 Belcastel, Gabriel, (comte de), ancien député
996 Cazenove de Pradines, Édouard, ancien député
1002 Cathelineau, Henri de, ancien général
1111 Guibert, Joseph-Hippolyte
1141 La Rochejaquelein, de
1223 Pie
1271 de Sonis
1541 Culte catholique, 1870–90; Jésus Roi (société de), Cœur Miséricordieux de; Union royaliste
1654 François Veuillot (gérant du journal)

Archivio Segreto Vaticano (Vatican Archives)

Segretario di Stato 1878
> Rubrica 220, fasc. 5

Segretario di Stato
> Rubrica 248: Nunziatura di Francia, fasc. 1, 2, 3 [1868–76]

Segretario di Stato
> Rubrica 283: Vescovi esteri, 1870, f. 1
> 1870, f. 1
> 1871, unico .
> 1872, f. 1 e 2
> 1873, f. 7
> 1874, f. 6
> 1875, f. 6
> 1876, f. 1
> 1877, f. 6
> 1878, f. "francia"
> 1879, f. "francia"
> 1880, f. "francia, vescovo di Parigi"
> 1881, f. "francia, vescovo di Parigi"

PUBLISHED SOURCES

Journals and Newspapers

L'Ami de la religion et du roi: Journal ecclésiastique, politique, et littéraire. Consulted 1815–17.

L'Ami du roi. Consulted 1790–91.

"Association de secours mutuels des zouave pontificaux sous la protection du Sacré-Coeur," ca. 1890

Bulletin de l'oeuvre du voeu national au Sacré-Coeur de Jésus. Published as part of *La Semaine religieuse de Paris* until 1873. Consulted 1873–1919.

Le Constitutionnel: Journal de commerce, politique et littéraire, 1827.

La Croix. Consulted 1885, 1886, 1891, 1897, 1914, 1917, 1919.

Journal de la montagne. Consulted 1793.

Journal officiel de la république française. Consulted 1870–75, 1881–82, 1889–93.

Mémoires particuliers formant avec l'ouvrage de M. Hue et le journal de Cléry l'histoire complète de la captivité de la famille royale à la tour du Temple. Paris: Audot, 1817.

Le Messager du Sacré-Coeur de Jésus: Bulletin mensuel de l'apostolat de la prière. Consulted 1862, 1881, 1889, 1892, 1893, 1914–19.

Le Moniteur universel. 1870–71.

Le Pèlerin: Organe du conseil général des pèlerinages. Consulted 1873–75, 1889, 1914–19.

La République française. Consulted 1873–74.

La Semaine catholique de Luçon. Consulted 1876–80.

La Semaine liturgique du diocèse de Poitiers. Consulted 1870–72, 1914–19.

La Semaine paroissiale de Montbert (Loire Atlantique). Consulted 1918.

La Semaine religieuse de Paris. Consulted 1871–73, 1914.

La Semaine religieuse du diocèse d'Angers. Consulted 1871–74, 1878–79.

La Semaine religieuse du diocèse de Nantes. Consulted 1870–75, 1889.

Anonymous and Unsigned Works

A la Memoire de M. Thibeaud-Nicollière, Avocat, Conseiller-Général de la Loire-Inferieure, ancien batonnier, ancien membre du Conseil de l'Ordre, ancien président de la Jeunesse Royaliste de Nantes, 11 septembre 1830–20 juin 1904. Vannes: Lafolye, 1904.

Association de quarante jours. Paris: Crapart, 1790.

Authentic Trial at Large of Marie-Antoinette, Late Queen of France, before the Revolutionary Tribunal at Paris, on Tuesday, October 15, 1793 on a Charge of having been accessory to, and having cooperated in divers maneuvers against the Liberties of France, entertained a Correspondence with the Enemies of the Republic, and participated in a Plot tending to kindle Civil War in the Interior of the Republic by arming Citizens against each other. London: Chapman, 1793.

Bernard de Quatrebarbes, volontaire pontifical, blessé à Monte-Rotondo, mort à Rome pour la cause du Christ. Paris: Poussielgue, 1868.

La Congrégation des filles de la charité du Sacré-Coeur de Jésus. Paris: Letouzey, 1923.

[D. L.] *Seconde Lettre à Louis XVIII, roi de France et de Navarre, sur le salut de la monarchie française.* London: Booker, 1798.

"Ermite de Jérusalem" [ancien missionnaire, auteur de lettres à un ministre protestant]. *Écho de trente années de prédications pour carêmes, missions, jubilé.* Paris: Bloud et Barral, 1885.

Exercices de la dévotion au Sacré-Coeur de Jésus, à l'usage de la confrérie établie à Semur en Brionnois, et confirmée par N. S. P. le Pape Pie VII. Lyon: Rusand, 1818.

Faisons pénitence pour le salut de la France. Paris: Imprimerie de l'Oeuvre des pauvres du Sacré-Coeur, 1903.

"Fête de la croix de Charette à la Chabotterie (6 août 1911)." In *Revue de Bas-Poitou* (1911): 263–331.

Guide officiel du pèlerin au Sacré-Coeur de Montmartre. Paris: Imprimerie des Arts et Manufactures et Dubuisson, 1892. [In Archives nationales, F19 2371, Église du Sacré-Coeur de Montmartre.]

L'Institution Notre-Dame de Chartres à Loigny, le 18 juin 1891. Chateaudun: Pigelet, 1891.

Instructions, pratiques, et prières pour la dévotion au Sacré-Coeur de Jésus: L'Office, vespres et messe de cette dévotion. Paris: Valleyre, 1752.

Les Légitimistes à Sainte-Anne-d'Auray le 29 septembre 1887. Paris: Librairie Légitimiste, 1887.

Manuel et souvenir de la mission prêchée à Nantes par les RR PP Rédemptoristes en 1890. Nantes: Libaros, 1890.

[MM. les Vicaires généraux, administrateurs du diocèse de Poitiers.] "Consécration du diocèse de Poitiers au sacré-coeur de Jésus par ordonnance de MM. les Vicaires généraux, le siège épiscopal vacant." *Les Archives religieuses du pays poitevin* 6 (1902): 99–104. [orginally published as a brochure, Poitiers: Barbier, 1816]

Mois du Sacré-Coeur de Jésus. Paris: Poussielgue-Rusand, 1850.

Montmartre, la basilique du voeu national au Sacré-Coeur: Guide. Paris, n.d. [after 1918].

Notice biographique sur madame la comtesse Donairière de Bouillé, née de Bonchamps. Nantes: Bourgeois, 1877.

Notice sur le calvaire de Pontchateau. Nantes: Bourgeois, 1873.

Pèlerinage au calvaire de Pontchateau, presidé par Mgr l'Evêque de Nantes, le 24 septembre 1873. N.p., n.d.

Pèlerinage breton à la Salette, à Tours, à la Chartreuse, à Fourvière, à Ars, et à Paray-le-Monial du 12 au 23 juin 1883. Nantes: Imprimerie de l'Ouest, 1883.

Petit manuel des adoratrices du Sacré-Coeur. Paris: Adoratrices du Sacré-Coeur, 1894.

Recueil des cantiques à l'usage des élèves du Sacré-Coeur de Jesus. Lyon: Pélagaud, 1851.

Réponse aux attaques contre l'oeuvre de Loigny par un catholique de Lyon. Saint-Malo: Commerce, 1890.

Saints and Servants of God. Vol. 2, *The Lives of the Venerable Mother Margaret Mary Alacoque, Religious of the Order of the Visitation and of Saint Catherine of Bologna.* London: Thomas Richardson, 1850.

Les Soldats du Pape: Journal de deux zouaves bretons. Nantes: Libaros, 1867.

Souvenirs du Sacré-Coeur de Paris. Tours: Mame, 1878.

Souvenirs sur le Cardinal Guibert par un de ses anciens familiers. Tours: Mame, 1886.

La Vénérable Anne-Madeleine Remuzat [sic], *la propagatrice de la dévotion au Sacré-Coeur de Jésus, d'après les documents de l'ordre.* Lyon: Vitte, 1894.

Les Volontaires de l'ouest. Nantes: Libaros, 1873[?] [Musical score].

Les Zouaves pontificaux. Marseille: Chauffard, 1873.

Books, Pamphlets, Musical and Dramatic Works, and Secondary Sources

Agulhon, Maurice. "Politics, Images, and Symbols in Post-Revolutionary France." In *Rites of Power: Symbolism, Ritual, and Politics since the Middle Ages,* edited by Sean Wilentz, 177–205. Philadelphia: University of Pennsylvania Press, 1985.

Aillery, Eugen-Louis [abbé]. *Archives du diocèse de Luçon: Chroniques paroissiales.* Luçon: Bideaux, 1908.

Alacoque, Marguerite-Marie. *Vie et oeuvres de sainte Marguerite-Marie Alacoque.* 2 vols. Paris: Poussielgue, 1920. Reprint Paris: Éditions Saint-Paul, 1991.

Alet, Victor. *La France et le Sacré-Coeur.* Paris: Lethielleux et Dumoulin, 1871, 1904.

Alexander, Bobby C. *Victor Turner Revisited: Ritual as Social Change.* Atlanta: Scholars Press, 1991.

Allard, Julien S. [abbé]. *Le Volontaire Joseph Louis Guerin du corps des Zouaves Pontificaux, Franco-Belges, né à Sainte-Pazanne, le 5 avril 1838, mort à Osimo, le 30 octobre 1860.* Nantes: Mazeau, 1860.

———. *Les Zouaves pontificaux, ou Journal de Mgr Daniel, aumônier des zouaves.* Nantes: Bourgeois, 1880.

Anizan, Félix. *Les Hommes de France au Sacré-Coeur.* Paris: 1913.

———. *Qu'est-ce que le Sacré-Coeur?* Paris: Lethielleux, 1910.

Archives parlementaires de 1787 à 1860: Recueil complet des débats législatifs et politiques des Chambres françaises. Paris: Dupont 1867–.

Ashworth, William, Jr. "Natural History and the Emblematic World View." In *Reappraisals of the Scientific Revolution,* edited by David C. Lindberg and Robert S. Westman, 303–32. Cambridge: Cambridge University Press, 1990.

Aubineau, Léon. *Paray-le-Monial et son monastère de la Visitation.* Paris: Douniol, 1873.

Aulard, Alphonse. *Christianity and the French Revolution.* Translated by Lady Frazer. London: Ernest Benn, 1927.

Babonneau, P. *La France et le XIXe siècle: Discours prononcé lors du Triduum séculaire en la Basilique Saint-Nicolas de Nantes, les 28, 29, et 30 décembre 1900.* Nantes: Lanoe-Mazeau, 1901.

Bainvel, Jacques. "Dévotion au coeur-sacré de Jésus." In *Dictionnaire de Théologie Catholique,* vol. 3, 271–351. Paris: Letouzey, 1938.

Baird, Henry. *History of the Rise of the Huguenots of France.* New York: Scribner's, 1970.

Baker, Keith. *Inventing the French Revolution.* Cambridge: Cambridge University Press, 1990.

Barnes, Andrew. *The Social Dimension of Piety: Associative Life and Devotional Change in the Penitent Confraternities of Marseille, 1499–1792.* Mahwah, N. J.: Paulist Press, 1994.

Barrows, Susanna. *Distorting Mirrors: Visions of the Crowd in Late Nineteenth-Century France.* New Haven: Yale University Press, 1981.

Barruel, Augustin [abbé]. *Mémoires pour servir à l'histoire du jacobinisme.* Chiré-en-Montreuil: Diffusion de la pensée française, 1973.

Bataille, Georges. *Against Architecture: The Writings of Georges Bataille.* Translated by Betsy Wing. Cambridge, Mass.: MIT Press, 1989.

Baudrillart, Alfred [Monsignor]. *Dictionnaire d'histoire et de géographie ecclésiastiques.* Paris: Letouzey, 1930.

———. *Vie de Monseigneur d'Hulst.* 2 vols. Paris: Poussielgue, 1912.

Baunard, Louis [Monsignor]. *Adelaide de Cicé.* Wetteren, Belgium: Meester, n.d.

————. *Le Général de Sonis d'après ses papiers et sa correspondance.* Paris: Poussielgue, 1890.

————. *Histoire de la vénérable mère Madeleine-Sophie Barat, fondatrice de la Société du Sacré-Coeur de Jésus.* 2 vols. Paris: Poussielgue, 1892.

————. *Histoire du cardinal Pie, évêque de Poitiers.* 2 vols. Poitiers: Oudin, 1886.

Bécel, J. M. [abbé]. *Souvenir du pèlerinage de Sainte-Anne d'Auray.* Paris: Adrien, 1860.

Beckwith, Sarah. *Christ's Body: Identity, Culture, and Society in Late Medieval Writings.* London: Routledge, 1993.

Beik, Paul. "The French Revolution Seen From the Right: Social Theories in Motion." *Transactions of the American Philosophical Society* 46 (1956).

Bellanger, Claude, and others. *Histoire générale de la presse française.* Vol. 1, *Des Origines à 1814.* Paris: Presses universitaires de France, 1969.

Benoist, Jacques. *Le Sacré-Coeur de Montmartre de 1870 à nos jours.* 2 vols. Paris: Éditions ouvrières, 1992.

————, ed. *Le Sacré-Coeur de Montmartre: Un Voeu national.* Paris: DAAVP, 1995.

Bercé, Yves-Marie. *History of Peasant Revolts: The Social Origins of Rebellion in Early Modern France.* Translated by Amanda Whitmore. Ithaca, N. Y.: Cornell University Press, 1990. Originally published as *Histoire des Croquants: Étude des soulèvements populaires au XVIIe siècle dans le Sud-Ouest de la France* (Geneva and Paris: Droz, 1974).

Biré, Edmond. *Paris pendant la Terreur.* Paris: Perrin, 1890.

Bittard des Portes, René. *Histoire des zouaves pontificaux.* Paris: Bloud et Barral, 1894.

Biver, Marie-Louise. *Fêtes révolutionnaires à Paris.* Paris: Presses universitaires de France, 1979.

Blanchet, Louis. *Qui es-tu, Vendéen?* N.p. 1994.

Bliard, Joseph. *Le Salut de la France: Considérations philosphiques sur l'histoire contemporaine.* Bordeaux: Feret, 1871.

Bloch, R. Howard. "*Mieux vaut jamais que tard:* Romance, Philology, and Old French Letters." *Representations* 36 (1991): 64–86.

————. "Naturalism, Nationalism, Medievalism." *Romanic Review* 76 (1985): 341–60.

Bois, Paul. *Histoire de Nantes.* Toulouse: Privat, 1977.

————. *Paysans de l'Ouest.* Le Mans: Vilaire, 1960.

Boissé, Claudie, ed. *Boulogne-sur-Mer: La Cathedrale et basilique Notre-Dame, Pas-de-Calais.* Images du Patrimoine, Ministère de la Culture 56. Lille: Dieudonné, 1988.

Boisseleau, E. [abbé]. *Le Sacré-Coeur des Vendéens.* Luçon: Bideaux, 1910.

————. *Le Sacré-Coeur et la France: L'Étendard du Sacré-Coeur à Loigny.* Luçon: Bideaux, 1911.

Bonin, Jacques, and Paul Didier. *Louis XVIII, roi de deux peuples, 1814–1816.* Paris: Albatros, 1978.

Bony, M. [père, oblat de Saint-François de Sales]. *Vie et oeuvres de M. Alexandre Legentil.* Paris: Victor Retaux, 1893.

Bottineau, J. *Les Portraits des généraux Vendéens.* Cholet: Musée d'histoire de Cholet, 1975.

Bougaud, Louis-Victor-Émile [bishop of Laval]. *Life of the Blessed Margaret Mary Alacoque: Revelations of the Sacred Heart to Blessed Margaret Mary.* Translated by "A Visitandine of Baltimore." Baltimore: Benziger, 1890.

Bourcier, Arm [curé de Saint Donatien]. *Le Chanoine Hillereau, curé de Saint-Donatien à Nantes: Sa Vie, ses oeuvres, 1837–1907.* Nantes: Lanoe-Mazeau, 1909.

————. *Le Couronnement du Sacré-Coeur.* Nantes: Landreau, 1906.

Boutry, Philippe. "'Le Roi martyr': La Cause de Louis XVI devant la cour de Rome (1820)." *Revue d'histoire de l'Église de France* 76 (1990): 57–71.

Boutry, Philippe, and Michel Cinquin. *Deux Pèlerinages au XIXe siècle: Ars et Paray-le-Monial.* Paris: Beauchesne, 1980.

Bowman, Frank Paul. *Le Discours sur l'éloquence sacrée à l'époque romantique.* Genève: Droz, 1980.

————. *French Romanticism.* Baltimore: Johns Hopkins University Press, 1990.

————. "Le Sacré-Coeur de Marat, 1793." In *Les Fêtes de la Révolution,* edited by Jean Ehrard and Paul Viallaneix, 155–79. Paris: Société des études robespierristes, 1977.

Brown, Peter. *The Cult of the Saints: Its Rise and Function in Latin Christianity.* Chicago: University of Chicago Press, 1981.

Bugnot, Paul. *Réponse aux attaques de la Franc Maçonnerie contre l'église.* Auxerre: Imprimerie auxerroise, 1906.

Burnichon, Joseph [S. J.]. *Histoire d'un siècle, 1814–1914: La Compagnie de Jésus en France.* 4 vols. Paris: Beauchesne, 1922.

Bury, John P. T., and Robert Tombs. *Thiers, 1797–1877: A Political Life.* London: Allen and Unwin, 1986.

Bynum, Caroline Walker. *Holy Feast and Holy Fast.* Berkeley and Los Angeles: University of California Press, 1987.

————. *Jesus as Mother.* Berkeley and Los Angeles: University of California Press, 1982.

————. "Why All the Fuss About the Body? A Medievalist's Perspective." *Critical Inquiry* 22 (fall 1995): 1–33.

Cabanes, Auguste. *Marat Inconnu: L'Homme privé, le médecin, le savant.* Paris: Albin Michel, 1891.

Canetti, Elias. *Crowds and Power.* Translated by Carol Stewart. New York: Viking, 1962.

Carrière, Charles, Marcel Courdurié, and François Rebuffat. *Marseille, ville morte: La Peste de 1720.* Marseille: Garçon, 1968.

[Abbé Carle and others.] "Un comité d'archéologues." *L'Église du Sacré-Coeur à Montmartre sera-t-elle de notre style national ou sera-t-elle d'un style étranger?* (Paris, 1875).

Cate, Phillip Dennis, and Mary Shaw. *The Spirit of Montmartre: Cabarets, Humor, and the Avant-Garde, 1875–1905.* New Brunswick, N. J.: Jane Voorhees Zimmerli Art Museum, 1996.

Catta, Étienne. *La Visitation Sainte-Marie de Nantes, 1630–1792: La Vie d'un monastère sous l'ancien régime.* Paris: Vrin, 1954.

Cauvin, Charles. *Les Légitimistes devant la Révolution, et la restauration morale de la France.* Paris: L'Oeuvre de Saint-Paul, 1878.

Cerbelaud-Salagnac, Georges. *Les Zouaves pontificaux.* Paris: France-Empire, 1963.

Chaigne, Louis. *Les Bénédictines de la rue Monsieur.* Strasbourg: Le Roux, 1950.

Champré [abbé]. *Les Zouaves pontificaux, ou Volontaires de l'Ouest: Poème dramatique et lyrique.* J.-L. Boivin, composer. Paris: Gautrot, 1873.

Charbonneau-Lassay, Louis. "L'Iconographie du Sacré-Coeur dans les armées contre-révolutionnaires de la Vendée." *Regnabit: Revue universelle du Sacré-Coeur* (1922): 448–63.

————. *La Mysterieuse emblematique de Jésus-Christ: Le Bestiaire du Christ; Mille cent cinquante-sept figures gravées sur bois par l'auteur.* Paris: Desclée, de Brouwer, 1940.

Charette de la Contrie, Athanase Charles Marie [baron]. *Legion des volontaires de l'Ouest, commandement supérieure.* Rennes: Oberthur, 1871.

———. *Noces d'argent du régiment des zouaves pontificaux, 1860–1885: Basse-Motte, 28 juillet 1885—Anvers, 30 août 1885.* Rennes: Oberthur, 1886.

Chartier, Roger. *Cultural Origins of the French Revolution.* Translated by Lydia G. Cochrane. Durham, N. C.: Duke University Press, 1991.

Chassin, Charles-Louis. *La Préparation de la guerre de Vendée, 1789–1793.* 5 vols. Mayenne: Floch, 1973.

Chauveau, Jacqueline. *La Conjuration de Satan: La Persécution religieuse sous la Révolution de 1789.* Paris: Nouvelles Éditions Latines, 1969.

Chelini, Jean. *Les Chemins de Dieu: Histoire des pèlerinages.* Paris: Hachette, 1982.

Chevalier, Louis. *Montmartre du plaisir et du crime.* Paris: Robert Laffont, 1980.

Chirol, Pierre. "La Basilique du Sacré-Coeur de Dijon: Julien et Gérard Barbier, architectes." *La Construction moderne* 54 (1939): 130–34.

Cholvy, Gérard. *Le Diocèse de Montpellier.* Paris: Beauchesne, 1976.

Cholvy, Gérard, and Yves-Marie Hilaire. *Histoire religieuse de la France contemporaine.* Vol. 1, *1800–1880.* Paris: Privat, 1985.

Christ, Yvan. *Cathédrales de France.* Paris: Éditions Mondes, 1952.

Ciammitti, Luisa. "One Saint Less: The Story of Angela Mellini, a Bolognese Seamstress (1667–17??)." In *Sex and Gender in Historical Perspective,* edited by Edward Muir and Guido Ruggiero, 141–76. Baltimore: Johns Hopkins University Press, 1990.

Clément, Maurice [évêque de Monaco]. *Vie du cardinal Richard, archevêque de Paris.* Paris: Gigord, 1924.

Clenet, Louis-Marie. *Cathelineau, le "saint de l'Anjou."* Paris: Perrin, 1991.

Connerton, Paul. *How Societies Remember.* Cambridge: Cambridge University Press, 1989.

Corbin, Alain. *The Village of Cannibals: Rage and Murder in France, 1870.* Translated by Arthur Goldhammer. Cambridge, Mass.: Harvard University Press, 1992.

Coudart, Laurence. *La Gazette de Paris: Un Journal royaliste pendant la Révolution française, 1789–1792.* Paris: Harmattan, 1995.

Crespelle, Jean-Paul. *La Vie quotidienne à Montmartre au temps de Picasso, 1900–1910.* Paris: Hachette, 1978.

Crétineau-Joly, Jacques. *Histoire de la Compagnie de Jésus.* 6 vols. Paris: Lecoffre, 1859.

Croiset, John [S. J.]. *The Devotion to the Sacred Heart of Our Lord Jesus Christ.* Translated by Patrick O'Connell from the French of the final edition published at Lyon, 1864. Newman Press, Westminster, Md., 1948.

Croiset, Paul. *De Sonis à Loigny.* Paris: Haton, 1898. [Play in three acts.]

Crouzet, Denis. *Les Guerriers de Dieu: La Violence au temps des troubles de religion.* 2 vols. Paris: Champ Vallon, 1990.

Cucherat, François, chanoine aumônier à Paray-le-Monial. *Album-guide des saints pèlerinages de Paray-le-Monial et de Verosèvres en l'honneur du coeur de Jésus et de la Bienheureuse Marguerite-Marie.* Paris: Palmé, 1873.

d'Hulst, Maurice Lesage d'Hauteroche. *Allocution prononcé dans l'église de Loigny par Mgr. d'Hulst, vicaire-général de Paris, le 2 décembre 1876, à l'occasion du sixième anniversaire de la Bataille de Loigny et de la bénédiction d'un monument élevé au Sacré-Coeur dans le bois des Zouaves.* Paris: Imprimerie des apprentis catholiques, 1876.

———. *Religion et patrie; discours prononcé à la consecration de l'église de Loigny. Le 18 septembre 1893 par Mgr. d'Hulst, recteur de l'Institut Catholique de Paris, député du Finistère.* Chartres: Garnier, 1893.

Dakyns, Janine R. *The Middle Ages in French Literature, 1851–1900.* London: Oxford University Press, 1973.

Dansette, Adrien. *Histoire religieuse de la France contemporaine: l'Église catholique dans le mêlée politique et sociale.* Paris: Flammarion, 1965.

Darricau, Raymond. "Poitiers." In *Catholicisme hier, aujourd'hui, demain.* Vol. 11:51, *Plérôme–Prédestination,* edited by G. Mathon and others. Paris: Letouzey et Ané, 1988.

Davis, Natalie Zemon. *Women on the Margins: Three Seventeenth-Century Lives.* Cambridge, Mass.: Harvard University Press, 1995.

de Barral, Edgard [comte]. *Les Zouaves pontificaux, 1860–1870.* Paris: Dauphin, 1932.

de Beauchesne, Alcide. *La Vie de Madame Élisabeth, soeur de Louis XVI.* Paris: Plon, 1869.

de Bertier de Sauvigny, Guillaume. *The Bourbon Restoration.* Translated by Lynn Case. Philadelphia: University of Pennsylvania Press, 1966.

———. *Le Comte Ferdinand de Bertier, 1782–1864, et l'énigme de la Congrégation.* Paris: Presses continentales, 1948.

———. *La Restauration, 1815–1830.* Nouvelle histoire de Paris. Paris: Hachette, 1977.

de Cabrières, François-Marie Anatole de Rovérié. *Cinquantième anniversaire de la création du regiment des Zouaves Pontificaux: Allocution de Monseigneur de Cabrières, Montmartre, le 5 juin 1910.* Montpellier: Manufacture de la Charité, 1910.

de Chateaubriand, François-René. *Mémoires d'outre tombe.* Paris: Garnier, 1924.

de Falloux, Alfred Frédéric [comte]. *Mémoires d'un royaliste.* Paris: Perrin, 1888.

de Franciosi, Xavier [S. J.]. *La Dévotion au Sacré-Coeur de Jésus et au Saint-Coeur de Marie.* Nancy: Chevalier Frères, 1885.

de Guibert, Joseph [S. J.]. *The Jesuits: Their Spiritual Doctrine and Practice.* Chicago: Institute of Jesuit Sources, 1964.

de La Faye, Jacques [Mlle Marie de Sardent]. *Histoire du général de Sonis.* Paris: Bloud et Barral, 1890.

de La Gorce, Pierre. *Histoire religieuse de la Révolution française.* 5 vols. Paris: Plon, 1922.

de Lagenevais, F. "Ultrix poesis 'Les Châtiments,' par Victor Hugo." *Revue des Deux Mondes* 90 (1870): 154–69.

de Lamennais, Félicité. *Essai sur l'indifférence en matière de religion.* In Vol. 1 of *Oeuvres complètes de Félicité de Lamennais.* Paris: Daubrée et Cailleux, 1836–37.

de La Rochejaquelein, Marie-Louise. *Mémoires de Madame la Marquise de La Rochejaquelein.* 2 vols. Paris: Michaud, 1815.

de Liguori, Alphonse-Marie. *La Dévotion au Sacré-Coeur de Jésus et au Saint Coeur de Marie, ou le Salut de la France précédée de la neuvaine au Sacré-Coeur.* Clermont: Thibaude-Landriot, 1853.

de Llobet [archevêque d'Avignon]. *Le Cardinal de Cabrières.* Paris: Bonne Presse, 1944.

de Maistre, Joseph. *Considérations sur la France: Essai sur le principe générateur des constitutions politiques.* London [Basle], 1797.

de Mun, Albert. "Les dernières heures du drapeau blanc." *La Revue hebdomadaire* 11 (1909): 141–63.

de Propiac [M. le Chevalier]. *Histoire de France à l'usage de la jeunesse, depuis l'établissement de la monarchie jusqu'au 1er juillet 1820.* Paris: Gérard, 1820.

de Quatrebarbes, Théodore [comte]. *Souvenirs d'Ancône, siège de 1860.* Paris: Douniol, 1866.

———. *Une Paroisse vendéenne sous la Terreur.* Rennes: Salmon, 1837.

de Rorthays, Emmanuel. "Le Cardinal Richard en Vendée." *Revue de Bas-Poitou* 21 (1908): 5–17.

de Sivry, Louis, and Jean-Baptiste Champagnac. *Dictionnaire des pèlerinages anciens et modernes et des lieux de dévotion les plus célèbres de l'Univers,* 2 vols. Paris: La Bibliothèque universelle du clergé, 1851.

de Tourzel, Louise Elizabeth. *Mémoires de Madame la duchesse de Tourzel.* 4 vols. Paris: Plon, 1884.

de Valori, Henri [prince, zouave pontifical]. *Charette, Troussures et les zouaves pontificaux: Campagne de France.* Nîmes: Giraud, 1871.

de Verneilh, Félix. *L'Architecture byzantine en France: Saint-Front de Périgueux et les églises à coupoles de l'Aquitaine.* Paris: Didron, 1851.

de Vésly, Léon. "Concours de la maison de répression de Nanterre et de l'église du Sacré-Coeur à Montmartre." *Le Moniteur des architectes* 8 (1874): 113–20.

Debidour, Antonin. *Histoire des rapports de l'Église et de l'État en France de 1789–1870.* Paris: Alcan, 1898.

Delaporte, Albert. *L'année du Sacré-Coeur: Second Centenaire du culte public du Sacré-Coeur, 21 juin 1886. Discours du R. P. Delaporte, missionnaire du Sacré-Coeur au Congrès de Lille et de Rouen.* Paris: Librairie Catholique Internationale, 1886.

Delécluze, Étienne Jean. *Journal de Delécluze, 1824–1828.* Paris: Grasset, 1948.

Delumeau, Jean, and Yves Lequin. *Les Malheurs des temps: Histoire des fléaux et des calamités en France.* Paris: Larousse, 1987.

Des Buttes, E. *Le Scapulaire du Sacré-Coeur.* Paris: Tolra, 1878.

Devigne, Paul. *Charette et les zouaves pontificaux.* Paris: Béduchaud, 1913.

Diefendorf, Barbara. *Beneath the Cross: Catholics and Huguenots in Sixteenth-Century Paris.* New York: Oxford University Press, 1991.

Drevon, Victor [S.-J.]. *Le Coeur de Jésus consolé dans la sainte Eucharistie: Recueil de différentes publications concernant l'Oeuvre de la Communion réparatrice.* 2 vols. Avignon: Aubanel, 1866.

Driskell, Michael Paul. *Representing Belief; Religion, Art, and Society in Nineteenth-Century France.* University Park: Pennsylvania State University Press, 1992.

Drochon, Jean-Emmanuel [des Augustins de l'Assomption]. *Histoire illustrée des pèlerinages français de la Très Sainte Vierge publiée sous le patronage des R. R. P. P. Augustins de l'Assomption.* Paris: Plon, 1891.

———. "Les Pèlerinages à la Sainte Vierge dans le diocèse de Luçon." *Revue de Bas-Poitou* 3 (1890): 231–44.

Duc, Joseph-Louis. *Rapport sur le concours de l'église du Sacré-Coeur.* Paris: Imprimerie de Le Clère, 1874.

Duchâtellier, Armand. *Histoire de la Révolution en Bretagne,* 5 vols. Paris: Desessart, 1836.

Dugan [Dugar?] [abbé]. *Le Pèlerinage du Sacré-Coeur en 1873; histoire et documents.* Moulins: Desrosiers, 1873.

Dumas, Alexandre. *The She-Wolves of Machecoul* [*Les Louves de Machecoul*]. Boston: Little, Brown, 1894.

Duncan, Carol. "Ingres's *Vow of Louis XIII* and the Politics of the Restoration." In *Art and Architecture in the Service of Politics,* edited by Henry Millon and Linda Nochlin, 80–91. Cambridge, Mass.: MIT Press, 1978.

Dupanloup, Felix [éveque d'Orléans]. *Oraison funèbre du général de la Moricière, prononcé dans la cathédrale de Nantes, le mardi 17 octobre 1865 par Mgr. l'Evèque d'Orléans.* Paris: Douniol, 1865.

Dupront, Alphonse. *Du Sacré: Croisades et pèlerinages, images et langages.* Paris: Gallimard, 1987.

———. "Pèlerinages et lieux sacrés." In Mélanges en l'honneur de Fernand Braudel. Vol. 2, *Méthodologie de l'Histoire et des sciences humaines,* edited by Raymond Aron and others.Toulouse: Privat, 1972.

Durand, Yves, and others. *Le Diocèse de Nantes.* Paris: Beauchesne, 1985.

Duroselle, Jean-Baptiste, and Jean-Marie Mayeur. *Histoire du Catholicisme.* Paris: PUF, 1949.

Eade, John, and Michael J. Sallnow. *Contesting the Sacred: The Anthropology of Christian Pilgrimage.* London: Routledge, 1991.

Eliade, Mircea. *Images and Symbols: Studies in Religious Symbolism.* Translated by Philip Mairet. New York: Sheed and Ward, 1961.

Fauchois, Yann. *Religion et France revolutionnaire.* Paris: Herscher, 1989.

Faugeras, Marius. "Les fidélités en France au XIXe siècle: Les Zouaves pontificaux, 1860–1870." In *Fidélités, solidarités et clientèles.* Vol. ii of *Enquêtes et documents,* edited by Raymond Darricau and others. Nantes: Presses de l'Université de Nantes, 1986.

Favreau, Robert. *Le Diocèse de Poitiers.* Paris: Beauchesne, 1988.

Fillon, Benjamin. *Pièces contre-révolutionnaires du commencement de l'insurrection vendéenne.* Fontenay: Robuchon, 1847.

Fitzpatrick, Brian. *Catholic Royalism in the Department of the Gard, 1814–1852.* Cambridge: Cambridge University Press, 1983.

Fleury, Michel, and others. *Paris Monumental.* Paris: Flammarion, 1974.

Fonssagrives, J. *Le Sacrifice de Loigny: La Bataille du 2 décembre 1870.* Paris: Poussielgue, 1898.

Ford, Caroline. *Creating the Nation in Provincial France: Religion and Political Identity in Brittany.* Princeton, N. J.: Princeton University Press, 1993.

Forrest, Alan. *Conscripts and Deserters: The Army and French Society during the Revolution and Empire.* New York: Oxford University Press, 1989.

Foucart, Bruno. "'L'éternelle discussion': From the Introduction to the Published Journal of Fontaine, Which Describes the Development of the Tuileries au Louvre." *Architecture d'aujourd'hui* 253 (1987): 46–53.

Foucart, Bruno, and others. *Paul Abadie, architecte, 1812–1884.* Angoulême: Jean Ebrard, 1984.

Foucault, Michel. *Language, Counter-Memory, Practice; Selected Essays and Interviews.* Translated by Donald F. Bouchard and Simon Sherry. Ithaca, N. Y.: Cornell University Press, 1980.

Foulon, J. A. [archevêque de Lyon]. *Histoire de la vie et des oeuvres de Mgr. Darboy, archevêque de Paris.* Paris: Poussielgue, 1889.

Frayssinous, Denis. *Oraison funèbre de très-haut, très-puissant et très-excellent prince Louis XVIII, roi de France et de Navarre, prononcée dans l'église royale de Saint-Denis, le 25 octobre 1824 par M. l'évêque d'Hermopolis, premier aumônier du roi.* Paris: Imprimerie royale, 1824.

Freppel, Charles-Emile [Monsignor]. *Oeuvres polémiques de Monseigneur Freppel,* 8 vols. Paris: Palmé, 1881.

Furet, François. *La Révolution: De Turgot à Jules Ferry, 1770–1880.* Paris: Hachette, 1988.

———. *Revolutionary France, 1779–1880.* Translated by Antonia Nevill. Oxford: Blackwell, 1992. Originally published as *La Révolution: De Turgot à Jules Ferry, 1770–1880.* Paris: Hachette, 1988.

Furet, François, and others. *Critical Dictionary of the French Revolution.* Translated by Arthur Goldhammer. Cambridge, Mass.: Harvard University Press, 1989. Originally published as *Dictionnaire critique de la révolution française.* Paris: Flammarion, 1988.

———. *Dictionnaire critique de la révolution française.* Paris: Flammarion, 1988.

Fustel de Coulanges. "La Justice royale au moyen âge." *Revue des Deux Mondes* 94 (1871): 536–56.

Gabory, Émile. *Les Bourbons et la Vendée.* Paris: Perrin, 1923.

———. *La Révolution et la Vendée d'après des documents inédits.* Paris: Perrin, 1927.

Gadille, Jacques. *Guide des archives diocésaines françaises.* Lyon: Centre d'histoire du catholicisme, 1971.

———. *La Pensée et l'action politiques des évêques français au début de la IIIe République, 1870–1883.* 2 vols. Paris: Hachette, 1967.

Gaétan de Wismes [baron]. *Les Loup de la Biliais: Martyrs du Sacré-Coeur d'après des documents inédits.* Vannes: Lafolye, 1898.

Gaffarel, Paul, and [marquis] de Duranty. *La Peste de 1720 à Marseille et en France.* Paris: Perrin, 1911.

Galtier, Révérend Père E. *Les Congrès Eucharistiques.* Montréal: Oeuvres eucharistiques, 1910.

Garnier, François, and others. *L'Église de Vendée fait mémoire.* Luçon: 1993.

Genet-Delacroix, Marie-Claude. "Esthétique officielle et art national sous la Troisième République." *Le Mouvement social* 131 (1985): 105–20.

Gérard, Alain. *Pourquoi la Vendée?* Paris: Colin, 1990.

Germain, Élisabeth. *Parler du Salut? Aux origines d'une mentalité religieuse: La Catéchèse du Salut dans la France de la Restauration.* Paris: Beauchesne, 1968.

Gildea, Robert. *The Past in French History.* New Haven: Yale University Press, 1994.

Gillet, Louis. *Histoire des Arts.* Vol. 11 of *Histoire de la nation française,* edited by Gabriel Hanotaux. Paris: Plon, 1922.

Girard, René. *La Violence et le sacré.* Paris: Bernard Grasset, 1972.

Girault de Coursac, Paul, and Pierrette Girault de Coursac. *Louis XVI et la question religieuse pendant la Révolution.* Paris: OEIL, 1988.

Godechot, Jacques. *La Contre-révolution: Doctrine et action, 1789–1804.* Paris: PUF, 1961.

Goyau, George. "France. État religieux actuel." In *Dictionnaire de Théologie Catholique,* vol. 6:630–57. Paris: Letouzey, 1924.

Grégoire, Henri. *Histoire des sectes religieuses,* 2 vols. Paris: Baudouin, 1828.

Grégoire, Pierre Marie [abbé]. *Les Religieuses nantaises durant la persécution révolutionnaire.* Nantes: [privately printed], 1920.

Grente, Joseph. *Les Martyrs de septembre 1792 à Paris*. Paris: Téqui, 1926.

Grubb, Alan. *The Politics of Pessimism: Albert de Broglie and Conservative Politics in the Early Third Republic*. Newark: University of Delaware Press, 1996.

Guéroult, Adolphe. "La République." *Revue des Deux Mondes* 90 (1870): 104–21.

Guillaume de Saint-Thierry. *On Contemplating God: Prayer and Meditations,* translated by Sister Penelope. In vol. 1 of *Works*. Spencer, Mass.: Cistercian Publications, 1971.

Guillon de Montléon, Aimé [abbé]. *Les Martyrs de la foi pendant la Révolution française*. 4 vols. Paris: G. Mathiot, 1821.

Guiral, Pierre. *Adolphe Thiers; ou De la nécessité en politique*. Paris: Fayard, 1986.

Gumbrecht, Hans Ulrich. "'Un Souffle d'Allemagne ayant passé': Friedrich Diez, Gaston Paris, and the Genesis of National Philologies." *Romance Philology* 40 (1986): 1 37.

Hacquet, Pierre-François. *Mémoire des missions des montfortains dans l'ouest, 1740–1779*. Fontenay-le-Comte: Lussaud, 1964.

Halbwachs, Maurice. *Les Cadres sociaux de la mémoire*. Paris: PUF, 1952.

———. *The Collective Memory*. New York: Harper, 1980.

Hamon, Auguste [S. J.]. *Histoire de la dévotion au Sacré-Coeur de Jésus,* 5 vols. Paris: Beauchesne, 1923–39.

Hanet-Cléry, Jean-Baptiste Cant. *Mémoires de M. Cléry, valet-de-chambre de Louis XVI, ou Journal de ce qui s'est passé à la tour du Temple pendant la captivité de Louis XVI, roi de France*. London: 1798.

Hardman, John, ed. *French Revolution Documents*. Oxford: Blackwell, 1973.

Hardy, Paul. *Discours prononcé à l'occasion de la bénédiction du drapeau du groupe Saint-Martin de Vertou*. Nantes: Bourgeois, 1906.

Harvey, David. "Monument and Myth: The Building of the Basilica of the Sacred Heart." In *Consciousness and the Urban Experience: Studies in the History and the Theory of Capitalist Urbanization,* edited by David Harvey, 221–49. Baltimore: Johns Hopkins University Press, 1985.

Hautecoeur, Louis. *La Fin de l'architecture classique, 1848–1900*. Vol. 7 of *Histoire de l'architecture classique en France*. Paris: Picard, 1957.

Héron de Villefosse, René. *Solennités, fêtes, et réjouissances parisiennes*. Nouvelle histoire de Paris. Paris: Hachette, 1980.

Hilgers, Joseph. *Livre d'or du Coeur de Jésus, pour les prêtres et pour les fidèles: Indulgences et privilèges de la dévotion au coeur de Jésus*. Paris: Lethielleux, 1911.

Hillairet, Jacques. *Dictionnaire historique des rues de Paris,* 2 vols. Paris: Minuit, 1966.

Howard, Michael. *The Franco-Prussian War: The German Invasion of France, 1870–1871*. New York: Macmillan, 1962.

Hue, François. *Dernières années du règne et de la vie de Louis XVI*. Paris: Imprimerie royale, 1816.

Hunt, Lynn. *The Family Romance of the French Revolution*. Berkeley and Los Angeles: University of California Press, 1992.

Irvine, William. *The Boulanger Affair Reconsidered: Royalism, Boulangism, and the Origins of the Radical Right in France*. New York: Oxford University Press, 1989.

Jacquemont, Sauveur. *La Campagne des zouaves pontificaux en France sous les ordres du Général Baron de Charette, 1870–1871*. Paris: Plon, 1871.

Jonas, Raymond. "L'Année Terrible, 1870–1871." In *Le Sacré-Coeur de Montmartre: Un Voeu National,* edited by Jacques Benoist.Paris: DAAVP, 1995.

———. "Anxiety, Identity, and the Displacement of Violence during the *Année Terrible:* The Sacred Heart and the Diocese of Nantes, 1870–1871." *French Historical Studies* 21 (1998): 55–75.

———. "La Colonne Sherman et la Vendée dans l'imaginaire américaine." In *Guerre et répression: La Vendée et le monde,* ed. Jean-Clément Martin. Nantes, 1993.

———. "Monument as Ex-Voto, Monument as Historiosophy: The Basilica of Sacré-Coeur." *French Historical Studies* 18 (1993): 482–502.

———. "Restoring a Sacred Center: Pilgrimage and the Sacré-Coeur." *Historical Reflections/Réflexions historiques* 20 (1994): 95–123.

———. "Sacred Mysteries and Holy Memories: Counter-Revolutionary France and the Sacré-Coeur." *Canadian Journal of History/Annales canadiennes d'histoire* 32 (1997): 347–60.

Jordan, David. *Transforming Paris: The Life and Labors of Baron Haussmann.* New York: Free Press, 1995.

Joséfa, M. T. *Le Général de Sonis, le héros de Patay.* Paris: Tolra et Simonet, 1904.

Kingdon, Robert. *Myths About the Saint Bartholomew's Day Massacres, 1572–1576.* Cambridge, Mass.: Harvard University Press, 1988.

Kleinberg, Aviad M. *Prophets in Their Own Country; Living Saints and the Making of Sainthood in the Later Middle Ages.* Chicago: University of Chicago Press, 1992.

Krautheimer, Richard. *Early Christian and Byzantine Architecture.* Harmondsworth: Penguin, 1975.

Kselman, Thomas. *Miracles and Prophecies in Nineteenth-Century France.* New Brunswick, N. J.: Rutgers University Press, 1983.

Lacouture, Jean. *Jésuites: Une Multibiographie.* 2 vols. Paris: Seuil, 1992.

Laligant, Pierre [abbé]. *Montmartre: La Basilique du Voeu national du Sacré Coeur.* Grenoble: Arthaud, 1933.

Laprie, Félix. *Dieu et le peuple Nantais: Discours prononcé pour la bénédiction de la première pierre de la basilique de Saint-Donatien, le 12 septembre 1873.* Nantes: Mellinet, 1873.

Larignon, Gilberte, and Héliette Proust. *Edouard de Monti de Rezé: L'Inébranlable certitude; Le Mouvement légitimiste dans l'Ouest.* Laval: Siloë, 1992.

Launay, Marcel. *Le Diocèse de Nantes sous le second empire.* Nantes: Cid, 1982.

Le Bras, Gabriel. *L'Église et le village.* Paris: Flammarion, 1976.

Le Brun, Jacques. "Politics and Spirituality: The Devotion to the Sacred Heart." In *The Concrete Christian Life,* edited by Christian Duquoc. New York: Herder and Herder, 1917.

Le Chauff de Kerguenec, François. *Henri Le Chauff de Kerguenec: Souvenirs des zouaves pontificaux, 1861 et 1862, recueillis par François Le Chauff de Kerguenec.* Poitiers: Oudin, 1890.

Leclerc, Jean-Baptiste. *Essai sur la propagation de la musique en France, sa conservation et ses rapports avec le gouvernement.* Paris: Imprimerie nationale, 1797.

Le Clère, Marcel. *Paris de la préhistoire à nos jours.* Paris: Bordessoules, 1985.

Le Doré, Ange. *Le Sacré-Coeur de Jésus: Son Amour d'après la doctrine du bienheureux Jean Eudes, père, docteur, et auteur de la dévotion au Sacré-Coeur.* Paris: Lethielleux, 1909.

Le Gentil, Jean-Philippe-Gui [comte de Paroy]. *Mémoires du comte de Paroy: Souvenirs d'un défenseur de la famille royale pendant la Révolution, 1789–1797.* Paris: Plon, 1895.

Le Goff, Jacques, and René Rémond. *Histoire de la France religieuse,* 3 vols. Paris: Seuil, 1988.

Le Gouvello, Hippolyte. *Henri de Bellevue, capitaine des zouaves pontificaux.* Nantes: Forest et Grimaud, 1871.

Lebrun, François. *Le Diocèse d'Angers.* Paris: Beauchesne, 1981.

Lebrun, François, ed. *Histoire des Catholiques en France du XVe siècle à nos jours.* Toulouse: Privat, 1980.

Lebrun, François. *Parole de Dieu et Révolution: Les Sermons d'un curé angevin avant et pendant la guerre de Vendée.* Paris: Imago, 1988.

Lecanuet, Edouard. *L'Église de France sous la Troisième République: Les Dernières années du pontificat de Pie IX, 1870–1878.* Paris: Alcan, 1931.

——. *Montalembert.* Paris: Gigord, 1925.

Lefebvre, Henri. *The Production of Space.* Translated by Donald Nicholson-Smith. Oxford: Blackwell, 1991.

Leith, James A. *Space and Revolution; Projects for Monuments, Squares, and Public Buildings in France, 1789–1799.* Montreal: McGill-Queen's University Press, 1991.

Lelièvre, Henri. *Les Ursulines de Bordeaux pendant la Terreur et sous le Directoire.* Bordeaux: Feret, 1896.

Lenfant, Alexandre Charles Anne. *Mémoire ou correspondance secrète du Père Lenfant, confesseur du roi pendant trois années de la Révolution, 1790, 1791, 1792.* 2 vols. Paris: Mame, 1834.

Léniaud, Jean-Baptiste. *Jean-Baptiste Lassus, 1807–1857, ou Le Temps retrouvé des cathédrales.* Paris: 1980.

Lenoir, P. V. *Éloge funèbre de Louis XVI, roi de France et de Navarre; prononcé à Londres, le 27 mars; le 2, le 11 et le 23 avril 1793.* London: 1793.

Lequinio, Joseph-Marie. *Guerre de la Vendée et des chouans.* Paris: Pougin, 1794.

Leroy, Michel. *Le Mythe jésuite de Béranger à Michelet.* Paris: PUF, 1992.

Lesourd, Paul. *Montmartre.* Paris: Éditions France-Empire, 1973.

Lever, Evelyne. *Louis XVIII.* Paris: Fayard, 1988.

Levillain, Philippe. *Albert de Mun: Catholicisme français et catholicisme romain du Syllabus au Ralliement.* Rome: École française de Rome, 1983.

Levine, Neil. "The Romantic Idea of Architectural Legibility: Henri Labrouste and the Neo-Grec." In *The Architecture of the Ecole des Beaux-Arts,* edited by A. Drexler. New York: Museum of Modern Art, 1977.

Limouzin-Lamothe, Roger. *Monseigneur de Quelen, archevêque de Paris.* 2 vols. Paris: Vrin, 1955.

Loidreau, Simone. "Les Armes de la Vendée." *Le Vendéen de Paris* (1981): 5–7.

Loriquet, Jean Nicolas. *Le Salut de la France.* Poitiers: F. A. Barbier, 1816.

Loth, Arthur. *L'Echec de la Restauration Monarchique en 1873.* Paris: Perrin, 1910.

Lucas de la Championnière, Pierre Suzanne. *Mémoires sur la Guerre de Vendée, 1793–1796.* Paris: Plon, 1904.

MacCormack, Sabine. "*Loca Sancta:* The Organization of Sacred Topography in Late Antiquity." In *The Blessings of Pilgrimage,* edited by Robert Osterhout. Urbana-Champaign: University of Illinois Press, 1990.

Maingueneau, Dominique. *Les Livres d'école de la République, 1870–1914 (discours et idéologie).* Paris: Le Sycomore, 1979.

Mange, Christian. "Bernard Benezet et l'iconographie du Sacré-Coeur au XIXe siècle." *Histoire de l'art* 20 (1992): 79–87.

Martin, Benjamin. *Count Albert de Mun, Paladin of the Third Republic.* Chapel Hill: University of North Carolina Press, 1978.

Martin, Jean-Clément. *Blancs et Bleus dans la Vendée déchirée.* Paris: Gallimard, 1987.

———. *La Vendée et la France.* Paris: Seuil, 1987.

Martin, Malachi. *The Jesuits: The Society of Jesus and the Betrayal of the Roman Catholic Church.* New York: Simon and Schuster, 1987.

Martin, Thérèse [Saint Thérèse de Lisieux]. *Une Rose Effeuillée: Soeur Thérèse de l'Enfant-Jésus et de la Sainte Face, religieuse.* Paris: Saint-Paul, 1911.

Martin, Xavier. *Sur les droits de l'homme et la Vendée.* Bouère: Dominique Martin Morin, 1995.

Mathevon, Gustave [abbé]. *Les Pèlerinages au XIXe siècle.* Agen: Noubel, 1873.

Mauges, Charles des. *Vendée, Souviens-toi!* Angers: Siraudeau, 1910.

Maurain, Jean. *La Politique ecclésiastique du second empire de 1852 à 1869.* Paris: Alcan, 1930.

Maury, Jean Siffrein [abbé]. *Sur la Constitution civile du clergé.* Paris: Imprimerie du Roi, 1790.

Mauviel, Maurice. "Révolution et Contre-Révolution: La Confrontation aux langues et cultures d'Europe et du monde." *Impacts* 1–2 (1990): 139–54.

Mayeur, Françoise. "Fustel de Coulanges devant la guerre et la Commune: Notes inédites." In *La Guerre de 1870–71 et ses conséquences,* edited by Philippe Levillain and others. Bonn: Bouvier Verlag, 1900.

Mayeur, Jean-Marie. "Les Conservateurs dans la crise de 1870–1871." In *La Guerre de 1870–71 et ses conséquences,* edited by Philippe Levillain and others. Bonn: Bouvier Verlag, 1900.

Mazé, Jules. *Les Derniers coups de feu de l'Armée de la Loire.* Tours: Mame, 1908.

McManners, John. *Church and State in France, 1870–1914.* New York: Harper and Row, 1972.

McNamara, Jo Ann Kay. *Sisters in Arms; Catholic Nuns through Two Millennia.* Cambridge, Mass.: Harvard University Press, 1996.

Méhier de Mathuisieulx, Henry [vicomte]. *Histoire des zouaves pontificaux.* Tours: Mame, 1913.

Michelet, George. "La Philosophie chrétienne en France." In *La Vie Catholique dans la France contemporaine,* edited by [monsignor] Alfred Baudrillart. Paris: Bloud et Gay, 1918.

Michelet, Jules. *Du Prêtre, de la femme, de la famille.* Paris: Atheneum, 1845.

———. *Witchcraft, Sorcery, and Superstition.* Secaucus, N. J.: Citadel, 1997.

Middleton, Robin. *The Beaux-Arts and Nineteenth-Century French Architecture.* Cambridge, Mass.: MIT Press, 1982.

Mitchell, Allan. "Crucible of French Anticlericalism: The *Conseil Municipal* de Paris, 1871–1885." *Francia* 8 (1980): 395–405.

Mitchell, Allan. *Victors and Vanquished: The German Influence on Army and Church in France after 1870.* Chapel Hill: University of North Carolina Press, 1984.

Monin, Hippolyte, and Lucien Lazard. *Sommier des biens nationaux de la ville de Paris conservés aux Archives de la Seine.* 2 vols. Paris: Cerf, 1920.

Montégut, Émile. "Ou en est la Révolution française? Simples Notes sur la situation actuelle." *Revue des Deux Mondes* 94 (1871): 872–98.

Nettement, Alfred. *Règne de Charles X.* Vol. 8 of *Histoire de la Restauration.* Paris: Jacques Lecoffre, 1872.

———. *Restauration de 1814-Cent Jours.* Vol. 2 of *Histoire de la Restauration.* Paris: Jacques Lecoffre, 1872.

Nolan, Mary, and Sidney Nolan. *Christian Pilgrimage in Modern Western Europe.* Chapel Hill: University of North Carolina Press, 1989.

Nora, Pierre, ed. *Les Lieux de Mémoire.* Paris: Gallimard, 1984-.

Ozouf, Mona. *L'École, l'Église et la République, 1871–1914.* Paris: Colin, 1963.

———. *Festivals and the French Revolution.* Translated by Alan Sheridan. Cambridge, Mass.: Harvard University Press, 1988. Originally published as *La Fête révolutionnaire, 1789–1799* (Paris: Gallimard, 1976).

———. *L'Homme régénéré: Essais sur la révolution française.* Paris: Gallimard, 1989.

Paguelle de Follenay, J. [abbé]. *Vie du cardinal Guibert, archevêque de Paris,* 2 vols. Paris: Poussielgue, 1896.

Palanque, Jean-Remy. *Le Diocèse de Marseille.* Paris: Letouzey, 1967.

Pano, E. [abbé]. *Pèlerinage des Lorrains à Paray-le-Monial, 12 juin 1873: Souvenirs et impressions.* Nancy: Collin, 1873.

Parenteau, Fé[lix?]. *Médailles vendéens.* Nantes: Guéraud, 1857.

Parfait, Paul. *Le Dossier des pèlerinages.* Paris: Alcan-Lévy, 1877.

Paris, Gaston. *La Poésie du moyen âge: Leçons et lectures.* Paris: Hachette, 1885–95.

Pelabon, Louis. *La Peste de Toulon en 1721: Poëme provençal en quatre chants dédié a cette cité et à la ville de Lorgues en mémoire de leurs anciennes et fraternelles relations.* Toulon: Castex, 1873.

Pelletan, Camille. *L'Assemblée au jour le jour du 24 mai [1873] au 25 février [1875]: Le Théâtre de Versailles.* Paris: Dentu, 1875.

Peltier, Jean-Gabriel. *Tableau de l'Europe.* London: Glindon, 1794.

Pergeline [abbé, vicaire-général du diocèse de Nantes]. *Eloge funèbre de Joseph Houdet, Fernand Le Lièvre de la Touche, et Hippolyte de la Brosse, Volontaires de l'Ouest, prononcé dans la chapelle des enfants nantais, le 6 mars 1871.* Nantes: Bourgeois, 1871.

———. *Victor Charruau: Allocution prononcée le 27 mars 1872, par M. l'abbé Pergeline, vicaire-général adressée aux anciens élèves de l'externat des enfants-nantais, et aux autres jeunes gens qui suivaient les exercices de la retraite pascale.* Nantes: Imprimerie Vincent Forest et Emile Grimaud, 1872.

Perrier, M. F. *L'Oeuvre du Voeu National et celle du Mont Pie IX.* Paris: Commission du Mont Pie IX, 1875.

Petitfrère, Claude. *La Vendée et les Vendéens.* Paris: Gallimard, 1981.

———. *Les Vendéens d'Anjou, 1793: Analyse des structures militaires, sociales et mentales.* Paris: Bibliothèque nationale, 1981.

Petronius Arbiter. *Satyricon.* Translated by P. G. Walsh. Oxford: Oxford University Press, 1996.

Pie, François Désiré Édouard [cardinal]. *Oeuvres de Monseigneur Pie, l'évêque de Poitiers.* 6 vols. Paris and Poitiers: Oudin, 1868–79.

Pierrard, Pierre. *Juifs et catholiques français.* Paris: Fayard, 1970.

———. "La Renaissance des pèlerinages au XIXe siècle." In *Les Chemins de Dieu: Histoire des pèlerinages,* edited by Jean Chelini. Paris: 1982.

Pinkney, David. *Napoleon III and the Rebuilding of Paris.* Princeton, N. J.: Princeton University Press, 1958.

Popkin, Jeremy D. *Revolutionary News: The Press in France, 1789–1799.* Durham, N. C.: Duke University Press, 1990.

Port, Célestin. *Dictionnaire historique, géographique, et biographique de Maine et Loire et de l'ancienne province d'Anjou.* Angers: Sirandeau, 1965.

———. *La Vendée angevine: Les Origines, l'insurrection, janvier 1789—31 mars 1793.* 2 vols. Paris: Hachette, 1888.

Pothier, Joseph [abbé]. *Monseigneur Fournier évêque de Nantes: Sa Vie, ses oeuvres.* 2 vols. Nantes: Libaros, 1900.

Poulat, Émile. *Les Semaines religieuses: Approche socio-historique et bibliographique des bulletins diocésains français.* Lyon: Centre d'histoire du catholicisme, 1973.

Provost [l'abbé Provost, chanoine de Chartres]. *Loigny-la-Bataille de 1870 à 1912.* Lille: Ducoulombier, 1912.

Quinet, Edgar. *Le Christianisme et la Révolution Française.* Paris: Fayard, 1984.

Ramière, Henry [S. J.]. *Apostolat de la Prière, sainte ligue des Coeurs chrétiens unis au Coeurs de Jésus: Pour obtenir le triomphe de l'église est le salut des âmes.* Lyon: Perisse, 1861.

Ramière, Henry [S. J.]. *L'École de la reforme sociale.* Tours: Mame, 1875.

Rapley, Elizabeth. *The Dévotes: Women and Church in Seventeenth-Century France.* Montreal and Kingston, Ontario: McGill-Queen's University Press, 1990.

Ravitch, Norman. *The Catholic Church and the French Nation, 1685–1985.* London: Routledge, 1990.

Rearick, Charles. *Pleasures of the Belle Epoque: Entertainment and Festivity in Turn-of-the-Century France.* New Haven: Yale University Press, 1985.

Reinhard, Marcel. *Religion, Révolution, et Contre-Révolution.* Paris: Centre de documentation universitaire, 1985.

Rémond, René. *L'Anticléricalisme en France de 1815 à nos jours.* Paris: Fayard, 1976.

———. *The Right Wing in France from 1815 to De Gaulle.* Translated by James M. Laux. Philadelphia: University of Pennsylvania Press, 1966. Originally published as *La Droite en France de 1815 à nos jours.* Paris: Aubier 1954.

Ricordel, Emile [chanoine]. *Nantes et le XIXe siècle.* Nantes: Lanoë-Mazeau, 1901.

Robinet, Jean-François. *Le Mouvement religieux à Paris pendant la Révolution, 1789–1801.* 2 vols. Paris: Cerf, 1896–98.

Roë, Art[hur]. "L'Assaut de Loigny." *Revue des Deux Mondes* 126 (1894): 605–48.

———. "Au Polygone." *Revue des Deux Mondes* 126 (1894): 268–301.

Rohault de Fleury, Charles. *Mémoire sur les instruments de la passion de Notre Seigneur Jésus-Christ.* Paris: Lesort, 1870.

Roland, Marie-Jeanne. *Lettres de Madame Roland.* Paris: Imprimerie nationale, 1900.

Rubin, Miri. *Corpus Christi: The Eucharist in Late Medieval Culture.* Cambridge: Cambridge University Press, 1991.

Saint-Montan, Jeannette. *Nos Pèlerinages en 1900, 15 août-19 octobre: Souvenirs, lettres intimes.* Balan-Sedan: Imprimerie du patronage, 1901.

Sevrin, Ernest [chanoine de Chartres]. "Croyances populaires et médecine supranaturelle en Eure-et-Loir au 19e siècle." *Revue d'histoire de l'Église de France* 32 (1946): 265–308.

———. "Le Général de Sonis et la Franc-Maçonnerie: Mémoire composé en mai 1952 par le chanoine Ernest Sevrin de Chartres, suivie d'un appendice: L'État de conservation du corps de Sonis." Typescript, Chartres, 1952 [in Archives du diocèse de Chartres].

———. *Les Missions religieuses en France sous la Restauration, 1815–1830.* 2 vols. Saint-Mandé: Procure des Prêtres de la Miséricorde, 1948.

Shennan, J. H. *The Parlement of Paris.* Ithaca, N. Y.: Cornell University Press, 1968.

Sigal, Pierre-André. *Les Marcheurs de Dieu: Pèlerinages et pèlerins au Moyen Âge.* Paris: Colin, 1974.

Sirinelli, Jean-François, ed. *Histoire des droites en France.* 3 vols. Paris: Gallimard, 1992.

Smith, Michael L. *Ionian Vision.* London: Allen Lane, 1973.

Sorlin, Pierre. *La Croix et les juifs, 1880–1889: Contribution à l'histoire de l'antisémitisme contemporain.* Paris: Grasset, 1967.

Starobinski, Jean. *1789: The Emblems of Reason.* Translated by B. Bray. Cambridge, Mass.: MIT Press, 1988.

Tabaraud, Mathieu. *Essai historique et critique sur l'état des Jésuites en France depuis leur arrivée dans le royaume jusqu'au temps présent.* Paris: Pichard, 1828.

Tackett, Timothy. *Becoming a Revolutionary.* Princeton, N. J.: Princeton University Press, 1996.

———. *Religion, Revolution, and Regional Culture in Eighteenth-Century France: The Ecclesiastical Oath of 1791.* Princeton, N. J.: Princeton University Press, 1986.

Taine, Hippolyte-Adolphe. *Le Régime moderne.* Vol. II of *Les Origines de la France contemporaine.* Paris: Hachette, 1899.

Terdiman, Richard. *Present Past; Modernity and the Memory Crisis.* Ithaca, N. Y. : Cornell University Press, 1993.

Terrier, Charles. "Le Concours pour l'église du Sacré-Coeur." *Gazette des architectes et du bâtiment* (1874): 74–75.

Téry, Gustave. *Les Cordicoles.* Paris: Cornély, 1902.

Tilly, Charles. *The Vendée.* Cambridge, Mass.: Harvard University Press, 1964.

Tombs, Robert. *Nationhood and Nationalism: From Boulanger to the Great War.* London: Harper Collins, 1991.

Touchet, Stanislas-Xavier [évêque d'Orléans]. *Oraison funèbre du général Baron Athanase de Charette, prononcée dans la cathédrale de Nantes, le Samedi 2 décembre 1911.* Paris: Lethielleux, 1911.

Tulard, Jean, and Marie-Hélène Parinaud. *The French Revolution in Paris Seen through the Collections of the Carnavalet Museum.* Paris: Indre, 1989.

Turner, Victor. *Image and Pilgrimage in Christian Culture: Anthropological Perspectives.* New York: Columbia University Press, 1978.

———. "Pilgrimages as Social Processes." In *Dramas, Fields and Metaphors: Symbolic Action in Human Society.* Edited by Victor Turner. Ithaca, N. Y.: Cornell University Press, 1974.

Van Dam, Raymond. *Saints and their Miracles in Late Antique Gaul.* Princeton, N. J.: Princeton University Press, 1993.

Van Kley, Dale K. *The Religious Origins of the French Revolution.* New Haven: Yale University Press, 1996.

Vance, Eugene. "'And the Flag was Still There': Image, Intentionality, and the Semiotics of Flag Burning." In *Other Intentions: Cultural Contexts and the Attribution of Inner*

States, edited by Lawrence Rosen. Sante Fe, N. M.: School of American Research Press, 1995.

———. "Semiotics and Power: Relics, Icons, and the *Voyage de Charlemagne à Jérusalem et à Constantinople.*" In *The New Medievalism,* edited by Marina S. Brownlee and others. Baltimore: Johns Hopkins University Press, 1991.

Van Zanten, David. *Designing Paris: The Architecture of Duban, Labrouste, Duc, and Vaudoyer.* Cambridge, Mass.: MIT Press, 1987.

Verdet d'Adhemar, Marie Blanche Angeline [vicomtesse]. *La Femme catholique et la démocratie française.* Paris: Perrin, 1900.

Veuillot, François. *Le Sacré-Coeur et les hommes de France.* Langres: Maitrier et Courtot, 1902.

Vidalenc, Jean. *La Restauration, 1814–1830.* Paris: Presses universitaires de France, 1973.

Vovelle, Michel. *1793: La Révolution contre l'église: De la raison à l'être suprême.* Lausanne: Éditions complexe, 1988.

———. *Piété baroque et déchristianisation en Provence au XVIIIe siècle: Les Attitudes devant la mort d'après les clauses des testaments.* Paris: Plon, 1973.

Walter, Gérard, ed. *Le Procès de Marie-Antoinette, 23–25 vendémiaire an II (14–16 octobre 1793): Actes du tribunal révolutionnaire.* Paris: Éditions complexe, 1993.

Waquet, Françoise. *Les Fêtes royales sous la Restauration, ou L'Ancien régime retrouvé.* Geneva: Droz, 1981.

Watkin, David. *Morality and Architecture: The Development of a Theme in Architectural History and Theory from the Gothic Revival to the Modern Movement.* Oxford: Clarendon Press, 1977.

Wright, Beth Segal. *Painting and History during the French Restoration: Abandoned by the Past.* Cambridge: Cambridge University Press, 1997.

Zola, Émile. *The Debacle [1870–1871].* Translated by Leonard Tancock. Harmondsworth: Penguin, 1972. Originally published as *La Débâcle* (Paris: Charpentier, 1892).

———. *Lourdes.* Paris: Charpentier, 1922.

———. *Les Mystères de Marseille.* Paris: Charpentier, 1921.

INDEX

STUDIES ON THE HISTORY OF SOCIETY AND CULTURE

Victoria E. Bonnell and Lynn Hunt, Editors